THE STRATEGY OF CAMPAIGNING

¶ 'Heresthetic (Riker) frames (manu-
pulas)

For Professor Axelrod — 7/08
with best regards

The Strategy of Campaigning

....

Lessons from
Ronald Reagan *&* Boris Yeltsin

Kiron K. Skinner

by Kiron K. Skinner,
Serhiy Kudelia,
Bruce Bueno de Mesquita, *and*
Condoleezza Rice

Foreword by
George P. Shultz

The University of Michigan Press • *Ann Arbor*

Copyright © by the University of Michigan 2007
All rights reserved
Published in the United States of America by
The University of Michigan Press
Manufactured in the United States of America
⊗ Printed on acid-free paper

2010   2009   2008   2007   4   3   2   1

A CIP catalog record for this book is available from the British Library.

Library of Congress Cataloging-in-Publication Data

The strategy of campaigning : lessons from Ronald Reagan and Boris
    Yeltsin / by Kiron K. Skinner ... [et al.] ; foreword by George P.
    Shultz.
        p.   cm.
    Includes bibliographical references and index.
    ISBN-13: 978-0-472-11627-0 (cloth : alk. paper)
    ISBN-10: 0-472-11627-4 (cloth : alk. paper)
        1. Political campaigns—United States.   2. Presidents—United
    States—Election—1980.   3. Reagan, Ronald.   4. Presidents—Russia
    (Federation)—Election.   5. Political campaigns—Russia (Federation)
    6. Yeltsin, Boris Nikolayevich, 1931–2007.   I. Skinner, Kiron K.

JK2281.S73   2007
324.7'2—dc22   2007023387

Contents

Foreword
George P. Shultz   vii

Acknowledgments   xi

1   Campaign Strategy   1

2   The New South Rises
*Competition for the Republican
Presidential Nomination in 1968*   32

3   Down to Political Defeat
*Reagan's Inability to Break Ford's
Coalition in the 1976 Primaries*   91

4   Reshaping the Domestic and
International Landscape, Part 1
*The Long Road to the 1980
Presidential Election*   124

5   Reshaping the Domestic and
International Landscape, Part 2
The 1980 Presidential Election   163

6   Fighting the Nomenklatura's Privileges
The Rhetorical Campaign of 1986–88   205

7   Yeltsin's Winning Campaigns
*Down with Privileges and Out of the USSR,
1989–91*   225

8   Conclusions   249

Notes 261   *Bibliography* 305   *Index* 321

Foreword

....

George P. Shultz

The authors of *The Strategy of Campaigning* have done us a great service. They have done careful research, and lots of it. They present detailed accounts of three successful campaigns—Richard Nixon's in 1968, Ronald Reagan's in 1980, and Boris Yeltsin's in 1991—along with a considerable amount of reference material to other campaigns. The writing is clear and the material is lively. That makes the book interesting and readable. What makes the book important is the ability of the authors to relate this rich factual material to ideas about strategy—ideas from which future campaigners can benefit.

I was especially fascinated by the book because of my personal involvement: I was a participant in the Nixon and Reagan campaigns and in the negotiations with the Soviet Union and Mikhail Gorbachev in the 1980s, and I was an observer of the fall and rise of Boris Yeltsin. I served in the administrations following the two successful U.S. campaigns. The result is that I almost instinctively react to the strategies of campaigns with an eye on the subsequent success of the campaigners as holders of the office of president.

From this standpoint, I would judge Ronald Reagan to be a clear success. His ideas prevailed, they worked, and the outcome produced changes for the better in the United States and in the world, very much as he said they would during his campaign. Richard Nixon and Boris Yeltsin leave records that have positive elements, but in the end, each left us with a more ambiguous legacy. This raises the question: Does the nature of the campaign have any impact on the process of governance that comes afterward?

Richard Nixon was exceptionally gifted intellectually and well informed, with a great knowledge of world affairs. As the description of his successful campaign brings out, he was also a master of maneuver who could readily shift his gears. My own experiences with him were mostly positive, as he supported what I regarded as good positions in the effort to deal with discrimination in employment and education, to revive the vitality of the collective bargaining process, to stand up to the pressures involved when he created the volunteer armed forces, and to move toward a system of flexible exchange rates. I was deeply disappointed, however, when he imposed wage and price controls, a move that in the end damaged the U.S. economy, much as I, and many of my economist colleagues, predicted it would. However, the maneuver worked politically in the 1972 election. I also saw a dark side as Nixon tried unsuccessfully to persuade me, as secretary of the Treasury, to use the IRS in ways that I regarded as improper.

Ronald Reagan's basic views and the principles from which they were derived stayed much the same through his presidential campaigns described in this book. The fascinating point is the way he put them to the electorate in his dramatically successful 1980 campaign. Basically, he didn't change, but he changed the way the electorate saw issues. Knowing him as a campaigner and as a president, I can't imagine him trying to use the IRS improperly or imposing wage and price controls, as Nixon did despite his earlier promises not to do so. The reason is that Reagan took positions in the campaign based on principles that he well understood, and he stuck to those principles during his presidency. His rhetoric came from the strength of his ideas.

I don't have the same feel for Boris Yeltsin, although I did have a ringside seat in the evolution of Soviet affairs and the dramatic change that took place during the latter part of the 1980s and the early 1990s. The authors develop Yeltsin's role, as opposed to that of Mikhail Gorbachev, in a way that I found revealing and extraordinarily interesting. His "Russian" instinct had more to do with the breakup of the Soviet Union than I had realized. Gorbachev got the "blame" in the eyes of the Russian people, but it was Gorbachev who opened the political process that made possible both Yeltsin's rise and the end of the Cold War. Sadly, Yeltsin didn't govern effectively, didn't develop any lasting political structure, and didn't leave a lasting legacy, even though he had hit on a winning campaign strategy.

All of this is simply to say once again how intriguing and stimulating *The Strategy of Campaigning* is. That shouldn't be too surprising because the authors possess an extraordinary mixture of talent, with scholarly credentials as well as deep experience in the process of governance. I tip my hat to them for producing this volume, and I know that readers will enjoy, as well as learn from, reading this book. I include those readers who may aspire to high office.

Acknowledgments

....

The Strategy of Campaigning began as a casual conversation in Condoleezza Rice's office at the Hoover Institution many years ago. Our discussion of the success of Ronald Reagan and Boris Yeltsin despite their seeming remoteness from their respective society's political mainstream led us to undertake what we thought would be a modest project culminating in a brief article. Thanks to the encouragement of many colleagues, friends, and the University of Michigan Press, and following hundreds of conversations among various mixes of the four authors, our project has grown into a book that explores our original question and many others. We owe, therefore, a deep debt of gratitude to the many people who encouraged the development of this work.

We are indebted to the Hoover Institution at Stanford University for its unflagging support of our effort. John Raisian, the Director, has been a source of support throughout. We benefited greatly from the expertise, wisdom, and guidance of Richard V. Allen, Annelise Anderson, Martin Anderson, Jeff Bliss, David Brady, Rita Ricardo Campbell, John Dunlop, Morris Fiorina, John Lewis Gaddis, Gordon Hahn, Charlie Hill, Stephen Krasner, Ed Meese, Charles Palm, Thomas Schwartz, Richard Sousa, and especially George Shultz. Kiron Skinner thanks Tad and Dianne Taube and the Taube Family Foundation for generous funding for her research on Ronald Reagan.

Carnegie Mellon University also provided enormous support and encouragement. We are especially grateful to Caroline Acker, Jared Cohon, Robyn Dawes, Gail Dickey, Baruch Fischhoff, Mark Kamlet, Steve Klepper, John Lehoczky, George Loewenstein, Allan Meltzer, John Miller, Amy Paterson, Scott Sandage, Steve Schlossman, Donald Sutton, Joel Tarr, Joe Trotter, and the late, much-missed Otto Toby Davis.

George Downs, Leslie Johns, and Alastair Smith at New York University gave us excellent feedback and, in Leslie's case, also superb research assistance.

In addition to others we have already thanked, we wish also to express our gratitude to Bruce Parrott, Anatoliy Cherniaev, the Hoover Library staff, and then-anonymous reviewers for their comments on earlier drafts of the chapters on Boris Yeltsin's and Ronald Reagan's campaigns.

We received invaluable comments at the University of Michigan, where an early draft of a portion of this research was presented in a Department of Political Science seminar. We benefited especially from the counsel of James D. Morrow and William Zimmerman. Phil Pochoda, Director of the University of Michigan Press, was the first to inspire us to turn our project into a book. Sarah Remington and Christina L. Milton at the Press have provided invaluable assistance in seeing our manuscript through the production process. Jim Reische, Executive Editor for Law, Politics, and Economics, has been as fine an editor, commentator, critic, and supporter as anyone could ever hope for. He helped transform our efforts into a coherent book and was brilliant in his ability to recognize and bring out ideas while sustaining the historical thread.

We also presented a very early draft at the Council on Foreign Relations. Peter Katzenstein served as an outstanding commentator. Leslie Gelb, then the President of the Council, was generous with his time and in making the Council available to us as a forum for presenting and developing our ideas.

This book could not have been written without the able assistance of numerous archivists and other experts on our subject. We are grateful to James Cannon, Lou Cannon, William P. Clark, Hank Cooper, Peter Hannaford, and Tom Reed as well as to numerous people at the Ronald Reagan Presidential Library. We especially thank Duke Blackwood, Joanne Drake, and Sherrie Fletcher. We cannot adequately express our appreciation to Nancy Reagan for making President Ronald Reagan's papers available to the public. We also thank the staff of the other libraries and archives cited in this book.

No project can succeed without able editorial and research assistance. Susan Schendel and Rosa Stipanovic have provided tireless editorial assistance. Excellent research assistance was provided by Emily Clise, Lela Gibson, Neil Guzy, Ioan Ifrim, Lauren Ingram, Jennifer LaCoste, Alex Porfirenko, Natasha Porfirenko, Inyoung Song, and Breanna Zwart.

Many others also gave us their help and guidance. We are especially appreciative of the guidance given to us by Stephen Ansolabahere, and the late, deeply missed, exceptionally generous Nelson Polsby.

Each of our families has been an inspiration and a rock-solid, unwavering source of support. Kiron Skinner especially thanks Byron, Gloria, and Ruby Skinner for their love and support. Serhiy Kudelia extends his warmest gratitude to his parents, Yuliy and Liudmila Kudelia, for fostering his youthful curiosity about Soviet politics and for providing him with unwavering support as his youthful passion turned into his present academic endeavors. Bruce Bueno de Mesquita is deeply grateful to Arlene, his children Erin, Ethan, and Gwen and their families, and to his sisters, Mireille Bany and Judy Berton, for their willingness to listen to his innumerable retellings of the ideas in this book. Condoleezza Rice is grateful to her family for their support, encouragement, and faith in her throughout her academic career and beyond.

We beg the forgiveness of anyone we have neglected to mention, and we, of course, remain solely responsible for any errors of omission or commission in this work.

I

Campaign Strategy

....

Baseball fans with enough gray hair to remember what the game was like fifty years ago will know that the complete game, today nearly an extinct species, was once the hallmark of a successful pitcher. Those who lament its passing may blame Casey Stengel, the legendary manager of the New York Yankees, who saw more clearly than others before him that extra games could be won by removing starters and bringing in power pitchers in late innings. Thus, while he did not invent the professional relief pitcher, he did more than anyone else to establish specialized relief pitching as a way to reframe baseball competition. In the process, he succeeded in defeating more opponents than any other manager of his day.[1]

Similarly, Benny Friedman, elected to the Pro Football Hall of Fame in 2005, redefined how teams gained yards by making the forward pass a routine, rather than an extraordinary, weapon. Friedman recognized that his team's blockers could create a pocket to shield the passer. As he observed, "Charging tackles, bearing down on the passer, come at the original position of the passer, which is the apex of the angle. . . . The passer, [by stepping into the pocket] if he delivers the ball properly, will escape the tacklers. They will converge behind him."[2] There is no football team today that does not exploit the pocket for exactly the benefits that Benny Friedman first saw.

Finding better ways to defeat opponents is the mark of a genius in sports, and it is the mark of a genius in politics as well. Genius is, of course, uncommon. Most competitors aim at incremental improvements within the prevailing understanding of strategy, rather than by redefining competition itself. This book is about political analogs of Casey Stengel and Benny Friedman: two extraordinary politicians, Ronald Reagan and Boris Yeltsin, whose strategies reframed the possibilities of political campaigns. Whether one likes or dislikes their policies, it is hard not to recognize that each reconfigured the political landscape of his day. Their success did not depend exclusively on skillful pursuit of office under the usual terms of competition. Instead, they redefined the rules of the game.

Although we examine campaigns by two politicians, this book is not primarily a biographical undertaking, another application of the "Great Man" view of history. Rather, it is a comparative study of campaign strategy. We use theory, archival evidence, and secondary sources to gain insight into how politicians thought to be extremists within their own political setting were able to redefine issues and change institutions so as to relocate the political center to their advantage. We believe that Reagan's and Yeltsin's campaigns illustrate general characteristics of political competition.

As in sports, so too in politics: defeat is the greatest enemy, to win the greatest goal. Those who lose often fade rapidly from public view. How many of us remember the American presidential candidates defeated during our own time, let alone before? George Romney, once a leading contender for the Republican presidential nomination, disappeared from national prominence following his failed 1968 primary campaign. Edwin Muskie likewise faded from electoral politics in 1972, as did the Democrat's 1988 nominee, Michael Dukakis. The 1964 Republican vice presidential nominee, William E. Miller, became so obscure that American Express used him in an advertising campaign that emphasized the once famous but now forgotten.

Defeat in politics usually ends public life. Yet some succeed in reviving their political career. Abraham Lincoln proceeded from defeat to defeat before achieving the presidency. After serving in the Illinois Assembly, Lincoln won one term in Congress, followed by a long electoral dry spell, including two failed attempts at election to the United States Senate, before he gained the presidency in 1861 and again in 1865. He relied in part on institutional innovation to win his second term, providing absentee ballots to soldiers so that they could vote from the front. Winston Churchill lost his first campaign for Parliament, only later to become a fabulously successful prime minister. He then lost to Clement Atlee in 1945, but overcame defeat and reemerged as prime minister in 1951. Richard Nixon, defeated for both the presidency and the governorship of California, resurrected himself in 1968, only to self-destruct in the Watergate scandal and then resurface as a prolific and influential writer and thinker on foreign policy.

The puzzle of how individuals return from the wilderness of political defeat deserves close attention. It may be that most failed politicians are just unlucky, while a few find an opportunity to win, hitting on the right argument at the right moment by dumb luck. If serendipity is the dominant factor separating winners from losers, those of us who are trying to understand historical outcomes should not portray victors as clever strategists when good luck is a better explanation. Indeed, we do not doubt the importance of serendipity in any politician's rise to high office. Quite the contrary. We are mindful of Napoleon's response when asked what qualities he most desired in his generals: "I want them to be lucky." It is a candidate's bad luck, in a sense, to adhere to uncommon opinions. Holding views judged by the majority to be wrong—however right those views may later prove—may create an impediment too difficult for a candidate to overcome. (On the other hand, holding popular but wrong views—the wrongness of which is only established in the fullness of time—may lead to a successful run for office, and failure once there.) However important luck is in politics, we believe it is never the whole or even the main story. Anyone who strives long enough in any arena is bound to have runs of bad luck and good luck. But some people are better at exploiting the opportunities that come their way, seizing chances that others miss. Here we examine how Ronald Reagan and Boris Yeltsin each rose, phoenixlike, from defeat, and we do so with the supposition that more than luck was at play.

Reagan's rise to the presidency in 1981 followed on his failed 1968 campaign for the Republican nomination and his close defeat by Gerald Ford at the Republican convention. In the 1980 election, Republican candidates benefited from Carter's bad luck in being saddled with a hostage crisis and a weak economy (if those were matters of luck). But, as we will show, Reagan's successful strategy was taking clear shape well before these fortunate breaks came his way. He capitalized on the opportunity when his Republican rivals failed to do so. Success depended on his creativity in redefining issues, rather than on his convincing voters that he had the right position on issues as they had previously been understood.

Boris Yeltsin's creation of and ascent to the Russian presidency followed his 1988 expulsion from the Politburo by Mikhail Gorbachev.

Like Reagan, Yeltsin benefited from the difficult economic conditions faced by his country. He also benefited from the attempted coup d'état against Gorbachev, an event that both provided Yeltsin with a bully pulpit and opened the door for dramatic institutional change. Yeltsin, after being expelled from the Politburo, could not have realized his great political success without redefining the very institutional framework within which political competition took place. How he did so while other contenders in the Soviet Union failed is an important part of our story.

We present historical evidence suggesting that Yeltsin was unlikely to be victorious solely within the confines of Communist Party competition, the arena in which political success had previously been determined. Instead, he suggested ways to improve the welfare of the average Russian, often at the expense of party officials. In the context of the USSR's rigged electoral structure, such an approach was likely to fail. Campaigning to limit private benefits for party members—the very people whose support was required for victory—made him a loser in 1987; similar appeals made him a winner in a newly shaped electoral environment that had, by November 1991, outlawed the Communist Party. The times were right for him, that is clear. Yet others could not see how to exploit the opportunities of the moment. Yeltsin seized the day, turning luck into political opportunity and employing his genius for campaigning to spark a remarkable political resurrection. Even though they benefited from propitious circumstances, both Reagan and Yeltsin were ingenious at creating opportunities for themselves.

Our purpose lies, therefore, not in illuminating the luck of the moment or the unique personal qualities of this or that candidate, but in specifying generalizations about the strategies of campaigning. Indeed, our primary goal is to understand how candidates who appear to be out of the mainstream of political life—as many thought Reagan and Yeltsin were before their rise to the highest offices in their respective lands—can maneuver themselves into position to win office through democratic processes.

A secondary goal is tied to the dramatic international consequences of Reagan's and Yeltsin's quests for high office. In our view, the end of the Cold War is as much a story of leadership as of anything else. Most scholars who have investigated the role of political leaders in ending the Cold War have typically done so in biographical terms, emphasizing idiosyncratic factors over general principles.[3] While these studies stimulate thinking about common patterns, they do not contribute directly to knowledge about how individual campaign strategies affect international outcomes. For more than a decade, however, certain political scientists have been working to understand definable characteristics of political leaders as key variables in international relations and politics more generally.[4] One of our objectives is to appreciate the transformation of the international system in the late 1980s and 1990s from the perspective of the domestic political maneuvers of Ronald Reagan and Boris Yeltsin. Our study is thus rooted in the growing body of research on strategic politicians. As such, this book contributes to a more focused investigation of the intertwining of domestic politics and foreign policy.

We have two additional, narrower interests. These are to stimulate further research into a cross-national theory of campaigning, and to illustrate through the Reagan analysis how archives can be used to assist in testing equilibrium-based theories of political action through the method of analytic narrative.[5]

All of our goals can be summarized as efforts to move beyond anecdotal accounts of political campaigning. While anecdotes are entertaining, they usually make a particular point rather than establish what is generally true. As such, anecdotal studies may be misleading guides to general principles of campaign strategy. Here we build on systematic theorizing about campaigns, coupled with an institutional theory of incentives that identifies when it makes sense for politicians to offer special rewards to elite backers, and when to offer general rewards to all in the polity through public-goods-oriented initiatives.[6]

This study is not a rigorous, scientific demonstration of the veracity of the theoretical principles we examine. Such an undertaking would require an investigation of many more campaigns within the same theoretical framework, as well as the juxtaposition of the generalizations set out here with those that follow from other perspectives on political campaigns. We hope that our investigation will stimulate more studies of campaigning that rely on an explicit theoretical perspective and the hypotheses that follow from it, and that those studies will motivate further archival research into whether campaigners approach their challenges according to the general principles we articulate.

Our work is a step along the way. But it is a step we believe helps answer the question that motivated us at the outset: How can politicians whose ideas are seemingly at odds with mainstream political thought nevertheless rise to hold the highest office in the land?

....

Overview of the Book

Most studies of campaigning are chronicles of particular political com-petitions, not analytical investigations of the campaign. Yet campaigns are one of the most important features of the contract between the gov-erned and the politician in a democracy. During campaigns, politicians present their ideas and are judged; intense debates about policy occur; political coalitions form; and political parties set new directions. Cam-paigns, failed and successful, are our units of analysis. In this introduc-tory chapter we delineate the puzzles that motivate the study and set out our theoretical perspective on how to resolve them.

Chapter 2 focuses on Reagan's failed effort to win the Republican Party's presidential nomination in 1968. Here we see how important the structure of party competition was and how skillfully Richard Nixon exploited it. In 1968 Reagan failed to grasp how difficult it was to gain the nomination based on a grassroots campaign in a political environ-ment dominated by party bosses.

By 1976, the structure of competition for the Republican nomination had changed in ways that were advantageous for Reagan. As chapter 3 demonstrates, he manifested considerable skill in competing for the nomination against the incumbent president, Gerald R. Ford. Although Reagan failed to secure the nomination, he positioned himself as the leading contender in 1980. Chapter 4 draws our attention to Reagan's maneuvers within the Republican Party in preparation for his cam-paign in 1980 against an impressive list of competitors. We will see how Reagan progressed in his politicking, from a candidate in 1976 who made rhetorical arguments about well-defined issues, to a more sophis-ticated strategist who recast political debate in order to construct a coalition that could win him the nomination without weakening his prospects in the race against Jimmy Carter. Chapter 5 continues this theme, turning attention to Reagan's successful bid during the 1980 presidential election. Here we see that luck played a part—he could not have anticipated that Jimmy Carter would face a disastrous Iranian hostage crisis or a Soviet invasion of Afghanistan—but also that Rea-gan laid out his winning strategy well before Carter's woes set in.

Reagan's strategic insights into reshaping political competition not only helped him win the presidency, but also launched what has come to be known as the Reagan Revolution. His revolutionary reframing of the issues was an example of what William Riker calls *heresthetic*. We discuss the meaning of this term subsequently in this introduction.

Chapters 6 and 7 parallel the Reagan chapters, examining the campaigns of Boris Yeltsin between 1986 and 1991. In chapter 6 we examine his efforts between 1986 and 1988 to gain national prominence by arguing against the special privileges afforded members of the Communist Party. This strategy was doomed to failure so long as political control resided in the hands of the very Communist Party officials Yeltsin criticized.

Following his seeming political demise, Yeltsin resurrected himself by redirecting his campaign against privileges as a vehicle to restructure political competition. As we show in chapter 7, Yeltsin shifted strategies between 1989 and 1991. Early on he relied primarily on rhetoric to improve his political position within the Soviet system, but later he realized that he could not rise to great heights within the existing political framework. Whereas a less skillful politician might have satisfied himself with a middling career, Yeltsin was able to restructure political institutions and reframe debate, calling into question the unequal economic and political treatment of the Russian Republic as compared to the other Soviet republics. In the course of doing so, he redefined political competition in such a way that the existence of the Soviet Union itself became a central issue. His main political rival, Mikhail Gorbachev, could not move toward Yeltsin's positions without losing important elements of his core coalition, nor could he forgo doing so without losing still other elements. Thus, Yeltsin's redefinition of the debate over economic policy prevented anyone from competing with him for the loyalty of his newfound supporters. He deflected the rhetoric of his rivals by reducing their policy positions to obsolescence.

Finally, our concluding chapter pulls together the key generalizations that follow from this study. Now, however, we turn to the theoretical approach that defines our investigation.

The Theoretical Argument

Every political contest occurs within a unique context defined by its time and place. The context always includes a particular configuration of issues thought to be important by competitors for office and those who choose among them. We believe that a small set of general principles governs all campaigning, but that the particulars of their implementation depend on a separate set of principles unique to individual institutional contexts. We will first set out these context-specific principles, and then turn to the more general principles of campaign strategy that help resolve the puzzles at the core of our study.

Institutional Context and Policy Choices

In *The Logic of Political Survival,* Bruce Bueno de Mesquita and his coauthors set out a theory in which a politician's motivation to gain and retain power and the institutional context in which he or she operates powerfully influence the content of political debate and the allocation of resources among contending policies.[7] As the authors of that study see it, the governmental structure of every polity is defined by its location in a two-dimensional institutional space. One dimension is the size of the *winning coalition,* the group whose support is essential if a leader is to remain in office. The other dimension is the size of the *selectorate,* the people in a polity who have a say in choosing leaders. The winning coalition is a subset of the selectorate.

Democratic national governments are characterized by large selectorates and large winning coalitions. Still, there are systematic differences in the sizes of those coalitions in different types of democracies. For example, systems with directly elected presidents foster larger winning coalitions than do British-style parliamentary democracies. These, in turn, rely on larger coalitions than many proportional representation systems.

Autocracies and other nondemocratic systems sometimes have smaller selectorates, and always have smaller winning coalitions than democracies. Military juntas and monarchies normally rely on both small selectorates and small winning coalitions, while rigged-election autocracies are typified by small winning coalitions drawn from relatively large selectorates.

Leaders provide both public and private goods. The latter—the special privileges that all leaders and regimes dole out to supporters—are given only to members of the winning coalition. For our purposes, the key feature of the selectorate theory is its logical and empirical demonstration that leaders who rely on small coalitions retain power primarily by providing private, personal rewards to their winning coalitions, while leaders in large-winning-coalition systems maintain their hold on power by providing broad public goods, such as personal freedoms, effective economic policies, and national security. When the coalition is small, as was true in competitions for national office in the Soviet Union, membership involves valuable personal benefits. If the small coalition is drawn from a large pool of selectors, then a would-be defector to a rival politician incurs a high risk of losing those valued rewards. Naturally, the combination of personal benefits and the risk of their loss induces fierce loyalty to the leader who provides the rewards and who, in turn, demands support for his or her continued hold on office.

In contrast to the special-privileges focus of small-coalition, rigged-election systems, personal rewards to members of large coalitions, such as those typical of the American system, are swamped by the greater value of public goods that everyone enjoys through the policy choices of the leadership. Because the coalition is inherently a large proportion of the selectorate, the risk of losing private benefits by being excluded from future winning coalitions is relatively small. As a consequence, leaders who rely on large coalitions tend to provide successful public policies and have relatively short tenure in office. Because the loyalty of coalition members to the incumbent leader is greatest when the coalition is small and the selectorate is large and weakest when both are large, it is easier for autocrats to survive in office despite failed national policies than it is for democratically elected officials.

The selectorate theory implies what sort of campaign is most likely to be successful in different political contexts. In this regard it is important to recognize that even the most democratic political system may, at the local or the party level, operate along institutional principles quite different from arrangements at the national level. Party politics in the United States, for instance, especially before the explosion in importance of primary elections starting in the 1970s, were (and sometimes still are) the politics of the "smoked-filled room." The 1968 Republican campaign was the last in which a majority of convention delegates were chosen by party barons rather than through primary elections.[8] That is, party politics before 1970 were governed by small coalitions that determined which candidates would receive backing and funding from the party. In such a small-coalition setting, successful candidates needed to offer personal benefits for members of the coalition, rather than focus on broad-based national priorities.

As we will see in chapter 2, Richard Nixon understood the importance of emphasizing rewards to party insiders in his 1968 campaign for the Republican presidential nomination. An analysis of the campaigns of his competitors, Ronald Reagan, Nelson Rockefeller, and George Romney, indicates that they did not understand this principle, or at least failed to act on it. Chapter 2 reveals a nomination process largely controlled by a few barons who could deliver the vote in exchange for the right commitments from the successful candidate. Reagan, Rockefeller, and Romney all eschewed the support of the party barons in favor of appealing to a broad swath of voters. They tried to persuade voters of the soundness of their policy proposals, while Nixon was busy persuading party elites, especially in the South, that he could and would protect their interests.

By the time Ronald Reagan secured his party's nomination in 1980, the process had been changed by institutional reforms, especially the surge in the significance of primaries. The coalition needed to secure the nomination and win the presidency had become much larger than that required in 1968. Even in primaries that attracted only party activists to the polls, the size of the coalition—and therefore the variety of policy orientations—required to win was much greater than that needed in the smoke-filled room. In the institutional context of internal party competition in 1980, having the right agenda of solutions to national problems had become more important than it was in 1968, when party politics was dominated by an elite group of party leaders.

The principles of the selectorate theory will prove even more important for our analysis of Boris Yeltsin's campaigning. After all, in the Soviet Union he operated in the context of a rigged election autocracy at the national level and a small-coalition, small-selectorate "junta" at the party level. President Mikhail Gorbachev understood the fundamental selectorate principle: when you rely on a small coalition—and the leadership of the Communist Party was inherently a small coalition—you succeed by protecting and enhancing private rewards. Yeltsin's initial campaign sought to eliminate the economic, educational, housing, and social privileges that came with top party positions. Such an appeal might have worked well in a large-coalition environment, but it was anathema in the institutional context within which he competed in 1986 and 1987. By 1991, however, that context had been radically transformed by internal and external pressures, including Yeltsin's own political maneuvers.

In the new, larger-coalition environment, Yeltsin's call for radical economic reform, even at the price of the Soviet Union's dissolution, could have great appeal. An expanded coalition required more emphasis on public policy than private rewards. One of the striking aspects of Yeltsin's political ascent was his effectiveness in redefining the institutional landscape, shifting it from a small-coalition system of privilege to an inclusive system of competition over policy ideas, especially in the economic arena. This change was essential if Yeltsin was to realize his comparative advantage as a campaigner, and he did everything in his power to make it happen.

Principles of Campaigning: Heresthetic and Rhetoric

Institutional context may shape the extent to which a successful campaigner emphasizes private rewards or public benefits, but whatever the institutional context, one must also have the requisite skills as a campaigner to exploit one's opportunities. William Riker's investigation of the Federalists' campaign to overturn the Articles of Confederation, replacing them with the Constitution, is the exemplar around which our study is constructed. Riker observes that campaigners persuade people to support them even though voters know that campaign promises often prove meaningless. He suggests a theory designed to resolve this conundrum. His theory not only provides our analytic focus, but also suggests a resolution of the puzzle of campaign persuasion that stands in contrast to the received wisdom as articulated by James A. Farley, Franklin Roosevelt's campaign manager, who is reputed to have said, "[M]ost elections were decided before the campaign began."[9]

Riker's initial point of departure is to examine the ways in which campaigners use language to argue and persuade. He enumerates three traditional liberal arts of language: Logic concerns the truth-value of sentences; grammar concerns their communications-value; and rhetoric concerns their persuasion-value. He then identifies a fourth art, which he calls *heresthetic*. Derived from the Greek root for choosing and electing, heresthetic concerns the strategy-value of sentences. "In each case," Riker writes, "the art involves the use of language to accomplish some purpose: to arrive at truth, to communicate, to persuade, and [in the case of heresthetic] to manipulate."[10] Heresthetic is about framing the situation so that others want to join you. Put simply, heresthetic is "structuring the world so you can win," or at least improving the odds of winning.[11] Although closely linked to rhetoric, the art of persuasion, heresthetic is distinctly concerned with manipulation.[12]

Generally, the competition of ideas and issues takes place during the rhetorical phase of a campaign. Rhetorical interaction produces a sifting of issues that "set[s] the scene for heresthetical manipulation."[13] Heresthetic becomes relevant when the landscape of issues in dispute is relatively clear and is susceptible to redefinition. A successful heresthetician is a politician who has found a way to uniquely combine issues in order to create a coalition that would not otherwise be possible.

Rhetoric and heresthetic are two elements in agenda setting. Rhetoric can play a role in agenda setting if the campaign is about sifting through issues. But agenda setting does not always occur in a rhetorical campaign, for persuasion can occur without an agenda being set. This is what occurred in the 1968 Republican primaries and in the general election. In both stages, Richard M. Nixon, the victor, ran a campaign based on rhetoric.

Heresthetic, in contrast, is a strategy of (1) uniquely combining issues that have become salient in the rhetorical phase of a campaign; and (2) showing how these issues work together. It is not enough for a candidate to merely combine issues; he or she must present a convincing "story" of why this particular combination is the best alternative. The manipulation of issues that is central to heresthetic goes to the heart of agenda formation. The very linking of issues is a form of agenda setting; it entails laying out policy alternatives.

Richard Nixon's 1968 campaign illustrates the key features of a rhetorician. Nixon seized control over the agenda without taking many transparent positions on policy. Instead, he neatly summarized his claim to exceptional competence with his campaign theme, "Nixon's the One." Ronald Reagan's 1980 campaign, in contrast, illustrates the master heresthetician at work. Reagan emphasized an unprecedented view that linked growth-oriented economic policies with greatly increased military spending intended to provoke a peaceful end to the Cold War. Reagan argued vigorously that these policies could be linked to forge a stronger America, and by doing so he built a coalition of voters that included socially conservative, hawkish, blue-collar workers and fiscally conservative conventional Republicans. That coalition persists to this day as central to the Republican Party.

The effective heresthetician redefines the debate—as both Reagan and Yeltsin did—so that policies previously viewed as distinct are combined to create a new context for political debate. A central component of heresthetical maneuvering, then, is linking issues to create new and durable coalitions. Successful heresthetics do not merely break up an opponent's coalition; they realign issues so that the opponent cannot repair the damage.[14] While purely rhetorical campaigners try to persuade voters that their solutions to previously defined problems are superior to those of their rivals, the heresthetician tries to persuade voters that the rivals have not recognized the true nature of the issues.

Rhetoric, Riker wrote, is the "principal feature" of campaigns, and "campaigns are rhetorical exercises: attempts to persuade voters to view issues in the way the candidate wishes them to."[15] Heresthetic is not a principal feature of most campaigns because few politicians develop the skills needed to reframe issues or reconfigure coalitions to isolate opponents. Riker equates a successful heresthetician with a great painter or mathematician: "[T]he level of genius and creativity is roughly the same for the heresthetician as for these other innovators."[16]

Heresthetical campaigners argue that their opponents do not understand the real issues and that their policies, therefore, are aimed at the wrong problems. While Jimmy Carter discussed the right trade-off between guns (that is, national defense) and butter (quality of life), Ronald Reagan argued that the choice itself was wrongheaded. Reagan maintained that the American voter could have guns *and* butter, rejecting the standard view that one had to choose one or the other. While his view prompted derision from rivals, with George H. W. Bush describing it as "voodoo economics," none of Reagan's rivals could find a rhetorical means to undo the coalitional gains he derived by reframing the debate over national security and individual consumption. As Reagan aptly demonstrated, the heresthetical cross-fertilization of manipulation and persuasion can transform a campaign.

Reagan reframed the discussion about the Cold War by arguing that the existing policy of peaceful coexistence failed to address the real issue. He argued that the morally compelling question was not how to survive within the Cold War, but how to win it. All of his predecessors and contemporaries, in contrast, had debated how to manage U.S.-Soviet relations, presuming the inevitability of a persistent Cold War. As we will see, Reagan's linkage of guns and butter, victory in the Cold War and economic prosperity at home, allowed him to disassemble existing coalitions and reassemble them in a way that promoted his electoral success and propelled him to the center of American politics.

Although heresthetic and rhetoric are distinct, we should not overstate the clarity of that distinction, or the ease with which it is observed. At times the line between them "is wavy and uncertain," as Riker warned.[17] One useful marker that distinguishes the two is the audience to which each is targeted. Rhetoric is directed at the voter. Candidates use it to persuade voters to support them. Heresthetic is directed at both the voter *and* the opponent. Candidates use it to structure the contest so that voters feel compelled to support them and opponents are unable to adjust to the new landscape of issues.

Heresthetic, Credible Commitments, and Policy Equilibrium

Heresthetic is perforce radical. By definition, it combines issues in new ways, and the unique recombination it creates is the basis upon which a diverse coalition is held together. Once in office, politicians may find that they cannot easily abandon the implications of this reconfiguration. At the very least, they must look to the next election, where a major departure from prior campaign themes could hurt them. In this way, a successful campaign strategy exerts a binding effect on any campaigners.

This binding commitment, however, may be less chafing to herestheticians than other politicians. By reframing issues, heresthetic campaigners move voters to their viewpoint. Rhetorical campaigners, in contrast, present themselves as advocating what they believe are the dominant preferences among voters; they move themselves to the voters' preferred position, not the other way around. Thus, a successful heresthetician is more likely to show her hand during a campaign than a rhetorician.

The Dependent Variable

Following Riker, we seek to explain how candidates who are political or ideological outliers can exceed expectations about their "performance," while others who either are in the political center or have had a broad-based following fail to perform at or above expectations.

For us, "performance" does not mean that the candidate must win the election. We mean that the candidate must receive a greater number of votes than was predicted: she wins more supporters than she started with; or, in the case of a novice politician, comes through a contest without having damaged her future in politics. She may even have improved her future chances. Harking back to Jim Farley's observation that elections are decided before campaigning even begins (or its more recent incarnation in models that predict electoral outcomes based on economic indicators and other noncampaign variables), we can think of the successful candidate as one whose vote performance exceeds expectations based on these precampaign models.

In essence, we investigate the phenomenon of candidates who outperform expectations. Our primary focus is on political outliers who become acceptable contenders. All campaigns include more than one contender; they are classic examples of strategic interaction. Thus, we also investigate those politicians whom the outlier challenges. Some-times the political outlier is competing against another, more or less like-minded outlier, as may have been true with Yeltsin and Gorbachev in the late 1980s; sometimes the outlier runs against someone from the opposite end of the political spectrum, as in the case of Reagan and Nelson Rockefeller in 1968. We are looking to see how an outlier per-forms in comparison to expectations. We also investigate how the out-lier candidates interact with each other.

The political outlier's main challenge, however, is the candidate who commands the political center. Hence, we also investigate the per-formance of the centrist candidate, as well as the interaction of the cen-trist with the outlier, a vivid example of which is found in chapter 2. Our objectives in studying the American campaigns are not only to track the evolution of Reagan's strategies, but to give considerable attention to the campaign strategies of Reagan's competitors (Nixon, Rockefeller, and Romney) and the strategic interaction among all four (see chapter 2, which examines the Republican contest of 1968).

There is a copious body of scholarly literature on elections, and there are standard theories, such as retrospective economic voting, that are seen as reliable explanations for and predictors of electoral out-comes. These explanations tend to be high-altitude, macro explana-tions of elections, but they are not about politicking, which is the main-stay of campaigns. We do not seek to supplant these theories; indeed we do not answer the questions they do, though, as stated earlier, our performance variable is sometimes associated with a successful elec-toral outcome for the candidate under investigation.

We are interested in the practice—really the art—of politics, the pol-iticking that takes place during a campaign. We offer a probabilistic contribution to the electoral outcome, not a causal, deterministic expla-nation of election outcomes.

This takes us, then, to the specifics of how candidates maneuver within campaigns. Our analysis begins by evaluating two general prin-ciples outlined by Riker, and which we believe will help readers under-stand the strategy of campaigning.

The Dominance and Dispersion Principles

The "two principles for the choice of rhetorical effort" are the principle of dominance and the principle of dispersion.[18] The dominance principle maintains that when an issue attracts a net increase in support for one side in a campaign, then that side reiterates the importance of the issue and the solution it advocates, while the other side, to the extent permitted, abandons the issue. The dispersion principle indicates that if neither side gains from a particular issue, then that issue is abandoned by both sides and so ceases to be a feature of the ongoing campaign.[19] Taken together, these principles dictate that actors do not talk about the same issues in campaigns. They suggest that the winner will be the actor who dominates on issues that matter most to voters. These principles are about the rhetorical aspect of a campaign.

Riker built a theory of campaigning around these two and related ideas, but he also recognized that, because they were derived from his study of the Federalist campaign, it could not provide an independent test of them. In his final, posthumously published book, *The Strategy of Rhetoric,* he urged others to subject his propositions to investigation, using other campaigns. As others before us, we do so here.[20]

The dominance and dispersion principles hardly seem surprising. One might be tempted to think that they say no more than "do what works and give up whatever doesn't." Yet they carry important normative implications about politics, politicians, and citizens. These implications speak to the factors contributing to political success, and those creating the essential political tension between the desires of citizens and the actions of their leaders.

Normative Implications

The dominance and dispersion principles strongly imply that successful politicians do not and cannot act solely on the basis of high ideals and deeply held philosophical commitments to a particular approach to government. Rather they must be committed to winning, tailoring their campaign to that goal and that goal alone. This suggests a corruption of the language arts of logic and grammar.

The former, recall, concerns the truth-value of sentences. When the truth is not advantageous for a politician, she must choose how far to deviate from it: when to tell the truth but not the whole truth. As we will see in our case studies, effective campaign rhetoric often compels persuasive candidates to tell partial truths, making clear the inherent tension between the exercise of logic and of rhetoric. One of the most effective ways to bridge the gap between the incentive to persuade and the urge to tell the truth is to strategically alter the communication-value of campaign utterances. The widespread, discernible corruption of logic and campaign grammar is, of course, the reason that voters are skeptical of campaign promises, and is thus at the core of the fundamental puzzle of campaigning: why are voters persuaded by what politicians say, when they know that politicians have incentives to mislead and obfuscate? After all, voters understand that campaigns are at least in part about personal advancement for the candidates, who may place expedience and pragmatism ahead of civic virtue. Therefore, voters need ways to ensure that candidates are committed to fulfilling their campaign promises—that is, committed to the truth-value of their utterances.

Ensuring that the successful candidate is bound to deliver the goods is more easily done in a small-coalition institutional setting than a large-coalition environment. When the winning coalition is small, victors must deliver private benefits. These are easily seen and evaluated by their recipients. If the rewards fall short of what coalition members think they can get from someone else, they switch sides. The risk that they will defect binds the incumbent, ensuring that she or he delivers. And the possibility that coalition members can be replaced with other selectors constrains their demands so that rewards doled out to the coalition's members fall within feasible levels. Thus, Communist Party officials in the Soviet Union could demand special privileges, confident that their party general secretary would deliver the goods. Perversely, the promises of Soviet leaders to their party's elite (but not to citizens in general) were likely to hold considerable truth-value as a result.

In a large-coalition setting, competition is essentially an arms race over policy ideas. Because the coalition is large and rewards are enjoyed more or less equally by those inside and outside the coalition, it is difficult for supporters to discern when a promised policy fails to materialize because of factors beyond the leader's control, and when it fails because the incumbent has reneged. Consequently, incumbents in such situations live on the brink of being deposed. They are never as secure in their jobs as their autocratic counterparts. And, perhaps surprisingly, the grammar of democratic policy campaigning is thus likely to be fraught with a looser vocabulary, weak in truth-value.

Of course, successful politicians can hold high ideals or strong beliefs, but, especially in large-coalition political settings, they must be prepared to massage their message to satisfy a massive number of voters. Those seemingly principled, issue-driven candidates—like John Calhoun, Ralph Nader, or Gary Bauer—who act as if they would rather be right than win may be profiles in courage, but they have virtually no prospect of election. Such candidates, therefore, are not the subject of this study. That is not to say that Ronald Reagan, Boris Yeltsin, or any other successful politician must be unprincipled. A lucky few enjoy a convergence between their circumstances and their principles. We mean to say that successful politicians know how to bend; they present their principles in a manner that first and foremost wins over supporters, even if that requires some intellectual gymnastics.

One critical normative observation is that politicians who frankly say what they mean and believe, uncensored by concern for the impact of their words on voters, rarely hold office. Citizens say they want principled people to hold high office, but when voters think the candidate's principles are not the same as their own, they vote for someone else.[21] Consequently, successful campaigners must know what to say, when to say it, and how to say it. They must also know which among their beliefs are best left unsaid. We will see in chapter 5 that Ronald Reagan quite consciously chose not to raise the idea of missile defense in his 1980 presidential campaign, even though he passionately believed in it long before he became president. During the campaign he did not deny his principles, he simply chose to emphasize some issues and not others. We are confident that, had missile defense become a major topic, he would have made a forthright statement of his position,[22] but—and this is an important part of his political success—it did not come up because hardly anyone else in mainstream politics was thinking about missile defense as a strategic option.

Conversely, both Boris Yeltsin and his hard-line rival, Yegor Ligachev, made early efforts to gain political advantage over Mikhail Gorbachev, as detailed in chapter 6, by advocating principled positions that inevitably diminished their political fortunes, at least in the short term. Yeltsin argued against the economic and educational privileges bestowed on party leaders and their families, thereby alienating a constituency whose support was vital to political success. At the same time, Ligachev attacked excessive political liberalization, making himself a spokesman for the party conservatives. In doing so he angered Gorbachev, who viewed Ligachev's platform as a challenge to his policy of perestroika. Both Yeltsin and Ligachev were subsequently demoted and lost influence within the party. However, as detailed in chapter 7, Yeltsin ultimately shifted ground and found a way to satisfy his political ambitions. By combining issues that appealed to the wider public, he transformed the political setting from a small-coalition, private-goods orientation to a large-coalition, public-policy outlook. Ligachev was unable to do the same.

The Negative Campaign: A Dominance Imperative

Because voters hold different views of how government should function, campaigners are driven to use negative messages rather than positive arguments. Positive statements of policy intent must be crafted so as not to alienate people who might otherwise have voted for the candidate. But any clear policy statement is likely to alienate at least some voters. Therefore, at the first sign that such messages are costing support from more voters than are being attracted, the message must be abandoned. This is the dominance principle at work. Negative messages are less risky, as we explain later. They are aimed at convincing voters not to vote for the campaigner's rival. With luck, negative campaign messages shift voters from the rival to the message-sender, but even if negative campaigning merely persuades some of the opponent's supporters to stay home, the effort has paid off. If some of the rival's backers do not vote, fewer votes are needed to overcome any electoral advantage that the rival may have held.

This gloomy view of *homo politicus* forces us to ask questions about the effectiveness of campaign rhetoric. Why do voters care what politicians say, if politicians routinely subsume principles to expediency? Why do campaign promises have any impact in persuading voters, when such promises may be easily broken after the election? Why do voters look at anything more than a candidate's previous record?[23] What can they learn from words that will mean more to them than the candidate's actions? Voters know that campaign rhetoric is often "cheap talk" offered by candidates eager to get elected. Yet politicians since time immemorial have tried to persuade voters with promises that the voters have surely looked upon with skepticism.

The great orator Cicero successfully pursued the office of consul of Rome, relying on campaign advice given to him by his brother, Quintus Tullius, in an essay, *Commentariolum Petitioni,* to "change his air and his statements in accordance with the opinions of the people he meets" and—anticipating Riker's strategy of rhetoric by two millennia, to "[s]lander your opponents as often as possible, reckon their crimes, their sexual depravity, or their attempts to bribe other candidates—all according to the character of the individual opponent."[24]

Quintus Tullius provided the essential rationale behind the use of slander and deception in campaigns. Disproving the negative—denying allegations of personal depravity—is always difficult. Telling people what they want to hear always gratifies listeners, as long as they are not inalterably opposed to the speaker from the outset. Telling the whole truth does not provoke the same gratification in listeners and so is less likely to persuade. Politeness toward one's rivals does not stimulate the kind of doubt necessary to erode an opponent's support. Therefore, slander is a better means to gain support than generosity toward one's foes. We say this not as a normative endorsement of such behavior, but in recognition of its effectiveness as a strategy of campaigning. Indeed, the heresthetician, by recasting political debate, may be able to escape the pressure to use negative campaigning. But for the rhetorical campaigner, such escape is exceedingly difficult.

One Winning Position or Many Winning Positions?

Perhaps the best-known insight in political science is the median voter theorem: when an issue is one-dimensional (that is, the set of alternatives can be positioned along a single line) and preferences are single peaked (that is, any policy closer to the chooser's ideal policy than the status quo will be more desirable to the chooser than the status quo), and a majority is needed to win, then the position of the median voter will be the predicted political outcome.[25] Building on the insights of Harold Hotelling, Anthony Downs has shown that in such a one-dimensional, winner-take-all political landscape, politicians will gravitate toward the political center.[26] In converging on the median voter's position, they ensure that no rival can gain political advantage by staking out a different policy position. Indeed, quite the contrary: if one candidate moves closer to the median voter's policy preference and another candidate moves farther away, then the latter, more "extreme" candidate will lose support. Downs's account helps explain why most American presidential elections are close, with candidates who appear to be, like Tweedledum and Tweedledee, virtually indistinguishable.

The median voter theorem highlights how the more centrist candidate in a two-person race gains the advantage by keeping issues separate in the minds of the voters. To illustrate this we briefly consider the contest between Mikhail Gorbachev and Boris Yeltsin in 1990, foreshadowing our more extended discussion in chapter 7. Figure 1 illustrates the advantage Gorbachev would have gained if he had succeeded in keeping separate the political debates over economic reform and the degree of autonomy—if any—to be granted to the Russian Republic. The top half of the figure shows the policy preferences regarding reform of the Soviet economy among three critical factions: Gorbachev and his backers, Yeltsin and his supporters, and the nomenklatura. In 1990, Gorbachev still held the center on this issue. His position enjoyed the support of the median "voter" (or, in this case, the median official in the Communist Party and the Soviet Congress) and so was the "winning position." The top party nomenklatura, though more conservative than Gorbachev, certainly preferred his economic stance to Yeltsin's radical reformist position. Therefore, Gorbachev could count on their backing in a head-to-head contest.

When debate turned to the prospect of Russian sovereignty, Yeltsin again took a radical stance, far from the political center. On this issue, however, the nomenklatura (and general public opinion), rather than Gorbachev, were the relative centrists, although they were shifted closer to the right than to the left. They saw some value in expanding Russia's rights, thereby improving their own welfare or power position; but they were not yet ready to embrace full-fledged Russian sovereignty, at least not in the economic sphere. Thus, the nomenklatura included the median voter, probably forcing Gorbachev to be more receptive to modest improvements in the Russian Republic's well-being than he otherwise would have been. In a contest over Russian autonomy, we can infer from the assumption of single-peaked preferences that the nomenklatura would have sought modest concessions from Gorbachev while continuing to back him rather than throwing their support behind Yeltsin, whose position was farther from theirs.

Figure 1 looks at preferences on two important issues facing decision makers in Russia and, more broadly, the Soviet Union, in 1990–91. It shows us that as long as the economy and Russian sovereignty were treated separately, Yeltsin could expect to lose, as was confirmed by the results of the 1991 referendum, when the majority of Russians voted in favor of Gorbachev's plan to preserve the Soviet Union. Yeltsin needed to alter the terms of debate if he was to rise to power through direct elections.

The median voter theorem, of course, holds only under the condi-

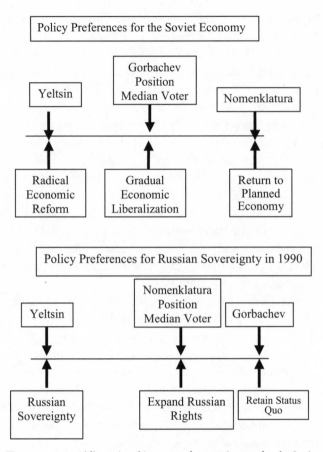

Fig. 1. Two separate, unidimensional issues, preferences in 1990 for the Soviet economy and for Russian autonomy

tions from which it is derived. If preferences are not single-peaked, or majority rule does not hold, or issues are not unidimensional and treated separately, then the median voter's preferred policy need not be the winning position. For instance, the chaos theorems of Richard McKelvey and Norman Schofield show that when issues are multidimensional or policy choices across issues are linked together, then there is a rational path to any policy stance so that neither the median voter's position, nor any other position, is privileged as the likely outcome unless some additional constraint is added to the decision-making environment.[27] Examples of such constraints include tie-breaking authority (such as is often granted to a committee chair), a fallback policy position (such as the existing policy), or agenda control (such as might be seized by a skillful campaigner).

Yeltsin could not alter the underlying, fundamental preferences of the decision makers. Nor was he yet in a position to change the decision-making procedure. So as long as the issues of economic well-being and Russian autonomy were framed as distinct political questions, there was little prospect that Yeltsin, as a rhetorician, could be persuasive enough to win. But as a heresthetician he could reframe the debate, tying the issues together inextricably. By linking issues he could find a path through the debate that would defy the median voter theorem, defeat Gorbachev, and win the election. To see how this could be done, we return to the two issues from figure 1, but now inquire about what would happen if Yeltsin bound these two questions to one another. We already know that Gorbachev had no interest in doing so. He profited from their being kept separate. Therefore, Riker's dominance principle tells us that Gorbachev, if left to his own strategic devices, would try to maintain that separation. Equally, we know that Yeltsin had to alter the terms of debate if he were to have a chance at political success.

Figure 2 shows what happens if Yeltsin succeeds in tying the issues together. While examining the figure, keep in mind that we continue to assume single-peaked preferences and majority rule among the few with a say, given the then-existing institutional arrangements. We continue to infer that a coalition of any two factions is sufficient to defeat the third. The solid dots show the ideal policies for each faction. They are located as in figure 1 on each issue. The solid oval shows the location of the existing policies on the two now-linked issues. It, too, is at the same location on each issue as was true in figure 1.

If we draw a circle (or ellipse if salience for the two issues is different) centered on a faction's ideal point so that the circumference of the circle is tangent to or just crosses through the position representing existing policies, then all policy combinations inside the circle are preferred by members of that faction to the existing policies. Figure 2 shows such circles for Gorbachev, Yeltsin, and the nomenklatura. If the circles for two factions intersect, as shown by the shaded area in figure 2, then the policy combinations that fall within the overlapping segment are preferred by both factions to the existing policies. Therefore, policy combinations in such overlapping areas reflect campaign positions around which a winning coalition could form to defeat the existing policies. In this case, the existing policies are the position of the median voter on each of the two dimensions: the degree of Russian

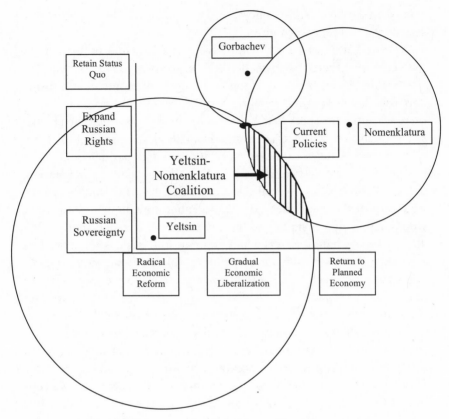

Fig. 2. Issue linkage and policy choice, an illustrative example

autonomy and economic reform. As separate issues, those policies favored Gorbachev over Yeltsin.

By arguing that the Russian economy could only be reformed through greater Russian independence, Yeltsin linked these two questions, opening the possibility that he could construct a coalition that could beat Gorbachev (and then restructure the institutional setting of coalition size and selectorate size in a more autonomous Russia). The shaded area in figure 2 shows the range of policy options regarding the economy and Russian independence that favored a political victory by Yeltsin.[28] We see that he could align himself with some in the party nomenklatura, as indeed he did. If Yeltsin behaved in accordance with Riker's dominance principle, then he not only would tie economic reform to greater Russian autonomy, but also would repeat his issue-linkage message—as indeed he did—because it won him more supporters than it cost him. We document this in chapter 7.

Taking figures 1 and 2 together, we see several important, well-established principles of politics. If issues are subject to the conditions of the median voter theorem, then centrist politicians are advantaged. In such cases, whoever occupies the policy stance desired by the middle voter is sure to win. If, however, issues are multidimensional, then positions far from the political status quo are advantaged. In such a setting, embracing the median voter policy on each dimension does *not* confer a political advantage. Rather, extreme policy stances offer an advantage, in that many variations from the status quo policy will be viewed by extremists as improvements, thereby fostering many opportunities for compromise. Strategic centrist politicians are therefore expected to keep issues separate, while extremists will link them together. Thus, whether issues are linked is probably not determined by inherent attributes of the policies in question, but is rather a consequence of heresthetical maneuvering; it is, in the vocabulary of game theorists, endogenous. Linkage is a critical path to political success for politicians whose policies lie outside the mainstream on important individual issues.

Centrists want to keep debate focused on separable, one-dimensional concerns because this form of campaign debate favors them. Those with policy preferences that are far from the center—Boris Yeltsin and Ronald Reagan both fit this description during the times they sought office—have an interest in introducing new policy combinations to political debate. By doing so, they improve their chances of breaking any existing coalition that favors their rivals, and replacing it with a coalition that improves their own chance of victory. Success in recasting political debate so that previously separate issues are seen as part of a single, larger problem, and in convincing voters that the candidate who links them has the right approach to solving the newly identified larger problem, depends on the campaigner both as a heresthetician and as a rhetorician.

The heresthetical component is essential. It is the creative means by which an otherwise losing candidate maneuvers into a position from which voters can be persuaded to deliver the support needed to win. Rhetoric is equally essential. It is the means by which those voters are persuaded. The candidate skilled at rhetoric is likely to improve her electoral prospects regardless of whether she is a centrist who successfully keeps issues apart or an extremist who links issues in a single, larger debate.

The Best Heresthetical Maneuvers

A politician vying for office attempts to satisfy a few simply stated—but difficult to implement—principles. Strategic politicians try to pick (and possibly link) positions so that if their opponents disagree with the selected position, the voters whom the opponents are counting on to elect them will most likely abandon them. Conversely, if opponents endorse the strategically successful politician's proposals, they will appear to compromise their core philosophy and thus lose constituents who subscribe to it. Furthermore, the incumbent will have conceded innovation on policy and control of the political agenda to the person he seeks to defeat. We will see in chapter 5 that Jimmy Carter faced these problems as a consequence of policy positions carved out by Ronald Reagan.

Successful heresthetical politicians advance their prospects by taking positions that bring new people into their camp and isolate their opponents by preventing them from embracing the positions the heresthetician has adopted. This is done by some combination of reshaping debate over issues and reshaping the institutions that determine who has a say in determining campaign outcomes. A skillful politician creates and capitalizes on such opportunities by acting on the dominance and dispersion principles. This is true even if—or perhaps especially because—the candidate is perceived as being well outside the political mainstream on individual issues.

Success through heresthetical maneuvers requires that a politician identify one or more issues that attract broad-based support among essential backers (voters in a democracy, military officers in a junta, etc.). If one or more issues exist that can attract broad support and cannot be endorsed or co-opted by other candidates, the politician has greatly improved his or her chances for success.

Rhetoric Redux

Finding issues that restructure political coalitions is difficult. With hindsight, students of American electoral politics are able to identify successful efforts to do so. The politician's challenge is much tougher than the scholar's: scholars need only recognize these realignments after they have occurred, whereas politicians must figure out how to bring them about. Recall that Riker asked how campaign speeches and promises could influence outcomes. In his study of the debates leading to the writing and ratification of the Constitution, he observed that politicians floated many new issues or new solutions to old issues.

Political history is strewn with examples of insightful politicians who nonetheless failed to advance their political prospects, even though their ideas eventually prevailed over those held by candidates who defeated them at the polls. We have only to think of a figure like Norman Thomas, who succeeded Eugene Debs as the Socialist Party candidate for president. Thomas, strongly anti-Soviet, was a founder of the American Civil Liberties Union and an early advocate of social security, racial equality, and efforts to combat poverty. Might he have risen to high office by employing the rhetoric of a mainstream politician? Thomas chose instead the rhetoric of an outlier, but apparently lacked sufficient heresthetical creativity or rhetorical panache to forge a strong base of support. Nevertheless, his ideas eventually became part of mainstream America. Franklin Roosevelt's Social Security program owed more than a little to Thomas's ideas, as did Lyndon Johnson's War on Poverty. Yet Norman Thomas is little more than a footnote in American political history.

Changing a losing coalition into a winning one is no small task. Consider the problem of entrenched policy positions. A candidate's core constituents typically hold well-formed preferences, and have concluded that their candidate's positions are close to their own. That is what makes them core constituents. It is rarely the case that the core constituency is so large that it alone ensures political victory. Therefore, rivals for office are likely to campaign for the support of swing voters. In addition, an aspiring candidate will seek to mobilize people who traditionally do not vote. The latter group typically does not hold well-formed political opinions, nor do they generally know much or care much about the candidates. If they did, they would already be in the fray.

How do candidates attract voters who are not members of their core constituency, or who would normally stay home? One significant answer, as Quintus Tullius so well understood, is negative arguments. Rhetoric about the virtues of one's own ideas is fine, but is unlikely to motivate new support. Those already committed to a candidate typically have weighed the costs and benefits of each candidate's positions and chosen the person they believe most likely to maximize the voter's welfare. But some people do not choose on this basis. Voters who have not committed to a candidate presumably believe they are as well off with one as with the other. One way to sway such voters or those planning not to vote is to make a persuasive case that their indifference exposes them to grave dangers. Negative campaigning does exactly that. It is a means by which candidates attempt to gain support by creating the belief that a victory for the other candidate will lead to disaster.

We know from the experimental research by Nobelist Daniel Kahneman and Amos Tversky that a considerable number of people choose on the basis of how issues are framed. Emphasizing the positive or negative aspects of a choice influences how these people respond to an otherwise comparable situation. Kahneman and Tversky found that people are more tenacious about preserving what they have—about avoiding losses—than they are about seeking new benefits. The risk of loss looms large in calculations. In such circumstances, many more prospective voters can be mobilized by raising their fear of losses than by promising future gains. When Ronald Reagan asked voters on the eve of the 1980 election to judge whether they were better off after four years under Jimmy Carter, he was invoking this principle. He was, in essence, encouraging voters to avoid the dangers that he claimed Carter embodied. The easiest way to do that, Reagan implied, was to vote for him.

Choosing on the basis of avoiding losses is one expression of a principle known as minimax regret. Simply put, those who act on the principle of minimax regret choose to do things that, if failure follows, will minimize their losses. Riker makes a persuasive case that it was negative campaigning, causing people to be in line with minimax regret, that drew out the extra, marginal support needed to pass the Constitution. Likewise, as just suggested, Reagan skillfully argued that the economic policies of his rival would lead to disaster in the form of persistently high inflation and high unemployment. Reagan's economic policies, untested before his election to the presidency, were surrounded with greater uncertainty than were Carter's. But through clever negative rhetoric Reagan made the case that the devil people knew—Carter's economic policies—was a bigger danger than the devil they did not— that is, Reagan's supply-side economics.

The Domestic Story of International Affairs

The twenty-first century in international affairs began around 1989, when democracy and market-based economies finally prevailed over

the third of their three most prominent twentieth-century rivals: mer-
cantilist monarchy (defeated in World War I), fascist dictatorship
(defeated in World War II), and authoritarian Communism (defeated in
the Cold War). As we look ahead to the challenges of the future,
prospective rivalries are brewing between, for example, religious fun-
damentalism and secular—increasingly democratic—governance.

The events that brought us to this emerging world order are not
exclusively nor even primarily the product of grand strategies in foreign
affairs that were sustained from one governing administration to
another. Nor are they solely the product of contests between superpower rivals. The end of the Cold War and the emerging new international order require a close focus on the role of leaders in their domestic context. Even political contests that ignore foreign affairs have the
potential to change fundamental international relationships. Without
attending to partisan domestic political competition, it is unlikely that
we can understand or illuminate what is possible in foreign affairs.

Our thesis is straightforward. Domestic political issues and competition over ideas shape choices about foreign policy. Whatever brings a
politician to national leadership, he or she must inevitably address foreign affairs. The intersection of ideas about foreign policy held by leaders in different countries determines the future course of international
relations. No one country can determine the course of events by mold-
ing a grand strategy that is independent of the domestic political context. Leaders select the issues that must be addressed and the direction
that policy takes. Their decisions reflect the choices they believe best
enhance their prospects of gaining or staying in high office. Therefore,
they must be attentive to the preferences of the citizens whose support
they require. Considerations of national power, national security, or
even the national interest play a more limited role in the choices leaders
make in foreign policy. Indeed, in political settings where leaders need
only the loyalty of the military and perhaps key civil servants, it will be
almost impossible to continue in power by enhancing the national
interest, if doing so comes at the expense of the few essential backers.
How else are we to explain the success of leaders like Cuba's Fidel Castro or North Korea's Kim Jong-il, who cling to power while beggaring
their people? They surely are not ruling on behalf of the well-being of
their citizenry.

Whether the focus of foreign affairs is on arms control, missile
defense, human rights, free trade, or counterterrorism, the solutions
chosen must be consistent with the incentives leaders and politicians

have to gain and maintain office. We investigate the end of the Cold War in the context of domestic political maneuvers in the United States and Russia. These maneuvers changed the structure of the international system, but they were designed and adopted with an eye toward control of domestic leadership, achieved through the give-and-take of local political competition.

Our focus on leadership probes general principles grounded in the individual motivations of prospective leaders. We show how those motivations translate into actions that can reshape the structural landscape of the international system. Although we illustrate our main propositions with the tactical and strategic maneuvers of Boris Yeltsin and Ronald Reagan, this is not a study of characteristics unique to these individuals. Rather, it is a study of how individual motives shape foreign policy, and how political choices, especially when made by someone at the helm of a major state, reshape international politics.

It is rare for world leaders to be selected on the basis of their foreign policy acumen or experience. Perhaps only when leaders are chosen against the backdrop of an international crisis do such skills predominate over everyday political ability. The German invasion of Poland in 1939 may have marked such an occasion, ensuring the downfall of Neville Chamberlain and the rise of Winston Churchill. But Adolf Hitler's rise to power through the ballot box did not depend primarily on his plans for foreign policy, even though, after the fact, it is evident that those plans were central to his policies as chancellor.

Most leaders are chosen over rivals because of skills in domestic politics. This is true whether the selection process is democratic or autocratic. Whether politicians are motivated by high-minded civic ideals or crass opportunism, they cannot fulfill their objectives without first coming to and then holding onto office. Consequently, those who shape international affairs are best understood first as politicians and only later perhaps as statesmen.

Whatever the domestic maneuvers that brought Ronald Reagan and Boris Yeltsin to their respective presidencies, their approaches to foreign affairs fundamentally changed the world. Their successes illustrate our central claim that individual leaders, rather than system structure, are fundamental to change or constancy in international politics. Understanding how leaders come to and stay in office is far more important to our grasp of major events in international politics than traditional ideas about the balance of power or bipolarity. Leaders make decisions constrained, but not determined, by the international environment in which they live. Those decisions include choices that can and do fundamentally change the international system.

....

Summary

We build on earlier work by William Riker and many others with the hope that we can offer additional insights into how campaign strategy, together with institutional context and rhetoric, influences electoral outcomes, policy formation, and the reshaping of international affairs. Our investigation focuses on five campaigns. These are Ronald Reagan's failed efforts to gain the Republic presidential nomination in 1968 and 1976, his successful effort to win the presidency in 1980, Boris Yeltsin's failed campaign against party conservatives in the period from about 1986 to 1988, and his successful effort to create an independent Russian state with himself at its head. In each case, we draw on ideas about heresthetic and rhetoric within the relevant institutional framework to explain the campaign strategies of Reagan, Yeltsin, and their rivals.

2

The New South Rises

....

Competition for the Republican
Presidential Nomination in 1968

Rhetoric can be viewed as a continuum: at one end is the verbal effort
to persuade one's audience, and at the other is the attempt to form an
issue-based agenda. A campaign in which rhetoric is a prominent feature can lean toward either end of the continuum or combine elements
of both. The contest for the 1968 Republican presidential nomination is
located at the persuasion end of the continuum. No major policy
agenda was set. In fact, none of the competitors presented a major policy program.

   The Republican competition for the 1968 presidential nomination
was characterized primarily by repeated rhetorical appeals from four
prominent politicians—Richard Nixon, Ronald Reagan, Nelson Rockefeller, and George Romney—each of whom attempted to persuade
party bosses, the rank and file, or both, that he could prevail in both the
primaries and the general contest. However, in the final weeks of the
primary season and throughout the Republican convention, Nixon
made a carefully crafted set of promises on civil rights, law and order,
and social unrest that came closer to heresthetical maneuvering than
anything else in the campaign. Although Nixon's strategy ultimately
thwarted the campaigns of the other contenders and satisfied the bloc
of southern conservatives who were central to securing his party's nom-

ination, it was not heresthetical. Unlike Ronald Reagan in 1980 and Boris Yeltsin in 1990 and 1991, Nixon did not present new or distinct policy alternatives that fundamentally reshaped policy debates.

Even when a rhetorical campaign does not set a political agenda, it may filter ideas; the give-and-take among candidates typically leads to some significant sifting of issues. Candidates adopt and repeat issues and themes that appeal to voters and abandon those that are not persuasive in order to "set the scene for heresthetical manipulation" in a future campaign.[1] Riker's analysis suggests that successful herestheticians often take many years to develop their skills. Even if they do not win, candidates who survive an earlier campaign may be prepared for future campaigning as heresthetecians.

Ronald Reagan lost the race for the GOP nomination in 1968, but he gained valuable experience in making rhetorical appeals in a presidential race, and in the process he also witnessed the powerful effect of Nixon's strategic combination of issues. Although he failed again in 1976 to win his party's presidential nomination, the 1968 and 1976 races provided him with the opportunity to hone his rhetorical appeals and heresthetical strategies, which in 1980 would play a major role in dramatically improving his performance against Jimmy Carter.

Although Riker was keenly attuned to the importance of the size and nature of the audiences candidates seek to court and the coalitions they hope to create, connecting such institutional factors to heresthetical strategies and rhetoric was not at the forefront of his intellectual project. As discussed in chapter 1, however, embedding our analysis of rhetorical and heresthetical strategies in the given institutional context allows for an extension of Riker's analysis along this feature of politics; it yields tests of the hypotheses about large and small coalitions associated with selectorate theory. A key hypothesis of selectorate theory is that when a small winning coalition exists, political actors typically use private benefits to keep their support group together.

In the nineteenth century and first half of the twentieth century, party power brokers dominated the process of nominating presidential candidates. As Nelson Polsby and Aaron Wildavsky have reported, the party bosses sought "to gain power, to nominate a man who can win the election, to unify the party, to obtain some claim on the nominee, to protect their central core of policy preferences, and to strengthen their state party organizations."[2] This system had been under assault for at least a decade before 1968 but it remained largely intact during the presidential race for a host of reasons, including, as political scientist Larry Bartels has written, the fact that it "was buffeted by an incredible series of political shocks" in American domestic politics in the first half of 1968.[3] In light of the fact that the old system largely remained in place, it would be virtually impossible to obtain the Republican presidential nomination in 1968 without the support of a small coalition of selectors—the conservative party leaders.

On a related note, primaries were not as central to securing the presidential nomination in 1968 as they would be in the future. In 1968, 17 states held Republican primaries and 34.3 percent of the delegate votes cast in the primaries were binding for the convention. By contrast, 35 states held Republican primaries in 1980 and 74.3 percent of the delegate votes during those primaries were considered binding at the convention.[4] The institutional makeup of the electoral system in 1968 reinforced the power of party leaders and made it more difficult for candidates to seek to broaden their political audience until, for the most part, after their party's convention because party leaders typically dominated all phases of the nomination process—from primaries through the national convention—through the old politics of decision making in smoke-filled backrooms.

Setting the Stage

In 1964, Senator Barry Goldwater gave prominent attention to the concerns of conservatives below the Mason-Dixon Line by opposing civil rights legislation and federal intervention in state desegregation efforts, but this "southern strategy" did not deliver the national triumph he had hoped for.[5] President Lyndon B. Johnson won the election by 16 million votes, one of the largest margins in any American presidential contest. With 61 percent of the popular vote and 486 electoral votes to Goldwater's 38 percent of the popular vote and 52 electoral votes, Johnson scored a decisive victory.

The Arizona legislator was not alone in defeat. Republicans lost 38 seats in the House of Representatives, leaving them with 140 members, their smallest delegation since 1936. They also lost two Senate seats, leaving a total of just 32, the weakest GOP representation since 1940. Republicans added one governor to their roster, but that only brought their national total to 17. Democrats also made substantial gains in state legislatures, while, as one observer noted, "more Republican defeats in the state and local contest[s] prompted talk of [the] eventual disappearance of the party from the American political scene."[6] Two months after the election, Ray Bliss, the new GOP national chairman, reported, "All the press wanted to ask me was whether or not I thought the Republican Party could survive as an effective force in our nation."[7]

Despite these grim predictions, the conservative wing of the party rose phoenixlike from the ashes in 1966, gaining 3 seats in the Senate, 47 in the House, and 8 governorships. Thirteen of the House seats won were from southern districts, 7 of which represented victories over Democratic incumbents.[8] The Democrats lost 24 of the 38 House seats they had won only two years earlier. Ronald Reagan of California and Claude R. Kirk, Jr., the first Republican to be elected governor of Florida since 1872, were among those who defeated Democrats in gubernatorial races.[9]

The Republicans were making impressive inroads in the South. In 1964, Goldwater had won his home state of Arizona and the five Deep South states of Alabama, Georgia, Louisiana, Mississippi, and South Carolina. The "Solid South" that had been a Democratic stronghold for almost a century was no longer solid. Power was shifting from the Northeast liberal wing of the Republican Party to conservatives in the South and West, where leaders representing the New Right worked efficiently to ensure that the realignment would lead to victory in the next presidential election.

After a long and acrimonious battle against Goldwater, party liberals and moderates such as Governor William Scranton, Governor Nelson A. Rockefeller, and Ambassador Henry Cabot Lodge saw their wing of the party demoralized and disoriented. Though still influential, these Northeast-based liberal Republicans found themselves in the unfamiliar position of struggling to recapture their influence in the party.

The rapidity of the GOP's recovery was due largely to the intense political and social changes of the time. Between the 1964 and 1968 elections, voter preferences were shaped and sharpened by numerous issues, including civil rights, law and order, school busing, and the Vietnam War. For nearly a week in August 1965, rioters ravaged Watts, California, leaving more than 30 people dead. Between January and September 1967, 164 "disorders," including the devastating race riots in Detroit, took place in 128 American cities. The Kerner Commission, appointed by President Johnson to investigate the causes of urban unrest and propose solutions, designated eight of the disorders as "major" on the grounds that they involved "many fires, intensive looting, and reports of sniping; violence lasting more than two days; sizeable crowds; and use of National Guard or federal forces as well as other control forces."[10] The period from 1964 to 1968 saw approximately 329 notable black riots in 257 cities.[11]

While the nonviolent movement spearheaded by Reverend Martin Luther King, Jr., progressed, other, more confrontational black movements were gathering steam. Stokely Carmichael, the newly installed president of the Student Nonviolent Coordinating Committee, helped usher in a distinctive language and attitude when he declared, "We want black power" at a rally in Greenwood, Mississippi, in June 1966. That same fall, Huey Newton and Bobby Seale formed the Black Panther Party in Oakland, California.

As these and other radical forces increased their participation in the political process, traditional Democratic leaders, including black centrists, began to lose control of the left-center coalition that had governed the party for so long. This breakdown exposed the uneasiness with which many whites regarded the civil rights movement. White liberals supported the redress of past injustices and the guarantee of equal rights, but many were frightened by black radical behavior and the more sweeping demands of the new generation of black activists. A groundswell of opposition to the black power movement was also building within the Democratic Party's working-class base.[12]

In April 1965, a few months before the Watts riots, 71 percent of northern whites polled said that the pace at which Washington was implementing racial integration was either "not fast enough" or "about right." Polls taken shortly after the riots showed that number dropping to 64 percent, and by the early fall of the following year, it had dwindled to just 48 percent.[13] Victorious in 1964, the Democratic Party was crumbling two years later beneath the weight of the very forces it had helped unleash.

Meanwhile, crime rates soared throughout the 1960s, with a dramatic 83 percent increase between 1966 and 1971. The number of blacks arrested for homicide jumped by more than 130 percent between 1960 and 1970, and the plight of poor blacks in inner cities had become a national crisis.[14]

Race, civil rights, and urban turmoil were not the only sources of dissension. Opposition to the Vietnam War was also growing, especially among college-educated youth. In 1962, Students for a Democratic Society issued a far-ranging statement in defense of civil rights and against Cold War foreign policy. And the New Left, which was

focusing much of its energy on opposing the Vietnam War, issued a call
to arms in its Port Huron Manifesto. Yet a large proportion of working-class Democrats viewed the antiwar movement as an even greater
problem for the United States than the conflict in Indochina.[15]

Law and order cut across the issues of civil rights, societal unrest,
and Vietnam, and became an issue in itself. Seventy percent of whites
who took a dovish position on Vietnam also rejected the statement that
"too much force" had been used by the police against the demonstrators at the 1968 Democratic National Convention in Chicago. A political science study published in 1969 reported that whites had generally
become more liberal on civil rights between 1964 and 1968, but were
disturbed by social unrest, accounting for their support of law-and-
order campaign policies.[16] For many working-class and southern
whites, the phrase *law and order* was code for issues of the utmost
importance to them, such as opposition to government-enforced racial
integration of public institutions, and school busing. Concern over law
and order was to play a major role in the 1968 election.

The Republican challenge in 1968 was to avoid repeating the defeat
of 1964, to exploit the fissures in the Democratic Party represented in
part by the challenges from the black power movement and the New
Left, and to continue the momentum of the successful 1966 election. In
other words, the party would need to reflect the preferences of New
Right voters on the presidential ticket without compromising the
acceptability of the GOP's message to a broader set of voters. From the
primaries through the convention, this meant gaining the support of the
emerging New Right bloc in the South. The main issues these voters
opposed were civil rights legislation, court-ordered racial integration,
school busing, and social protest movements. These voters supported a
continuation of U.S. involvement in the Vietnam War. The Republicans
needed a ticket during the actual presidential race that would appeal to
some Democrats and independents, since, according to some analyses,
46 percent of Americans were affiliated with the Democratic Party in
1968, 27 percent with the Republicans, and 27 percent labeled themselves independents.[17]

The Conservative Barons

The heirs to the 1964 conservative revolution—Senators Barry M.
Goldwater, Strom Thurmond, and John Tower—became important

gatekeepers on the road to the 1968 GOP nomination. Goldwater's hard-fought battle in 1964 had earned him a unique position of honor in the emerging conservative wing of the Republican Party.[18]

Through the highly effective and financially independent operation known as The Thurmond Speaks for Goldwater Committee, the senator from South Carolina helped Goldwater win the four southern states that Thurmond had carried as a segregationist presidential candidate under the Dixiecrat banner in 1948. Then, two months after Goldwater's victory at the Republican convention, Thurmond changed his party affiliation from Democrat to Republican. His successful run for reelection to the Senate in 1966 made him the first Republican to win statewide office in South Carolina in nearly 100 years.

The third member of the trio, John Tower, was the first Republican elected to the U.S. Senate from Texas since Reconstruction and the first senator to declare his stalwart support for Goldwater's presidential bid. Although Texas delivered its 25 electoral votes—more than any other southern state—to Johnson, significant Republican inroads were made that would have an important effect on the next round of elections.

A second tier of conservatives, principally composed of Republican Party state chairmen from southern states, rose from the 1964 race into positions of influence. This group included, among many others, Harry Dent of South Carolina, William F. Murfin of Florida, Peter O'Donnell of Texas, and Clarke Reed of Mississippi, who together formed an association that became known as the Greenville Group. The three met regularly at Reed's home in Greenville, Mississippi, to monitor the party's commitment to the South in the 1968 national election.[19]

The 1964 Goldwater campaign also attracted many southerners into the Republican Party's rank and file. Drawing on the party infrastructure and coffers they had built up during the 1964 campaign, southern Republican loyalists now had the means to influence the GOP's 1968 nomination and ensure that the new candidate would stand with the South as firmly as Goldwater had in 1964.[20]

Liberal and Moderate Leaders

Conservatives were gaining influence, but liberals and moderates continued to exert authority during the 1968 race. George Romney and Nelson A. Rockefeller were among the most influential of the GOP liberals. Romney found cover behind his favorite-son banner during the bitter 1964 battle between Goldwater and Rockefeller. In 1966, he won a third term as governor of Michigan by a half-million votes. Even before his widely expected victory, Romney was considered a serious front-runner for the presidential nomination.[21]

Rockefeller had been badly bruised in the 1964 presidential race. He received only 22 percent of the vote during the primaries, was booed at the convention when he accused Goldwater of political extremism, and received only 114 delegate votes to Goldwater's 883 on the first ballot. In winning his third term as governor of New York in 1966, he attracted an impressive number of votes from Democrats and independents, demonstrating his viability as a political contender within the GOP's northeastern liberal wing.

Senator Everett M. Dirksen and Vice President Richard Nixon were first among the centrists, having ridden the tide of the Goldwater movement.[22] Dirksen, the Senate minority leader, had been extremely influential in Republican politics long before Goldwater's presidential campaign. His close ties to President Johnson and his staunch support of the president's Vietnam policy enabled Dirksen to bridge the widening gap between the parties. His leadership for Senate approval of the Civil Rights Act of 1964, a reversal of his initial opposition to the bill, had boosted his credentials as a Republican moderate.[23] But his tireless work on Goldwater's behalf further elevated his political profile and sent an important signal to a broader constituency.

Nixon also emerged from the 1964 race as a prominent player in Republican politics. In 1964, he visited more than 30 states on behalf of Goldwater and scores of other Republican candidates. After the election he helped move the Republican Party in a more moderate direction by quietly assisting in the replacement of Goldwater's strategist, Dean Burch, with Ray Bliss. Bliss was an Ohio party leader who, as chairman of the Republican Party, had helped Nixon win the state in his 1960 battle against John F. Kennedy.[24] The support that Nixon was accumulating among the Republican Party elite was decidedly more centrist than the political forces that had elevated Goldwater in 1964.

Yet Nixon also maintained close ties with the conservatives. In January 1965—the same month that Bliss took over the party's top post—Goldwater publicly endorsed Nixon's candidacy for the 1968 presidential race.[25] The most vigorous campaigner for Republican candidates in the 1966 race, the vice president was widely acknowledged for his role in the party's turnaround that year.[26]

Other moderates, such as Congressman Gerald R. Ford, were important bellwethers, but Romney, Rockefeller, Dirksen, and Nixon represented the core group of GOP moderates.[27]

The Presidential Contenders

Nixon, Reagan, Rockefeller, and Romney were the Republican Party's most serious contenders for the presidential nomination in 1968. Of the four, Ronald Reagan was the only major GOP hopeful who was not a longtime party leader. Although he had been famous for decades, he had won his first major political office only two years before the 1968 national election. He was also the only truly conservative candidate in the field.

On October 27, 1964, the former actor and spokesman for the General Electric Company gave a 30-minute televised address supporting Goldwater's presidential bid. In "A Time for Choosing," Reagan warned against big government, a runaway bureaucracy, the welfare state, and the United Nations. He described the worldwide Communist movement as "the most evil enemy mankind has known in the long climb from the swamp to the stars."[28] This address was one performance of "The Speech," a concise statement of the general political philosophy that Reagan had been delivering to audiences for more than a decade. But this time was different.

Now, instead of addressing workers at a GE plant in the middle of the country, Reagan was speaking to millions of Americans from coast to coast, and they listened. The Speech raised more than a half-million dollars for the Republican Party, and when he finished delivering it Ronald Reagan was a national political figure. A group of conservative California businessmen quickly identified him as a future presidential candidate, but first they would have to persuade Reagan to run for statewide office.[29] They prevailed.

On November 8, 1966, Ronald Reagan won the governorship of California by almost a million votes. As the New York Times reported two days later, "Without a day in public office [Reagan became] the favorite Presidential candidate of Republican conservatives."[30]

"As governor," Reagan wrote in a letter, "I was asked to be a favorite son for president [in 1968] to hold our California party together. I agreed on the condition that that was as far as it would go. I would not be a real candidate."[31] Yet, secondary and primary sources, including the archival files of the main Republican challengers and many of their advisers, show that Reagan was an important force in the contest for the Republican presidential nomination in 1968 and courted the type of national exposure that would make him a politically viable candidate if the opportunity presented itself at the Republican convention in Miami Beach in August 1968.

The Wallace Insurgency

Another presidential contender in 1968 played a more important role in Republican deliberations about their nominee than in his own party's choice of a challenger. In the Democratic primaries of 1964, Alabama Governor George C. Wallace won 33.8 percent of the vote in Wisconsin, 29.8 percent in Indiana, and 42.7 percent in Maryland.[32] Emboldened by his respectable showing and determined to stop federally mandated integration from changing southern political institutions, Wallace considered competing as a third-party candidate in the general election. But Strom Thurmond persuaded the governor to abandon his plans; a Wallace candidacy would have doomed Goldwater in the South, the only region in which he would win a bloc of electoral votes. So instead of running in 1964, Wallace campaigned energetically for Goldwater.

But there was no stopping the Wallace candidacy in 1968. He formed the American Independent Party early that year, and his supporters successfully placed his name on the ballot in all 50 states. While he never expected to win, he hoped his electoral vote total would throw the election into the House of Representatives, which would enable him to influence the choice of the next president.[33]

Both Democrats and Republicans knew that Wallace's candidacy posed a threat to their electoral designs. In fact, Wallace carried five southern states in 1968, won a larger proportion of the popular vote (approximately 13.5 percent) than any third-party presidential candidate since 1924, and garnered a greater proportion of electoral votes than any third-party candidate since the election of 1860.[34]

If his campaign could not be stopped, then conservative Republicans would need to prevent southern whites from stampeding toward the American Independent Party. In order to do this, they needed a presidential candidate who could convincingly tell southerners what they wanted to hear on the issues and desegregation in particular.[35]

Setting Up the Game

Barry Goldwater, Strom Thurmond, John Tower, the GOP state chairmen, and other party leaders absorbed three key lessons from Goldwater's 1964 presidential bid that would influence their efforts in 1968:

1. Avoid the kind of divisive primary contests that had split GOP support between Goldwater on the one side and Scranton and Rockefeller on the other.

2. Secure delegates for the favored candidate well in advance of the party's convention, as had been done for Goldwater (who received 883 of his 1,308 delegate votes on the first ballot).

3. Select a candidate who could garner the support of both the growing conservative movement in the South and the wider electorate.

These lessons led conservative Republican leaders to search for a candidate who was, in essence, a pragmatist. And while rank-and-file conservatives shared the barons' political preferences—for a candidate who advocated continued engagement in Vietnam, states' rights, a desegregation policy sensitive to southern culture, and law-and-order measures that would address crime in American cities—they drew a different lesson from 1964 about the importance of nominating a true soldier. Unlike the barons, the rank and file did not want a candidate who would appease both conservatives and moderates. This bloc of voters could not be ignored because it would be particularly influential at the party's convention. Whoever was going to win the Republican nomination would have to reconcile these two very different, indeed conflicting, electoral strategies.

According to the Republican Party's accounting rules, a state that delivered its electoral votes to the presidential nominee in 1964 would receive six additional delegates. One additional delegate would be granted to a congressional district that cast more than 10,000 votes for Goldwater. Under the new configuration, the southern states could unite to nominate or block a candidate at the convention. Southern states controlled 356 of the 1,333 delegates to the 1968 convention, and a candidate required 667 delegate votes to win the party's nomination.[36] In short, it would be difficult, if not impossible, to forge a winning coalition without the support of the southern delegates, who had been organized by the barons into a cohesive voting bloc. The barons thus ensured their control over the nomination process and their likely future control over how the Republican Party distributed resources and selected candidates.

Faced with the challenge of keeping the rank and file under control, numerous liberal and conservative party elites designated themselves as favorite sons in their respective states. As a favorite son, a candidate would not necessarily expect to win the nomination, but he would, in principle, be able to deliver his entire delegation's vote to the candidate of his choice.[37] Party leaders also invoked the unit rule, which required that an entire delegation vote in concert with the majority of its delegates at the convention. This ensured that the effective size of a winning coalition within the Republican Party was actually smaller than the 667 delegates nominally required; it could, in fact, be won with support from as few as half that number if delegate votes were strategically mobilized under the unit rule.

For Reagan and Nixon, the challenge was to identify a set of issues and a political strategy that would enable the party elites and the rank and file to build a coalition that would deliver the necessary delegate votes. Both Reagan and Nixon had essentially written off the industrial Northeast to Romney and Rockefeller. Instead, the first step in their campaigns depended upon the undecided South. Reagan's strategy was to circumvent the barons and take his conservative message directly to the rank-and-file cadre. But the more he did so, the harder the barons worked to keep the cadre in line, and the less inclined they were to support him. Furthermore, Reagan never presented a policy message that the barons could embrace.

As the presidential candidates competed for the nomination, the barons prepared for the general election. And the more that Reagan's message resonated with the delegates, the tighter the barons banded together against him. So long as they remained unified and could deliver blocs of votes under the unit rule, they could still determine the Republican nominee. Thus, by trying to skirt this small coalition of elites, Reagan diminished his chances of gaining the nomination.

Nixon's strategy, in comparison, was to use code words that satisfied southern conservatives and at the same time enabled him to hold onto the political center. The barons liked his strategy, but many rank-and-file Republicans distrusted him.

Liberal and moderate Republicans supported Romney and Rockefeller, but neither enjoyed much, if any, support from conservatives and southerners. Both needed to find a way to bring the conservatives into their respective camps without jeopardizing the support of their natural political constituencies. The challenge was daunting. Each needed to court and gain the support of the conservative barons as well as the rank and file. Rockefeller described the situation at a campaign rally in San Francisco on July 8, 1968: "The key political issue of 1968 is whether the people or the bosses will make the final decisions at the Republican and Democratic national conventions."[38]

Rockefeller's presidential drive was further complicated by the fact that his entry into the contest depended on Romney's failure. The New York governor was gun-shy after the 1964 Goldwater upset. He and his advisers believed that he should initially support Romney and then enter the race himself only if Romney's presidential drive failed to gain momentum, something they hoped would happen late in the primary season.[39]

Phase 1: November 9, 1966, to April 3, 1968

After the 1966 election, Reagan, Nixon, and Rockefeller were all show-ing well in opinion polls on possible Republican presidential candi-dates. Romney was generally considered the front-runner in 1966 and 1967, and on November 18, 1967, he made his candidacy official. On February 1, 1968, six weeks before the New Hampshire primary, Nixon entered the contest. Rockefeller, once Romney's most influential backer, had quietly begun his own preparations to enter the competi-tion if circumstances became favorable. Romney's February 28, 1968, withdrawal from the race provided the New York governor with an opening. On April 30, 1968, Rockefeller announced that he would cam-paign for the Republican Party's presidential nomination. Reagan threw his hat in the ring on August 5, 1968, the first day of the Repub-lican convention, but, as mentioned earlier, he and the other candidates had been developing campaign strategies and reaching out to potential supporters throughout 1966 and 1967.[40]

Romney did not emerge from his 1966 reelection campaign with the support of the new power barons or the conservative rank and file within the Republican Party. During the summer of 1966, for example, Goldwater publicly predicted that Romney would not win the 1968 nomination, saying, "I don't believe the party will forget the fact that he took a walkout in 1964."[41]

A lengthy memo dated September 1, 1966—two months before Romney was reelected governor—outlined his campaign strategy. Written by Glen Bachelder, a Romney adviser, and titled "Timing, Issues & Strategy," the memo essentially urged the governor to adopt a southern strategy different from the one used by Goldwater in 1964:

> [T]he basic strategy must be directed at seeking Negro participation and support. This means a rejection of the Southern strategy of 1964. . . . Strategy must recognize that there is a new South— urban, industrial, suburban and technical. . . . The appeal must be to the racial moderates on the one big issue of that region— civil rights. There are community leaders, such as in Atlanta, who recognize reason and progress on this issue. They and their kind must be appealed to, not the outright segregationists of the old order. A final note on this: the number of registered Negro voters in the South will be very significant by November, 1968.

In other words, the memo called upon the governor to play to his natural political base but provided no framework by which he could expand his political reach. In fact, the memo surmised that the governor could not win in the Deep South: "There is a good possibility of winning Florida, Tennessee, and Virginia," and North Carolina and Arkansas were "within striking distance," but "the longest shots are the Goldwater-Wallace states—Alabama, Georgia, Louisiana, Mississippi, South Carolina."

Bachelder's memo also suggested that Romney situate himself between his two likely competitors for the Republican presidential nomination: Reagan, who had not yet been elected governor of California, and Nixon. Bachelder wrote that Romney would be politically strongest in the East, Midwest, and Mountain West; that Nixon would dominate the South; and that Reagan would command the Far West, with the possible exceptions of Oregon and Washington. The memo foreshadowed Romney's actual campaign strategy from the fall of 1966 until he withdrew his candidacy in February 1968.

Bachelder also declared the obvious: "Any national campaign must be based on issues."[42] Yet the difficulty of finding issues with which the governor could be distinctly identified plagued Romney's campaign, which was generally characterized by vague statements about foreign and domestic policy, and policy recommendations that clearly reflected the candidate's moderate positions.[43] The speeches he gave on several

1967 tours, for example, failed to produce a distinct understanding of his overall policy agenda. At no point did he give a comprehensive statement about any policy issue, although he presented a plan to end the Vietnam War toward the end of his campaign. In February, he traveled to Alaska, Utah, Idaho, New Mexico, and Arizona, where he espoused conservative themes, telling audiences, "In state after state, we proved that progressive state governments could meet problems with greater understanding, closer attention, better follow-through and wider citizen involvement and control."[44]

Some listeners may have been impressed, but the Michigan governor did not inspire a noticeable broadening of his political base. Alaska Governor Walter J. Hickel gave Romney "an excellent chance" of receiving Alaska's 12 delegate votes, but added that they were "not for sale." In fact, by the end of Romney's western tour, he began to lose ground among likely voters. For instance, in a Gallup Poll conducted on January 26–31, Romney beat President Lyndon Johnson with 50 percent of the vote to Johnson's 42 percent in a presidential trial heat and when pitted against Nixon in a Gallup survey on February 16–21, the Michigan governor was endorsed by 45 percent of those surveyed and Nixon received 41 percent. In a presidential heat against Senator Robert Kennedy on February 16–21, Romney was ahead with 48 percent to the senator's 46 percent. Yet, a March 9–14 survey of the likely Republican field placed Romney behind Nixon with 30 percent of voter support to the vice president's 39 percent. In a March 30–April 5 Gallup presidential trial heat where Johnson was the Democratic candidate, Romney the Republican candidate, and George Wallace was the third-party contender, Johnson received 43 percent of voter support, Romney 35 percent, Wallace 13 percent, and 9 percent of those questioned were undecided.[45]

Two months after concluding his tour, Romney gave what was planned as a major speech on the Vietnam War. Speaking to an audience in Hartford, Connecticut, he said, "[I]t is unthinkable that the United States withdraw from Vietnam. . . . Our military effort must succeed. I believe that we must use military force as necessary to reduce or cut off the flow of men and supplies from North Vietnam to knock out enemy main force units, and to provide a military shield for the South. We must give our gallant fighting men our full support. . . . We must stand immovably against all pressures which would preclude a just peace."[46] President Johnson immediately declared that the governor's speech reflected his own views. As authors Michael Kramer and Sam Roberts contend, LBJ's statement effectively denied Romney the opportunity to offer an independent voice on Vietnam.[47]

Romney was attracting the notice of at least one of the barons. Senator John Tower, favorite son of the Texas delegation, endorsed the Hartford speech in a letter to the governor: "Your remarks on Southeast Asia were thoughtful, constructive and well done. I have been in several places across the country in the interim and the comments I have heard are favorable. . . . None of the commanders I have talked with feel it wise or necessary for us to destroy North Vietnam. They advocate continued, controlled military pressure toward negotiations or an ultimate 'fading away' of communist efforts."[48]

Despite this expression of support from an influential colleague, Romney was not gaining in national approval. His ratings began to climb again in July following the Detroit race riots, but the improvement was short-lived.

Romney remained in contact with the barons, but a strategy document written on July 5, 1967, suggested that he should seek the political center of the Republican Party:

> The dynamics of the situation leave Romney without a major competition for the middle position. It is obvious that Nixon or Reagan will have little chance of uniting the [Senator Charles H.] Percy or Rockefeller factions behind them. Percy's Vietnam position has permanently ruled out support of conservative Republican opinion which has been in complete support of a "hard" line in Vietnam and on the world Communist tension front. Rockefeller has no chance at all of winning right conservative support because of his New York State domestic program, his anti-Goldwater campaign in '64, and his general symbolism of liberalism.
>
> But even more important, the more Reagan appears as a formidable threat with a real chance to win, the more moderate middle-of-the-road Republican leadership will turn to Romney to head off an extreme conservative takeover with a probable repeat of the '64 debacle.
>
> And the more Rockefeller appears as the true main candidate of the moderate-liberal Eastern Wing, the more moderate-conservative opinion will be alarmed and see Romney as the lesser of two evils.

In this situation Romney's strategy should be to let the left
and right wings quarrel among themselves and to let them volley
across the extremes on the opposite side.[49]

The fact that the memo pays no attention to issues or policy positions
may account for Romney's inability to impart a distinct perspective on
domestic and foreign policy, and for the "impression of confusion"
detected by his audiences.[50]

In fact, the governor fell victim to his own misstatements. On
August 31, 1967, during the taping of a Michigan television program, he
said that in 1965 he had received "the greatest brainwashing that anyone can get when you go over to Vietnam, not only by the generals, but
also by the diplomatic corps over there, and they do a very thorough
job." Upon further consideration, he explained, he could no longer
support U.S. policy, and now believed it had been a mistake for the
United States to become involved in the conflict at all. He blamed the
United States for the war, saying, "[W]e have created the conflict that
now exists between Communism and freedom there," and warning the
South Vietnamese government against "count[ing] on continuing supplies of men and material without limit." Romney's electoral prospects,
which had been waning even before his national tour, were greatly
diminished by his "brainwashing" pronouncement, which made
national headlines.[51] But he soldiered on.

The next day, Romney Associates, the governor's own campaign
and polling organization, took the position that "only he, can defeat
the incumbent Democratic President."[52] Soon thereafter, Romney commenced a more ambitious tour. He traveled to 13 states over 19 days in
September 1967, investigating and discussing the social and economic
conditions of inner cities.[53] But instead of unveiling a plan to cure
urban ills, he simply called for improved race relations. A devout Mor-
mon, Romney advocated a "restoration of faith in America and the
Constitution."[54] On the issue of Medicaid, he adopted a middle position between Reagan and Rockefeller, limiting his criticism to the lack
of flexibility in the program and its encroachment on private sources of
health care for the indigent.[55]

In light of the race riots and rising crime rates plaguing American
cities in the late 1960s, the issue of law and order was a major concern
for the American public. Conservative Republicans wanted a presidential candidate who would advocate tough measures. Romney attempted
to tackle the issue on September 30 during his final statement on his

urban tour: "While we must maintain law and order, we must either achieve orderly progress or change will be inflicted with mortal wounds. Either we shall join hands, hearts, and minds and march together on paths of fulfillment for all, or we shall find ourselves torn asunder."[56] Muted and inconclusive, the statement, like the tour, failed to persuade the public that the governor of Michigan should be president.

In the fall, it was Reagan and Rockefeller, not Romney, who were featured in a *Time* magazine cover article about the presidential race.[57] Rockefeller would continue to support his fellow governor, but it was becoming clear to Romney that he would not recapture his earlier standing as the front-runner, even among moderates who had hoped to be persuaded by him. In fact, fellow Republican politicians told the Romney team that they were hearing a rumor "that Governor Romney was being used by Governor Rockefeller" to pave the political ground for the New Yorker's entry into the race.[58]

At the end of October 1967, the Michigan governor began yet another tour, this time to New England. While in New Hampshire he described himself as the underdog for the nomination. He reviewed familiar themes, including the excesses of the federal government and the need for racial tolerance. He charged that the Johnson administration's foreign policy had damaged the United States' international standing, and declared himself "a dissenter on our government's policy in Vietnam."[59] His visit to the home of the first primary failed to ignite deep interest in his candidacy.

Romney made another series of attempts to bolster his national standing later that fall. On November 18 he officially announced his intention to seek the nomination. In early December, he declared that underdevelopment, not Communism, posed the greatest threat to U.S. interests.[60] Later in December he traveled to Europe and Asia, where he looked into the idea of declaring Indochina a neutral, alliance-free zone, as a means of ending the conflict on the peninsula. On January 15, 1968, after more than a year on the campaign circuit, Romney unveiled his plan of "guaranteed neutralization" at Keene State College in New Hampshire:

> There would be a removal of foreign military troops or bases in the area and there would be no alliances by nations in the area with outside blocs, either Eastern or Western. The principle of self-determination would hold sway internally. The nations con-

cerned would be free to pursue and should be assisted in achieving economic development cooperatively on a regional basis.[61]

A month later, after more than a year of touring the country to discuss social issues such as crime, discrimination, health care, and unemployment, Romney elaborated on his Vietnam policy, telling an audience in Manchester, New Hampshire, that until the Vietnam War ended, "there can't be adequate progress" on social policy. He called Nixon "a me-too candidate on Vietnam" because the former vice president had not taken a strong stance against the Johnson administration's execution of the war. Romney also issued a foreign policy paper in which he said that Americans must "apply the enormous wealth and technology of our society in helping poverty-stricken peoples."[62]

The Michigan governor's speeches, tours, and position refinements failed to reverse the slippage in his political standing. Gallup surveys at the end of the year showed a clear reversal in Romney's political fortunes. In an October 27–November 1, 1967, survey about who would be the best Republican presidential nominee, Nixon was supported by 42 percent of those questioned, Rockefeller was endorsed by 15 percent, Romney took 14 percent of the vote, and Reagan received 13 percent of voter support. In a December survey of Republican county chairmen, Gallup reported that 52 percent of the Republican officials endorsed Nixon, 24 percent were for Reagan, 14 percent supported Rockefeller, and Romney trailed with 5 percent of support among the officials.[63]

On February 25, 1968, William Johnson, Romney's New Hampshire campaign director, and Leonard Hall, his national campaign chairman, met in Washington to review the results of a poll by Market Opinion Research, the governor's Detroit-based firm. The results showed that in the upcoming New Hampshire primary Nixon would receive 70 percent of the vote to Romney's 10.[64] Three days later, Romney withdrew from the race.

The governor had disregarded the lessons that his party's leaders had drawn from the 1964 campaign. By attacking Nixon on Vietnam, he showed a propensity to instigate the same type of internecine conflict that had plagued the GOP primaries of 1964. Southern and conservative leaders would not support his policy stances, and even Romney's natural base in the North and Midwest remained unconvinced by his pronouncements on important issues. His negative campaigning against Nixon was not of the persuasive sort discussed in chapter 1, and it failed to persuade voters that his opponent's stance on Vietnam would lead to policies as disastrous as some of Johnson's had been. By Romney's own admission, he failed to win "wide acceptance with rank-and-file Republicans."[65] The governor of Michigan never hit his rhetorical stride, and had gained the support of few delegates.

Ronald Reagan began seeking the Republican nomination for president shortly after the 1966 midterm election. On November 17, just nine days later, the governor-elect held what was in effect his first planning session. He and his advisers concluded that the real contest for the Republican nomination would take place at the convention, not in the primaries. Tom Reed has recorded in his notes that Reagan authorized him, as the governor-elect's director of national political operations, to retain F. Clifton White, the strategist who had delivered 883 delegates to Goldwater in 1964, to deal with "the delegate-hunting business."[66]

The Californian's political views resonated with the barons, with other conservative Republican leaders, and with the Republican rank and file. Indeed, Reagan was the only conservative candidate, as defined by the New Right. His challenge was to find a combination of issues and policy stances that would appeal to a wider constituency. It was a goal he would have to achieve in order to enlist actual support from the barons, who wanted a candidate capable of winning the general election.

Reagan's first year as governor in 1967 was devoted in part to testing the national political waters. It was also a year in which the barons sought to decide which of the contenders, Reagan or Nixon, would make the best nominee. Tom Reed, who chronicled Reagan's political activities in his diary of the campaign, understood at the time that "with the support of these four men [Dirksen, Goldwater, Thurmond, and Tower] Reagan might win the nomination. With their opposition—no chance."[67]

Reed retained Stuart Spencer, of Spencer-Roberts—the political consultant who had helped Reagan during his gubernatorial campaign—for the first six months of 1967. Early in 1967, Reed and Spencer agreed that Reagan would hold the delegates in California by announcing as a favorite-son candidate for president. They also concurred that Reagan should compete in three "must opt-out" primaries. As opt-out states, Wisconsin, Nebraska, and Oregon held primaries in which a state official would select individuals who were prominent in the press as possible presidential contenders and place their names on the ballot. The only way to remove one's name from the ballot was to file an affidavit disavowing candidacy. Although his advisers did not expect him to win in Wisconsin or Nebraska, they hoped the governor would make a respectable showing and then build enough momentum to win the Oregon primary in May. Their main objective was to coast untarnished through the primary season while gunning for victory at the convention.

A few weeks after Reagan's gubernatorial inauguration, White presented Reed and Spencer with a preliminary delegate count. With 667 delegates required to win the Republican nomination, White's analysis showed Romney as the leader with 320 delegates, Nixon following with approximately 310, and Reagan holding between 200 and 300.[68]

Reagan began touring the country six weeks after White presented his count. In March he traveled to Washington and New York, where he participated in several social events. But it was his participation on May 15, in an internationally televised dialogue with Senator Robert F. Kennedy before an audience of students in London that gave Reagan his greatest exposure to date as a potential presidential candidate. Kennedy struggled to make convincing arguments about the Vietnam War and other international issues, and he seemed uncomfortable with the television format. In contrast, Reagan made commanding assessments of domestic and foreign policies and even corrected the statistics cited by one of his questioners. He played to his conservative base by calling for the six-year-old Berlin Wall to be torn down and by advocating the exclusion of the Vietcong, as a "rebellious force," from negotiations between North Vietnam and South Vietnam. Reagan seemed to have won a debate against a prominent Democrat and potential presidential candidate.[69]

In June Reagan visited Nebraska. His speech to a convention of Young Republicans in Omaha included his standard warnings against big government and the Soviet Union's lack of reciprocity in its relations with the United States. He also employed the law-and-order code words when he declared, "We will not tolerate those who use civil rights or the right of dissent as an excuse to take to the streets for riot and mob violence—even when it is called civil disobedience," and again when he said, "Let us reaffirm that the national purpose is the ultimate freedom for the individual, consistent with law and order."[70] As Reed observed, "Reagan did a great job, and the core of a future Draft Reagan headquarters was assembled."[71] Yet Reagan never veered from the conservative heart of his message; he was not broadening his political base.

Reagan looked like a presidential candidate whenever he spoke, but he was unwilling to clarify his intentions even to the party elite who were interested in supporting him. On September 17, for instance, a "Texas Summit" was held at the governor's residence in Sacramento. The meeting included John Tower; Peter O'Donnell; Anne Armstrong, a member of the Republican National Committee; Tobin Armstrong, Anne's husband and a major rancher; the Reagans; William P. Clark, Reagan's executive assistant in the California governor's office; Lyn Nofziger, Reagan's communications director in Sacramento; Tom Reed; and Gordon Luce, a recent addition to Reagan's presidential advisory team. When asked if he planned to run, "Reagan never answered the question," said Reed. Two weeks later Tower returned to San Francisco, but Reed was still unable to give him an answer.[72]

The governor may have wanted to keep his options open, galvanizing support among the rank and file in case he decided to run while remaining cautious in conversations with the party leaders who would actually control the outcome. Reagan was at his best when he took his message directly to the people, but his plebiscite-type approach to capturing the nomination in 1968 did not reflect the modus operandi of the party leadership.

On September 29, Reagan spoke at a meeting of the South Carolina Republican State Central Committee, preaching his anti-big-government message to a chorus of southern elites and rank and file. But again the speech did not reveal much about his ability to craft a message with more national appeal. Perhaps of even greater concern was his continued indecisiveness when Thurmond asked him about his presidential plans during a private meeting that also included Dent (of the Greenville Group), Nofziger, and Reed.[73]

On October 2, Reed met with John Tower, who by this time had abandoned his own presidential aspirations. Instead, Tower was working to secure the South's interests in the Republican contest, and he had been offered a position on Nixon's campaign team. Reed, who was still unable to offer Tower a definitive answer about Reagan's candidacy, said, "Reagan left the impression with these high priests of conservatism that his campaign was a vague and headless monster, that he was going to wing it."[74]

Reagan was also taking a much harder line on certain policy issues than any other potential nominee. On November 11 in Albany, Oregon, for instance, he insisted, "The war in Vietnam must be fought through to victory. We have been patient too long. . . . Stop the bombing [of North Vietnam] and we will only encourage the enemy to do his worst."[75]

Southern and conservative leaders agreed with Reagan but they were determined to back a candidate who could actually win the election. Percy, Rockefeller, Romney, and Nixon had also spoken out on the Vietnam War, but Nixon was the only one of the group to advocate the continued use of American military power against the North Vietnamese. A *New York Times* article reviewing the candidates' positions found that "Governor Reagan waxes even more hawkish" than Nixon.[76]

Public sentiment, however, was moving in the opposite direction. The Citizens for Peace with Freedom in Vietnam, a nonpartisan commission, was formed on October 25. The group, which included former presidents Harry Truman and Dwight D. Eisenhower, stated that it believed the United States had a "vital national interest" in Vietnam but warned against an escalation of U.S. military activities in Indochina that might lead to "a general war in Asia or a nuclear war in the world."[77]

Unlike Rockefeller, Romney, and Nixon, Reagan was serving his first year in a major political office. A solid record of leadership would bolster his image as a politician, but it was threatened by a homosexuality scandal in his inner office that undoubtedly diverted some of the governor's attention from the campaign.[78] A conflict was also brewing between, on the one hand, Reed and White, who were working on Reagan's 1968 presidential bid, and, on the other, Reagan's older Los Angeles trust, which included Holmes Tuttle and Taft Schreiber. The latter had become distrustful of Reed and White's youthful arrogance and sought to wrest control of Reagan's national activities.[79] Reagan's failure to find a decisive resolution to the conflict cost him valuable time.

Richard Nixon and his team, on the other hand, were highly organized, focused, and efficient. With his Congress '66 group, Nixon campaigned in approximately 35 states and 165 congressional districts on behalf of Republican candidates. As the most vigorous GOP campaigner of that year, the former vice president established himself as a major player in the party's rebound from its 1964 losses.[80] "With those wins came promissory notes," one observer of the 1968 presidential campaign remarked, "notes that could be cashed at the Republican convention in Miami Beach in 1968."[81] On November 13, five days after the 1966 election, Nixon met one last time with Congress '66 in New York and then announced that he would consider running for president.[82]

The Republican bosses were quickly lining up behind Nixon. As Congress '66 was being transformed into a de facto presidential campaign, Goldwater wrote that he "support[ed] Nixon because . . . I consider him to be the best qualified man in the country today, including the incumbent, to be President."[83] The other barons eventually followed suit.

The first planning sessions for Nixon's expected presidential run were held in New York on January 7 and 8, 1967. A Washington campaign office was opened in May, and members of Nixon's team quickly went to work in New Hampshire.[84] George Romney was Nixon's main concern at the time. The Nixon camp believed that Romney would prevail in the Northeast, so their own candidate's pathway to the presidency would have to be secured with the support of southern delegates.[85] He would need the Northeast in the general contest, but Nixon wrote off those industrial states in the primary. His advisers believed that a heavy expenditure of campaign funds in the region would be unlikely to yield more delegate votes, since Nixon had never developed a strong constituency among the eastern Establishment.[86]

The campaign required campaign issues and themes that would allow him to simultaneously hold the center and court the South. On the domestic side, Nixon chose law and order and states' rights as his main talking points. As noted earlier, a strong stand on the crossover issue of law and order appealed to white conservatives in the North and South alike, providing common ground for southern voters and many from the center.

Although there was some national support for states' rights, the issue was especially popular among southerners who opposed federal desegregation laws and court decisions. There was little overlap between these voters and the political center on the issue, but having learned from Goldwater's defeat, Nixon planned to broach the subject in a southern strategy that would "have its overtly racist form subtly modified."[87] His invocation of emotion-laden issues related to social order reassured conservative southerners who would not otherwise support him to join his camp.

Dent, a key strategist on the South, convinced Nixon of the necessity of a southern operation in 1965 and 1966.[88] The operational dimension of their strategy was to give "high priority to nailing down early commitments from Dixie's most prominent conservatives."[89] Nixon clearly understood how to operate in an institutional context in which the coalition of essential supporters was very small.

As noted earlier, the Vietnam War was the most salient foreign policy issue for voters in the 1960s. The southern barons supported a continuation of U.S. military involvement and wanted victory—defined as the soonest possible establishment of a non-Communist government in Saigon. Nixon had long been known as a staunch anti-Communist, but his campaign rhetoric on Vietnam lacked the vitriol characteristic of earlier phases in his career. His message was now tailored to address centrists who were concerned about escalation into a wider Indochinese conflict and alarmed by the lack of military and political results in the face of growing American military commitment.

In keeping with his electoral strategy, Nixon steered a middle course in a 1967 *Foreign Affairs* essay entitled "Asia after Vietnam." He advocated an end to the war that preserved the honor of the United States; a peace settlement that disallowed a coalition government in the North (which he felt would pave the way for Communist victory); and continued military involvement, to avoid seeming weak in the eyes of the Soviets or Chinese. He defended U.S. involvement on the grounds that it had prevented an ambitious People's Republic of China from interfering in other parts of Asia. But Nixon's essay and his other campaign statements on the war still lacked specificity. In fact, sometimes Nixon was so muted on the issue that voters thought "he sounded like Johnson."[90] Yet, in his memoir, Nixon boasted about his Vietnam posture during the 1968 campaign:

> As a candidate it would have been foolhardy, and as a prospective President, improper, for me to outline specific plans in detail. . . . And even if I had been able to formulate specific "plans," it would have been absurd to make them public. In the field of diplomacy, premature disclosure can often doom even the best-laid plans. To some extent, I was asking the voters to take on faith my ability to end the war. A regular part of my campaign speech was the pledge: "New leadership will end the war and win the peace in the Pacific."[91]

Nixon took cover under the rules of diplomacy, but he was actually holding the political center. Romney criticized Nixon for his measured response, calling it "the Johnson-Nixon Vietnam policy."[92] That was precisely the message the Nixon team sought to convey. As Lou Cannon, Reagan's biographer, has observed, "Nixon followed a shrewder strategy [than Reagan] of playing the middle and saying as little as possible about Vietnam. It made him seem more moderate and would help him win the election."[93] Nixon did not always say what the conservative bloc wanted to hear on the war, but, as will be discussed later, he offset his moderate stance on Vietnam by promising conservatives that he would have a robust national defense policy.

As plans progressed for his 1967 campaign, Nixon took a six-month hiatus from publicly discussing the presidency. During this period, he traveled to South Vietnam, among other foreign countries, and reported on his experiences in *Reader's Digest*.[94] The former vice president was waiting for the right time to officially enter the fray.

In the fall of 1967, Romney was still holding his place as a possible candidate; Rockefeller was still backing Romney; and Reagan was touring the country, giving speeches that resonated with rank-and-file conservatives but delivered no delegates.

As 1968 began, the Reagan camp was riven with arguments about who was in charge, but all involved agreed that Reagan should continue to deliver distinctly conservative messages on his speaking tours.[95] His name would not be removed from the ballots in the opt-out states of Wisconsin, Nebraska, and Oregon, and, as the favorite-son candidate, he would more or less automatically control the 86 California delegates who were pledged to the unit rule of voting for the favorite son unless he released them. Reagan also let it be known that he thought the Republican gathering in Miami Beach would be a real contest. Thus, the first half of 1968 would be devoted to harvesting delegates. For the Reagan camp, that meant focusing on the Republican rank and file.

Reagan's challenge was heightened when Nixon officially entered the race on February 1. The California governor offered Republican voters an ideological alternative to Romney, or, to a lesser degree, Nixon. But Nixon had been campaigning for the southern barons' vote for at least two years. Even though Reagan had stronger support among rank-and-file southern Republicans, the barons held the key to the delegates. And Goldwater, one of these barons, publicly endorsed Nixon on March 7.[96]

Four weeks after Nixon entered the race, Romney withdrew, thereby making Nixon the only official Republican presidential contender. Maryland governor Spiro Agnew immediately formed a "Draft Rockefeller" movement, but Rockefeller was reluctant.[97] He had been accused of dividing the party by battling with Goldwater in the 1964 primaries and then refusing to campaign on the Arizonan's behalf.

Rockefeller did not want a repeat of that episode. He also knew that it would be nearly impossible for him to build a coalition that would include the New Right, that he would not be a big winner in the primaries, and that his main hope for snatching the nomination would come at the party's Miami Beach convention in August.

Romney's withdrawal from the race complicated Rockefeller's plan to avoid the primaries until the Oregon vote in May. He had won the Oregon primary in 1964 and hoped to be victorious there again in 1968. With Romney out, Rockefeller would most likely be a write-in candidate in more primaries than he desired and would need to enter the race well before the convention. Once he became an official candidate, he would face a conservative attack that would gather strength as soon as he began explaining his position on contentious policy issues.[98]

Strategists from the Reagan, Rockefeller, and Nixon camps projected that Nixon would have difficulty winning the nomination on the first convention ballot, and that he would lose if the voting went beyond the first ballot; whereas successive rounds of balloting would improve Rockefeller's chances. More popular nationally than within his own party, Rockefeller would be stronger in the general contest than Reagan. If Reagan split the conservative vote on the first ballot, the door would be open to a Rockefeller victory in later balloting. In such a scenario, Rockefeller could appeal to the delegates' desire for a Republican win in the general election. Reagan was Rockefeller's main hope.

On the other hand, Rockefeller's imminent entry into the race was potentially advantageous for Reagan.[99] Voting beyond the first ballot could result in a victory for the California governor because the rank and file would be released from the barons' control and delegates would be free to vote their preferences. So Rockefeller in turn was Reagan's main hope.

George Wallace's candidacy, however, loomed over the Reagan camp like a dark cloud. On January 2, Wallace's American Independent Party qualified for the ballot in California's primary, having registered 34,000 more voters than required. On February 8, Wallace announced that he would seek the presidency on a law-and-order platform. His party would qualify to be on the ballot in all 50 states, and his ratings in the polls revealed an ever-increasing political viability. A Harris survey showed that if the election were held in January 1968, Wallace would receive 14 percent of the vote and place second behind Johnson in the South.[100] Reagan counted southern conservatives as part of his political base, but Wallace had the capacity to frustrate his plans.

As the lineup of Republican and conservative candidates took shape, the California governor fought to maintain his public stance as a noncandidate. During one of his weekly news conferences in Sacramento, he promised to "support the nominee of the Party" even if Rockefeller were chosen, and added, "I reiterate, I'm not a candidate."[101] But events were about to take a dramatic turn.

On March 12, Nixon won approximately 78 percent of the vote in the New Hampshire primary. But the big news was on the Democratic side. Senator Eugene J. McCarthy had been campaigning on a peace platform in the wake of the Vietcong's Tet Offensive, which Americans had watched with horror. President Johnson won the primary with almost 50 percent of the vote, but the Minnesota legislator received nearly 42 percent and took 20 of the state's 24 delegates. It now appeared that Johnson could be beaten.

On March 13, Senator Robert F. Kennedy announced that he was reconsidering his bid for office. Three days later he officially joined the Democratic field. All of the Republican hopefuls immediately reassessed their positions. Nixon, according to his aide, Richard Whalen, "showed no hesitancy about taking on the brother of the man who had beaten—and awed—him in 1960." Whalen reports that, following Kennedy's announcement, Nixon asked his advisers how his campaign "might 'pre-empt' positions [on Vietnam] and thereby narrow Rockefeller's room for maneuver."[102] The former vice president felt that Kennedy would take the steam out of the Rockefeller candidacy because the two men had similar positions on issues such as the Vietnam War.

In early 1968, Nixon started to assert himself more decisively on the conflict in Indochina: "Let's help them [the South Vietnamese] fight the war and not fight the war for them," he remarked. Shortly thereafter he criticized the Johnson administration for "failing to train the South Vietnamese to take over the major share" of the combat operations, and called for "a diplomatic offensive with the Soviet Union and others who might influence the North Vietnamese to come to the conference table."[103] Nixon declared his commitment to "keeping the pressure on militarily" and asserted his opposition to either a coalition government in Saigon or unilateral withdrawal by the United States.[104] At a rally in early March he promised, "I pledge to you that new leadership will end the war and win the peace in the Pacific."[105] The pledge persuaded the media that a more complete statement about the war was forthcoming. In actuality, however, "nothing had been decided [by the Nixon forces] on the Vietnam statement, not even whether there would definitely be one," according to Whalen.[106]

Meetings in late March found Nixon and his advisers pondering a definitive statement on Vietnam. His earlier public pledge to end the war had raised expectations that he would enter the fray with a comprehensive proposal. Now he told his aides that his commitment to "end the war and win the peace" should not be expressed "in the form of a promise."[107] The candidate known as an old Cold Warrior wanted to disarm his critics by staking out the political center. Whalen, who was enlisted to draft Nixon's major speech on the subject, felt that his candidate had clarified his position to his advisers.

> I soon discovered that he [Nixon] did not wish to be persuaded of the validity of our ideas. Rather, he sought guidance in the procedure that was the sum of his "centrism"—the pragmatic splitting of differences along a line drawn through the middle of the electorate. The line could go left or right, depending on the persuasiveness of claims made for the popularity of competing views. Nixon's aim was to find the least assailable middle ground. The grand theme interested him less than the small adjustment, which might provide an avenue of escape.[108]

Nixon, in keeping with the dominance principle, chose arguments based on the "popularity of competing views." In the context of the Vietnam debate, this translated into a decision not to speak about victory in Vietnam, but to encourage the Soviet Union to use its influence with the North Vietnamese to help bring an end to the war. The final draft of the speech was ready on March 30, and Nixon was to deliver it as a radio address the next day.[109]

The collapse of Romney's campaign on February 28 and Kennedy's entry into the race a little more than two weeks later reverberated throughout the Rockefeller camp. On March 10, the governor met with more than 30 Republican leaders and members of his staff at his New York apartment. Governors Agnew of Maryland, Rockefeller of Arkansas, Shafer of Pennsylvania, LeVander of Minnesota, Chafee of Rhode Island, Love of Colorado, and McCall of Oregon pledged to support Rockefeller, as did William E. Miller, Goldwater's running mate in 1964, among others. Some campaign analysts observed that these endorsements were "inconclusive," because "no one from the big Midwestern states or the South, or from the party leadership in Congress" signed on to the Rockefeller movement.[110]

It was nonetheless widely believed that Rockefeller would soon become an official candidate. But during a March 21 press conference at which he was expected to declare his candidacy, the New Yorker shocked his audience by saying, "I am not a candidate campaigning, directly or indirectly, for the Presidency of the United States." Instead, he accepted the fact "that a considerable majority of the party's leaders want the candidacy of former Vice President Richard Nixon, and it appears equally clear that they are keenly concerned and anxious to avoid any such divisive challenge within the party as marked the 1964 campaign." He revealed that he had filed an affidavit affirming that he was not a candidate so that his name could be withdrawn from the Oregon ballot, the contest he had hoped to win. But he added a proviso that he would enter the race if there were a "true and meaningful call" from the Republican Party.[111] Rockefeller was obviously still waiting for the right moment to throw his hat into the ring.

Reagan, meanwhile, had decided that he had to reconstitute his national effort. He had recently reemphasized his noncandidacy to the press, but Kennedy's entry into the race had changed the political equation, inasmuch as the Reagan camp did not believe that Nixon could defeat a member of the Kennedy family. On March 25 the Reagans and some of their advisers laid out the strategy that they would use throughout the spring. Reed described their plan in his diary: "Our opportunities to recruit the Republican barons were gone, but the prospect of another Kennedy-Nixon fiasco gave us access to the grass roots. Ron and Nancy Reagan agreed. They authorized an escalated travel schedule and a serious television campaign in our target primary states." Reagan had invoked solidly conservative themes during his speaking tours in 1967 and early 1968, but Reed reported that in the upcoming phase of his candidacy the governor would more pointedly address "Vietnam, inflation, civil disturbances, national priorities and defense. The case would have to be made that these crises were the product of Kennedy-Johnson policies. RFK must not be allowed to run as an outsider."[112] A sweeping analysis of domestic and foreign policy issues was to become the central feature of the revised campaign.

Reagan would in effect undertake negative campaigning against the Johnson administration. Yet, Reagan's negative campaigning, like Romney's, lacked the persuasive qualities that such campaigning generally requires. It did not raise fear among voters and encourage them to support Reagan. Despite being a powerful orator, Reagan was not a major rhetorician in the 1968 Republican presidential race. His message did not reach out beyond his core constituency.

Nixon was scheduled to deliver his radio address on Vietnam on March 31, six days after Reagan's strategy meeting. But upon learning that President Johnson had requested television network airtime for March 31, Nixon informed the press that he would refrain from making a "comprehensive statement on Vietnam."

Johnson's March 31 call for peace talks with the North Vietnamese and his declaration of a bombing halt north of the 20th parallel were not wholly unexpected. The nation was stunned, however, by his announcement on his political future: "I shall not seek and I will not accept the nomination of my party as your President." The statement was a war-weary president's admission that his authority had been eroded by the unending conflict in Indochina and the disparity between White House pronouncements about the war and the televised battles in Saigon and Hue during the Tet Offensive of early 1968. New Hampshire voters spoke for the larger electorate. Republicans were now even more firmly convinced that Kennedy would be the Democratic nominee.

On April 1, Nixon again postponed his comprehensive statement on Vietnam, but he offered a few uncontroversial remarks: "I believe that the key to peace in Vietnam probably lies in Moscow." He modestly endorsed Johnson's partial bombing halt: "I hope the President's initiative succeeds. In my judgment, a bombing halt by itself would not be a step toward peace. But if the United States has finally gotten assurances that it would be reciprocated, then further steps toward peace may become possible." He reemphasized his commitment to a peace settlement consistent with the long-standing objectives of the United States: "The [war] has been a war not for the freedom and independence of South Vietnam alone, but to make possible the conditions of a wider and durable peace. A settlement in Vietnam that would encourage further aggression by its weakness would betray these larger purposes, and would thus render futile the terrible costs already sustained."[113]

As one writer explains, "The president's announcement offered him [Nixon] a fortuitous way to keep his Vietnam policy vague and general. Until March 31, pressure had been building on the Republican front-runner to be more specific about his program for Southeast Asia."[114] Nixon had not bowed to the pressure, and his political centrism was working. On April 2, he won the state of Wisconsin with nearly 80 percent of the vote. McCarthy was the Democratic winner, receiving 56 percent of the vote.

··

Phase 2: April 4 to June 11, 1968

There was barely time for Nixon to savor his Wisconsin victory. Just two days later Reverend Martin Luther King, Jr., was shot in Memphis. His assassination posed a dilemma for Nixon, who was anxious about his image among southern Republicans. Some of Nixon's advisers were concerned that a significant number of delegates from Dixie would defect if the former vice president attended King's funeral. Nixon split the difference of opinion among his advisers: he attended the service and called Mrs. Coretta Scott King to express his condolences, but did not take part in the funeral procession.

This dual strategy of careful centrism and genuflection to the Right was bearing fruit. A nationwide Gallup Poll showed that, as of early April, Nixon was the consistent winner when pitted against Vice President Hubert Humphrey and Robert Kennedy, the Democratic hopefuls, and George Wallace, the third-party candidate.[115]

Nixon put as much effort into retaining the centrist vote as he did into reassuring the Right. In what Whalen describes as the "high point of the campaign," Nixon used his April 25 radio address, "Bridges to Humanity," to take up the cause of black Americans, declaring that "programs of welfare, of public housing, of payments to the poor" merely served to buy off black Americans instead of solving problems. "Much of the black-militant talk these days," he went on, "is actually in terms far closer to the doctrines of free enterprise than those of the welfarists of the '30s. What most of the militants are asking is . . . to have a share in the wealth and a piece of the action. It ought to be oriented toward more black ownership, for from this can flow the rest— black pride, black jobs, black opportunity, and, yes, black power."[116] As a result of this address and others, Nixon was labeled a supporter of "Negro capitalism."

Despite such grandiloquent declarations, the former vice president was mindful of the small coalition of barons who governed the environment in which he was operating. According to Whalen, Nixon later "rebuked those of us who had urged him to go to Atlanta [to King's funeral], calling it 'a serious mistake that almost cost us the South.'"[117]

Reagan, the only Republican contender with deep support among the party's southern rank-and-file members, did not attend the funeral, but he did speak publicly about King's death and its implications, proclaiming, "The murder of Martin Luther King was a shocking act of violence that solves none of our nation's problems. It is more evidence of a moral sickness that seems to be inflicting our nation. I want to extend my deepest sympathy to the family of Reverend King. I urge all Californians to remain calm in the face of one single act of violence."[118]

In a speech in Phoenix, Arizona, a few days later, Reagan spoke about King and civil rights in terms on which all could agree: "Whatever you may think of Martin Luther King, whether you approved or disapproved, something of America was buried today. It began with the first acceptance of compromise of the law—acceptance of those who would apply the law unequally because of race or religion, and acceptance of those who advocate breaking those laws with which we are in disagreement." The California governor also reassured his conservative political base on the Vietnam War issue by disagreeing with Johnson's decision to commence peace talks with the North Vietnamese.[119] And he used a series of speeches throughout April to rail against excessive government spending, the budget deficit, rising inflation, and other issues of concern to conservatives.

As much as the barons agreed with Reagan's message, they and other Nixon supporters were disquieted by his activities. The threat the California governor posed to Nixon became apparent during a visit to Idaho on April 26–27. Speaking to a large gathering in Boise, Reagan invoked a variety of Goldwater-like themes, including opposition to Great Society government programs. Nixon visited the Idaho capital on the day of Reagan's speech and publicly described the California governor as a "more active non-candidate." Nixon had good reason to be concerned. Idaho governor Don Samuelson, a conservative Republican for whom Nixon had campaigned two years earlier, was calling Reagan "a new dynamic voice in the Republican party." And Clif White, Reagan's key delegate-hunter, had close lieutenants in the state. It was expected that Idaho's delegates would be pledged to Nixon, but as political analyst Tom Wicker reported at the time, "Most of the 14 delegates will be Republicans who supported Goldwater in 1964 and who will swing comfortably into the Reagan camp if and when the time comes—maybe on the second or third ballot at Miami Beach."[120] Reagan was in Boise to rally the rank and file to his side; Nixon was there to hold the line.

Two days after Reagan's tour of the Mountain West, Rockefeller finally announced his much-anticipated decision before a national television audience, promising that he would ensure his party "a choice of candidates and programs."[121] As planned, Rockefeller had missed most of the primaries. Instead, his strategy was to persuade as many uncommitted delegates as possible to cast their votes for him in Miami Beach. He also hoped to convince committed delegates that it was in their best interest to release themselves from their pledges to the other candidates in order to hold an open convention in which ideas and candidates could be debated and tested. In attracting support from Democrats and independents, he also wanted to demonstrate to the party that he was the candidate who could prevail in November.[122] It was a tall order with the convention looming only three months away.

As expected, the high priests of Republican conservatism were skeptical about Rockefeller's entry into the race. Goldwater remarked, "It is quite important that his philosophies be made clear now since he has not run in any of the primaries where people traditionally get a chance to take a good hard look at the candidate."[123]

The New York governor was prepared for this reaction. After all, he had actually been planning his campaign for some time. In fact, the Romney camp, along with many others throughout the country, suspected that Rockefeller had long been waiting for Romney to withdraw from the race. Their conjecture that he had planned to enter the fray once the moderate Romney had smoothed the way for him is consistent with confidential campaign documents from the Rockefeller archives.[124] Rockefeller felt that he had found the right moment to enter the contest. By the end of July, he would have traveled to 45 states, delivered 120 speeches, and campaigned actively for 68 days.[125]

The New Yorker's campaign got off to a propitious start. On the same day that he announced his candidacy, he won the Massachusetts primary, defeating Governor John A. Volpe, the state's favorite-son candidate, by less than 1 percent. Rockefeller's campaign strategy was designed to rally the support of his natural base of liberal and centrist Republicans and Democrats. He claimed that there was no "purely military solution" in Vietnam and suggested that the United States should increase its "contact and communication" with the People's Republic of China in order to "significantly affect the whole future of our relations with the Communist world." Political analysts believed that Rockefeller was "attempting to stake out a position less 'hawkish' [on

Vietnam] than that of his chief rival, Mr. Nixon, but less 'dovish' than those of Senators Robert F. Kennedy and Senator Eugene J. McCarthy."[126]

This analysis is borne out by the way in which the governor began his first month as an avowed presidential candidate. Before a cheering crowd of students at the University of Iowa, Rockefeller proposed replacing the existing draft laws with a national lottery system that would subject individuals to the draft for no longer than one year. He also advocated lowering the voting age from 21 to 18.[127] He continued to drum out his liberal message during campaign stops in Minnesota, Kansas, Massachusetts, and Pennsylvania, but changed his approach when he began his southern tour on May 19.

On May 20, Rockefeller attended a breakfast meeting with the southern Republican state chairmen in New Orleans. While in Gainesville, Florida, later that day, he declared that he did not see a significant ideological difference between himself and Governor Reagan. The tour, which also included visits to Georgia and South Carolina, failed to cut into Nixon's Dixie support. During the trip, Harry Dent, the South Carolina Republican chairman, told the press that he did not expect many delegates to swing to Rockefeller.[128] But Rockefeller persisted, issuing thinly disguised critiques of Nixon's recent overtures to black Americans: "It is not straight talk to propagate notions of unity in terms of a 'new alignment'—particularly in incongruously pretending to merge new Southern leadership and the new black militants."[129] These negative statements did not score many points; Nixon's fusing of political constituencies was exactly what the southern leaders wanted to see from their candidate. Rockefeller lacked the capacity to undermine Nixon in the South, and he left the region without having won the support of the former vice president's delegates.

The governor ended the first month of his campaign with a major loss in a primary. On May 28, Rockefeller, a write-in candidate, received approximately 11 percent of the vote in Oregon to Nixon's 70 percent. He had undertaken a vigorous and expensive campaign, but by entering the ring late in the primary season he had deprived himself of the time required to fine-tune a political message that would appeal to voters across the political spectrum. Instead, Rockefeller was racing to catch up with Nixon's highly organized political machine.

As discussed earlier, Ronald Reagan had decided to renew his pursuit of the Republican nomination after a meeting with his advisers in late March. By May, the plan to revive his national activities was in full swing in the form of a series of talks criticizing the Kennedy-Johnson policies. On May 11, Reagan presented a speech titled "The History and Significance of the US Role in the Pacific" at the Western Governors' Conference in Honolulu, attacking the Kennedy-Johnson record on Vietnam.[130]

The clearest example of Reagan's national political message came the next day when he commenced what was described in his daily schedule as an "Eastern Tour."[131] His first stop was New Orleans, where on May 19 he gave a rousing speech titled "National Priorities and the Negotiations in Paris" at Tulane University. "Civilization," he said, "cannot afford politicians who demand that Social Security be tripled; that the national duty in Vietnam be discarded to provide huge make-work programs in the city slums with money diverted from Vietnam; that no youth need honor the draft; that Negroes need not obey the law; that there will be pie in the sky once the country gets moving again." As he had done in Honolulu, Reagan again condemned the Johnson administration's policies toward Hanoi. He then recited a laundry list of general positions that both Nixon and Wallace could embrace, though he sounded closer to Wallace in his Tulane address and other speeches down South. As some campaign observers noted, "Reagan was building himself a limited, but emotional, national constituency."[132]

Hosting a dinner for the Southern Association of Republican State Chairmen later that evening, Reagan further narrowed the possibility that he would be the Republican Party's presidential nominee. The party chairmen were in agreement with his pronouncements at Tulane, but they wanted to know if he planned to become an official contender. Reagan replied that he would remain a favorite-son candidate for the time being, but would accept a grassroots-based draft. "The trouble was it was too late for that kind of draft," Clif White lamented. The convention was only two months away and the Reagan shop was miniscule in comparison with the operation that had delivered Goldwater's resounding first-ballot victory in San Francisco four years earlier.[133] Furthermore, the grassroots strategy was in complete defiance of the party's elite-governed institutional structure.

But Reagan continued his national activities. On May 20, he delivered a speech entitled "Atlantic and Caribbean Foreign Policy" before a Tampa audience in which he charged that, despite the availability of intelligence data confirming the presence of Soviet missiles in Cuba,

President Kennedy had responded to the Cuban threat only after U-2 photos provided indisputable proof and the midterm elections were a few weeks away. Reagan repeated this charge in Miami the following day. Discussing "Defense Preparedness" in Cleveland on May 22, he argued that there was no "missile gap" as Senator Kennedy had claimed during the 1960 presidential race; that the Johnson administration had mishandled the seizure of the *Pueblo;* and that its management of the Vietnam War was dangerously off course. Reagan further warned of the implications that Soviet nuclear parity held for the United States and Western Europe, and suggested that a real missile gap was in the offing.[134]

But such grand foreign policy speeches were nevertheless no match for Nixon's aggressive moves to sew up delegate support. Instead of campaigning in person in Oregon, where he would compete in his third primary, Reagan authorized the showing of a documentary film on his life. His hopes for the state were dashed when he received only 20 percent of the vote on May 28. He and his supporters took little solace in their anticipated June 4 victory in California. Nixon went on to win primaries in New Jersey and South Dakota that same day, along with the final contest in Illinois on June 11. Tom Reed, one of Reagan's campaign advisers, recalled this period in his diary: "When the smoke had cleared, on May 29 and again during the first week of June, I met with Reagan to tell him it was all over. . . . To this day, I am not sure if he heard me or if the message sank in."[135] Whether it did or not, Reagan decided to quicken the pace of his national appearances in June and July.[136]

Like Reagan, Nixon prepared a series of policy pronouncements for conservative audiences. His May 8 statement on law and order, "Toward Freedom From Fear,"[137] endorsed an omnibus crime bill that would reassess the Miranda rule. The bill would allow court-ordered wiretapping in investigations of major crimes or national security threats, increase pay for policemen, and launch a "major overhaul" of the prison system. The 25-page document also blamed the Supreme Court for the increase in crime during the Kennedy-Johnson years. Nixon sounded like Reagan during his May 15 appearance in Pendleton, Oregon, when he characterized the April 23 student uprising at Columbia University as "the first major skirmish in a revolutionary struggle to seize the universities of this country and transform them into sanctuaries for radicals and vehicles for revolutionary political and social goals."[138] He urged university administrators to swiftly punish the student organizers.

The following day, the CBS radio network broadcast Nixon's conversation with the nation. Titled "A New Alignment For American Unity," the address was a call to replace the "old power bloc" with a "new alignment" of black militants committed to capitalism, the "new liberal" who desired "more personal freedom and less government domination," and the "new South," which was no longer bound to a "racist appeal" or one-party voting. Nixon identified himself as the man to lead this new alignment, which he called the "silent center, the millions of people in the middle of the political spectrum who do not demonstrate, who do not picket or protest loudly." This bold attempt to amalgamate diverse factions of the electorate into a single centrist majority appealed to voters. Roy Innis, associate director for the Congress of Racial Equality, said that Nixon was the only presidential candidate who understood the national aims of black Americans.[139]

There were other significant indications in mid-May that the Nixon campaign was gaining support and momentum. On May 16, two days after Nixon roundly defeated Reagan in the Nebraska primary, Senator Howard Baker of Tennessee endorsed the former vice president, thus becoming the first Republican to shed his favorite-son status in order to commit his delegation to an official contender. In a statement to the press, Nixon acknowledged that Baker's "decision provides us with first-ballot delegates we had not counted on before," and called the decision "tangible proof . . . that our ideas and new programs are winning increasing support."[140] Six primaries remained, but the Nixon camp already sensed victory.

Indeed, Nixon was only a matter of days away from an even more significant triumph. In late spring, the Republican front-runners traveled to the South to meet with the Republican state chairmen. Rockefeller and Reagan had accepted the southerners' invitation to meet in New Orleans. Rockefeller made a few nods toward conservative ideas, but Reagan, as noted earlier, turned in an ideologically conservative performance in New Orleans.[141] Neither man succeeded in sharply defining the issues or winning the endorsement of the party chairs. Meanwhile, Nixon met with Republican leaders in Atlanta on May 31. Harry Dent, the South Carolina party chairman, asked most of the questions, focusing on law and order, the Supreme Court, school busing, and national defense, among other issues. Nixon assured the group that, as president, he would uphold the 1954 desegregation decision, but would oppose school busing as a means to integrate public schools. While he advocated compliance with Supreme Court decisions, Nixon said that he would allow the states to decide how to abide by those decisions, and said he favored appointing strict constructionists to the courts.

The former vice president also continued his coalition-building efforts during the meeting, informing the group that he would not "balance" the ticket by choosing a liberal running mate, but would instead select someone who shared his philosophy. The southern leaders liked what they heard, and Dent called Thurmond to tell him that they had found their candidate. Dent asked Thurmond to meet with Nixon in Atlanta the following day.[142]

On June 1, Nixon met with Thurmond and other southern leaders. He emphasized the points he had made the previous day and declared his support for a strong national defense. Nixon was confident that he had outmaneuvered the conservative governor of California: "I emerged from this meeting with Thurmond's pledge of support, which would become a valuable element in my ability to thwart any moves by Reagan on my right."[143] Ironically, one of Nixon's defter moves was to express interest in missile defense, an issue that Reagan would identify as the central item of his presidential defense policy 15 years later. According to authoritative accounts, Nixon's specific promise of support for the development of an antiballistic missile (ABM) system, in addition to his stance on social issues, convinced Thurmond to support his candidacy.[144] The senator had been advocating an ABM defense for several years and had called for research and development of its feasibility in his book, *The Faith We Have Not Kept*, published earlier that year.[145] Nixon endorsed the deployment of an ABM system during his campaign, and although his memoirs do not explicitly confirm that he made any specific promises to Thurmond on the subject of ABMs that day, they do acknowledge his commitment to a robust policy of national defense. Nixon also agreed—albeit reluctantly—to support Thurmond's call for tariffs to protect South Carolina's textile industry.[146]

After the Atlanta meeting, White flew to Washington to ask Thurmond if the reports that he was supporting Nixon were correct. The senator expressed great affection for Reagan but confirmed his choice.[147] Thurmond was a segregationist but he was also a master politician. He knew that a far-right candidate could not prevail in the

November election and that desegregation could not be stopped. He took no umbrage at Nixon's apparent centrism on issues of concern to conservative southerners.[148]

Nixon was no heresthetician in 1968, but his commitments to Thurmond, the most influential politician among the southern Republican delegates in 1968, were deal-makers. He had found the precise language and policy positions that would satisfy the center and the right concurrently, making it difficult for Reagan and Rockefeller to gain a hold.

By the close of the primary season, Nixon had secured a public endorsement from Goldwater, one of the barons; Thurmond had committed to making a major public statement of support; and Tower was leaning in his direction. Furthermore, Dirksen, another power broker, had joined party leaders such as House Minority Leader Gerald R. Ford in lending tacit support.[149] But the contest was not over. Although Thurmond was leaning toward Nixon, many of the South Carolina delegates favored Reagan and planned to vote their preference if balloting at the convention went beyond the first round. Could the barons really hold the cadre in place? As Nixon mused later, "There was always the possibility that Southern delegates could be lured at the last minute by his [Reagan's] ideological siren song."[150] The threat of a revolt among the rank and file brewed just beneath the surface.

At the same time, Rockefeller's campaign was posing an increasing challenge from the left and the center. His three terms as governor and, indeed, his whole political career, had been built on his capacity to attract Democrats and independents as well as Republicans. And he enjoyed a longer history with, and deeper ties to, Republican moderates than did Nixon, the old anti-Communist. In effect, Rockefeller was surrendering the South and the conservative wing of the party to Reagan and Nixon, while hoping to convince them of his ability to beat the Democratic nominee in the fall. With this prospect in mind, Rockefeller made a bid for supporters of Robert Kennedy. On June 11, six days after Kennedy fell to an assassin's bullet, the New York governor told a National Press Club audience that he considered it his personal responsibility to perpetuate Kennedy's "unfulfilled dreams" of peace, freedom, and justice for all. He presented the same message in a nationally televised address later that evening.[151] On the hustings from the middle of June to the beginning of the Republican convention on August 5, Rockefeller sounded like the dovish heir-apparent to Robert Kennedy.[152]

His campaign aides encouraged this strategy. A few days after

Kennedy was assassinated, Henry Kissinger wrote a memo to the governor titled "Where Are We Now in the Campaign?" in which he disagreed with the pundits' contention that Kennedy's fall secured the nominations for Nixon and Humphrey. Instead Kissinger offered this advice:

> The Kennedy supporters in their majority will look for a new focal point. So will much of the youth. . . . Anybody who can appeal to idealism and the desire for commitment may start a groundswell which is bound to express itself in public opinion polls. . . . You can still create the groundswell which will change the situation dramatically. . . . The focus should be less on attempting to sway delegates directly than in gaining such widespread popular support that the delegates have to reconsider their commitments.[153]

Rockefeller heeded this advice in the weeks that followed.

As the primary season came to a close in Illinois on June 11 with another overwhelming victory for the former vice president, the Republican contenders were faced with a challenge that was more obvious than it had been at any point during the campaign: Nixon, the front-runner, would have to continue to beat back attempted raids from Reagan on the right and Rockefeller on the left and in the center. Wallace, too, was a threat, with conservative white constituents, mostly from the South but increasingly from working-class communities in northern cities. This struggle, waged on three fronts, dominated Republican Party politics during the two months leading up to the convention in Miami Beach.

....

Phase 3: June 12 to August 4, 1968

During the two months prior to the convention, Nixon and his advisers relentlessly analyzed the three-front challenge and devised operations to thwart it. Wallace's support among Republicans had risen from 2 to 8 percent following King's assassination, meaning that the job of swaying Wallace voters could not wait until after the convention. In early June, Pat Buchanan, a Nixon speechwriter and strategist, wrote a memo on how to cut into Wallace's support, in which he contended that a targeted undertaking *might* yield one million black votes, while a similarly scaled effort to reach Wallace supporters would most assuredly deliver a million votes. He then asked, rhetorically, "Which is easier for RN to accomplish?" Another of Buchanan's campaign memos analyzed California, a state whose seven million voters could determine the whole election. A major undertaking might deliver 100,000 black votes for Nixon. On the other hand, Wallace, a former Democrat, might receive one million votes in California. Again, Buchanan asked, "How many of these [votes from the Wallace camp] can a good tough campaign get?"[154] The Nixon adviser was not urging his candidate to abandon his support for "Negro capitalism." Indeed, he and other advisers sought to avoid the racist appeal and fractious nature of the Goldwater effort, but they were urgently searching for a plan to attract Democratic votes.

Alan Greenspan, Nixon's director of domestic research, also considered Wallace supporters crucial. In June, he wrote: "It is my judgment that we can win five percentage points back from Wallace, at a cost of one, or at the most two points moving from RN to Humphrey. . . . [W]e need a strong gut issue to swing a large bloc of Wallace votes to us. I wouldn't want to guarantee that such an issue would win us the election, but I am concerned that if a major effort is not made against Wallace, we may not make it past November." Nixon had already been using his law-and-order theme as a gut issue. He now endorsed Buchanan and Greenspan's recommendations.[155]

Nixon's choice of vice presidential running mates was widely viewed by those inside his campaign as a means to undercut Wallace and hold the South. Staffer John Sears suggested Reagan for the number two slot on the grounds that the California governor was "the only officeholder in the country who can outtalk and outcampaign George Wallace." Richard V. Allen, Nixon's director of foreign policy research, also supported a Nixon-Reagan ticket: "With him, there is no crude appeal—his 'old time religion' is founded on the very elements which are missing today: law, order, patriotism, thrift—and in language which the common man can understand."[156] Although Nixon was disinclined to call on Reagan, he clearly agreed with the more general point that he needed to move to the right.

In a mid-July strategy meeting, Nixon concluded that Vice President Hubert Humphrey had "bedrock" strength at 40 percent of the electorate to his own 35 percent. He told his staff that "this game will be won or lost by the sixteen percent Wallace vote and the six or eight percent vote of the true independents."[157] He knew he needed to move to the right, but he was prepared to do so only on an issue-by-issue basis, as he had done in his June 1 meeting with Strom Thurmond. Law and order and national defense were conservative themes he had already endorsed. The war in Vietnam was another matter.

On the war, Nixon had so far taken cover behind President Johnson's surprise announcement of March 31 and the RFK assassination; he would refrain from discussing the war during a time of national emergency and mourning, or while the negotiations in Paris were under way. He continued to keep a low profile throughout the summer. In a July 20 press conference in Los Angeles, he informed reporters that his classified briefing from the State Department two days earlier suggested that progress was possible in the Paris Peace Talks, and that he would refrain from making a major assessment until he had firm evidence to the contrary.[158]

But as the convention approached, aides such as Whalen urged their candidate to make a comprehensive statement. The need to work on the Republican platform provided the right opportunity for such a statement, yet Nixon decided to continue his moratorium. He authorized his aides to include cautious statements in his speeches and submissions to the Republican Platform Committee, such as the claim that he would not engage in "partisan interference" by remarking on the negotiations in Paris. In one example, he rejected a line written by Whalen—"The B-52 is an extremely costly and irrelevant weapon against the Vietcong terrorist armed with a knife"—because it might offend the U.S. Air Force. "At the end of the session," Whalen reports, "the language of the statement had been toned down and the challenge to the administration muted, but the central promise remained—to 'de-Americanize' the war." After learning that a recent Gallup Poll found him to be the only Republican who could defeat Humphrey and McCarthy, Nixon called Ray Price, who, like Whalen, was a speechwriter for the campaign, to express concern about including the term *de-Americanization* in his statements on the war.[159] The front-runner had found safety from the Vietnam firestorm in the political center, and he did not want to move left or right.

The statement that Nixon offered to the GOP platform panel on August 1 reflected his safe position. His criticisms of the Johnson administration were relatively mild. First, he said, "The Administration has done far too little, too late, to train and equip the South Vietnamese." Second, "The Administration has either not recognized that this is a new and more complex kind of war, or has not seen its significance." And, third, "The Administration has failed in candor at home and in leadership abroad." Nixon declared that the war could no longer be won primarily through military means because "it is primarily a political struggle, with this enemy conducting military operations to achieve political and psychological objectives." He also called for phasing out American troops as the South Vietnamese took greater responsibility for the war, as well as engaging the Soviet Union in a dialogue about ending the conflict.[160] In sum, the document failed to present any bold or new ideas.

There was little evidence, however, that Nixon's centrism on Vietnam was damaging his standing with conservatives during the summer of 1968. On June 22, Thurmond announced that South Carolina's 22 delegates would switch their pledge from him, as his state's favorite-son candidate, to Nixon on the first ballot. On July 1, Senator John Tower endorsed Nixon for president and said he was releasing his own 56-member delegation as Texas's favorite son.[161] Throughout 1968, and especially during the two crucial months leading up to the convention, the former vice president had been carefully mobilizing his center-right coalition. Those on the left and in the center were particularly concerned about the Vietnam War, and supporters in these camps were reassured by Nixon's statements of support for the Johnson administration's peace negotiations in Paris. Those on the right were attracted by his toughness on law and order, his opposition to busing, his promises to favor strict judicial interpretations of the Constitution, and his readiness to substantially increase defense spending. Nixon the candidate offered something for everyone.

The seasoned politician seemed to move effortlessly from the center to the right and back again. In a June 27 address on the CBS radio network, he again found common cause with black America: "If we listen, we'll discover that the white man in the Boston suburb shares many of the same frustrations as the black man in the Chicago ghetto. Not all, of course. But he, too, wants to be heard. He too, wants a voice in the decisions that shape his life. He, too, wants dignity—the dignity of being a man, not a number, not a category or a census statistic." Nixon then proposed a commission on reorganization of government to investigate "new patterns of direct Federal involvement in the cities, and in education; new ventures in regional co-operation; and new layers upon layers of authority for the individual to fight his way through." Two days later he continued to speak in terms that today might be labeled as compassionate conservatism: "You simply can't have order without progress. All the police in the world are not adequate to deal with men and women who have no hope."[162] This was the pragmatic and centrist Nixon.

But Nixon the centrist coexisted with Nixon the conservative. On June 23, the former vice president reassured his more hawkish supporters that his commitment "to restore stability to the economy and strength to the dollar" did not entail sacrificing defense "programs upon which the future security of the American people will depend." On July 6 he issued "A New Direction for America's Economy," a 17-page campaign document charging the Johnson administration with implementing inflationary fiscal and monetary policies, and declaring the administration's efforts to spur urban renewal a failure. Nixon argued that American cities would be improved more by keeping the wealth they produced within their own municipal boundaries than by accepting "federal handouts."[163] The next day he announced that John Tower would chair a new issues committee that he had formed to advise him on domestic and foreign affairs. He was more firmly embedding his conservative constituency into his campaign.

Nelson Rockefeller was running a different type of campaign. Unlike Nixon's deft moves between the center and the right and his deliberate evasions on Vietnam, Rockefeller's statements were intended to appeal to the moderate and liberal wings of his party. Like Romney before him, Rockefeller unveiled a detailed plan to end the Vietnam War. And, in a series of statements during June and July, he struck a moderate tone on crime, law and order, the inner city, poverty, and race relations. In a June 11 speech, he rejected Nixon's positions on law and order: "I don't believe, as my opponent for the Republican Presidential nomination has stated, that the Supreme Court has given the 'green light' to crime. And I do not believe, as he has also stated, that poverty has been 'grossly exaggerated' as a source of crime in America." He expanded on this in subsequent appearances, promising to combat poverty by creating federally funded programs to provide low-interest loans, loan guarantees, and technical assistance to impoverished communities, while also encouraging private investment. He proposed reducing the crime rate through proper rehabilitation and advocated further research on the causes of crime. During this period, he also vetoed a New York state bill that would have instituted a sentence of life in prison for anyone convicted of selling marijuana to minors.[164]

Rockefeller was clearly courting Kennedy supporters, independents, and moderate Republicans. Also, the governor tended to deemphasize issues of law and order when addressing black voters. And his brand of political centrism was reaping political dividends in the form of endorsements from black leaders including Omar Ahmed, James Farmer, Rev. Martin Luther King, Sr., and Dr. Benjamin Watkins, as well as from Kennedy Students for a New America, Governor Daniel J. Evans, Mayor John Lindsay of New York City, and Senator Charles Percy, the Illinois Republican who was now on Nixon's short list of vice presidential running mates.[165]

Rockefeller had attracted Democrats and independents throughout his political career, a fact that was not lost on Republican leaders, and especially the moderates who sought to stop their party's move to the right. But, as stated earlier, the influential New Right wanted a candidate who could both prevail in November *and* satisfy the emerging Republican majority at the convention. Even as Rockefeller demonstrated his electability, he was also revealing his distance from the policy preferences of the New Right. As he succeeded in the larger political arena, his prospects within his own party dimmed.

The governor challenged Nixon's position—or lack thereof—on Vietnam in a Sioux City, Iowa, speech on June 27: "There is no moratorium on courage—or casualties—in Vietnam. . . . No man seeking the Presidency, whatever political advantage he might imagine to exist in evading discussion of the issues has any right to retreat into silence when his country is in crisis at home and abroad."[166] Nixon was unmoved. But Rockefeller continued to discuss the Vietnam War and, on July 13 he unveiled a detailed plan to end it. His proposal entailed the withdrawal of North Vietnamese troops from Cambodia, Laos, and the demilitarized zone, followed by gradual American troop redeployments, ultimately leading to complete removal. The plan also called for free elections, which would be honored by the United States even if a Vietcong government were elected, and an international peacekeeping force that would secure the border between North Vietnam and South Vietnam, and which would be withdrawn following successful negotiations to reunify the country.[167] His Vietnam plan did not provoke a stampede of uncommitted and moderate delegates to his camp.

Reagan was now campaigning more aggressively than at any time since his November 1966 meeting with Tom Reed and Clif White to begin preliminary discussions about running for president. In the two months immediately prior to the convention, he undertook to convince conservatives that he was an alternative to Wallace, arguing, as had the barons, that Wallace could hurt the Republican nominee in the general election.[168] He also sought to establish himself as the only Republican challenger with a well-defined conservative philosophy. Earlier in the campaign, Reagan had often sidestepped the party leadership by taking his message directly to the rank and file. Now he had no choice but to continue on this path because most of the party leadership was already firmly behind Nixon. A powerful dose of populism was necessary to undo the alliance between Nixon and the barons. Reagan had to take his bottom-up campaign into high gear.

All of the Republican contenders exposed themselves to serious political risks when they confronted the Wallace challenge.[169] Nixon had nothing to gain by delivering a frontal attack on the third-party candidate because he had already established his credentials with the center: any overture to Wallace supporters would shake the faith of his base and alarm the barons.[170] Rockefeller sometimes mentioned his differences with the former Alabama governor, but, having entered the race late, he had to reserve most of his energy for challenging the frontrunner.

Like the other candidates, Reagan continually repeated the mantra that a vote for the third-party candidate was a wasted vote. His relationship with the Wallace faction, however, was different from that of Nixon or Rockefeller—or the barons, for that matter. Reagan was no Wallace, but as Reagan biographer Lou Cannon has observed, "Wallace posed a special problem for Reagan. Without Wallace, Reagan was the strongest potential nominee of any party in the South. With Wallace, he was a question mark, for their appeal to white conservatives overlapped."[171] Throughout the campaign, Reagan and his advisers had calculated that the emerging power bloc of Republicans in the South was their most important constituency, but now more than ever they felt that the southern bloc was essential to the one task before them—stopping Nixon on the first ballot at the convention. In some instances, this meant using stock-in-trade themes that appealed to conservatives across the political spectrum, including Wallace supporters.

Reagan's strategy was so specifically geared to preventing a Nixon victory on the first ballot that it failed to acknowledge its obvious risks: unless his appeals were broadened he could not expand his political base, but a broader message might weaken his ties with die-hard conservatives. Reagan's indecisiveness about his candidacy finally came home to roost. In one way or another, the California governor had been campaigning for the GOP nomination since late 1966. Yet he waited until the summer of 1968, shortly before the convention, to begin his first major tour directed toward a specific audience. He would receive maximum media attention for his efforts, but his message would perforce be narrow—much narrower at times than his own thinking. He was seeking the vote of conservative Republicans, especially, though not exclusively, in the South.

In numerous speeches after primary season, such as those in Indianapolis on June 13 and in Omaha 10 days later, Reagan advocated law-and-order policies and railed against "the growth of government."[172] These boilerplate speeches reinforced the image of Reagan as a conservative, but they were inconsistent with some of his policies as governor and with the image he was seeking to develop in California. This inconsistency became glaringly evident when Reagan discussed equal opportunity in his July 14 appearance on *Report to the People,* an occasional policy series carried on statewide television in California. He said that "it is imperative—and it is morally right" to address the grievances of minorities, and that his administration sought to "remove unnatural barriers" and wanted to "guarantee equal rights to all of our citizens regardless of color or creed." He also repeated the assertion, which he had made on numerous previous occasions, that he had hired more minorities to executive positions in state government than any previous governor.[173]

In the 1966 gubernatorial race, Reagan won all of the districts in the greater Los Angeles area except two composed mainly of blacks and Hispanics and one made up primarily of Jewish residents. Well aware of his need to become involved with minority communities, Reagan held a series of meetings with African-American leaders and activists from other minority groups during the spring and summer of 1968. He enlisted the help of H. C. "Chad" McClellan, an industrialist, to create jobs for black youths in the riot-torn areas of Watts and South Central Los Angeles.

Although some of his initiatives were criticized for failing to produce the expected outcomes, Governor Reagan received high marks and good statewide recognition for his efforts.[174] Undeclared presidential candidate Reagan, however, was running into trouble on his right flank. "When Reagan was meeting with minority groups," Cannon recalls, "polls showed Wallace receiving 14 percent of the vote nationally and a higher percentage in the South."[175] This threat could impede Reagan's attempt to undo Nixon at the convention. Thus, two days after expounding on equal opportunity, he undertook what might be thought of as a rebalancing act.

Cannon reports that in July, White and Reed were given the "limited goal of trying to avoid alienating southerners with an attack on Wallace."[176] The result was a statement by the governor at a July 16 press conference. To the question, "What views of George Wallace do you disagree with?" Reagan responded:

> Well, now, lately on the basis of his speeches this would be kind of hard to pin down because he's been speaking a lot of things that I think the people of America are in agreement with. But I would have to say on the basis of his past record . . . that I can't believe that he has the philosophy that I believe in, and the Republican party at heart because on his past record and as a Governor he showed no opposition particularly to great programs of federal aid and spending programs, etc. Right at the moment he's dwelling mainly on law and order, patriotism, and so forth, and these are attractive subjects. I'm sure that there are very few people in disagreement and I think this perhaps is responsible for some of the gains he's made.

Another journalist probed further: "You listed things in George Wallace's past record that you don't like. You left out his stand at the schoolhouse door and his opposition to school integration. Was that on purpose or would you include that as things that you don't like?" Reagan responded: "I would have to include a number of those things that I don't like." But it was his longer statement, not this caveat, which caught the public's attention. The result was a series of headlines equating Reagan with Wallace.[177]

In the context of his announcement that he was launching a speaking tour in southern states, the governor was asked again about the third-party candidate: "Why, Governor, do you think that you are regarded as a man who can head off possible defection of Republican voters in the South to George Wallace? Do you see yourself as an alternative in any way?" He replied that he was invited to help "stimulate a little interest in the Republican Party" in what had historically been Democratic territory.[178]

On July 19, the Californian began his "southern solicitation,"[179] a series of invited talks and fund-raisers for the Republican Party. His first stop was a rally in Amarillo followed by appearances in Char-lottesville, Little Rock, and Dallas. On July 21, he headed for Baltimore to woo delegates from Maryland, Delaware, Pennsylvania, and New Jersey. A few hours later he moved on to Cincinnati, where he spoke at a large rally before heading for the National Governors' Conference. The next day he harvested delegate votes in Louisville at the home of Kentucky governor Louie B. Nunn.[180]

Throughout his southern solicitation, Reagan gave his standard stump speech: Soviet military superiority was a near-term possibility; "no man can have real freedom without law and order"; the courts increasingly safeguard the rights of the accused more than those of soci-ety at large; and American citizens want guns because government has failed to protect them.[181] During this tour, Reagan was mindful of his speech on equal opportunity and the comparison to Wallace. He spoke directly to these issues in Amarillo: "We have in California programs to provide employment in the minority areas, to help break the deadly stalemate of welfare programs. We try to provide jobs and education. Contrast his [Wallace's] record in office with mine. Compare my state-ments on discrimination with his." While in Little Rock on July 20, he addressed what had been labeled as his two-faced domestic policy:

> I realize that when a Republican talks "law and order" there are those who say he is using a code word appealing to the white backlash. The implication is that we cannot be for law and order and at the same time be for improving the lot of our minorities. This is nonsense. Those who demand law and order are not racists and those who want to help the underprivileged should recognize that they can accomplish their goals better within a framework of law and order. No man must be above the law and no man beneath it. All men must stand equal before the law, regardless of race, religion or station in life. The criminal is no bigot and he is color-blind. Members of minority communities are victims out of all proportion to their numbers.[182]

The Republican rank and file liked what they heard. But meanwhile Nixon had been deriding aspects of the Great Society, declaring the Viet-nam War to be in the national interest, and accusing President Johnson of failing to protect the Americans taken hostage in the seizure of the USS *Pueblo*. Even though he was not the true conservative the rank and file would have liked to support, Nixon was saying what they needed to hear—enough so that voters were not crossing over to Reagan.

Reagan continued with familiar themes on July 24 in Birmingham, Alabama—Wallace country. He had a private session with delegates from Alabama, Georgia, Mississippi, North Carolina, and South Carolina, and gave several public stump speeches that the local press described as "paralleling the Wallace platform point for point." The *Birmingham News* declared Reagan's foray a failure: "California's Ronald Reagan—having tried to out-Wallace George Wallace in the Alabamian's own territory—flew home before dawn today, leaving behind in Birmingham a disappointingly small turnout and a thinly disguised effort to line up some 90 Southern Republican convention delegates in a closed door meeting." Evenly split between Reagan and Nixon, Alabama delegates were polled after Reagan's visits, and the results "showed no great shifts in their preference."[183] As Reagan headed home on July 25, Nixon's support among southern delegates remained strong. The barons had taken no chances. While Reagan was meeting with southern delegates in Alabama, Goldwater was sending telegrams to the Alabama delegation urging them to hold fast for Nixon because the former vice president could "best unite our party."[184]

Reagan had failed in his mission. After a brief return to California to carry out various gubernatorial duties, he headed back to the South. Before making an appearance in Winston-Salem, North Carolina, the governor traveled to Atlanta, where he sounded more like a presidential candidate than ever before. He stated that his delegation would place his name in nomination at the convention and that "if there are other delegations that want me as a candidate then obviously I will be a candidate." His near-candidacy had an immediate effect on delegates such as Jack Cox from Texas, who announced that he would switch his convention vote from Nixon to Reagan. The majority of the 56-member delegation, however, remained committed to Nixon.[185]

The governor made one more major preconvention appearance when he spoke before the Platform Committee on July 31. As in the remarks he had delivered throughout his southern tour, Reagan sprinkled his platform speech with conservative themes: lapses in law and order, the Great Society's ineffectual federal programs, and the Paris Peace Talks as North Vietnamese propaganda, among others. But he failed to deliver a message more compelling than Nixon's.[186]

As the convention drew near, the Nixon team declared victory, while Reagan and Rockefeller, hoping to create the expectation of a real contest in Miami Beach, continued to call for an open convention. The Reagan camp remained cautiously optimistic even though their candidate's summer tour had failed to secure the firm support of many new delegates. Their preliminary survey gave Nixon 570 delegates, approximately 100 less than were needed for the nomination, suggesting the possibility of open competition at the convention.[187] As discussed earlier, any need to move beyond the first round was widely expected to result in delegates releasing themselves from the bosses' control; in many southern and border states, this would likely lead to additional ballots being cast for Reagan.

Rockefeller's private polling in eight states (California, Massachusetts, Michigan, New Jersey, New York, Ohio, Pennsylvania, and Maryland) showed him beating Humphrey, compared to Nixon carrying only California, New Jersey, New York, and Ohio in a similar survey. But the polling was inconsistent with events. A few days before the convention, Romney, who had become the favorite son for Michigan, which had 48 delegates, issued a statement about his position on the convention: "I go to Miami to fight for the principles I know this country must follow to find peace. I wish I could enthusiastically go to fight for a particular candidate. At this point, I cannot."[188] Rockefeller had targeted the industrial Northeast in his campaign, but he was entering the convention without the support of delegate-rich Michigan.

Nixon's aides based their victory claim on indicators such as a late July Gallup Poll, which showed Nixon beating the Democratic presidential candidates and Rockefeller tying with them.[189] Other surveys, however, reported quite different results. A Harris Poll in late July found Nixon losing to Humphrey and McCarthy, and Rockefeller defeating Humphrey but losing to McCarthy. According to the vote count by United Press International on the eve of the convention, support for Nixon had eroded enough in the southern and border states to deny him victory on the first ballot.[190]

Phase 4: August 5 to August 8, 1968

When the Twenty-ninth Republican National Convention opened in Miami Beach on Monday, August 5, Nixon and Rockefeller were widely regarded as the leading candidates. Reagan joined them as an official candidate on the first day of the convention. Building on his July tour of the South, the California governor arranged a lunch meeting with Harry Dent of South Carolina; Alfred W. Goldwaithe, chairman of the Alabama delegation; William F. Murfin, chairman of the Florida delegation; and Clarke Reed, leader of Mississippi's delegates. He discussed with the group his plans to announce, but Dent sought to dissuade him on the grounds that Nixon was unstoppable; Reed and Murfin concurred that Reagan's candidacy was unlikely to have a major effect on Nixon's chances. Despite attempts by the party bosses to hold the South for Nixon, Goldwaithe pledged to Reagan.[191]

Following the lunch, William Knowland, the former U.S. senator from California and publisher of the *Oakland Tribune,* encouraged Reagan to announce himself as a bona fide candidate. The California delegation passed a resolution calling for the governor's official candidacy, and at around 4:00 p.m., Reagan publicly declared: "As of this moment, I am a candidate." The announcement was considered part of a southern strategy: "The strategy behind his move was simple: To shake loose enough delegates, especially in the South, who . . . felt they had to stick with Nixon as long as the California governor was playing coy."[192]

But Nixon was tightening his grip on the southern delegations. He arrived in Miami soon after Reagan's announcement, and by 10:00 p.m. was meeting with Dent and Thurmond. The former vice president restated his opposition to busing as a means to achieve school desegregation, which he supported. Thurmond presented Nixon with a *New York Times* article stating that moderates John Lindsay, Charles Percy, and Nelson Rockefeller were his most likely running mates. Nixon immediately restated the promise he had made to southern leaders during his springtime meetings in Atlanta: he would select a running mate who would be acceptable to the South.[193] Having already sent a telegram to the delegates urging them to support Nixon because of his stances on law and order, Vietnam, the Supreme Court, military superiority, and what he called "fiscal sanity," Thurmond was now prepared to launch an all-out campaign on the candidate's behalf.[194] He enlisted the help of Tower and Goldwater and undertook a blitzkrieg of the southern delegations.[195] Nixon's statements on a host of issues besides busing and his selection of a running mate provided the final assurance to southerners who might otherwise have leaned toward Reagan. A delegate from South Carolina noted that Nixon had "take[n] the conservative edge off Reagan's positions."[196]

Rockefeller continued to sound the themes of his campaign. He had a proven record of electoral support from Democrats and independents, and his support throughout the big industrial states of the Northeast made him the Republican contender who could prevail in the presidential election. Reagan and Nixon also courted delegates from the Northeast, but Nixon was the only contender who came to the convention with the support of party leaders from across the political spectrum. His candidacy was endorsed by Senator Mark Hatfield on one end of it and Thurmond on the other. As mentioned earlier, centrist party leaders including Gerald Ford, House minority leader and chairman of the convention, and Dirksen, chairman of the Platform Committee, were also essentially in the Nixon camp.[197]

Reagan posed the most important challenge to Nixon at the convention. Like the barons and the rank and file, the California governor opposed Great Society programs. Like the conservatives, he favored strong law-and-order policies, the continued application of military power in Vietnam, states' voluntary compliance with judicial decrees, and postponing peace talks with the North Vietnamese until they withdrew from South Vietnam. Nixon agreed with the conservatives on many points but differed on several substantial issues, including the value of the Great Society, the legitimacy of the Civil Rights and Voting Rights Acts, and the future of military engagement in Vietnam.

The second day of the convention, Tuesday, August 6, was one of southern strategies and solicitations for both the Nixon and Reagan camps. In a morning closed-door session with delegates from seven southern states, Nixon unleashed his full-blown southern strategy. The meeting was secretly taped, and a transcript published in the next day's *Miami Herald* revealed Nixon reaffirming the promises he had made to southern Republicans in Atlanta that summer. Although he had made these promises privately in Atlanta, Nixon was now combining the issues more emphatically and, most importantly, expounding his opinions to a larger number of delegates.

Nixon's combination of centrism and southern-style conservatism not only persuaded delegates, but also enabled him to outmaneuver Reagan with powerful rhetorical appeals. The barons, in particular, were concerned about a repeat of 1964. Nixon demonstrated his ability to take a stance that was conservative enough to satisfy southerners yet sufficiently moderate to carry the center. In other words, the former vice president was able to convince conservatives that although he held some of Goldwater's beliefs, he was otherwise unlike Goldwater. Reagan had no hope of outmaneuvering Nixon in the center, which the former vice president had worked assiduously to dominate. Even the Reagan team's backroom negotiations to select a politically centrist running mate from a big northeastern industrial state (Ohio governor Jim Rhodes, with Pennsylvania governor Raymond P. Shafer as the second choice) did not persuade delegates that he could form a moderate-conservative coalition, as Nixon was doing.[198]

Of Nixon's performance at his meeting with southern delegates, Garry Wills writes: "If Nixon gave more, and more flamboyantly, to the South, that was because the whole convention hinged on the South. Others he could soothe or try to placate; those delegates he had to serve."[199] Thurmond was pleased with the meeting and used Nixon's vice presidential assurance to shore up support from southern delegates who were still undecided. Nixon's maneuvers and Thurmond's efforts produced impressive results. Prior to the meeting, half of the Mississippi delegation was behind Reagan, but by the end of the day the entire delegation had pledged its support to Nixon. The Florida delegation was divided and would remain so through Wednesday. But Nixon was on the move. Tower was holding the line in his delegation in the face of strong support for Reagan. Ultimately, 41 out of the 56 Texas delegates would vote for Nixon.

Despite Thurmond's well-orchestrated campaign, which included close collaboration with Tower and Goldwater, the Reagan team remained in high gear. Congressman James Gardner, chairman of the North Carolina delegation, endorsed Reagan, but for the most part there was no substantial delegate movement in the Californian's direction.[200]

Rumors swirled throughout the convention hall that Reagan and Rockefeller had joined forces to stop Nixon on the first ballot. Clif White claims that while the two camps stayed in close contact, there was no collusion.[201] Even if Reagan and Rockefeller had coordinated their strategies, by the end of Tuesday it was clear that Nixon could not be stopped. Neither Reagan nor Rockefeller had a message that would appeal to delegates across the political spectrum. Reagan was too far to the right, and although Rockefeller had been arguing that he was the only GOP contender who could prevail in November, Nixon was actively demonstrating that he could build the center-right coalition needed to win.

The Reagan team continued their efforts to raid the southern delegations on Wednesday, August 7. Many delegates from Alabama, Florida, Louisiana, and Mississippi favored the California governor but were being pressured by the Thurmond group to vote for Nixon. As mentioned earlier, Goldwaithe of Alabama supported Reagan. Jim Martin, a delegate from Alabama, was pushing for Nixon. The Alabama delegation delivered a split vote of 14 for Nixon and 12 for Reagan. Clarke Reed held Mississippi for Nixon, and the delegation delivered all of its votes to him. Charlton Lyon, the chairman of the Louisiana group, expressed his preference for Reagan even though he cast his ballot for Nixon, just as 19 of the state's 26 delegates would do.

There was more uncertainty among Florida's delegates. Governor Kirk pledged his support to Rockefeller, but 17 of the 34 delegates were women who favored Reagan. Bill Murfin, chair of the delegation and a member of the Greenville Group, was a Nixon man, but he was unable to wield sufficient influence over his delegates. Thurmond's intervention saved the day for Nixon. When he assured the Florida contingent that he had been given control over the selection of Nixon's running mate, 32 of the 34 delegates decided to support Nixon.[202]

Nixon and his strategists believed that they had secured southern support, but they took no chances on the possibility of last-minute defections to Reagan. Turning to the North, they began working to win over the delegations of Ohio, Michigan, and New Jersey, states held by favorite sons in territory that Rockefeller claimed he could command. They were unsuccessful in Ohio and Michigan, where they won over only a few votes on the first ballot. Nixon's greatest victory came in New Jersey, where his strategists succeeded in breaking Senator Clifford Case's favorite-son stronghold. When New Jersey delivered 18 of its 40 delegates to him, Nixon and his team felt confident that they had clinched the nomination.[203]

At approximately eight o'clock on the evening of August 7, the Reagan forces circulated a *Miami Herald* article with the headline "Delegates Talk Nixon-Hatfield; Choice Narrows."[204] Dent, Clarke Reed, Thurmond, and others immediately fanned out to refute this rumor that Nixon might offer the moderate senator from Oregon the second slot on the ticket.

The balloting took place later that night. Despite strenuous efforts by Reagan and Rockefeller to prevent a Nixon victory on the first ballot, the former vice president prevailed, receiving 692 votes on the first ballot, 25 more than were needed for the nomination. Rockefeller took 277 votes, and Reagan received 182. It was close to two o'clock on the morning of August 8 when Reagan strode to the podium and encouraged the delegates to support Nixon. Later that day, Rockefeller issued a statement in which he declared, "The convention has spoken and I support the decision of the convention, all the way."[205]

Nixon and his aides quickly turned their attention to selecting a running mate. Earlier in the campaign, Pat Buchanan, a campaign aide, had written a memo on the complexity of naming a vice presidential candidate: "The Nixon campaign is confronted with the old German problem—the two-front war . . . We are going to have to stave off the assaults of Wallace from the right, to keep him from making any further inroads, and we are going to have to defeat the challenge of Humphrey in the center of American politics. It is almost impossible for one candidate to do both at the same time." Reagan would release Nixon of "the burden of fighting George Wallace, a burden we would otherwise have to assume totally, a burden which would necessarily cost us something in the center." The match did not make sense for either man for numerous reasons, including the fact that they were both perceived as Californians.[206]

Nixon met with party leaders in the early morning hours between three and five o'clock to discuss the number two spot on the ticket. Maryland Governor Spiro Agnew and Massachusetts Governor John Volpe made the final list. Agnew was ultimately chosen for his ability to fight off Wallace from the right.[207] Southern conservatives like Thurmond admired Agnew's handling of the riots in his state following the assassination of Rev. Martin Luther King, Jr.; the governor had called out thousands of members of the Maryland National Guard and supported the deployment of federal troops. Meeting with black leaders a few days later, Agnew said, "You were beguiled by the rationalizations of unity; you were intimidated by veiled threats; you were stung by insinuations that you were Mr. Charlie's boy, by epithets like 'Uncle Tom.' God knows I cannot fault you who spoke out for breaking and running in the face of what appeared to be overwhelming opinion in the Negro community. But actually it was only the opinion of those who depend upon chaos and turmoil for leadership." His deprecating tone provoked civic and religious leaders to walk out of the meeting in protest, and the episode made the national press.[208] Agnew's actions were considered good enough for Thurmond and the "southern kingmakers," who agreed to place him on the ticket with Nixon.[209]

Throughout the campaign, all of the Republican contenders used rhetoric in an attempt to shore up existing support, but Nixon also employed it to broaden his political base, becoming more of a strategist as he formulated his campaign promises. His command of the center, combined with significant promises to southern concerns, convinced even those who disliked and distrusted him that they had found a presidential contender who could win in November and bring the South along with him. Nixon completed his strategizing by selecting a running mate who was liked by conservatives and who governed a border state. It was one more in a series of persuasive measures.

For their part, Reagan, Rockefeller, and Romney never found an effective way to challenge Nixon. The former vice president's consistent straddling the fence on controversial issues such as Vietnam and his stalwart political pragmatism helped him undermine these politicians and prevent them from building their own alternative constituencies.

Romney's and Rockefeller's hopes of becoming president ended in 1968. But as Richard Reeves, author of a recent book on Reagan's political career, writes, the California governor's attempt to win his party's nomination in 1968 was not a complete impossiblity.[210] His viability was not reflected in the first-ballot votes, but Reagan never expected to be successful immediately. Had balloting gone beyond the first round, the unit rule and favorite-son control of delegations would have disappeared and the durability of Nixon's strategic manipulation would have been tested, for there were many true believers among the convention-goers, and Reagan was their man.

Although later races would take place in a much more open political system, the 1968 Republican race was tightly controlled by a few party bosses and their supporters. In such a scenario, any serious contender had to buy off his key supporters with benefits. Nixon understood this logic, his promises to the South were political payoffs, and the convention win was his return on the investment.

Reagan had not been a great rhetorician or an architect of the institutional environment in the 1968 race, but he had weathered the contest without political damage, and he most likely regarded his campaign experiences as the beginning of a learning curve. A decade later, when pitted against President Jimmy Carter, he would combine issues into a package convincing to voters and more difficult for his opponent to maneuver around than the strategy Nixon had devised in the 1968 GOP contest. Beyond cleverly combining issues, Reagan would succeed in producing a fundamental redefinition of the policy landscape.

The only major conservative Republican contender in the 1968 race,

Reagan, would go on to command the political center in 1980. He would accomplish this without embracing centrist positions such as those taken by Rockefeller and Romney, and without abandoning the basic philosophy he had professed to voters in his first presidential bid. As the following chapters show, the lessons Reagan learned in 1968 clearly influenced his impressive showing in the 1976 Republican contest and contributed to his successful campaign in 1980.

3

Down to Political Defeat

Reagan's Inability to Break Ford's
Coalition in the 1976 Primaries

At a news conference on December 30, 1974, at the Los Angeles Press Club, Governor Ronald Reagan announced the impending launch of his nationally syndicated column and radio program in early 1975. His second term as governor officially ended in early January, and by the end of the month, he was recording his first batch of radio commentaries in a Hollywood studio. For nearly five years (from January 1975 to October 1979, except for a hiatus between November 1975 and September 1976), Reagan enjoyed access to an unparalleled rhetorical testing-ground through his nationally syndicated radio program and newspaper column. He also took on an almost endless series of engagements across the country in support of Republican candidates and causes.[1]

Although many of the columns were drafted by former Reagan aide Peter Hannaford, co-owner with Michael Deaver of the Los Angeles–based public relations firm that managed Reagan's activities throughout the late 1970s, the Reagan Presidential Library holds approximately 700 draft radio commentaries in Reagan's own handwriting. He recorded and broadcast more than 1,000 commentaries in all. The radio commentaries, as Reagan wrote in a January 1980 letter, addressed "virtually every subject mentionable and stated my views on those subjects."[2]

It is estimated that Ronald Reagan's commentaries were broadcast on 200 to 400 or so radio stations and reached between 20–30 million Americans a week.[3] The radio and newspaper commentaries proved to be an ideal vehicle for rhetorical campaigning, securing his conservative base while simultaneously extending his reach to new constituencies.

No other contender was appealing to voters on such a grand scale. In March 1975, the conservative journal *Human Events* reported: "Supporters of the 'don't declare now' philosophy contend that the governor, by plunging into the presidential contest immediately, would have to relinquish his nationally syndicated column and his widely heard radio program, two forums some strategists see as essential."[4] A similar assessment was made in the *Washington Post* three years later: "It would be grossly unfair to say that his nationwide public forum is devoted to advancing his personal cause. But it is an unprecedented opportunity to promote the conservative causes that are at the basis of his candidacy."[5]

Reagan's original handwritten drafts, full as they are of edited sentences and rephrased paragraphs, depict a man completely focused on improving his rhetorical performance. Some of the commentaries echo what came to be known as "The Speech"—an adaptable set of remarks about the social, economic, and political ills of big government—while others revealed the more mature rhetorical style of later stages in the campaign.

As Riker observed, the heresthetician has to convince voters that the conventional wisdom on a policy issue (such as containment as a means of managing U.S.-Soviet relations) is fundamentally wrong, and that a "new alternative" (peace through strength, for example) will produce better outcomes.[6] Reagan's essays from this period are an important step toward a heresthetical candidacy. The tax revolt that Reagan championed in so many of his radio commentaries from this era was slowly drawing together diverse interests and blocs of voters. Reagan argued in his commentaries that leading economists such Milton Friedman, Arthur Laffer, Paul McCracken, and Allan Meltzer advocated an economic philosophy that could radically improve the economy: "Each [theorist] made it clear that government can increase its tax revenues and create the jobs we need *without* inflation by lowering tax rates for businesses and individuals." In his 1980 presidential campaign, Reagan would refashion this statement to bolster his promise of tax cuts accompanied by economic growth and general prosperity. One of Reagan's first radio commentaries, taped in January 1975, also presented the broad outline of a 1980 campaign theme. In this radio commentary titled "Inflation," Reagan bluntly declared, "If we had less regulation we could have lower prices."[7]

Reagan's economic philosophy—stated in a radio commentary in early 1979—typified the economic policy ideas that he refined during his five years on the air: "My own belief is that cutting taxes will have the effect of cutting spending if government can no longer run a deficit and that will bring the end of inflation. . . . I think we need both a limit on spending and a ban on unbalanced budgets. One will reduce the inordinate amount of private earnings the government is taking and which is a drag on the economy, the other will make sure government doesn't evade the limit by running up a debt."[8]

In his radio commentaries and newspaper columns (as well as in other speeches and writings), Reagan presented alternative ways of thinking about the Cold War. In an April 1975 radio commentary titled "Peace" he articulated his idea that a robust military policy was part of a strategy to help create the conditions for better and more stable U.S.-Soviet cooperation. A month later, in "Communism, the Disease," he committed what was essentially intellectual heresy at the height of U.S.-Soviet détente. Détente signified a kind of stable status quo between the superpowers, yet Reagan declared that the Soviet system was "a temporary aberration which will one day disappear from the earth because it is contrary to human nature."[9]

As a prolific correspondent, Reagan was always in close contact with detractors and supporters. His letters were a source of information about what worked rhetorically; they enabled Reagan to fine-tune his radio messages, communicate with his listening audience, and sharpen his ideas.[10] Taken together, his writings offer a Rosetta stone for understanding Reagan's presidential strategy.

The Republican contest in 1968 had been a small selectorate process in which the party barons and their associated cadre played the role of selectors. By 1976, however, this system had become largely obsolete. This evolution was the result of a variety of forces, including greater access to television, which allowed candidates to appeal directly to the electorate over the heads of state party organizations; and reforms growing out of the Democratic Party's 1968 convention in Chicago (including the findings of the McGovern-Fraser Commission), which sought to make the process of selecting delegates more democratic.[11]

These and other factors led to a proliferation of primaries and an increase in the number of delegates bound by the popular vote in the primaries. Austin Ranney has reported that there were 16 "states using a primary for selecting or binding national convention [Republican] delegates" in 1968. Also in that election year, 458 (or 34.3 percent) of "votes [were] cast by delegates chosen or bound by primaries." By contrast, 28 states used primaries in 1976 for deciding or binding delegates, and 1,533 (or 67.9 percent) was the number of delegate votes chosen or bound to decisions in the primaries.[12]

In contrast to 1968, when a number of candidates had avoided entering the primaries or even announcing their candidacies during the early months of primary season, the main Republican challengers in 1976 announced their intentions well in advance of the Iowa caucuses, and competed in all of the primaries. The primaries were a source of major competition among the challengers, and delegates were open to persuasion. Reagan's improved performance in 1976 was primarily due to his skillful use of rhetoric in this new context.

The party bosses that had been so central to clinching the Republican Party's presidential nomination in 1968 remained influential, but they could not easily undo the many points of candidate-voter contact that were now available. The weakening of the system of party bosses in control of election-year politics was evident in the fact that Reagan came close to winning the Republican Party's presidential nomination despite his having limited support among Republican leaders. Senator Jesse Helms (R-NC) and Senator Paul Laxalt (R-NV) were his biggest supporters in the U.S. Senate. Other leaders such as Senator Barry Goldwater threw their support to President Ford largely on the grounds that it was safer to support the Republican occupant of the White House than to change course in the wake of the Watergate scandal.[13]

The Contenders

One has to know Ronald Reagan's challengers and the other relevant political actors in the 1976 presidential race in order to understand the campaign strategies of the two main contenders.[14] House Minority Leader Gerald R. Ford, a 25-year veteran of Congress and Reagan's most serious rival, had taken an unusual path to national prominence. He had become Nixon's new vice president after Spiro Agnew was indicted on tax-evasion charges in October 1973. Then, in late July 1974, the House Judiciary Committee adopted three articles of impeachment against the president himself. Nixon resigned on August

9, and according to the rules laid out in the Twenty-fifth Amendment, Gerald Ford was sworn in as the first unelected president in American history.

These were unpropitious circumstances in which to run for a full term, and Ford was never able to overcome them. His initial approval rating of 71 percent plummeted to 50 percent after he pardoned Nixon on September 9. By early 1975, only 37 percent of the public approved of his job performance. His rating surged periodically but never exceeded 50 percent during Ford's last full year in office.[15]

By late 1975 Ford was not even considered the Republican front-runner. When the Gallup Poll gave respondents a list of prominent Republicans and asked who they would like to see as the Republican presidential candidate, only 32 percent chose Ford compared to 40 percent for Reagan.[16]

Ford's choice of Nelson Rockefeller for vice president weakened the incumbent's already shaky standing among conservatives. Rockefeller's December 1973 resignation from the governorship of New York—supposedly to devote more time to the national commissions on which he served—had been perceived by many conservatives as his unofficial declaration of a fourth bid for the GOP nomination and an effort to build a national base that would undermine a Reagan candidacy. They were dismayed by Ford's choice, and many began to advocate for a Reagan bid instead.[17]

The president was walking a fine line: on June 16, 1975, he endorsed Rockefeller as his running mate, but he also proposed that the convention delegates should choose his partner on the ticket. This dual move did little to assuage conservatives. By late summer, Gallup was reporting that Republicans favored Reagan, not Rockefeller, as Ford's running mate. Pressure continued to mount from the right. Ford, already suffering from lukewarm approval ratings, met with Rockefeller on October 28. A few days later, Rockefeller announced that he would not be the president's running mate.[18] But he also let it be known that he might toss his own hat in the ring if the opportunity presented itself. A June *New York Times* article had the following headline: "Rockefeller Acting as If He's Running." It was not to be. Ultimately Rockefeller endorsed Ford. The president had the support of one of the most influential political figures in the Northeast, a region rich in delegates. On July 8, 1975, Gerald Ford formally announced his intention to campaign for the presidency.[19]

History was on Ford's side: since 1884, every president who had sought a second term had been renominated. But Ford's vulnerability quickly became apparent after he and Reagan emerged from the primaries in a virtual tie. His failure to appease conservatives improved Reagan's chances of winning the nomination. John Sears, Reagan's campaign director, thought that strategic choice of the number two spot on his candidate's ticket could diminish support for Ford among the delegates. In Sears's scheme, if Reagan announced his running mate before the convention, Ford would be forced to do the same. Ford's selection would most likely be less acceptable to the conservative wing of the party than any selection Reagan would make, thus eroding the incumbent's slim lead in delegate count.

Reagan approved. On July 26, he informed the public that he was "departing from tradition and announcing my selection," Senator Robert Schweiker of Pennsylvania, not coincidentally the state with the third-largest number of delegates. In addition to forcing the president's hand, the selection of a moderate Republican as Reagan's running mate was supposed to unite the Republican Party.[20]

That strategy failed. The widespread appeal of the Reagan-Schweiker ticket that Sears hoped for never materialized, and some prominent conservatives actually withdrew their support from Reagan. Nor did Ford respond by announcing his running mate before the convention. It was not until the last day of the convention that the president announced his partnership with Senator Robert Dole, a politician with acceptable conservative credentials.[21]

On the Democratic side, it was Jimmy Carter, the governor of Georgia, who showed a number of surprising similarities to Reagan. Carter was 14 years younger than Reagan, but had been preparing to run for president almost as long as the Californian had. In 1966, when aides met with Reagan to discuss a presidential bid just two weeks after he won the California gubernatorial race, Carter was tasting defeat in the race for the governorship of Georgia, becoming a born-again Christian, and beginning to form close ties with men like Stuart Eizenstat, Hamilton Jordan, Jody Powell, and Gerald Rafshoon, who, along with Peter Bourne, Patrick Caddell, and a few others, would become key advisers to Carter's 1976 and 1980 presidential campaigns.

Carter won the Georgia governor's race the second time around, in 1970, and at some point in the next two years decided to run for president.[22] A lengthy and detailed memo sent by Hamilton Jordan to Carter in November 1972 offered some projections about the Democratic outlook for 1976. It included sections on potential contenders George Wallace and Edward Kennedy, and discussed subjects such as establishing Carter's national image, campaign tactics for a governor seeking the presidency, and the need for staff and advisers.[23]

On December 12, 1974, Carter announced his campaign for the Democratic nomination. It was an ambitious gambit inasmuch as the Georgian was not a nationally recognized political figure. In fact, some analysts labeled him a dark horse.[24] If elected, he would be the first southern president since Zachary Taylor had carried the Whig ticket in 1848. Nor did Carter have a national platform to raise his national profile as Reagan did with his radio program, newspaper column, and many speaking engagements. Instead, he embarked on a grueling campaign schedule, traveling half a million miles in 22 months.[25]

In 1976, both Carter and Reagan were campaigning as Washington outsiders. In the wake of Watergate and the debacle in Vietnam, the two rivals portrayed themselves as leaders who, free of Beltway ties, could steer the country in a new direction. But beyond these commonalities of form, Carter's platform contrasted starkly with Reagan's small-government and anti-Communist ideas. In his campaign, the Georgia governor endorsed traditional Democratic social policies based on large amounts of funding from the federal government, deep cuts in defense spending, and a de-emphasis on U.S.-Soviet competition and conflict.[26]

Carter insisted that his running mate share his views. He also wanted his partner to be a member of Congress, thus offsetting his own lack of Washington experience. His choice of Walter Mondale, the senior senator from Minnesota, did not create an ideologically balanced ticket, but it certainly gave the Democrats broad geographic appeal.[27]

Among Carter's Democratic rivals in the early stages of the race, George Wallace was perhaps the most prominent. Wallace had a long history in presidential politics. Having repressed his national ambitions in favor of Goldwater in 1964, Wallace had won 13.5 percent of the popular vote in 1968 under the American Independent Party banner. He had run as a Democrat in 1972, winning primaries in Florida, Tennessee, North Carolina, Maryland, and Michigan, before an assassin's bullet struck his spinal cord during a Maryland campaign stop, paralyzing him from the waist down and ending his candidacy in that race. On November 12, 1975, Wallace announced that he would again compete for the Democratic nomination. His platform would be devoted to "the survival and salvation of the average, middle class," which he argued was under attack from ultraliberal policies. He promised to compete in most of the primaries, and cannily refused to reject the idea of a third-party candidacy.[28] But Wallace's campaign was hurt by Alabama's history of burgeoning government expenditures under his leadership as well as by the fact that, as he himself recognized, "it's impossible for a wheelchair man to get out into the crowd."[29] Wallace failed to carry even a single primary, and he ultimately endorsed Jimmy Carter's nomination.

Analysts have debated whether Wallace's 1976 bid had a major impact on the Carter, Ford, and Reagan candidacies.[30] There is general agreement, however, that his truncated campaign did not have the same effect as his full-blown 1968 campaign.

Seizing the Conservative Mantle: November 1968 to early 1975

In winning the 1968 and 1972 presidential races, Richard Nixon had carefully crafted a campaign strategy rooted in centrism and political pragmatism. Ronald Reagan, too, would need to command the center, but it is doubtful that Reagan could have simply adopted Nixon's strategy without compromising his credibility. In the years following his 1968 bid, Reagan had become convinced that the Republican Party could permanently capture the political center without compromising its traditional principles. His national activities after 1968 suggest that he believed himself to be the rightful defender and promoter of the conservative doctrine. His party, meanwhile, was increasingly looking to him for political leadership, electing him president of the Republican Governors' Association in 1968 and 1970.

Governor Reagan was often asked during the early 1970s if he would again seek his party's presidential nomination. His usual response, typified in a 1973 interview, was, "I don't think an individual makes that decision. I think the people make that determination."[31] But behind the rhetoric Reagan was leaving nothing to chance. Immediately after the 1968 presidential election he undertook a strenuous schedule of national political activity that continued almost unabated until 1980. It was a run unmatched by any GOP contender, with the possible exception of Rockefeller, who seemed determined to make a fourth presidential run.

While simultaneously governing California and stumping to keep up his national profile, Reagan was also solidifying his reputation as heir of the conservative movement, identifying the type of coalition needed to elevate the GOP out of its minority-party status, and crafting a message that would hold that coalition together in the face of Democratic challenges. Everything that Reagan did on the national level during these years contributed to the agenda he had set for himself. It was in the context of fulfilling this agenda that Reagan evolved from a great orator and rhetorician to a heresthetician.

Many people were watching and writing about Reagan during the late 1960s and 1970s, but few perceived his subtle rhetorical changes or appreciated his increasing political momentum. In a few short years, Reagan both recast his message and redefined the institutional context within which the selectorate would be asked to support him. It is when seen from this perspective that Reagan most closely resembles Boris Yeltsin during his own rise to power in the late 1980s and early 1990s.

The American political landscape itself was evolving during the 1970s. In 1968 Richard Nixon had received 43.3 percent of the popular vote to Hubert Humphrey's 42.7 percent. Many in the Nixon camp argued that had George Wallace not been in the race, Nixon would have taken his 13.5 percent share. The implication was that Nixon's victory was actually a mandate.

The president may have seen his 1968 victory in these terms, but conservatives and Republicans did not unanimously agree with this interpretation. By 1971, prominent conservatives had begun to complain that Nixon was abandoning the Republican voters who had been so essential to his election. They publicly reminded him that he had won the GOP nomination thanks to the "conservative constituency" of party kingmakers and delegates that had lined up behind him.[32]

The discontent began to take shape in early 1971, when the conservative Young Americans for Freedom initiated a movement to draft Reagan for president.[33] On July 26, William F. Buckley, Jr., led a group of conservatives in a public declaration that they were suspending support for the Nixon administration in objection to continued inflation and unemployment, as well as what they called "excessive taxation and inordinate welfarism." They also denounced Nixon's overtures toward the People's Republic of China and his policies toward Southeast Asia and the Soviet Union as being at odds with America's national security interests. "We do not plan at the moment to encourage formal political opposition to President Nixon in the forthcoming primaries," they wrote, "but we propose to keep all options open in the light of political developments in the next months."[34]

Although the conservatives did support Nixon's reelection bid in the end, some of them broke off to encourage Republican congressman John Ashbrook of Ohio in his protest presidential campaign.[35] Meanwhile, various independent conservative organizations—Americans for Constitutional Action, the Free Society Association, the American Conservative Union, and Young Americans for Freedom—were becoming openly disenchanted with Nixon's policies.

Federal spending and government regulation increased more during the Nixon administration than they had during the Johnson years, and social spending outpaced defense spending. Nixon created new government agencies, such as the Environmental Protection Agency and the Occupational Safety and Health Administration, massive bureaucracies that conservatives disliked and distrusted. And they derided Nixon's new Cost of Living Council, directed by future defense secretary Donald Rumsfeld, as an effort to control prices and wages, labeling it "America's most concerted attempt to introduce state control of the economy since the Second World War."[36] Conservative political analyst Frank Meyer's statement about Nixon in 1961—that "neither Disraeli nor Nixon ever stood firmly upon principle"—now seemed eerily prescient to many conservatives.[37] William Rusher, the *National Review*'s publisher, wrote that "in 1972 . . . Nixon's departures from conservative principle had become too numerous and too painful to ignore."[38]

The conservatives' claim of a national mandate was reinforced by Nixon's performance in 1972. The incumbent moved easily through the primaries and trounced his liberal GOP challenger, Congressman Paul N. McCloskey, Jr., leaving him with only one delegate vote on the first ballot. Nixon's reelection also signaled substantial GOP inroads into the traditional Democratic base. For the first time in its history, the AFL-CIO had refused to back the Democratic presidential nominee. As a result, Nixon took 57 percent of the blue-collar vote, a bloc that had voted solidly Democratic only a few years earlier. He also prevailed in every region of the country, including the South, where he won 71 percent of the vote. This southern defection was yet another blow to the Democrats' traditional strength. In fact, Democrats everywhere were defecting in record numbers. When it was all over, Nixon claimed 33 percent of the Democratic vote and 69 percent of the independent vote.

The District of Columbia and Massachusetts were the only two electoral units in which Democratic senator George McGovern received more of the popular vote than Nixon. The incumbent easily won the general election with 60.7 percent of the popular vote and 520 electoral votes to McGovern's 37.5 percent and 17 electoral votes.

Watergate and its associated scandals were already looming on the horizon. A few months after the election, White House staffers G. Gordon Liddy and James W. McCord, Jr., were convicted of crimes related to their break-in to Democratic campaign headquarters the previous year. Nixon staffers H. R. Haldeman and John Ehrlichman resigned, as did others. In the spring of 1973, the Senate began holding nationally televised hearings, during which White House counsel John Dean admitted that he had discussed a cover-up with Nixon on numerous occasions. In the midst of all this, Vice President Spiro Agnew resigned on October 10 under the shadow of an indictment on tax-evasion charges. On November 5, *Time* magazine's cover story speculated about Nixon being impeached. Two weeks later, Nixon declared, "I'm not a crook." He resigned nine months later.

Reagan remained a Nixon loyalist throughout the crisis, proclaiming that the Watergate conspirators were "not criminals at heart."[39] The California governor also continued to position himself as a key defender of the 1972 mandate, which he defined in terms of the Republican Party's commitment to creating a coalition based on "a libertarian philosophy, a belief in the individual freedom and the reduction of government."[40]

Reagan believed that the 1972 mandate was the result of efforts to make the conservative Republican philosophy attractive to a wide range of voters. He built on that idea in his December 1973 speech to the southern GOP convention in Atlanta:

> The battle we won in 1972 must be won again. Millions of Democrats must be made to see that philosophically they have more in common with us than with those who would erode our defenses, pawning our weapons to pay for some new experiment in social reform. . . .
>
> You don't have to sell your Democratic neighbors and friends on the Republican philosophy. Most of them already subscribe to it. What really is needed is to show them that what they believe is what we officially as a party stand for.[41]

But the California governor had not yet figured out how to show conservative Democrats and independents that the GOP was their natural home. Any attempts to do so were being eclipsed by Watergate, which had by then engulfed Washington and put the future of the Republican Party in question.

In speeches and interviews, Reagan implored conservatives to remain focused on the party's mission, saying: "The '72 election gave us a new majority, a long-overdue realignment based not on party labels—but on basic philosophy. The tragedy of Watergate and the traumatic experience of these past years since then [have] obscured the meaning of that '72 election. But the mandate registered by the people still remains. The people have not changed in philosophy."[42]

Reagan seemed like the right person to be preaching this sermon. Conservatives had been speculating about his potential to become a figurehead for American conservatism ever since he had won the governor's race in 1966. Russell Kirk's postprimary 1966 essay on conservatism in the *New York Times* magazine is one important illustration of the conservative consensus:

> Mr. Reagan is something of a surprise. Previously he was a man of One Speech—and that chiefly an address to those already converted. But clearly he has been doing much reading and thinking and conferring, so that now he is ready with persuasive answers to nearly all questions.
>
> Whether he can develop into a genuine leader of responsible conservatives will depend upon his performance as Governor—if he is elected. He is more supple than Mr. Goldwater, and willing to work. He will have to go a great way beyond his famous Speech, which was almost wholly a rapid-fire attack on a variety of afflictions without alternative courses being presented, if he is to lead the conservative interest out of simple negativism.[43]

Kirk's essay identified Reagan's most urgent challenge: could he move beyond a mere critique of existing policies to present voters with a clear set of alternatives? The questions that Kirk had raised in 1966 were still unanswered in the mid-1970s, as Reagan ended his tenure in Sacramento and geared up for his first full-scale presidential campaign. By this time Reagan had successfully staked out the position of defender, if not yet leader, of the conservative movement. But he had yet to build a coalition unified by anything more than conservatives' opposition to the failures of current policy. He was not yet anything more than a talented rhetorician.

But that change was already in the works. In late 1972, Governor Reagan had invited a group of domestic policy experts to meet with him at the Century Plaza Hotel in Los Angeles. There he expressed concern that Nixon's landslide victory might not lead to restraints on government spending. He asked the experts in attendance about the feasibility of constructing a constitutional amendment to control California's taxation and spending authority. The group had soon drafted an amendment to the state constitution, which Reagan put before California voters as Proposition 1 on November 6, 1973.[44] Proposition 1 was defeated 54 percent to 46, thanks in large part to a massive opposition campaign launched by the California Teachers Association, the California State Employees Association, and the League of Women Voters, among other groups. But Reagan believed he had found an issue that mattered to voters. In a letter penned soon after the vote, he wrote: "We planted a seed and we won't stop now. A number of other states have picked up the idea and may implement it before California does. We'll keep on trying."[45]

Five years later, Californians passed Proposition 13, a property tax reduction measure. Voters in many other states passed similar measures. Reagan believed that Proposition 1 had paved the way for Proposition 13, and in the late 1970s he devoted numerous radio commentaries to his "tax revolt," noting that it had attracted support from unexpected quarters, including the labor rank and file.[46]

The journalist Peter Schrag has written that Proposition 13 "set the stage for the Reagan era and became both fact and symbol of a radical shift in governmental priorities, public attitudes, and social relationships that is as nearly fundamental in American politics as the changes brought by the New Deal." Reagan biographer Lou Cannon concurs: if Schrag is right, then "Reagan helped set the stage for his own presidency when he put forward Proposition 1."[47] The tax cuts that Reagan advocated throughout the late 1970s became the core of his first economic agenda as president, and of his Economic Recovery Act of 1981.

The prairie fire that Reagan lit with anti–tax and spend sentiment would powerfully shape his heresthetical appeal in the 1980 presidential campaign. This message had not yet come together in the early 1970s, however. Nor had Reagan yet devised a way to present his prodefense views without seeming hawkish. While in Sacramento—and during subsequent years—he had maintained his national profile, but he had done so without a grand strategy for how to link his message to a new coalition.

There were various failed attempts throughout this period. For instance, at one point the Reagan camp contemplated creating a new foundation that would support Reagan's "undeclared campaign for the presidency." This foundation would allow Reagan to stump the "mashed potato circuit" in support of Republican candidates.[48] The idea, which did not seem to include a set of messages specifically tailored to broadening Reagan's own political base, was abandoned.

Soon thereafter, however, Reagan and his aides embraced a different and more ambitious plan. In May 1974, Reagan held a gathering at his Pacific Palisades home with longtime aides and advisers Justin Dart, Mike Deaver, Peter Hannaford, Jim Jenkins, Jim Lake, Ed Meese, Holmes Tuttle, and Robert Walker. They discussed Reagan's political future in light of rapidly unfolding events in Washington.[49]

Three months after the meeting, Nixon resigned and Gerald Ford was immediately sworn in as president, prompting one *Los Angeles Times* reporter to write, "The last hope of Gov. Reagan ever to become President probably went glimmering." Reagan didn't see things in quite the same terms; instead, he declared his candidacy the year after Ford became president. When questioned about his decision, Reagan replied that Ford's adherence to the conservative mandate of 1972 would determine his course of action.[50]

Ford had known that Reagan was a potentially formidable rival, going back at least as far the wave of telegrams in 1973 urging him to select Reagan, not Rockefeller, as his vice president.[51] Reagan's prominence among Republicans most likely influenced Ford's fall 1974 invitation for Reagan to join his administration as secretary of transportation. Reagan declined the offer and instead agreed to a set of activities that would enhance a presidential bid, should he decide to run. His aides prepared two strategy documents in 1974 that described how Reagan's national activities could be used to best advantage. The first, "Ronald Reagan: Building a National Organization," suggested "testing the potential strength of a Presidential bid, without RR overtly stepping out of the 'mashed potato circuit' role he has described for himself." The second, "Ronald Reagan: A Program for the Future," described the radio program, newspaper column, and speaking tours as significant means by which the governor could "maintain influence in the Republican Party; strengthen and consolidate leadership as *the* national conservative spokesman; and enhance [his] foreign affairs credibility."[52]

By this time, Reagan had made a sort of mantra out of the need to build a broad-based coalition around conservative principles. But nothing in the ensuing litany of strategy documents, speeches, press conferences, or letters from this period indicates that he and his team had yet identified which groups they should recruit for their new majority beyond some grand and vague ideas about bringing Democrats, Republicans, and independents together.

As Reagan entered into his postgubernatorial phase, Republicans were busy assessing the disappointing results of the November 5, 1974, midterm elections, which had given the Democrats 43 new seats in the House and three in the Senate. The Democrats had also made a 5 percent gain in governorships and increased their numbers by 14 percent in the lower houses and 12 percent in the upper houses of state legislatures nationwide. While the 1974 results were not a complete negation of the GOP's 1972 victory, many Republicans worried that they represented the beginning of a trend.

The experts were analyzing polling data for signs of such a trend. In January 1975, pollster Robert Teeter painted a bleak picture of the Republican Party for a meeting in Chicago of the party's state chairmen. Teeter reported that the GOP could only claim 18 percent of Americans as members, explaining that there were "unbelievable increases in cynicism toward politics and American institutions in general and toward the Republican Party in particular." Watergate and the Agnew scandal had taken their toll on the reputation of a party that not long before had been considered more honest and upright than the Democrats.[53]

But Teeter's findings were juxtaposed against more hopeful statistics. William Rusher began his 1975 book *The Making of the New Majority Party* by citing a May 1974 Gallup Poll in which 38 percent of those polled said they would choose a conservative party. Rusher also cited the results of a Harris survey in which 43 percent of Americans described themselves as "middle of the road," 30 percent as "conservative," 15 percent as "liberal," 3 percent as "radical," and 9 percent as "not sure." Rusher concluded that, while the Republican Party might be in trouble, conservatism more generally was on the rise. He sought to describe the realignment that would bring conservatives together in one party: "In this book, I am proposing that America's conservatives set out to . . . form a new party that will replace the Republican Party *in toto* as one of America's two major parties."[54]

Rusher's new party was to be composed of social and economic conservatives. Social conservatives, such as blue-collar workers, had typically voted Democratic, whereas economically conservative business elites and upper-income suburbanites were generally Republican. But Rusher argued that the economic division between the "haves and the have-nots" was disappearing. Blue-collar workers were finding common cause with businessmen and manufacturers against what he called "a new and powerful class of non-producers comprised of a liberal verbalist elite (the dominant media, the major foundations and research institutions, the educational establishment, the federal and state bureaucracies) and a semi-permanent welfare constituency, all coexisting happily in a state of mutually sustaining symbiosis." "It is this new economic and social cleavage," he added, "that has produced the imposing (though not yet politically united) conservative majority detected by Dr. Gallup."

The Making of the New Majority Party argued that this cleavage could be exploited if social and economic conservatives joined forces. "The social conservative," Rusher wrote, "like the economic conservative, is at heart a stout individualist. He has an acute sense of individual as well as group identity, and shares the dream of personal success. . . . Social conservatism can also serve to moderate the near-Puritan severity of traditional conservative economics without undermining its basic structure. And that is a contribution almost beyond price."[55]

Rusher readily admitted that this was not a novel idea. He acknowledged that a political movement in this direction had been in the works for at least 15 years, thanks to the work of conservative thinkers such as Kevin Phillips.[56]

Phillips, too, published a treatise on American political realignment in 1975. Although his argument in *Mediacracy: American Parties and Policies in the Communications Age* was not articulated in terms of economic and social conservatives, his analysis was nonetheless consistent with Rusher's. Phillips was interested in the inexorable splintering of the Democratic Party. "Opposition to liberal elitism," he wrote, "is strongest among the groups historically in the vanguard of opposition to conservative elites." He later observed that "the hostility between the two wings of the Democratic Party was more pronounced than the hostility between the two parties. On the one side were the key blocs of the New Deal coalition: Southerners, ethnics, and blue-collar workers.

Leading the other side were the advocates of the New Politics (suburban liberals, skilled professionals, collegians) and their minority-group allies." This fracture was prompting a historically unprecedented move to the right in which disaffected Democrats were increasingly open to leadership alternatives.[57]

These books by Rusher and Phillips, along with other analyses,[58] signaled a conservative tour de force—an attempt to remake the American political landscape by shifting the political center of gravity away from the New Deal coalition and toward a revamped Republican Party, augmented by key elements of the Democratic Party's traditional base.

Two objectives would have to be met in order for this transformation to occur. The first was the creation of a unifying appeal that would attract socially conservative Democrats to the Republican Party and convince social and economic conservatives of their common interests. The second was the designation of a leader who could make such an appeal convincing.

These issues formed the basis for the agenda of the Conservative Political Action Committee's February 1975 meeting in Washington, DC. At the meeting, the CPAC created a Committee on Conservative Alternatives to consider how conservative Democrats, Republicans, and independents could be brought together and represented. The committee's members included William Rusher (whose book was on the verge of publication) as well as Jesse Helms, who had been elected as the first-ever Republican senator from North Carolina. The group vowed to look at all alternatives, including the creation of a new party—a notion that Helms endorsed in his condemnation of the Ford administration. "The loudest applause from the 500 delegates . . . [went] to those [speakers] urging a third-party option in 1976," columnist David Broder reported.[59] Rusher was interested in jettisoning the Republican Party in favor of a new conservative movement.

Reagan responded to the call for a third party during his speech to the conference: "Is it a third party we need, or is it a new and revitalized second party, raising a banner of no pale pastels, but bold colors which makes it unmistakably clear where we stand on all of the issues troubling the people?"

Reagan's speech also made use of the Gallup data that would soon appear in Rusher's book: "I know you are aware of the national polls which show that a greater (and increasing) number of Americans—Republicans, Democrats and Independents—classify themselves as 'conservatives' than ever before." To support this finding, Reagan also cited a political science study showing that the delegates to the 1972 Republican convention held views similar to the party's rank and file, while Democratic delegates were far removed from the opinions held by their party's base. Reagan offered no policy positions that might have brought together a new majority, nor did he even describe the nature of that majority, as Rusher would do in his book. Instead, he quickly slipped back into "The Speech."

Reagan had long advocated obedience to the eleventh commandment: "Thou shall not speak ill of a fellow Republican."[60] But his address bluntly attacked the Ford administration's policies. His litany of grievances included budget deficits, a shrinking commitment to national defense, and a compromise of American interests symbolized by the second Strategic Arms Limitation Agreement (SALT II).

As the country's leading conservative politician, Reagan was the only plausible leader for a conservative third party, and his decision not to endorse the idea marked the end of the movement. His decision was based in part on an aversion to Wallace, who had been suggested as his running mate, and with whose positions he largely disagreed.[61]

The Ford administration took a keen interest in these activities. In early 1975, the president continued his recruitment effort. Ford sent Donald Rumsfeld, his White House chief of staff, to meet with the governor. Peter Hannaford recalls that "this effort to co-opt him—and those that followed—in fact served to inch him a little closer to entertaining the idea of running."[62]

Two Presidential Contenders, Two Rhetorical Campaigns

A White House briefing paper had been commissioned in April 1975 to cover such topics as selecting a campaign chairman and determining how the White House would relate to the Republican National Committee.[63] The President Ford Committee (PFC) was formed that June, with Howard "Bo" Callaway as its chairman. Callaway was not only secretary of the army, but he was also a Georgia conservative who had campaigned in the South for Nixon in 1968.[64]

The Ford campaign would rely on the Rose Garden effect throughout the race. A July 1, 1975, memo from Jerry Jones, director of the White House Scheduling and Advance Office, to Chief of Staff Rumsfeld and his deputy Richard Cheney urged Ford to announce his bid from the White House. Ford had the distinction of being the only unelected president in American history, and he and his advisers wanted to minimize the salience of that distinction by portraying him as an incumbent. And, indeed, when Ford eventually announced his candidacy on July 8, he did so from the Oval Office.[65]

The president's aides were concerned about the need for a theme or package of issues, both for Ford's presidency and his campaign. In a November 12, 1975, memo to Cheney (who would become chief of staff just a few days later), Stuart Spencer, who had worked on Reagan's 1966 gubernatorial campaign, and the pollster Robert Teeter expressed concern that the president was seen as a tactician without an overall strategy for the country. They suggested a variety of themes including opposing "big government, big unions, big businesses, big school systems and the concentration of power in general" in favor of "helping the individual live his life as independently as possible." They also advised that the campaign take on a tone of morality and hope.[66] These themes would be as central to Ford's campaign as his incumbent's advantage.

Ford knew he was vulnerable among conservative Republicans. He had inherited the legacy of Nixon's détente along with a set of domestic policy decisions that many conservative Republican leaders considered betrayals of party values. Mindful of this charge, Cheney submitted a memo urging the president to "be very firm with Senator Goldwater [in their upcoming meeting]. He has to know that the bottom line is that you need him now, not later, and that you need him publicly, not just privately."[67] A November 5, 1975, *New York Times* article titled "The Ford Strategy" reported that "the new Ford strategy is based on the conviction that the President can successfully compete with Mr. Reagan for the votes of conservative Republicans in the South and Southwest," both Reagan strongholds.[68] As Craig Shirley has written, "Ford's drift to the right" greatly displeased some moderate Republicans. The president persisted in his strategy, however.[69] He worked to attract conservative support away from Reagan, who was ideologically much more in sync with conservative voters. In this regard at least, Ford's 1976 campaign somewhat resembled Nixon's strategy in 1968.

Unfortunately for Ford, the strategy didn't work. The incumbent began to slip in the polls by late 1975. A national poll placed his disapproval rating at 44 percent and found that 60 percent of respondents could not think of anything that "particularly impressed them" about the president. To counter the slippage, Teeter suggested to Callaway that they "put the bright light on Reagan."[70] He advised that the president refrain from taking part in negative campaigning, recommending instead that someone of high standing in the Republican Party should question Reagan's gubernatorial record and the proposals that he had endorsed in his speeches.

The Reagan camp had expected that their man would compete as the Republican front-runner in an open field. But Nixon's resignation had changed the game. It would be difficult for Reagan to honor the eleventh commandment while challenging a member of his own party, especially a sitting president. Reagan and his advisers took the position that because Ford had not been elected, he was not a genuine incumbent, nor had he ever won a national office.[71] Furthermore, they questioned Ford's commitment to the conservative philosophy that they believed truly represented the principles of the Republican Party and much of the nation. Their campaign would be based on the idea that this fellow Republican, although well liked within the party, was ineffective and should be unseated, whereas Reagan, a two-term governor of the most populous state in the nation and the declared representative of Republican conservatism, deserved the party's nomination.

In "Thoughts on Campaign Strategy," apparently written by John Sears, Ford's ability to lead was discussed early in the document:

> Among the Republican Party rank and file, it would be fair to say that Mr. Ford has alienated a significant number of conservatives because of his endorsement of deficit spending. He is unloved by the moderate-to-liberal wing of the Party because of his general lack of initiative. By so clearly handing over control of foreign policy to Dr. Kissinger and, at the same time blessing Vice President Rockefeller with major control over domestic policy Mr. Ford has perhaps robbed himself of the ability to demonstrate leadership to either the people or the Republicans.[72]

Sears did not suggest that the Reagan campaign openly call the president an inadequate leader, but that would be the subtext of the campaign. Sears suggested the following diplomatic language be used when a Reagan-for-president committee was announced:

> [O]ur perception tells us that the next few years will be as difficult as the preceding three and we feel a moral obligation to

do something constructive in anticipation of this fact. Lest anyone misconstrue our purpose, it is to be both loyal to Mr. Ford's
leadership while he is President and loyal to our obligation to the
country in assuring that we consider carefully our responsibility
as Republicans to nominate the best available candidate for President in 1976.

Such "a general statement is appropriate for us," the document continued, "rather than a pointed statement which would be more easily
interpreted as divisive. . . . [W]e want to make it as easy as possible for
Mr. Ford to withdraw up to the time we are forced to run against him
in the primaries."

There was a real sense throughout the document that Reagan's
actions might encourage Ford to abandon his presidential campaign. It
was suggested that "an early 'break' with Mr. Ford might force him to
stay in the race and certainly we would not want to be responsible for
that."

For many years, Reagan had been citing the Washington buddy system as a root cause of many of the nation's ills.[73] He continued to make
this case by campaigning against Ford as the ultimate Washington
insider. After all, Ford had first been elected to Congress in 1948. As the
chair of Reagan's presidential committee, Nevada senator Paul Laxalt,
put it, "We're not saying President Ford is not doing a good job. We
feel he is. But Governor Reagan could do a better job, because he is
totally independent of the federal government scene."[74]

Reagan's 1976 bid was characterized by more concrete policies and
sharper distinctions between himself and his opponent than his 1968
effort. But the two resembled each other in the sense that the campaigns
were still based on rhetoric rather than any more advanced type of
strategic maneuvering.

Ford versus Reagan: 1975

As Reagan made his rapid transition from governor to policy pundit in
January 1975, President Ford was putting forth economic plans that
were not wholly inconsistent with the governor's ideas. On January 13,
for example, the president proposed to cut income taxes by $16 billion.
But he submitted his fiscal year 1976 budget to Congress less than a
month later, on February 3, and its proposals for $349.4 billion in

spending and a record peacetime deficit of $51.9 billion irritated many conservatives. Ford was aware of the need to defuse their anger. That spring he signed the Tax Reduction Act of 1975, which promised $23 billion in tax cuts.[75] By mid-1975, he had made reasonable headway against inflation and unemployment.[76]

On aid to South Vietnam, too, Ford adopted a position largely congruent with Reagan's views. In early 1975, the president asked Congress to approve his financial and military assistance package for Saigon. On February 4, 1975, he said, "I believe that if the Congress funds the additional money that I've proposed for this fiscal year and continues the money that I have recommended for next fiscal year the South Vietnamese can and will be able to defend themselves against the aggressors from the North."[77] Although they approved $405 million in aid to Vietnamese refugees, Congress rejected Ford's request to supply South Vietnam with direct economic and military aid. In April, with a Communist takeover of his country imminent, President Thieu resigned. The Vietcong took over the country on April 30. Both Ford and Reagan could claim that they had warned that this might happen.

On another Cold War issue, however, their positions did not coincide, and Reagan promptly exploited this fact. Soviet dissident Alexander Solzhenitsyn criticized the Soviet regime in a speech in the United States on June 30. Following the speech, Ford was advised by members of his national security team, including his secretary of state, Henry Kissinger, not to receive the dissident at the White House because the encounter would be a violation of the terms and the spirit of U.S.-Soviet détente. Reagan derided this decision in speeches and writings and received national media attention for his stance. He was joined by leading conservative opinion makers in his opposition to the president's decision.[78]

Reagan's political momentum was typically tempered by Ford's ability to make slight gestures to the right. For instance, on July 25, the president met with leaders of European ethnic organizations to explain his decision to attend the East-West conference in Helsinki, a move that was opposed by leading conservatives, including Reagan, as well as by some European groups. The president told them that having the United States and the Soviet Union sign a document mandating the freer flow of people and ideas was an important step forward for superpower relations, and promised that the United States would continue "to support the aspirations for freedom and national independence of the peoples in Eastern Europe."[79] He left the next day on his ten-day trip to Europe.

Meanwhile, Reagan was speaking out against Ford's signing of the Helsinki Accords, as the various clusters of East-West agreements were known. In late July, Reagan urged "all Americans" to oppose the Helsinki documents because they abandoned those behind the Iron Curtain. On July 31, Soviet general secretary Leonid Brezhnev gave a speech to the Helsinki conference in which he declared that no nation had the right to interfere in the internal policies of another. For many conservatives, Brezhnev's statement confirmed Reagan's suspicions.[80]

The Final Act of the Conference on Security and Cooperation in Europe, as the agreements were officially titled, was signed on August 1 by Canada, the United States, the Soviet Union, and a host of European countries. That same day, Ford gave a talk that the *New York Times* described as "the most forcefully delivered address of his year in the Presidency," and the *Washington Post* labeled an "unexpectedly firm speech." In his comments, the president said the new agreements must not be "empty words and unfulfilled pledges," and that the signatories "will not be judged by the promises we make but by the promises we keep."[81] Secretary of State Henry Kissinger reportedly tried to convince the president not to give the speech, fearing that it would compromise U.S.-Soviet détente. The president, however, continued to take a tough line on superpower relations, following his August 1 remarks with a similarly stern speech in Minneapolis 18 days later.[82] Ford was not adopting the conservative position on Helsinki, but he was certainly co-opting Reagan's rhetoric.

Reagan, however, was undaunted, and continued to combine his hard rhetorical line with his well-known oratorical strengths. One such effort occurred on September 26, when he gave a speech in Chicago titled "Let the People Rule." In it, he proposed "nothing less than a systematic transfer of authority and resources to the states—a program of creative federalism for America's third century." He argued that the transfer of authority would reduce federal spending by $90 billion.[83] The speech was not so much a direct attack on Ford as it was a move beyond him, to call for a radical change in American social policy.

Two days before his "Let the People Rule" speech, Reagan had attacked Ford more directly during a speech in Memphis. Criticizing the president's support for transferring authority over the Panama Canal to the Panamanians, Reagan cautioned that "the Soviets would like to control the world's waterways . . . the Panama Canal would be a tempting prize [and] . . . the Canal is an important defense and commercial lifeline" for the United States. He summed up with a line that would become famous in his stump speeches: "We bought it. We paid for it. We built the Canal."[84]

In early December, Ford traveled to Asia, where he outlined a carefully framed Pacific Doctrine that reaffirmed his commitment to normalized relations with the People's Republic of China while simultaneously reassuring our allies in the region: "The preservation of the sovereignty and the independence of our Asian friends and allies remain a paramount objective to American policy." The speech also described America's alliance with Japan as a "pillar" of U.S. strategy in the region.[85] By the late 1970s, Reagan would become the leading conservative critic of normalizing relations with the PRC; but Ford was not advocating a move away from existing American commitments throughout Asia. The president was closing the rhetorical gap between him and Reagan through his actions and statements.

Ford versus Reagan: 1976

As primary season got under way in early 1976, Reagan continued to challenge Ford's policies, and Ford continued to deftly counter by making statements subtly tinged with conservatism. On January 4, the *Times* was reporting that Ford was responding to Democratic calls for increased government spending with a statement that he wanted to limit the federal budget to $395 billion. Sounding like Reagan, Ford said that inflation, not unemployment, should be the government's primary economic concern, and advocated reduced government regulation of business.[86]

On January 4, the *Times* also reported that Ford's upcoming State of the Union speech was going to endorse a $10 billion tax cut, and that his proposal for holding down federal spending was a preemptive maneuver against Reagan. In his address to the nation on January 19, the president indeed offered policies consistent with the ideas that Reagan had been endorsing in his speeches, radio commentaries, and writings. For instance, he called for an adjustment in federal estate tax laws to help those who inherited farms and small businesses, and demanded a decrease in federal government's involvement in the lives of Americans.[87]

Throughout the primaries Reagan hammered away on détente and rearmament. In a speech in Jacksonville, Florida, on January 14, Reagan had reviewed his stance on foreign and defense policy: "As a nation we must commit ourselves to spend whatever is necessary to remain strong, to consider our interests first in international dealings. . . . [W]e must not cast aside our nation's interests just for the sake of making a deal." He built on this idea in remarks made during a visit to Manchester, New Hampshire, on February 21: "I favor the concept of détente, but it must be pursued with the understanding that we shall be second to none in our military defense capability."[88]

Ford won the Iowa caucus on January 19, garnering 45 percent of the 20,000 votes to Reagan's 42 percent.[89] Following this victory, the Ford administration had issued defense budget projections that included long-term increases in defense spending.[90] The president was well positioned to co-opt Reagan's stance on defense and détente.

The next big test was New Hampshire on February 24. In their quest for issues that could be used against Reagan, the president's strategists returned to the challenger's "Let the People Rule" speech. In a November 3, 1975, memo to Dick Cheney, the White House advance chief Jerry Jones suggested challenging the figures Reagan used in the speech.[91] By January, the speech was back in the headlines. And in the run-up to the New Hampshire primary, the Ford team pointed to it as proof that Reagan lacked a firm grasp of fiscal issues. Lou Cannon contends that the speech actually lost Reagan the nomination.[92] In any case, Reagan's rhetoric clearly was not working. Ford left New Hampshire with 49.4 percent of the vote to Reagan's 48.0 percent.

With the momentum of wins in Iowa and New Hampshire behind him, the president rolled on to a string of primary victories in Massachusetts, Vermont, Florida, and Illinois. Prior to these primaries, Ford declared, "I don't use the word 'détente' any more. I think what we ought to say is that the United States will meet with the superpowers, the Soviet Union and with China and others, and seek to relax tensions so that we can continue a policy of peace through strength."[93] Once again he was adopting Reagan's rhetoric—even though he disagreed with the governor on the substance of defense policy.

Fighting to protect his rhetorical turf, Reagan told an Orlando audience in early March that the United States "is no longer the first military power on earth. . . . There is little doubt in my mind that the Soviet Union will not stop taking advantage of détente until it sees that the American people have elected a new President and appointed a new Secretary of State."[94]

It was not until the March 23 North Carolina primary that Reagan was finally able to halt Ford's progress. Following Riker's dispersion principle, Reagan shifted his rhetorical focus to the Panama Canal and détente, both hot-button issues for many conservatives. Jesse Helms, one of Reagan's few supporters in the Senate, had tipped the challenger that voters in his home state were deeply concerned about maintaining American control over the canal. Indeed, one presidential historian has described Reagan's heightened attention to the canal issue as "the turning point in the campaign."[95] It was a telling rhetorical blow that Ford could only counter with the relatively weak promise that the United States would never give up operational control of the canal, and would retain the right to defend the waterway. Reagan, having found an effective issue, adopted the dominance principle, declaring that the Ford administration lacked resolve in the face of Soviet and Cuban military involvement in Angola and that Secretary of State Henry Kissinger helped produce a flawed policy of détente.[96] Reagan won 52.4 percent of the North Carolina vote to Ford's 45.9 percent. The Reagan candidacy was revived.

A week after the North Carolina contest, Ford threatened a veto if Congress cut his defense spending bill.[97] He was very convincingly taking steps that were consistent with the interests of conservative Republicans. Two days later, on March 31, Reagan continued his critique of Ford's foreign policy. In a nationally televised address, the governor once again critiqued U.S. participation in the Helsinki Accords on the grounds that it put a "stamp of approval on Russia's enslavement of the captive nations."[98]

Although Ford regained momentum on April 6, winning Wisconsin with 55.2 percent to Reagan's 44.3 percent, his campaign was on the run. In an April 9 memo from Dave Gergen to Dick Cheney, the latest political assessment of Al Sindlinger, a public opinion analyst, was reported: "Continuing an upward surge that began a few weeks ago, the President moved up to a 56.9% overall approval rating in mid-March. His toughness on détente and foreign policy along with more good news on the economic front were the buoying factors. However, the North Carolina primary and the flap over HAK [Henry A. Kissinger]—fueled by the Reagan attacks—began cutting into the President's popularity in the last several days of March. It sank to 49%—a 7 point drop—in the final week of March, and Sindlinger thinks it has dropped some more since then. The President's foreign policy rating is the most interesting: from a high of 61.7 in mid-March to 46.9 by the end of the month."[99] In an April 12 memo to the president's chief of staff, Gergen continued to review Sindlinger's reading of the political landscape. The former California governor "[c]ontinues to haunt GRF

[Gerald R. Ford] on foreign policy/détente but has failed to take advantage of economic situation. Apparently doesn't understand it."[100] Reagan's rhetorical attacks on foreign and defense policy became the chief concern of the Ford campaign.

The president stepped up his counterattack on the Panama question. On April 23, he called Reagan's position on the canal treaties "irresponsible." Six days later, he added that ceasing the negotiations could lead to "guerrilla warfare" and "bloodshed" in Panama.[101]

Ultimately, though, Reagan's strategy was insufficient to beat Ford decisively. Instead, the two men ran almost neck-and-neck throughout the primaries. On April 27, Ford won a landslide victory in Pennsylvania, 92.1 percent to Reagan's 5.1. A week later Reagan beat the president in Georgia with 68.3 percent of the vote to Ford's 31.7 percent. The challenger went on to take the Indiana and Nebraska primaries in quick succession. Ford rallied with victories in West Virginia on May 11 and in Maryland and Michigan on the eighteenth. On May 25, Reagan took Arkansas, Idaho, and Nevada, while Ford prevailed in Kentucky, Oregon, and Tennessee. On June 1, Reagan won Montana and South Dakota, while Ford won Rhode Island.

Soon thereafter, the Ford campaign distributed a radio spot that amplified Reagan's June 2, 1976, response to a hypothetical question in which he stated that "in the interest of peace and avoiding bloodshed," the United States might consider sending troops to Rhodesia. When the Ford campaign proceeded to air a radio commercial suggesting that, if elected, Reagan might start a war, the Reagan campaign immediately inveighed against the charge. President Ford acknowledged his role in making the radio commercial and even admitted on television that he thought Reagan would make a good president. Ford's victory was that his mea culpa did not detract from the message that he, not his opponent, could deliver *peace through strength*.[102] The primary season was nearing its end, and Reagan had not been able to launch a substantive rhetorical challenge to Ford.

Unsurprisingly, California went to Reagan on June 8, with Ford taking New Jersey and Ohio that same day. He also prevailed in New York's delegate-selection primary, while Reagan was the favorite in the delegate-selection primary in Texas.

To win the Republican presidential nomination, a candidate needed at least 1,130 delegate votes. At the close of primary season, Ford claimed 961 votes, and Reagan 856.[103] The convention in Kansas City would be a real contest.

The Reagan team had two tactics that they planned to use to pick off Ford delegates at the convention. The first was a procedural measure, Rule 16c, which would force Ford to announce his running mate before the final balloting. As noted earlier, Reagan had already announced his choice of Richard Schweiker, a moderate Republican from Pennsylvania who lent the ticket both ideological and geographic breadth. The choice had cost Reagan the support of some hard-line conservatives, but his core coalition remained intact. Reagan's campaign manager, John Sears, who masterminded the Schweiker selection, thought that forcing Ford to select his running mate before the balloting might cause a stampede of delegates to Reagan, especially if the president chose a partner unacceptable to conservatives.[104]

When the Rule 16c tactic failed, the team turned to its second plan. Martin Anderson and Peter Hannaford (with help from Richard Allen, Reagan's foreign policy adviser) wrote a statement for the platform titled "Morality and Foreign Policy"—a theme that had helped Reagan win a number of primaries—in which they attacked the Nixon-Ford-Kissinger version of détente. The statement expressed admiration for Soviet dissident Alexander Solzhenitsyn, whom President Ford had refused to see a year earlier: "We recognize and commend that beacon of human courage and morality . . . for his compelling message that we must face the world with no illusions about the nature of tyranny." The statement criticized détente, lamenting, "We . . . grant unilateral favors with only the hope of getting future favors in return," and then turned to lambaste the Helsinki Accords: "Agreements that are negotiated . . . must not take from those who do not have freedom the hope of one day gaining it." The statement neatly linked morality and foreign policy in a way that discredited the version of détente with which Ford had historically been associated.

Convinced that their statement was a true representation of the party's position, and confident that the delegates would approve its inclusion as a plank in the GOP platform, many in the Reagan camp hoped for a floor fight. They believed that an open dispute over such a substantive issue would prompt delegates to switch their allegiance in significant enough numbers to give Reagan the nomination.

It was a well-conceived strategy, but one that failed to allow for the possibility of compromise. A few hours before the balloting began Ford approved the new plank, which had already received an affirmative voice vote from the convention floor. His advisers had convinced him that he was too close to clinching the nomination to enter into a fresh battle with Reagan. But his decision cost him the support of delegates from both ends of the ideological spectrum. Liberal Republicans like John Anderson argued that the statement was an affront to the president's aspirations for U.S.-Soviet relations, while conservatives like Jesse Helms wanted stronger, more direct language. Kissinger saw the plank as being directed squarely at him and urged the president to fight back.

On August 19, Gerald Ford just squeaked past Ronald Reagan by a vote of 1,187 to 1,070. After giving his acceptance speech, the president invited Reagan to join him on the podium. In discussing a request he received to write a letter that would be kept in a time capsule for 100 years, the governor expressed concern about "the erosion of freedom taking place under Democratic rule in this country." He then said:

[W]e live in a world in which the great powers have aimed and poised at each other horrible missiles of destruction, nuclear weapons that can in minutes arrive at each other's country and destroy virtually the civilized world we live in.

And suddenly it dawned on me; those who would read this letter a hundred years from now will know whether those missiles were fired.

They will know whether we met our challenge.

Whether they will have the freedom that we have known up until now will depend on what we do here. Will they look back with appreciation and say, "Thank God for those people in 1976 who headed off the loss of freedom? Who kept us now a hundred years later free? Who kept our world from nuclear destruction?"

And if we fail they probably won't get to read the letter at all because it spoke of individual freedom and they won't be allowed to talk of that or read of it.

This is our challenge and this is why we're here in this hall tonight.[105]

As one Reagan aide wrote, "Ronald Reagan left Kansas City not as a defeated candidate but as the leader of a large segment of his party and with the respect of those who had not supported him."[106] He had confirmed his right to the conservative mantle.

Reagan was an orator far superior to Ford, as became evident during his brief remarks at the convention. But oratorical skill does not automatically translate into rhetorical prowess. Reagan was never able to obtain rhetorical distance from Ford. This was due both to Ford's ability to co-opt Reagan's rhetoric and to the fact that Ford and Reagan were not actually that far apart on many policy issues. Both men believed that the Nixon-era decline in defense spending should be reversed. By virtue of his incumbency, Ford had the distinct advantage of being able to actually increase defense spending, while Reagan could only talk about doing so. Nor were they much different in the specifics, with both men advocating the addition of ships to the naval fleet, the modernization of America's nuclear force, production of the B-1 bomber, and development of a new land-based MX missile.[107]

Ford and Reagan were similar, too, on important social issues. Both advocated racial integration while opposing mandatory busing. Reagan favored a constitutional amendment against the use of federal funds for abortion, while Ford opposed the amendment but agreed that the 1973 Supreme Court decision in *Roe v. Wade* was not in line with his thinking.

The conservative party leaders were ideologically closer to Reagan, but Ford, like Nixon before him, had satisfied them enough in word and deed to garner their support. Furthermore, although he was not an elected incumbent, Ford was the occupant of the White House. In a letter dated June 29, 1976, Senator Barry Goldwater wrote, "[F]rankly, the philosophy presented by the two candidates is almost identical and the solutions offered to the problems, in most cases coincide." Not only was Reagan unable to gain rhetorical distance from Ford, but his negative campaign tactic of questioning Ford's commitment to conservative principles and of questioning his fitness for office was not as appealing as he had hoped. Goldwater continued: "[M]y decision [to support Ford] rests solely on the fact that at this time in our history I do not believe that our government can suffer through months and months of reorganization that would be necessary if we had a change in the office."[108] Although conservative party leaders agreed more with Reagan's philosophy than Ford's, the president had run a campaign that convinced them both that he could be elected president and that he would adhere to conservative principles.

Despite their similarities on some key policy issues, and despite Ford's ability to defuse Reagan's attacks by moving to the right, the two men differed profoundly on the issue of the Cold War. In his radio commentaries and other speeches and writings, Reagan had been advocating replacing détente and containment with a radically different military strategy, one that would encourage the Soviet Union to quit the fight. Reagan had not yet found the rhetoric with which to voice his ideas effectively. Not until 1980 would he identify a way to make his differences with his fellow Republicans fully apparent.

The Presidential Campaign: September to November 1976

Following the Republican Convention of 1976, however, Reagan began making his transition from rhetorician to heresthetician. Riker theorizes that herestheticians typically have had substantial prior practice and success as rhetoricians, and Ronald Reagan fit this description. By the fall of 1976, he certainly had substantial practice and success as a rhetorician, having been running for president in one way or another for almost 10 years.

Reagan's activities, after his close loss at the convention despite his having won 50.7 percent of the total vote in the primaries, offer compelling evidence that he was already planning his next presidential bid. Soon after the convention, Reagan restarted his nationally syndicated radio program and newspaper column, which would be distributed twice weekly by the King Features Syndicate.[109] The broadcasts, many of which Reagan wrote, were taped on September 1 and began airing on September 20.[110] The first radio commentaries focused on the convention, and Reagan boasted about his accomplishment in getting his "morality in foreign policy" statement into the GOP platform.

In addition to broadcasting to millions of listeners the imprint of his conservative philosophy on the Republican platform, Reagan also stumped his way across 25 states on behalf of the Ford-Dole ticket and made televised speeches and commercials for them, as well.[111] These activities kept Reagan at the forefront of American politics in the fall of 1976 despite his defeat in the primaries.

As two close Reagan observers have noted, "Reagan started running the day after Jimmy Carter's election, whether he admitted it to himself or not. He stepped up his schedule of speaking engagements and he had two other pretty good pulpits from which to preach his conservative message—his radio program and his newspaper column. . . . In short, it was apparent that Reagan was planning a comeback."[112]

In letters Reagan wrote to his supporters soon after the Republican convention, the governor revealed that he was already looking beyond the November election and that his radio commentaries, newspaper columns, and speaking engagements were central to his national plans. In one such letter he declared:

> [W]e must be ready in November, after the election, to reassess and mobilize the Democrats and Independents we know are looking for a banner around which to rally. To that end, I think I can be something of a voice and intend doing all I can to bring about a new majority coalition. Our cause is not lost and may even be more possible in the days ahead. Don't lose faith and don't think the war is over. I'm starting my five-day-a-week radio commentaries, newspaper column and speaking tours immediately.[113]

In another postconvention letter written around the same time, he stated, "It would have been easier the other way;" that is, having been chosen as the Republican Party's presidential nominee. But, he said, "we'll try by remote control," he assured his supporters, referring to his radio program and newspaper column.[114]

Even before the 1976 election was held, Reagan had already begun his heresthetical transformation. As Martin Anderson, one of Reagan's advisers in his 1976 presidential bid, has recalled, "On October 8, 1976, at the height of the presidential campaign between Jimmy Carter and Gerald Ford, and almost a year before the Kemp-Roth tax cut legislation was introduced, Reagan authored a national newspaper column entitled 'Tax Cuts and Increased Revenue.'" In the column, Reagan said: "Warren Harding did it. John Kennedy did it. But Jimmy Carter and President Ford aren't talking about it. That 'it' that Harding and Kennedy had in common was to cut the income tax. In both cases, federal revenues went up instead of down . . . the presidential candidates would do us all a service if they would discuss the pros and cons of the concept. Since the idea worked under both Democratic and Republican administrations before, who's to say it couldn't work again?"[115] Reagan's newspaper column was prescient.

The idea of tax cuts as a means of unleashing the productivity and creativity of the American people was present in Reagan's 1976 presidential bid and pre-1980 speeches and writings. By his 1980 presidential race, however, the governor had woven a plan to cut taxes into an overall economic package that carried the promise of prosperity for all Americans.

On the foreign policy front, Reagan would continue throughout the late 1970s to write and speak about morality in U.S. diplomacy.[116] In his 1980 presidential bid, though, his primary focus would be on defining what he meant by a strategy of strength, tying the strategy to the goal of securing the United States' position as the number one military power, and arguing that personal income taxes could be cut and defense spending markedly increased while the rate of inflation came down. The 1976 presidential bid both helped Reagan become a better rhetorician and find his way to heresthetic.

4

Reshaping the Domestic and International Landscape

Part One

*The Long Road to the
1980 Presidential Election*

It is easy to believe that Ronald Reagan's path to the presidency was never in question. He had emerged unscathed from the 1968 race for the GOP nomination and was reelected governor of the most populous state in the country by a half-million-vote margin two years later. His political prominence and viability seemed not to have suffered severely from his failure to win his party's presidential nomination in either 1968 or 1976. No other Republican presidential hopeful had such strong credentials going into the late 1970s. As to his Democratic competition, the incumbency advantage (every president since Herbert Hoover who sought reelection had been victorious) that should have helped President Jimmy Carter was clearly limited by the Iranian hostage crisis, the seemingly unsolvable energy crisis, and an economy that seemed to be spiraling out of control.

These macroeconomic and political factors may explain the outcome of the 1980 election; it is widely assumed that voters punished Carter for America's economic and political failures. But this version of events does not explain why Reagan emerged as the Republican nominee rather than some other leading contender such as George H. W. Bush, Senators Howard Baker or Robert Dole, or former Texas governor John Connally. And in emphasizing Carter's misfortune, it fails to acknowledge the artistry required to create an unusually broad coalition, especially from a politician who had long been associated with the Far Right. Explaining how this was done is our concern.

Despite mounting economic, energy, and foreign policy crises and news headlines predicting disaster upon further disaster, Dick Wirthlin, one of Reagan's key strategists, was sober about his candidate's prospects. With slightly more than four months remaining before the 1980 election, he warned that "unseating Jimmy Carter will be extremely difficult, even unlikely."[1] Wirthlin and others believed that in order to take advantage of voter dissatisfaction, particularly with Carter's economic policies, Reagan would have to present a message substantially different from that which he had offered in his 1976 presidential campaign and his more tenuous effort to win his party's 1968 presidential nomination.

Politics had changed since the era of the smoke-filled room. The expanded political environment still allowed for the influence of the party faithful, but as Wirthlin observed in 1980, "[T]he party bosses are gone and nothing has replaced them. Direct primaries have diminished the role and power of party organizations." Political scientist Gerald Pomper agreed with Wirthlin:

> By 1980, primaries were used in 37 states and territories, and determined three-fourths of the delegates. Aspirants to the White House no longer needed to win the favor of party leaders; they could take their case directly to the voters in these primaries (even if only a minority of those eligible actually voted). Because the delegates chosen also were pledged to particular candidates, the opportunities for any convention bargaining among uncommitted blocs were limited.[2]

The primaries could no longer be delivered to the Republican frontrunner or the person chosen by party leaders with the same certainty that was possible just a few years earlier. Rhetoric and heresthetic became much more valuable in the new, more open institutional context. As Pomper has also noted, "By 1980, a new system was established, in which individual candidates were the major actors who sought to influence the polls, the media, and the primaries, while paying little notice to party leaders."[3] Reagan thrived in this institutional environment in which the selectorate was much larger and less bound to party leaders and in which candidates had to communicate directly with millions of potential supporters on a regular basis. As the primaries became more important, Reagan's message—focused as it was on proposals for what he believed would be better public policies rather than delivering favors to party elites—expanded to encompass a broader and more diverse selectorate.

Selectorate theory hypothesizes that the large coalition needed to support a leader—a coalition of millions by 1980—is highly susceptible to defections or changes from within. Such challenges were apparent in the 1980 race. Carter was highly susceptible to defections as the size of the selectorate and winning coalition grew even within his own party. Carter needed political artistry more in 1980 than he did in 1976; he needed some appeal that would keep dissatisfied selectors from defecting.

The loss of power by the South in the Republican Party was an institutional feature of the 1980 presidential race that suggested that even at the stage of the primaries, contenders would have to present a broad message, as opposed to targeting a specific or narrow audience that in earlier campaigns was central to securing the nomination of one's party. Carter's success in 1976 was due in no small measure to the fact that he carried the South. He won all southern states except Virginia. While southerners basked in having one of their own in the Oval Office, 1980 Republican Party convention rules moved "southern Republicans . . . from the highest to the lowest number of delegates since the area suffered officeholder losses and only carried one state for president."[4] Unlike the 1976 Republican primaries, where Reagan spoke largely to his base, in the 1980 primaries he would need to speak to a truly national audience. This perforce meant that at the very start of the campaign season Reagan would be going after the potential defectors that Carter was trying to hold to his side.

Candidates typically build coalitions by means of rhetoric, but in 1980 Reagan took a heresthetical turn. His strategy was based on the politics of more—more defense spending, more wealth, more optimism, more everything—and a message of winning instead of managing the Cold War. This would have been a risky strategy for any presidential candidate. Indeed, no Cold War president had ever tried it. But Reagan was able to feel confident in his strategy because he had been testing it as a rhetorician for many years, especially during the late 1970s. Even during those periods when he was out of office, he had remained in close contact with his audience. As we noted earlier, he did so through his radio commentary, newspaper column, and speeches, as well as through prolific letter writing as a means of responding to questions and criticism about his statements and political activities. This unique opportunity to be in continuous contact with his audience allowed Reagan to identify messages that would appeal to a much broader set of voters than he previously had attracted.

Cast of Characters and the Political Context

As stated in the previous chapter, Ronald Reagan restarted his nationally syndicated radio program and nationally syndicated newspaper column soon after the Republican convention ended on August 19, 1976. In January 1977, he announced that he was creating another avenue to promote conservative ideas, Citizens for the Republic (CFTR), a new political action committee (PAC) funded with $1.5 million left over from his 1976 presidential campaign. Lyn Nofziger, who had served as Reagan's press aide during some of his years as governor, became CFTR's executive director. The CFTR office opened in Santa Monica on February 10. CFTR began sponsoring many of Reagan's speaking engagements to endorse Republican candidates and promote conservative causes. The PAC had become yet another vehicle by which Reagan could build his Republican base and keep his party's message alive. Although he was as yet an undeclared candidate, and many in his own camp were not even certain that he would run in 1980, Reagan had once again constructed the workings of an effective stealth campaign.[5]

The Carter campaign of 1976 galvanized a diverse constituency. Organized labor returned to the Democratic fold from its defection four years earlier. Carter won 63 percent of the union vote, 57 percent of the Catholic vote, and 82 percent of the overall Democratic vote. Ford received more popular votes than Carter in the Midwest and the West, but the South returned to the Democrats, with all states except Virginia delivering their electoral votes to Carter. Carter was also victorious in the East. The Georgian even made inroads into segments of society that had traditionally voted Republican, and a high percentage of those with college educations and in the professions, including business, delivered their vote to Carter-Mondale.

Despite his belief that he could revive the old New Deal coalition, Carter was not standing on terribly solid political ground when he assumed the presidency on January 20, 1977. He had won the South largely thanks to overwhelming support from poor whites and black voters.[6] Ford had begun to cut into his lead during the final days of the campaign, as was reflected in the final results, which showed Carter with 50.1 percent of the popular vote to Ford's 48 percent, and 297 electoral votes to Ford's 240. It was the closest presidential race since Charles Evan Hughes, a Supreme Court justice and former governor of New York, nearly defeated President Woodrow Wilson in 1916.

In a memo to Carter written a few weeks after the 1976 presidential election, his pollster, Patrick Caddell, assessed the outlook:

1. Governor Carter's political situation is precarious for a Democrat. Any loss that he sustains among the nontraditional groups which supported him in 1976 that is not compensated for among other groups would put his political future in danger.

2. The Democratic party is in serious national trouble—with a shrinking and ill-defined coalition. We need a new and broader political coalition that can attract new support. It would be a mistake, however, to try to create an all-inclusive coalition. Indeed, one decision that must be made is which groups ought not to participate in the coalition. A decision on who to exclude will make clearer both who should participate and how—strategy should be formed.[7]

Caddell's memo was prescient. After the inauguration Carter quickly began losing ground with both the traditional Democratic base and his nontraditional supporters. His approval ratings, according to Gallup Poll, reached as high as 75 percent during his first months in office, but then dropped into a downward spiral that continued for years (albeit with brief spikes tied to specific events): by late July 1978, his ratings were down to 39 percent, and by July 1980 they had declined even further to 21 percent. The national survey organization reported that the latter rating was "the lowest recorded for any president since the Gallup Poll initiated these measures in 1938." The final assessment of his job performance was 34 percent.[8] Carter was being negatively evaluated by virtually every segment of society.

Looking ahead to the 1980 race, Reagan was the Republican front-runner, but other contenders were important because, if for no other reason, they forced him to define his campaign and policy positions. And, of course, as the experience of 1968's front-runner, George Romney, showed, the leading candidate early in the process may well not be the nominee at the end of the process. With a Democrat as the incumbent, the Republicans had a much larger field of candidates in 1980 than they had in 1976. These included, in addition to Reagan, Representative John Anderson of Illinois; Senator Howard Baker of Tennessee; former Texas congressman and Central Intelligence Agency director George H. W. Bush; Representative Philip Crane of Illinois; former Texas governor and Nixon secretary of the treasury John Connally; Senator Robert Dole of Kansas; California businessman Benjamin Fernandez; Senator Larry Pressler of South Dakota; former Minnesota governor Harold Stassen; and Senator Lowell Weicker of Connecticut. Gerald Ford remained popular in the party and was also available to run if his party called upon him.[9]

Bush and Reagan were the only Republicans to take first place in any of the primaries, while Anderson, Baker, Bush, Connally, and Reagan took second place in various races. The balance of power in the Republican contest was reflected in a variety of statements made by the contenders. Five weeks after Reagan declared his candidacy, Baker said, "Ronald Reagan is the name of the game as far as I'm concerned, and we've got to play catch-up ball." Bob Dole quipped, "I tell people if they're looking for a younger Ronald Reagan with experience, I'm available."[10] While the others were campaigning to win the nomination, as political scientist Gerald Pomper has observed, Reagan "needed only to avoid losing it."[11]

Baker withdrew from the race on March 5, 1980, less than two months into the primary season, and Connally and Dole quickly followed suit. Crane announced his exit on April 17, and on April 24 Anderson declared that he would run as an independent. Bush abandoned his attempt to win the GOP nomination a month later, but did not formally withdraw. Anderson and Bush in particular remained actively involved in the race, vying for the support of liberal and moderate Republicans. Other candidates either closed their campaigns or failed to establish themselves as serious contenders. When the dust settled in July, it was Bush who accepted the number two spot on the Reagan ticket at the Detroit convention.

Bush had extensive experience in Washington. In addition to his service as CIA director, he had served as a two-term congressman from

Texas as well as U.S. ambassador to the United Nations, chairman of the Republican National Committee, and chief U.S. liaison officer to the People's Republic of China. Clearly, it was not Bush's credentials that worried his conservative Republican critics; they were more concerned that he would refuse to support Reagan's agenda and the party's platform. After all, this was the man who had called Reagan's tax proposals "voodoo economics" during the primaries. But Bush signed on to the Reagan plan, including its opposition to the use of federal funding for abortions. Many of those in the Reagan camp who had expressed reservations about this "marriage of convenience" gradually came to appreciate Bush's energetic and loyal efforts on behalf of the campaign.[12]

John Anderson was the main third-party candidate in the 1980 presidential race. A 10-term moderate Republican congressman from Illinois, Anderson had become disillusioned with his party and announced as an independent. He sought the support of a coalition of liberals and moderates who he believed were disillusioned with both parties and supported a platform based around a gas tax, the revenues from which would be funneled into Social Security while Social Security taxes would be reduced; protection for pro-choice legislation; the Equal Rights Amendment; and a reduction in federal spending without substantial cuts in personal income taxes.[13]

In 1980, 52 percent of the U.S. electorate identified itself as Democratic, 13 percent as independent, and 33 percent as Republican.[14] Both Carter and Reagan therefore needed to win substantial support from independents and moderates. Anderson's campaign posed a serious challenge to both contenders, but he was generally expected to cut most deeply into Carter's liberal base in key areas such as Illinois, New England, and New York.[15]

Four months after declaring himself an independent, Anderson selected Patrick J. Lucey, the former two-term Democratic governor of Wisconsin, as his running mate. Lucey was a progressive liberal who had supported both John F. and Robert Kennedy, and supported Ted Kennedy's 1980 presidential bid until resigning to join the Anderson ticket. "[I]t was hard," Mark Bisnow notes, "to avoid the conclusion that the campaign was making a bald appeal for Kennedy Democrats unhappy with Carter." Indeed, Anderson's campaign steadily drifted left as he reached out to traditional Democratic constituencies and various cause-oriented liberals.[16] The leftward move cost Anderson some of his Republican support, thereby relieving the pressure on Reagan, but it simultaneously forced Carter to appeal to the Kennedy wing of the party without alienating his more conservative base.

Anderson's third-party "national unity" campaign played an important role in the 1980 presidential contest. Unlike George Wallace, who withdrew from the 1976 competition in favor of his party's nominee, Anderson campaigned throughout the 1980 race, taking votes from Carter and Reagan along the way and influencing the manner in which both men framed issues and constructed coalitions.

On the Democratic side, California governor Jerry Brown and Massachusetts senator Ted Kennedy posed potentially serious challenges to Carter's renomination bid. Both campaigns invoked their candidates' commitment to liberal causes and policies, weakening Carter's hold on the left-center coalition he so urgently needed. Brown receded as quickly as he had emerged, withdrawing from the race on April 1 without having won a single primary. Kennedy announced his candidacy the day before Brown's November entry into the race, but the data suggested that the American electorate had considered him a serious contender since at least the early 1970s.[17] Carter himself was faltering in the polls in the fall of 1979, but his popularity ratings improved in the wake of the crisis at the Iranian embassy that began early that November, and he handily beat both Anderson and Reagan in presidential trial heats conducted by the Gallup Poll between January and July 1980. As the nation rallied around the president during the early months of the Iranian hostage crisis, Kennedy was unable to help his candidacy by criticizing the president's Iran policy. Thus, as Kennedy biographer Adam Clymer has written, Kennedy "dropped" the issue of Iran.[18]

Kennedy never succeeded in undermining the president's standing but posed a serious threat nonetheless. His 10 primary victories (to Carter's 24) allowed him to stay in the race until the Democratic convention in mid-August, pushing Carter steadily to the left.[19] Even as he was preparing to withdraw from the race and endorse Carter at the convention, Kennedy and his camp were still fighting for liberal planks in the party platform. Kennedy's proposals were approved by the delegates, and although Carter rejected the details of his rival's jobs-creation proposal, for example, he felt compelled to promise that he would "implement its spirit and its aims."[20]

During the first eight months of 1980, Carter had to fend off challenges from all sides. Brown and Kennedy were after his support base on the left. Anderson was now attracting support from liberals as well as those in the center. And Reagan's appeal among conservative Democrats was growing even as he continued to build a base among centrists in both parties.

....

The Long Run: January 1977 to January 1980

When Jimmy Carter first took office in January 1977, the American economy was on the upswing; inflation and unemployment were decreasing, and the recession had subsided. The president initially sought to beat back unemployment even further, but after almost two years in office declared that inflation was the greater problem.[21] By that time, however, Reagan had been broadcasting commentaries about the insidious effects of inflation for several years. He, rather than the president, was most closely associated with concern about inflation and its solutions. As noted in the previous chapter, one of Reagan's very first radio commentaries after he stepped down as governor of California in January 1975 was titled simply "Inflation."

By the fall of 1976, Reagan was pulling in the strands of his heresthetical argument, weaving together issues like tax cuts as a means to revive the American economy and replacing traditional policies of containment and détente with a military strategy that would peacefully replace the Cold War's domination of the international system with a larger community of free states. No matter how coherent a message is, however, it will be of little heresthetical value if it is not successfully connected to a coalition. On January 15, 1977, five days before Carter was sworn in as president, Reagan took a major step towards becoming a true heresthetician—and a successful presidential candidate— when he successfully identified the elements of this coalition in a speech to conservatives at the Mayflower Hotel in Washington, DC:

> You know, as I do, that most experts and commentators make a distinction between what they call "social" conservatism and "economic" conservatism. The so-called social issues—law and order, abortion, busing, quota systems—are usually associated with blue-collar, ethnic and religious groups themselves traditionally associated with the Democratic Party. The economic issues—inflation, deficit spending and big government—are usually associated with Republican Party members and Independents who concentrate their attention on economic matters.
>
> Now I am willing to accept this view of two major kinds of

conservatism—or, better still, two different conservative constituencies. But at the same time let me say that the old lines that
once clearly divided these two kinds of conservatism are disappearing.

Reagan then proposed a way to bind social and economic conservatives:

> It was only a few years ago that the word "inflation" was some-
> thing found only in the vocabulary of economists, Republican
> spokesmen and some editorial writers. But go into any super-
> market in America today, stop a man or woman pushing a cart
> filled with groceries, and mention the word "inflation." . . .
> Inflation has become what the political pros call a "gut" issue.
> It's no longer the exclusive worry of hard-line conservative econ-
> omists or spokesmen for free enterprise. It hits home because it
> hurts the working man and woman. . . .
> [I]s it possible to combine the two major segments of contem-
> porary American conservatism into one politically effective
> whole?
> Yes it is possible to create a political entity that will reflect
> the views of the great, hitherto, unorganized conservative major-
> ity. . . .
> What I envision is not simply a melding together of the two
> branches of American conservatism into a temporary uneasy
> alliance, but the creation of a new, lasting majority.
> This will mean compromise. But not a compromise of basic
> principle. What will emerge will be something new, something
> open and vital and dynamic, something the great conservative
> majority will recognize as its own, because at the heart of this
> undertaking is principled politics.

Later in his speech, he made a pitch for the black vote as part of this
same coalition:

> The New Republican Party I envision is still going to be the party
> of Lincoln and that means we are going to have to come to grips
> with what I consider to be a major failing of the party: its failure
> to attract the majority of black voters.
> [I]t's time black America and the New Republican Party move

toward each other and create a situation in which no black vote can be taken for granted.

Reagan went on to reiterate this vision in subsequent addresses. In a speech on June 8, 1977, in Westmoreland County, Pennsylvania, he discussed his goal of turning the Republican Party into a "new majority" party comprised of Democrats seeking a new political home, Republicans, and independents. By the time of his September 5, 1978, stump speech on behalf of a California legislator, Reagan was not only calling for the coalition of economic and social conservatives and a new majority, he was encapsulating this vision in the five words that would ultimately frame his campaign: family, work, neighborhood, freedom, and peace. Speaking before the California Republican Assembly in Los Angeles on March 24, 1979, Reagan continued to press his case, describing the Republican Party as a bigger tent than its reputation allowed: "I know I have said this before, but I repeat we are not a narrow band of ideologues. . . . We are the party of the people—the people of main street and the farm."[22]

From 1977 onward Reagan continued to refine his message and deliver it to millions of Americans. The core of his platform was that tax cuts and a robust defense policy could be accompanied by substantial decreases in inflation, and that a massive American military buildup would make the United States more secure because military superiority would dissuade any potential challenger from attacking the United States. Furthermore, military strength coupled with a restoration of international credibility, which Reagan believed was connected to both military power and living up to international commitments and agreements, would make the United States a more attractive alternative to the Soviet model. Reagan believed that as strength and credibility helped improve the post-Vietnam reputation of the United States, the international system would begin to be transformed from the bipolar status quo to a larger zone of economically and politically free states. He stopped short of declaring that his proposed direction for foreign and defense policy would end the Cold War, but he unabashedly charged that a radical departure from containment and détente was in order.[23]

One of the most prominent aspects of the economic message Reagan would advocate in his 1980 presidential campaign began to take shape in 1977. On July 14, Republican congressmen Jack Kemp of New York and William Roth of Delaware introduced a bill that would reduce personal income tax rates 10 percent a year for three years, lower corporate taxes, and provide tax relief for small businesses. Reagan immediately advocated the bill in his radio commentaries and speeches.[24] His early endorsement of the Kemp-Roth bill contributed to Reagan's already strong reputation as an advocate of tax cuts well before the 1980 presidential race began.

Of course, Reagan was not the first American to decide inflation was a national economic problem. By the late 1970s polls were consistently showing that Americans considered inflation an urgent issue. But Reagan, who had been speaking and writing about it for many years and on a regular basis since at least 1975, was positioned to exploit this concern. In his December 14, 1978, speech to the Los Angeles World Affairs Council, Reagan presented a refined position on inflation: "[T]here is but one cause of inflation, and that is government itself."[25] The text of his radio commentaries shows that Reagan was also sifting through scholarly and policy literature for proposals on reducing inflation. His comprehensive solution to the problem was still a couple of years away, but Reagan was already establishing himself as an anti-inflation warrior in much the same way that he had accrued his bona fides on the tax issue.

Reagan was not alone in discerning that, by 1978, large numbers of Americans had become concerned that Soviet expansionism was threatening American military power, and supported a robust defense policy. Public opinion polling confirmed these findings.[26] Reagan was convinced that the American public was prepared for peacetime rearmament, even with the humiliation of Vietnam still smoldering in recent memory. This belief fueled Reagan's heresthetical appeal, which held that massive increases in defense spending would make the United States more secure and help avoid war.

Reagan distinguished himself from Carter and from his Republican challengers by the way he interpreted the public mood, the issues he sought to make salient to voters, and the positions he took on those issues. He also set himself apart by interweaving public concerns with his own long-standing views. These tactics shielded him from efforts by other Republican presidential hopefuls to undercut support from within his own party, while simultaneously fracturing the loose coalition that had elected Carter president four years earlier. Carter needed the full support of those who voted for him in 1976 to retain the White House in 1980, but Reagan had been gaining their support from the moment the 1976 election was over.

Gary Hart, the former Democratic senator from Colorado and presidential candidate, recently captured the essence of heresthetical maneuvering in an essay for the *New York Times Book Review*: "Truly great leaders possess a strategic sense, an inherent understanding of how the framework of their thinking and the tides of the times fit together and how their nation's powers should be applied to achieve its larger purposes."[27] One could hardly imagine a more accurate description of Ronald Reagan in the late 1970s.

The governor's heresthetical appeal was that economic growth would be spurred by abandoning policies based on the old Keynesian theory of federal involvement in the economy. The economic malaise of the 1970s had not been a natural consequence of American decline, he argued, but was caused by excesses in government spending and regulation—excesses that could be reversed through tax cuts, a stable monetary policy, a reduction in the rate of growth of government spending, and less burdensome regulatory policies.

Reagan was not starting from scratch in 1980: his long climb up the economic learning curve reached across many campaigns. Nor was Reagan ever acting alone: over time, he had attracted an extremely savvy group of advisers and staff. But neither experience nor personnel would suffice: the campaign needed a clear strategy.

This strategy began to come together on March 7, 1979, when Senator Paul Laxalt (R-NV) announced the formation of the Reagan for President Committee. Unlike Reagan's 1976 campaign, which was announced with only a handful of supporters, his 1980 effort was launched with 365 backers from the GOP and nearly every segment of society. Laxalt, the committee's chair, made it known that this time Reagan would campaign as a centrist.[28]

Economic policies would be crucial to winning the center. In the months that followed, Martin Anderson, Reagan's domestic policy adviser, was nagged by his candidate's lack of a comprehensive economic plan that would appeal to the diverse segments of society that a centrist Reagan would need to reach. Anderson recalls, "Over the years he [Reagan] . . . studied and took positions on most major economic issues. He had not proposed any overall economic plan for the country, but he was convinced that tax rates, particularly those on people's earnings, were too high, that a lot of government regulations were of minimal benefit and hurt the economy. He felt our monetary policy was erratic and our currency unsound . . . [and this] in turn had a powerful impact on the economy."[29] Anderson undertook to put Reagan's economic ideas down on paper in one comprehensive statement.

By August, Anderson was ready to present Policy Memorandum Number 1. Relying on themes that Reagan had repeated in his broadcasts and speeches and arguments that noted economists had been making, Anderson identified inflation as "the main domestic problem facing the United States today, not only for its pure economic effects, but also because of its negative social and political consequences." He then proposed five measures to transform the American economy: (1) speed up economic growth through a reduction in taxation and government regulations; (2) eliminate government waste and excess spending and grant the president a line-item veto as a means of controlling government spending; (3) balance the budget; (4) establish a stable monetary policy and devise a constitutional amendment to ban wage and price controls, except in cases of national emergency; and (5) further amend the Constitution with an "Economic Bill of Rights" limiting government spending, requiring a balanced federal budget, prohibiting wage and price controls, creating the line-item veto, and requiring a two-thirds approval by Congress on major spending initiatives.[30] Reagan had already endorsed every component of this plan at some point in time, generally in his radio commentaries. But the memo was an important contribution to coalescing Reagan's heresthetical message in the 1980 campaign.

On another front, the governor's message on foreign and defense policy was also taking shape. Reagan had been an active anti-Communist throughout most of his professional life, and he campaigned on an anti-Communist platform in both 1968 and 1976. By the late 1970s, however, his hypotheses about U.S.-Soviet relations had evolved into an alternative way to think about the Cold War.

Reagan's thinking on the issue was solidly based on four separate hypotheses. Each of these ideas had been put forward by other conservative writers and politicians at various times. But no presidential contender had embraced them together as a complete way of analyzing the Cold War. Indeed, doing so was a kind of political and intellectual heresy at the height of U.S.-Soviet détente.

The first hypothesis, which Reagan had expounded as early as the 1960s, was that the Soviet economy was so weak that it could not survive an intense technology race with the United States. In a speech he delivered around 1963, Reagan spoke of "the shaky Russian economy" and its "limping industrial complex." He speculated that the Soviet economy would "come unhinged" if the United States stopped helping the satellite states of the Eastern bloc and forced the USSR to take up its full burden of obligations. He returned to this idea during an Oregon news conference in June 1977, in which he suggested that we tell the Soviets "we're going to turn our industrial machinery into developing weapons . . . and make them believe it." By doing so, he argued, the United States could force the Soviet Union to surrender the arms race.[31]

His second hypothesis held that the occupying Red Army was the Soviet Union's sole source of legitimacy in Eastern Europe. He did not see the Soviet bloc as a genuine alliance, and asserted that if the army pulled out, the bloc's client states would go their own way.[32]

Reagan's third hypothesis was that the American economy was strong enough to withstand a period of intense military competition with the Soviet Union. And his fourth hypothesis (mentioned earlier) was that, despite the recent failure in Vietnam, the American public was prepared to rearm for the purpose of transforming the international system away from the Cold War and toward a larger zone of economically and politically free states. His radio commentaries and speeches are replete with calls for military preparedness, and his July 7, 1978, newspaper column took issue with "McGovernites . . . . [C]onvinced that the American public and Congress would never support . . . increased defense expenditures."[33]

In a speech in Los Angeles on December 14, 1978, Reagan referred to "polls [that] show a majority of Americans wanting some kind of arms control agreement to ensure peace, while at the same time expressing concern about our falling behind the Soviets."[34] It was clear by then that Reagan was going to campaign on the proposition that America was over its Vietnam Syndrome of decreased military spending and wariness of foreign entanglements.

He did not go into detail on this matter during the campaign, but there was evidence throughout the years that Reagan was looking toward a post-Soviet world. In his early 1960s speech referred to earlier, Reagan embraced the belief "that in an all out race our system is stronger, and eventually the enemy gives up the race as a hopeless cause. Then a noble nation believing in peace extends the hand of friendship and says there is room in the world for both of us. We can make those rockets into bridge lamps by being so strong the enemy has no choice, or we can bet our lives and freedom on the cockeyed theory that if we make him strong enough he'll learn to love us."[35]

In January 1977, the same month during which he first defined his coalition of social and economic conservatives, Reagan offered his stark vision of the Cold War endgame to Richard V. Allen, an international relations scholar. "My view is that we win and they lose," he said. In Reagan's thinking it was that simple. An all-out race would force the Soviet Union to acknowledge America's economic and political superiority. Allen later wrote that he "was flabbergasted. I'd worked for Nixon and Goldwater and many others, and I'd heard a lot about Kissinger's policy of détente and about the need to 'manage the Cold War,' but never did I hear a leading politician put the goal so starkly."[36]

Impressed by these ideas, Allen joined Reagan's presidential campaign. By the summer of 1978, he was helping the governor develop a cohesive set of foreign and national security policy themes, akin to what Martin Anderson would do on the economic side the following summer. In a 14-page memo to Reagan titled "The 'Strategy for Peace' Theme," Allen outlined an overarching national security position for the campaign that built upon Reagan's criticism of U.S.-Soviet détente during his 1976 presidential campaign.[37] In effect, Allen was building an entire platform around Reagan's belief in the need for the United States to change the way it fought the Cold War. He offered a lengthy critique of détente, arguing that the Soviet Union had never accepted the code of conduct that President Nixon and his national security adviser Henry Kissinger had expected. The result, he argued, was "strategic asymmetry." Allen saw the Reagan "Strategy for Peace" as a radical alternative to the détente policies of the Nixon-Ford-Carter years.

Reagan's new foreign policy adviser cautioned that this would require a shift in rhetoric: "It will be crucially important to move away from discussing the merits of specific weapons systems (such as the great penetration capabilities of the B-1, the 'humaneness' of the neutron bomb) because it can be made to appear that you are fascinated with and 'like' weapons for what they can accomplish, and to move toward discussing the requirements of a *grand strategy*."

The first step toward this grand strategy would be to link defense policy to the economy. Allen wrote: "A sound and credible national security policy requires a strong and dynamic domestic economy, one in which the productive forces and creative genius of the American people are given free rein and are not stifled, by the Federal Government. Hence, the first line of our defense must be an economy capable of sustaining America's leadership position in the world and inspiring trust and confidence in our ability to manage well our own affairs." This line of reasoning was fully consistent with Reagan's Cold War hypothesis about the durability of the American economy in the face of revved-up military competition with the Soviet Union.

Reagan's grand strategy would also be based on what Allen described as an "enunciated national purpose capable of being understood by friend and foe alike." He did not outline the details of this deterrent strategy, but his memo suggested a clear break with traditional reliance on containment and détente. As Allen remarked in the concluding paragraph of his memo, "[T]he notion that there is a Ronald Reagan 'Strategy For Peace' will become an important part of your campaign arsenal."

The governor needed to run on a peace plan in 1980: a telephone survey taken by the Gallup Poll in the midst of the primaries had found that 46 percent of those questioned thought Carter would be more likely to keep the country out of war than Reagan, compared to 31 percent in favor of the challenger.[38] Encouraged by this finding, Carter would try to capitalize on Reagan's trigger-happy image throughout the campaign.

Meanwhile, Reagan was expressing a range of other, similarly radical views about national defense, questioning the wisdom of a deterrence strategy based on Mutual Assured Destruction and negotiated limits on antimissile defense: "There once was the beginning of a defense; an anti ballistic missile system which we had invented and which the Soviets didn't have. We bargained that away in exchange for nothing. Instead of a defense against their missiles we settled for something called mutual destruction. . . . Today there is reason to question that [MAD] is an adequate defense."[39] At the time of these words, spoken during a radio commentary taped in September 1979, Reagan stood alone among the Republican presidential contenders in his argument that the conventional deterrence strategy should be jettisoned.

Although missile defense would eventually become part of the 1980 GOP platform, Reagan did not emphasize his positions on missile defense and MAD during the campaign. It seems that the governor's camp chose not to publicize his unconventional views in order to avoid exposing themselves to attacks from Carter. The fact remains, however, that Reagan was campaigning on the radical notion that the American conventions of containment and deterrence were wrongheaded and had relegated the country to second-place status.

Despite widespread expectations that he would favor abandonment of nuclear arms control negotiations with the Soviets, the presumptive Republican presidential nominee in fact supported continued talks, although under dramatically revised terms. Speaking at a gathering of Republicans in San Diego on September 15, 1979, he pronounced SALT II to be "fatally flawed," but suggested that "the negotiators . . . go back to the table and come up with a treaty which fairly and genuinely reduces the number of strategic nuclear weapons."[40] By mid-1979, the *New York Times* was reporting that Reagan had softened his tone on defense policy: "Intentionally or not, the fact is that Mr. Reagan sounds much less aggressive on foreign affairs now than he did in 1976. . . . These days, however, his basic foreign-policy speech emphasizes the relative weakness of the American economy and Presidential indecision about defense priorities. It is a calm, reasoned, and even dull speech."[41] The radio commentaries often hinted more strongly at the fire in Reagan's belly: this was certainly due in part to the nature of the medium. There was a strategic preference in Reagan's 1980 presidential campaign, however, to employ measured rhetoric to turn conventional defense thinking on its head.

Reagan's official announcement of his presidential campaign in late 1979 laid out the candidate's unconventional ideas about the economy and defense policy, and his goals for arms-reduction talks with the Soviets. The announcement also endorsed the Kemp-Roth bill as the savior of the American economy: "The key to restoring the health of the economy lies in cutting taxes. . . . Proposals such as the Kemp-Roth bill would bring about . . . realistic reductions in tax rates." On foreign policy, Reagan warned that U.S.-Soviet negotiations "must never become appeasement," but he also said that "we should leave no initiative untried in our pursuit of peace." Furthermore, he took the opportunity to propose a North American Accord among Canada, Mexico, and the United States, on the grounds that such an agreement would enhance security in the Western Hemisphere.[42]

Reagan's proposals for the 1980 presidential race struck a much more modest rhetorical note than he had favored in 1976, but that modesty belied the fact that his proposals fundamentally challenged conventional economic and strategic assumptions. A rhetorician may accuse his opponent of incompetence or a lack of ideas, but only a heresthetician can convince voters that his opponent is so fundamentally misguided as to be talking about the wrong issues. Reagan was thinking heresthetically when he told voters that American leaders, including President Carter, had for decades completely misunderstood the Cold War. And he was doing it again when he claimed that his tax-cut plan would offset the negative effects of increased defense spending.

Of course, the adoption of unconventional policies is just the first step toward heresthetical success. After all, the American public always had the option of rejecting Reagan's ideas. The successful heresthetician must not only present a new way of thinking, but must also articulate positions in a way that backs opponents into a corner. If opponents so much as acknowledge any element of the heresthetician's argument, they risk losing large segments of their own coalition. In the end, the heresthetician must dominate the issues that will attract support. Reagan was applying all of these tactics in the late 1970s.

On January 7, 1977, two weeks before he was sworn in as president, Jimmy Carter proposed an economic stimulus package designed to reduce unemployment and create jobs. He amended this plan on January 22 and again on the twenty-fifth, adding a $50 tax rebate for individuals and tax credits for businesses that made new hires and increased their investments. He rescinded these proposals four months later out of concern that they might fuel further inflation. To bring inflation under control, the president now argued, business, government, and labor would have to work together more closely and the country would need "the voluntary cooperation and restraint of the American people."[43] In other words, Carter was calling for national sacrifice at the beginning of his White House tenure. The call for sacrifice was to become one of the most consistent themes of his presidency and 1980 reelection campaign. Early in his presidency, Carter was embracing a position on national sacrifice that would be difficult to abandon in his reelection campaign without, in effect, admitting failure and conceding that Reagan might have a good point.

By March 1980, inflation had reached 14.68 percent, its highest point so far that year. The main sources for the rise in inflation, according to Carter, were energy prices, the declining growth in productivity, and "failure in government and as individuals, as an entire American society, to live within our means." The *New York Times* ran a front-page story on the speech under the headline "Carter to Trim Budget $13 Billion and Curb Credit to Cut Inflation." The deck read: "Sees Need for Pain and Discipline."[44]

Reagan, on the other hand, neither blamed the American people nor advocated policies prescribing pain and discipline. He opposed the use of wage and price controls as an antidote to inflation, instead singling out government spending and interventionist polices as the underlying causes of the problem.

Herein lay Carter and Reagan's key difference on the economy. Reagan had two advantages: first, he did not bear any responsibility for the last four years of increasing inflation; and second, he had long been identified with anti-inflationary ideas. Carter was losing the inflation battle not only in real terms, but in campaign terms as well. His economic speeches and plans appeared to be reactions to economic shocks rather than innovative measures that could broaden his coalition.

Even so, Carter slowly moved in Reagan's direction on economic issues. "The Carter administration shifted gradually away from neo-Keynesianism to monetarist and supply-side thinking," Bruce Schulman has suggested, "from an emphasis on growth and unemployment to an all-out attack on inflation, from short-term fiscal management to long-term structural change."[45] This shift, however, failed to increase public confidence in Carter's ability to manage the economy.

In preparing policy priorities for 1978, Bob Ginsburg, a Carter administration staffer, remarked, "I do not think the President sees himself as, or will want to run for reelection as, a 'man of the economy.' . . . [W]e would *not* want to face an up or down vote from the public on the crucial issues of inflation, unemployment, and the budget deficit."[46] One could dismiss this statement as the musings of a lone official, but it is consistent with Carter strategist Pat Caddell's plan to emphasize the Rose Garden effect over specific policy positions.[47]

Carter also moved to embrace a number of other positions traditionally identified with Reagan. In January 1979, for example, he touted "reduc[ing] the growth of Federal spending" as a central component in his anti-inflation package. Sounding very much like Reagan, he went on, "I believe that we must firmly limit what the Government taxes and spends. . . . The Government has no resources of its own—its only resources are those it collects from the taxpayer."[48] This was not a unique position, nor was it an idea that had been at the forefront of Carter's economic thinking during his presidency. At a rhetorical level, the incumbent was finding it difficult to articulate distinct alternatives to Reagan's domestic and economic policy proposals.

It was his call for sacrifice that most fully distinguished Carter from his closest competitor. While Reagan promised a better economy without undue pain and sacrifice, the Carter team emphasized trade-offs. As his press secretary, Jody Powell, remarked, "The trade-offs [on battling inflation and the energy shortage] all along the line are extremely difficult. Everything you do in one area costs you something in another area."[49] Reality was taking its toll. In the summer of 1979, Carter asked Congress to grant him the authority to ration gasoline. Odd-even day gas sales went into effect on June 20 in some states.

Carter was scheduled to give a major address on the energy crisis on July 5, but he postponed it in favor of a series of meetings at Camp David with "people from almost every segment of our society." The president emerged from the sessions with a somber assessment, which he delivered in a speech on July 15:

> It's clear that the true problems of our Nation are much deeper— deeper than gasoline lines or energy shortages, deeper even than inflation or recession. . . . I want to talk to you right now about a fundamental threat to American democracy. . . . It is a crisis of confidence. . . . The erosion of our confidence in the future is threatening to destroy the social and the political fabric of America. . . . Energy will be the immediate test of our ability to unite this Nation, and it can also be the standard around which we rally. On the battlefield of energy we can win for our Nation a new confidence, and we can seize control again of our common destiny. . . . I do not promise a quick way out of our Nation's problems, when the truth is that the only way out is an all-out effort. . . . We can manage the short-term shortages more effectively and we will, but there are no short-term solutions to our long-range problems. There is simply no way to avoid sacrifice.[50]

In his speech, Carter emphasized increased domestic energy production and reduced government interference. These suggestions moved the president closer to the positions of his Republican challengers, but Carter still rejected their call to decontrol oil and gas prices.

Reagan, on the other hand, was promising the American people greater prosperity and peace. The major distinctions between their respective positions came down to Reagan's unswerving opposition to wage and price controls of any kind, and his commitment to relaxing federal environmental restrictions on energy exploration. For Carter, to embrace these policies would be to risk losing the support of his base.

On July 16, Reagan issued a response to Carter's speech, which he said was based on "massive new taxes . . . and on massive new government programs." He accused the administration of an inability to allocate gasoline supplies "fairly and rationally" and blamed the president for the energy crisis.[51]

Carter's speech failed to generate higher performance ratings in national polls. In fact, in its coverage of the speech, the *Washington Post* proclaimed that President Carter had succeeded in making "malaise a household word."[52]

"Carter's economic program attempted to walk a fine line between the demands of various Democratic constituencies and his own ideas on what was fiscally prudent," political scientist Henry Plotkin observed. "In all, as far as the economy was concerned, Carter was trapped by a need to limit spending while reconciling the values of traditional welfare-state Democrats."[53] Reagan, on the other hand, offered something approaching utopia for the American people: lower taxes accompanied by a balanced budget, a reduction (or at least deceleration) in government spending, and lower inflation.

Carter was also backed up against the wall on foreign and defense policy. The one-term Georgia governor had received his major education in international relations through his association with the Trilateral Commission. Formed in 1973 by leaders and private citizens from Europe, Japan, Canada, and the United States, the Commission sought "to foster closer cooperation among these core democratic industrialized areas of the world with shared leadership responsibilities in the wider international system."[54]

Carter was profoundly influenced by the trilateralists' dedication to enhance cooperation among industrialized democracies. He was particularly impressed with liberal-theory notions of bringing the nonmilitary dimensions of American power to bear in international crises. Through the Commission, he became friends with and was tutored by Zbigniew Brzezinski, the Columbia University political scientist who would later become his campaign adviser and national security adviser.[55]

Carter's foreign policy plan during the 1976 presidential race had been based on greater attention to North-South issues, human rights, and morality in foreign policy; deepening ties among North Atlantic countries; continuing America's commitment to Japan while simultaneously preparing to withdraw U.S. troops from South Korea; normalizing relations with the People's Republic of China; and encouraging and supporting negotiations between the Arab states and Israel. Carter's pledges also included halting production of the B-1 bomber and other weapons programs, reducing arms sales, making deep cuts in defense spending, and concluding the SALT II treaty with the Soviet Union.[56] This latter position was one expression of his unswerving commitment to nuclear arms control negotiations and antiproliferation measures.

In his first foreign policy speech as president, delivered on May 22, 1977, at the University of Notre Dame, Carter discussed the philosophy that would guide him. He declared that U.S. foreign policy should project "our essential character as a nation" and should be "based on fundamental values." He also said Americans "are now free of that inordinate fear of communism."[57] But there were at least two factions within the Carter White House when it came to foreign policy. The so-called regionalists, such as Secretary of State Cyrus Vance and Ambassador to the United Nations Andrew Young believed in dealing with international problems at the subsystem level, and giving greater weight to the nonmilitary dimensions of American power. Globalists such as Brzezinski favored a grand strategy that both viewed the international system through the prism of great power politics and gave greater recognition to the military dimensions of American power. Vance and Brzezinski, representing these positions, deeply disagreed over how much and what kind of foreign policy priority should be given to the Soviet Union. For Vance, détente required a de-emphasis on military competition and a focus on nuclear arms control. Brzezinski, meanwhile, advocated a more robust American military presence and a greater recognition that the U.S.-Soviet relationship was marked by both cooperation and conflict. Carter, who vacillated between these perspectives, was often accused of inconsistence and incoherence in his foreign policy.[58]

The Panama Canal negotiations provided the president with what Carter biographer Peter Bourne has called "a prime opportunity to apply moral values to foreign policy."[59] On September 7, 1977, Carter and Panamanian general Omar Torrijos signed a treaty to transfer the canal to Panama at the end of the twentieth century and a second treaty ensuring the canal's continued neutrality.[60] The U.S. Senate narrowly approved both treaties in the spring of 1978 and drained the president's political capital.

Meanwhile, Ronald Reagan had quickly distinguished himself as an outspoken critic of the treaties, a position that factored significantly in his late-1970s rise to prominence. Reagan was so closely identified with opposition to the negotiations that during his fourth month in the White House, Carter sent Ambassador Sol Linowitz, one of the U.S. negotiators on the canal treaties, to brief him on the issue. Peter Hannaford, one of Reagan's aides, attended the briefing at Washington's Madison Hotel with the governor and his wife, Nancy. Hannaford recalls that he and Reagan agreed that "it was something of a compliment for the Carter administration to assume that Ronald Reagan might have it in his power to mount so strong a campaign against a new treaty as a private citizen that he could derail its course."[61]

On May 1, Reagan discussed his opposition to the Panama Canal treaties on NBC's *Meet the Press:* "I do not believe that we should be . . . negotiating to give away the Canal or to give up our sovereign rights, and our rights of defense of the Canal, and I shall oppose that." A June 10, 1977, newspaper headline reflected the situation: "Carter policies draw active Reagan criticism." The *San Diego Evening Tribune* headline accompanied an article that discussed the implications for U.S. domestic politics of Reagan's relentless commentary on the canal treaties: "It was Reagan . . . who first made Panama Canal treaty negotiations a campaign issue [in 1976]."[62] On August 11, Reagan's Los Angeles office released a two-page statement summarizing his opposition. The statement described Reagan as believing that the existing treaties established U.S. sovereignty over the Canal Zone and thus should not be abrogated; that Fidel Castro sought to spread Marxism throughout the region through his friendship with the leader of Panama; and that the Soviet Union would enter the power vacuum left by the withdrawal of U.S. armed forces from the Canal Zone. On September 8, Reagan testified against the treaties before the Senate Judiciary Committee's Separation of Powers Subcommittee. He reiterated these views in his October 4 newspaper column, in a speech in Houston that October, and again repeatedly throughout 1978 and 1979. Reagan regularly spoke against the treaties in his radio program.[63] He did not succeed in derailing the negotiations, of course, but his estimable counteroffensive would pay a political dividend later on. He had associated himself with the Panama Canal treaties as closely as the president had—albeit from a very different angle.

Carter was as devoted to the SALT II treaty as he was to the Panama negotiations. Despite the fact that the nuclear arms talks had been languishing since the early 1970s, he was determined to conclude the nuclear arms control agreement with the Soviets. In remarks to a meeting of the Special Coordinating Committee at the White House on March 2, 1978, Cyrus Vance spoke about the arms control negotiations in a manner that illustrated the president's position: "I think the key still remains SALT. If we make progress on SALT, then a lot of things will fall into place that do not fall into place otherwise."[64] Brzezinski, too, wanted a second arms limitation treaty with the Soviets, but he did not prioritize nuclear arms control over increased Soviet activities around the world, including military buildups in Angola and Ethiopia.

The SALT II talks were held early in Carter's presidency, but it was not until June 18, 1979, that he and Soviet general secretary Leonid Brezhnev signed the treaty. Four days later, the president submitted the agreement to the U.S. Senate for consent deliberations. Extensive hearings by the Senate Armed Services Committee, the Senate Foreign Relations Committee, and the Senate Intelligence Committee were accompanied by growing doubts about SALT II's chances of success. International events in the summer—principally the "discovery" of a Soviet combat brigade in Cuba—fueled concerns in the Senate, and among treaty skeptics more generally, about America's ability to confidentially verify Soviet compliance with the terms of SALT II. It was becoming increasingly apparent that Carter lacked the two-thirds majority needed for Senate ratification.

The president pressed hard. Anticipating a battle, he declared on April 25, 1979, that if the Senate did not approve the treaty, "We would no longer be identified as a peace loving nation." At a White House meeting on May 10, 1979, he said: "I think the most important single achievement that could possibly take place for our Nation during my lifetime is the ratification of the SALT treaty." And he once again warned that the United States "would be looked upon as a warmonger, not a peace loving nation by many other people of the world" if the Senate did not vote to ratify.[65]

The differences between Reagan and Carter on foreign policy could hardly have been sharper. While Reagan was charging the Soviets with violating the expectations of reciprocity on which détente was founded, Carter was accusing American legislators of fostering aggression. As for the economy, Carter repeatedly assigned the American people at least partial responsibility for their own energy and economic woes, while Reagan saw the government, not the American people, as the cause of these problems. Carter's somber message of responsibility and sacrifice was a stark contrast to Reagan's optimistic, can-do message.

Even Carter's Democratic base was now beginning to defect to the Reagan camp. In his speech at an awards dinner of the Coalition for a Democratic Majority (CDM), an organization of conservative Democrats committed to a more militarily assertive U.S. foreign policy, CDM founder and senator Henry Jackson of Washington unequivocally opposed Senate ratification of SALT II: "To enter into a treaty which favors the Soviets, as this one does, on the ground that we will be in a worse position without it, is appeasement in its purest form." Jackson lamented the imbalance of U.S.-Soviet relations under Carter:

"All of this [the Soviet military buildup] is taking place in a misty atmosphere of amiability and good fellowship under a policy of détente." Jackson's June 12, 1979, speech attracted national media attention and heaped more pressure on the Carter administration from conservative Democrats.[66]

The administration vigorously sought to prove that its Soviet policy was being carried forward on a truly reciprocal basis, but members of the CDM remained skeptical. Conservative Democratic elites had been unhappy with Carter for a long time, but by 1980 their dissatisfaction was reaching a new level. In January, Carter met with CDM leaders at the White House. Their differences were made especially apparent when CDM representative Norman Podhoretz expressed interest in a campaign for human rights in the Soviet Union. Carter responded by saying that he needed help on Uruguay. According to Elliott Abrams, who was in attendance in his capacity as a Jackson aide, "[T]he meeting was a disaster, the straw that breaks the camel's back. Carter told us that he will continue to pursue a leftist McGovernite–Andy Young foreign policy." Upon leaving, Midge Decter, another conservative Democrat in attendance, asked Jeane Kirkpatrick what she thought about the session with the president. Kirkpatrick responded, "I am not going to support *that* man."[67] The movement of conservative Democrats away from Carter was becoming a stampede.

A similar redirection of loyalties had begun among the military after members of the top brass openly opposed the president's March 1977 decision to withdraw American troops from South Korea and his June 1977 decision to slow down the production of the B-1 bomber. The military leadership was also displeased with the fiscal year 1979 defense budget (put forward on January 23, 1978), which requested a far smaller increase in defense spending than the Ford administration had projected. There were also unpopular cuts to the navy's shipbuilding program and concerns about the April 1978 decision to defer production of the neutron bomb. In an unusual move, the Joint Chiefs of Staff broke ranks with the president and Secretary of Defense Harold Brown on May 29, 1980, by testifying to Congress that military spending should be much higher than the figure the White House had proposed.[68]

Carter did eventually seek larger increases in defense spending and invoked a tougher line with the Soviets, but he did so reactively, a strategy that hurt him politically. The years 1979 and 1980 were exceptionally eventful ones on the international stage: the Sandinistas seized power in Nicaragua on July 17, 1979; Iranian students took a group of

American hostages at the U.S. embassy in Tehran on November 4, 1979; the Soviets invaded Afghanistan in December 1979; Carter's efforts to rescue the American hostages in Iran failed catastrophically in April 1980; and the administration suspended economic and military aid to El Salvador after four American Catholic nuns were murdered by a Salvadoran death squad in December 1980.

These and other events transformed Carter's political rhetoric. Shortly after the Soviet invasion of Afghanistan, he was no longer stating that Americans were free of "that inordinate fear of communism," and instead he was declaring that "this action of the Soviets has made a more dramatic change in my own opinion of what the Soviets' ultimate goals are than anything they've done in the previous time I've been in office."[69] On January 4 and January 23 (during his State of the Union address), among other times, Carter made stern warnings to the Soviets and instituted a package of sanctions, including a partial grain embargo against the Soviet Union; recalling the U.S. ambassador in Moscow; a boycott of the Moscow Olympics; a request that the Senate halt its deliberations on SALT II; and additional development of the Rapid Deployment Force, a quick-reaction team that would be able to respond to Persian Gulf crises.[70] This package of foreign and defense policies did not, however, constitute a fundamental shift in Carter's political orientation. He and Vance, in particular, remained deeply and vocally committed to Senate ratification of SALT II and what remained of superpower détente.

For Carter, a complete change of course would have been a not-so-tacit admission of the failure of his decisions and policies during his first three years in office. In equivocating in his support of the shah of Iran, he had sacrificed a pillar of American foreign policy in the Middle East and a key post for monitoring Soviet ballistic missile activity along Iran's 2,000-mile border with the USSR. By refusing to endorse multilateral mediation efforts in Nicaragua, Carter had opened the door to the Sandinista seizure of power and the advent of another Marxist-oriented government in the Western hemisphere.

As the presidential contest was getting under way in 1979 and 1980, Carter was stuck in the awkward position of having to adjust his policies to new international realities while simultaneously defending his prior positions. At the same time, he also had to contrast himself to his chief Republican opponent. His campaign chose to go with a two-pronged strategy, defending Carter's record while portraying Reagan as a warmonger. But both claims rang hollow. Although he adopted a more aggressive military stance during his final year in office, Carter never made the leap to a major reorientation of U.S. foreign policy, something even critics in his own party were demanding.

One might be inclined to assume that Carter's political demise spelled success for Reagan. But it was not that simple. As Jay Winik has written of Carter's 1980 meeting with the CDM representatives, "[I]t was not clear, standing there on that chill January morning, that anyone in the CDM was included in Ronald Reagan's vision of America."[71] The political bloodletting in the Democratic Party offered Reagan an unheralded opportunity, but he would still have to work hard to win the support of discontented Democrats. In dozens of radio commentaries on the SALT II treaty and defense policy, Reagan constantly made reference to the defections among the military brass and the conservative Democratic factions. Instead of taking the lead, as he had done on the Panama Canal issue, Reagan now fell back on long citations from the congressional record and the speeches of military officials and defense experts to argue against SALT II. He openly courted members of both the CDM and the Committee on the Present Danger (CPD), a bipartisan group dedicated to ensuring continued American military superiority. The CPD claimed a roster of prominent members, including Reagan, who joined the organization's executive committee in 1979; George Shultz, president of Bechtel Corporation and future Reagan secretary of state; and Eugene Rostow, former dean of Yale's law school, LBJ's undersecretary of state, and director of the Arms Control and Disarmament Agency during the Reagan administration. As he wooed conservative Democrats, Reagan devoted six radio commentaries to a speech by Rostow.[72] And behind all this politicking was a clear message: massive increases in military spending would force the Soviets to cease their adventurism and make the world a safer place.

Other Republican challengers made similar appeals, but none had been doing so with the laser-beam focus that Reagan had demonstrated during the late 1970s. He pounded away at his message relentlessly through his daily radio commentaries, his biweekly columns, and his innumerable speeches on behalf of his Citizens for the Republic PAC. Reagan was everywhere, gaining dominance through his emphasis on international peace through strong defense.

Carter's shift toward a more hawkish defense and foreign policy was a net political gain for Reagan. As political scientist Seyom Brown has observed, "The Carter administration's new rhetorical and policy preoccupation with the Soviet threat appeared to legitimize the complaints of the unreconstructed cold warriors in the Reagan camp."[73] Carter's shift in effect validated the critique of détente that Reagan had so publicly expounded in his speeches and writings for nearly four years. Carter was moving toward a position that Reagan had already staked out, and the president's shift failed to improve the state of his relations with conservative Democratic elites and opinion makers.

Nor did the president's shift on defense help him among party faithful on the left. Early in his presidency there was vocal concern about his initial increase in defense spending. In December 1977, the month before Carter sent his FY 1979 budget to Congress, liberal Democrats began criticizing his defense proposals. Ron Brown, the vice president of the National Urban League, expressed concern that Carter was not sufficiently decreasing defense spending. Brown declared, "No longer can we have both guns and butter." Lee Alexander, the mayor of Syracuse and president of the U.S. Conference of Mayors, said that an increase in defense spending "indicated devastating consequences for urban America." Following the president's official presentation of the defense budget, House Speaker Thomas P. O'Neill, Jr., said that funding for jobs might be compromised by defense spending.[74]

The president was cornered. His defense spending increases were seen by conservative Democrats as pale imitations of Reagan's proposals, and by the liberals as expensive distractions from social policy. Carter was being pulled to the right by the Scoop Jackson Democrats and Ronald Reagan, and pulled to the left by the Kennedy Democrats. Unable to hold the middle, his campaign began to come apart.

The president's electoral troubles were not lost on his advisers. Prior to the primaries, for instance, Jerry Rafshoon, the media director for the reelection campaign, wrote a memo to the president in which he suggested that the president "should be careful never to cede your command of the political center to anyone" and noted a list of themes such as peace, prosperity, and trust that might be invoked throughout the campaign. At the same time, he delicately reported, "There is a general sense that, while you have been trying to do many good things, you have failed to provide the country with this 'vision.' That is why Brown, Connally, Reagan and Kennedy (in ascending order) are such threats. They each, for different reasons, suggest vaguely that they could fill the 'leadership gap.' . . . There is a widespread sense that you have let the country down on this score."[75]

Rafshoon was not alone. In a July 7, 1978, memo to the president,

Jody Powell, his press secretary, was blunt about the situation: "Our greatest vulnerability is the perception that we cannot govern." In a September 28, 1979, memo to Hamilton Jordan, Dick Moe, Mondale's campaign director, argued for developing campaign themes in advance of the primaries and suggested abandoning the current course, which he defined as a weak rhetorical strategy: "Instead of responding to vague charges about leadership with equally airy counter-charges, we can do a better job of showing the country the specific ways in which we are leading. Instead of dwelling on how difficult our plight is—how tough the nation's problems, how strapped the resources, how atomized the Congress and country—we can be mobilizing the enormous American desire to contribute and get the job done."[76] As the primaries approached, the Carter team knew it lacked a vision and a set of appeals to make to voters. They would continue to struggle with these issues throughout 1980.

The Republican Debates and Primaries and a Comment on the Carter-Kennedy Competition: January 6 to June 3, 1980

A large number of Republican candidates competed in the primaries. The lineup included Connally, Crane, and Reagan on the right, and Anderson, Baker, Bush, and Dole occupying various moderate-to-liberal positions, with Anderson decidedly more liberal than the rest. Conservatives were concerned that an intense rivalry between Crane and Reagan for control of the right wing of the Republican Party could open the door to a Bush victory.[77]

Following the recommendation of John Sears, his campaign chairman, Reagan declined to participate in the Iowa primary forum on January 6. Sears's position was that Reagan's abstention would cast him as the front-runner, above the fray.[78] But it did not turn out that way. Anderson impressed politicians and journalists as the candidate with the "strongest, freshest impression," while Reagan was accused of underestimating the importance of the Iowa forum. Throughout the debate, the challengers criticized Reagan's refusal to participate. Stephen Roberts, the state Republican chairman, remarked that "the biggest loser was Reagan, especially because we thought the debate worked, that it didn't turn out to be a farce that wasn't worth the effort."[79]

In the midst of the debate, Anderson made what was interpreted to be a thinly veiled reference to Reagan's economic proposals, "How do you balance the budget, cut taxes and increase defense spending at the same time?" he asked. "It's very simple. You do it with mirrors. And that's what it would take."[80] Reagan's core economic message was being attacked, and he was not present to defend himself. Two weeks later, Reagan lost the Iowa caucus to Bush, 30 percent to 32 percent.

The Reagan campaign quickly regrouped. On February 15, Reagan met with his chief foreign policy adviser, Richard Allen; adviser (and future attorney general) Edwin Meese; and pollster Dick Wirthlin in Massachusetts to discuss the direction of the campaign. William Casey, a Wall Street lawyer, former Securities and Exchange Commission chairman, and the group's choice to replace Sears (as well as being Reagan's future CIA director), was invited to join them. In the days surrounding the meeting, it was decided that Sears would be fired. The announcement would be held off until February 26, the day of the New Hampshire primary, so that the news would not interfere with the important campaigning in the days before the vote.[81]

In the debate among Republican contenders in Manchester, New Hampshire, on February 20, Reagan repeated the heresthetical message that economic growth and increased defense spending could be accompanied by a reduction in taxes, inflation, and the growth of government spending:

> I would in my first day as President put a freeze on the hiring of Federal employees. I would then start seeking a tax reduction in the income tax rates across the board over a three-year period, and reduce them by at least 30 percent in an effort to create jobs.
> . . .
> I would in addition to that, take the punitive taxes and regulations and remove them from the back of industry so that we could become more productive, and thus we wouldn't have to grind out that printing press imitation money that's destroying the value of our savings, our insurance and our pensions.[82]

According to Wirthlin: "The Manchester debate was the key event that turned the election from George Bush to Ronald Reagan . . . . [A]lmost 40 percent of those who voted said that they saw the debate. . . . Thirty-three percent said that Ronald Reagan won the debate, 17 percent Bush, 14 percent John Anderson, and 12 percent Baker."[83]

On Saturday, February 23, another debate was held in New Hampshire, yet another 20 miles farther south, in Nashua. Under the initial terms agreed to by Bush, Reagan, and the sponsoring *Nashua Telegraph,* this third debate would be limited to the two front-runners. Dole protested to the Federal Elections Commission on the grounds that the newspaper was illegally contributing to the Bush and Reagan campaigns by paying for the debate. The commission accepted this argument. In response, Reagan proposed that he and Bush pay for the forum themselves. When Bush rejected this proposal, Reagan offered to cover the fee himself and did so. He then invited the candidates snubbed by the *Telegraph* to join him. Anderson, Baker, Crane, and Dole accepted. They stood behind Reagan, who took a seat. Bush was already in his chair. There was a commotion in the audience as Reagan sought to explain what had occurred, and the *Telegraph*'s editor demanded, "Turn Mr. Reagan's microphone off." Reagan responded, "I am paying for this microphone, Mr. Green." Reagan recalled the incident in his memoir: "For some reason my words hit the audience, whose emotions were already worked up, like a sledgehammer. The crowd roared and just went wild."[84] Anderson, Baker, Crane, and Dole, the candidates who had been snubbed then left the stage, and the debate between Bush and Reagan began.

In Riker's theory, rhetoric alone is often sufficient to persuade voters, and in this instance Reagan, a master rhetorician, scored a huge rhetorical point with his audience. As Reagan himself later reminisced, "I may have won the debate, the primary—and the nomination—right there. After the debate, our people told me the gymnasium parking lot was littered with Bush-for-President badges."[85]

Something else happened that night that Reagan did not discuss in his memoirs. During the two-man Reagan-Bush debate, Reagan was able to articulate what the *New York Times* reported to be the "most persistent difference" between the two men.[86] When Bush argued that Reagan's 30 percent tax cut, to be dispersed over three years, would increase the federal deficit and inflation, Reagan stood his ground, asserting that under his plan everything could be achieved—fewer taxes, slower deficit growth, and lower inflation. It was another step toward binding together a coalition of social and economic conservatives.

The New Hampshire debates enabled Reagan to reclaim his front-runner status, and he won the state's primary with nearly 50 percent of the vote. Bush received 23 percent, Baker 12 percent, Anderson approximately 10 percent, Crane 1.8 percent, and Connally 1.5 percent. Sears, whom the Reagan camp held responsible for their loss in Iowa, was fired according to plan and replaced by William Casey.

Baker, Bush, Connally, and Reagan participated in the next debate, held on February 28 in Columbia, South Carolina. (Dole had suspended his campaign after his poor performance in New Hampshire.) Accusations flew back and forth, but the underlying tone was basically congenial. Connally accused Bush of being a liberal and told Reagan he was not prepared to be president. Baker was still reeling after his exclusion from the Nashua debate. The verbal posturing of the South Carolina forum did little to expose substantive policy differences among the candidates. The headline in Charleston's *News and Courier* read: "GOP Candidates Find Few Major Differences."[87]

Perhaps the most significant consequence of the debate came in the second rank of the field. As the *Washington Post* reported, "This debate probably helped Reagan consolidate the favorite's position he holds in the March 8 South Carolina Republican primary and the March 11 contests in Alabama, Florida and Georgia, by pitting Connally against Bush on a variety of issues."[88]

Reagan came in third behind Bush and Anderson in the March 4 Massachusetts primary but prevailed in Vermont that same day. On March 5, Baker said, "I don't like to do it, but it's clear that my campaign is not going anywhere," and withdrew from the race.[89] Reagan went on to an easy victory in South Carolina on March 8, taking 54.7 percent of the vote to Bush's 14.8. On March 11, Reagan defeated Bush throughout the South: in Alabama, he took 69.7 percent to Bush's 25.9 percent; in Florida, 56.2 percent to Bush's 30.2; and in Georgia, a sweeping 73.2 percent to Bush's 12.6.

Two days later, Anderson, Bush, Crane, and Reagan reconvened for a debate in Chicago. Party unity broke down as the group ganged up on Anderson, who was on his home turf. The three contenders derided Anderson's proposal for a 50-cent gas tax that would reduce Social Security taxes. Crane (who was also from Illinois) told Anderson, "You are in the wrong party." And Reagan (who had his own Illinois roots) warned that "when you raise one tax to cut another, the government always seems to come out ahead."[90] As the *New York Times* reported, Reagan also used the opportunity to reiterate his heresthetical message: "Mr. Reagan . . . [gave] a forceful exposition of his view that a [tax] cut now would actually increase Government revenues and lead to a balanced budget." Anderson answered that a tax cut would "make inflation even more virulent." When the discussion turned to Iran, Reagan said that the Carter administration should have helped the shah stay in power because his regime was "progressive" on issues such as education and land reform.[91] Reagan won the March 18 contest in Illinois with 48.4 percent of the vote. Anderson took second with 36.7 percent, and Bush trailed a distant third with 11 percent.

Although Anderson took the lion's share—50 percent—of the ballots cast by Democrats who voted Republican in the Illinois primary, Reagan received an impressive 28 percent of the crossover votes. The Reagan Democrats were almost entirely social conservatives, people whom Reagan had worked to include in his new coalition. A writer for the *New York Times* reported that many of the crossovers "oppose greater welfare spending, and combine that with strong opposition to abortion. . . . Yet, Reagan supporters also say that they favor larger military budgets and a stronger American posture around the world."[92]

In the midst of this Republican sparring, Ford ended public speculation by announcing that he would sit out the race for the sake of party unity.[93] Ford's decision gave the Reagan campaign team the opportunity to underscore its candidate's position as the Republican front-runner.

Anderson's plans were also the focus of much speculation. On March 19, John C. White, the chair of the Democratic National Committee, told reporters that if Anderson became an independent, he would take votes from Carter and Reagan.[94]

Bush's candidacy temporarily regained momentum on March 25 when he defeated Reagan in Connecticut by a vote of 38.6 percent to 33.9 percent. Reagan, however, was racking up endorsements. Crane, who had withdrawn from the contest just a few weeks before the Connecticut primary, asked his supporters to back the Californian. Connally declared Reagan the "champ" soon thereafter.[95] Reagan strengthened his lead in early April with victories in Kansas, Wisconsin, and Louisiana. Bush, however, again fought back, winning the April 22 Pennsylvania primary with 50.5 percent of the vote to Reagan's 42.5 percent.

The next day, the two contenders met in Houston for a Republican forum hosted by the League of Women Voters. Throughout the primaries, Reagan had proposed a response to the Soviet invasion of Afghanistan that included a naval blockade of Cuba, an idea with which Bush disagreed. His sharpest criticism, however, was directed at Reagan's plan to cut taxes by 10 percent annually for three years. Bush predicted that such a plan would add to the deficit and increase inflation, accusing Reagan of "overpromising" and countering with his own, more modest $20 billion cut. Reagan retorted by repeating his heresthetical mantra that the Kemp-Roth proposal would "not reduce Federal income, it will only reduce the increase in taxes."[96]

Anderson had declined to participate in the Houston debate, and one day later announced his decision to run on an independent ticket. He was more of a dark horse now than ever. Despite the fact that he had not won a single primary, and that a November 1979 Harris Poll had found that just 1 percent of the American people had even heard of him, the Illinois congressman was now embarking on a second full-scale campaign.[97]

As Kennedy challenged Carter for the Democratic nomination, the incumbent was facing the intractable crisis in Iran. On April 7, Carter broke diplomatic relations with the new Iranian regime and banned exports to the country. At a news conference 10 days later, he declared that "some sort of military action" would be necessary if sanctions did not end the hostage crisis. On April 24, he sent a rescue team to free the hostages; but mechanical problems aggravated by an unanticipated sandstorm forced them to abort, and in the ensuing melee two choppers collided, resulting in the death of eight military. The dead were abandoned in their burning helicopter as the survivors retreated. Secretary of State Cyrus Vance resigned in protest over the mission. One day later, Senator Edmund Muskie was named to replace him.

The candidates had until then largely refrained from openly criticizing administration policies on the grounds that private diplomatic efforts to free the hostages could be hurt by their campaign statements. As time went on, however, and the hostages remained in captivity, that criticism began to mount. After the imposition of sanctions, Reagan publicly declared, "It's just more of the same and it's been wrong from the first."[98] In the months to come, his critiques of Carter's Iran policy would become more pointed, and he would begin to incorporate them into his more general strategy of negative campaigning. Reagan's tactic was to continually urge voters to question the president's competence on all major policy issues.

Meanwhile, Reagan and Bush continued to trade electoral punches. On May 3, Reagan won the Texas primary with 51 percent of the vote to Bush's 47.4. Three days later, Bush won the District of Columbia election with 66.1 percent of the vote, while Reagan barely scored in that electoral unit. Reagan, however, was the big winner elsewhere that day, defeating Bush, Anderson, and the rest of the field in Indiana, North Carolina, Tennessee, and South Carolina.

As Reagan accumulated victories, Bush continued to focus his attack on Reagan's tax-cut plan. During a May 11 campaign stop in Michigan, Bush told his audience that Reagan's plan "may sound like a blueprint for paradise, but in my opinion it is a blueprint for economic chaos." The quote became part of the next day's *New York Times* headline: "Bush Says Reagan's Plan Would Be 'Economic Chaos.'"[99]

But Bush's challenge was not attracting voters to his base. On May 13, Reagan scored clear victories in Maryland and Nebraska. He also won the Oregon primary seven days later, but ceded Michigan to Bush, who carried 57.5 percent of the vote to Reagan's 31.8. The Oregon and Michigan primaries left Reagan with approximately 992 delegate votes—just six short of what he needed to win his party's nomination.[100] Acknowledging Reagan's momentum, on May 26 Bush asked his supporters to back Reagan and effectively ceased active campaigning. He did not make his withdrawal official, however, because he was still hoping to receive federal funds to pay down his campaign debt.

Needless to say, Reagan won all of the remaining primaries on May 27 and June 3, sending him into the Republican convention as the GOP's presumptive nominee.

Bush's campaign statements suggest that he understood Reagan's heresthetical advantage: the governor had fastened onto a set of economic arguments that any opponent would need to undermine if he were to undo the growing Reagan coalition. In response, Bush relied on criticism of Reagan's economic plan, which he memorably labeled "voodoo economics."[101] Yet George Bush failed to grasp that his rhetorical strategy, appealing as it was to his moderate Republican base, was unlikely to attract Republicans from the right or socially conservative Democrats in the center. Whereas Reagan not only shared socially conservative Democrats' views on abortion and school prayer but was also able to assure them that GOP economic policies wouldn't hurt them, Bush had nothing compelling to offer conservatives of either party. Rather than presenting an alternative plan or counterargument to Reagan's heresthetic, Bush relied primarily on a negative campaign strategy of criticizing Reagan's economic logic.

Nor did Bush offer voters a clear alternative foreign policy. In advocating indirect American aid for the anti-Soviet Afghan rebels in January 1980, the Texan was voicing the same idea that Reagan had been endorsing.[102] Reagan advocated that "we ought to be funneling weapons through [Pakistan] that can be delivered to those freedom fighters in Afghanistan to fight for their own freedom. . . . I think there's nothing wrong with giving weapons to a free people to defend their freedom." Several days later, Reagan proposed renewing arms sales to Pakistan "with full knowledge that some of the weapons will find their way across the border to the freedom fighters in Afghanistan."[103]

Bush's main criticism of Reagan's foreign policy amounted to a negative attack: "I've had experience in foreign policy, and he hasn't," he mocked.[104] But Reagan was working to persuade voters of the comprehensiveness of his agenda, which included both a robust foreign policy based on peace through increased defense spending and an economic program that promised those defense expenditures would neither stimulate inflation nor reduce social spending.

Reagan's other challengers ran into difficulties similar to Bush's. Crane, for example, had adopted a peace-through-strength message that echoed Reagan's attack on Ford four years earlier. Crane's statement in New Hampshire on February 20 could have been Reagan's in 1976: "I think we should keep in mind that George Washington gave us the soundest counsel and it's been counsel handed down since the ancient Greeks: that those who desire peace should prepare for war."[105] The problem was that Reagan did Reagan better than anyone ever could. Consistent with the dominance principle, Reagan had already established his ownership of the peace-through-strength idea. The other challengers could endorse the principle and respect the rhetoric associated with it, but through sheer effort—his seizure of the conservative mantle after Nixon's victories in 1968 and 1972; his tireless radio addresses, newspaper columns, and speeches throughout the late 1970s; and his full-scale challenge to Ford in 1976—Reagan had irrevocably identified himself with "peace through strength."

By 1980, Reagan had also refined his message of social conservatism. Thus, Crane's support for a school prayer bill endorsed by influential evangelicals including Jim Bakker, Jerry Falwell, James Robinson, and Pat Robertson was equally matched by Reagan's bid for the religious Right. While campaigning in California, Reagan reassured his born-again supporters: "[T]here are people who want to take the 'In God We Trust' off our money. I don't know of a time when we needed it more. . . . This nation is hungry for a spiritual revival."[106] The audience's enthusiasm left no doubt: Reagan was in rhetorical command of the religious Right.

Candidates such as Crane and Connally could not mount effective challenges to Reagan from the right, and Bush was unable to build on his natural support from the middle. All three, as well as the various lesser candidates, were running rhetorical campaigns. Yet even in this dimension Reagan proved the superior actor. His talents as a public speaker enabled him to turn the weapon of rhetoric against those who had no other device on which to rely. His rhetorical skills also effectively defended his heresthetical grand plan from criticism. No other Republican contender was better able to convince voters that he could deliver wealth and security for all.

Anderson was gaining some strength among liberal Republicans and Democrats, but it was not clear that this support amounted to a net loss for Reagan. The governor's heresthetical message was directed at a wing of the Democratic Party different from the one that found Anderson appealing.

Kennedy, on the other hand, posed a substantial challenge to Carter during the primaries. Although he only won 10 primaries to Carter's 24, by staying in the race until the Democratic convention in mid-August, he pushed Carter steadily to the left at the very time that the president was being pulled to the right by Reagan's challenge to the conservative center.

The Massachusetts senator's presidential campaign was clearly a liberal challenge to Carter's policies. His response to the energy crisis included rationing gas at the level of 11 gallons per week for each licensed driver for three years, after which the quantity would be increased to 14 gallons per week. He opposed lifting oil price controls and wanted to phase out the use of nuclear power plants. On the latter issue, Carter supported some development of nuclear energy.[107]

Sharp criticism of Carter's performance on the economy, foreign policy, and defense was another focus of Kennedy's campaign. He called the president's proposal to combat inflation "too little, too late, and too unfair," and he blamed the Carter administration for the Iranian hostage crisis. The senator also called for a tougher stand on the Soviet Union in the wake of its invasion of Afghanistan.[108] These negative rhetorical attacks did not constitute an alternative or comprehensive plan on domestic or foreign policy.

To be sure, Kennedy's rhetorical campaigning and his unmistakable embrace of liberal causes and policies led to endorsements by some opinion makers on the liberal wing of the Democratic Party. For instance, Congresswoman Bella Abzug (D-NY) and Gloria Steinem, a leading women's rights activist, supported his candidacy.[109] Such endorsements, however, did not mark a complete erosion of Carter's liberal base. The Rev. Martin Luther King, Sr., and Andrew Young,

Carter's first ambassador to the United Nations, came forward to declare their support for the president's renomination bid.[110]

The Carter campaign was clearly worried about Kennedy's ability to undermine their candidate with the voters he badly needed. But Kennedy's rhetorical campaign never proved to be an overwhelmingly attractive alternative to Carter's policies and rhetorical stance.

Like Reagan, Carter ended the primary season as his party's clear front-runner. By early June, Carter had tallied 1,964 delegate votes, almost 300 more than the 1,666 needed to guarantee him the Democratic nomination.[111] The incumbent had won a total of 51.2 percent of the primary vote, while Kennedy, his closest competitor, had only 37.1 percent. In 1856, Franklin Pierce became the only president not to be renominated by his party. Despite the substantial odds, the Massachusetts senator was determined to fight all the way to the convention, where he and Carter would have to wage a heated battle for the liberal vote.

5

Reshaping the Domestic and International Landscape

Part Two

The 1980 Presidential Election

The rivalry for the White House took on its final form immediately after the last primary. The conventions were still more than a month away, but it was already clear that Carter and Reagan would represent their parties, while Anderson seemed determined to stay in the race until the end. The politicking that ensued during the intense campaigning of late 1980 demonstrates in the starkest terms what happens when rhetoric runs up against heresthetic.

Rival Strategy Documents: June 1980

Pat Caddell and Richard Wirthlin played important roles in the 1976 and 1980 presidential campaigns of Jimmy Carter and Ronald Reagan. These two pollsters and strategists authored strategy documents for their candidates after the primaries ended in June, and watched closely as the campaigns implemented their strategies in the months that followed. Meanwhile, David Garth, a media specialist, and others were helping Anderson to make the transition from GOP contender to an independent candidacy.

Surveys revealed that Reagan was substantially ahead of Carter after the primaries. In a Gallup Poll presidential trial heat conducted in late June, 41 percent of registered voters surveyed said they would select Carter as president, while 46 percent chose Reagan. Fully 58 percent of those surveyed disapproved of Carter's job performance.[1] Despite these promising indicators, Wirthlin advised Reagan and his staff to prepare for a real fight: to capture "must win" states they had to develop an issue package that would create and sustain a diverse coalition of voters.

To capture the presidency, a candidate must win 270 of the total 538 electoral votes. Wirthlin had Reagan leading in the East and the West, although his western advantage was vulnerable to a challenge from Anderson. Concerned as he was about the Anderson threat, Wirthlin felt that the third-party candidate took a bigger bite of the Carter vote than he did of Reagan's. The major-party battle would be closer in the South and the Midwest, however, and Reagan might have to split the vote with Carter in those regions. Then Wirthlin analyzed the situation in small, medium, and large electoral states.[2]

The seven states with 20 or more electoral votes—California, Illinois, Texas, Ohio, Pennsylvania, New York, and Michigan—held a total of 211 votes, of which Reagan needed a minimum of 107 according to Wirthlin's calculations. Victories in California, Illinois, and at least two of the other four would lock up 117 electoral votes for Reagan. But California was the only safe bet in this group according to Wirthlin, whereas both New York and Michigan might have to be written off.

The states in the medium-size category (those with 10 or more electoral votes) controlled a total of 161 votes, with the top four—Indiana, Wisconsin, Virginia, and New Jersey—accounting for 53. In order to obtain the 82 electoral votes he needed from this group, Reagan would have to win not only all of these four, but also at least three of the others, Missouri, Tennessee, Florida, and Maryland. Wirthlin considered Wisconsin and New Jersey to be uncertain, at best, however, and warned that Reagan's lack of a strong base in this category would require him to make up the electoral difference from among large and small states.

Reagan also needed at least 84 of the 166 electoral votes controlled by small states (those with nine or fewer electoral votes). A Reagan victory in Idaho, South Dakota, Wyoming, Vermont, Utah, Nebraska,

North Dakota, New Hampshire, Kansas, Montana, New Mexico, Nevada, Arizona, Oregon, Alaska, and Iowa, and three of the four following states—Colorado, Washington, Maine, and Connecticut— would give him the electoral votes he needed in this category.

Wirthlin hoped that Reagan would garner more than the minimum from each group. His "best coalition of states" would give Reagan 149 electoral votes from large states, 62 from medium states, and 91 from small states, for a total of 302 and a 32-vote margin of victory. A broad coalition, held together by a compelling message, would be necessary to achieve this ambitious goal.

Reagan's pollster reported that 30 percent of voters identified themselves as Republican, 51 percent as Democrat, and 19 percent as independent. In addition to traditional Republicans, weak Republicans, and ticket-splitters, Wirthlin suggested that the Reagan campaign target "metropolitan, blue collar, ethnics," those in "rural areas in the non-south," and "disaffected white Southern Protestant voter[s] to reinforce our foothold in the South."

Wirthlin also urged the targeting of single-issue voters—conservative Republicans who were staunchly opposed to abortion, the Equal Rights Amendment, the Panama Canal treaties, or gun control. These voters were an important element of Reagan's base, and could be kept in his camp through the deployment of "appropriate messages." However, Wirthlin discouraged the campaign from relying on these ideological issues again, as it had done in 1976, believing that they were no longer the subject of widespread voter interest in 1980.

Instead, convinced that the American economy was the main issue in the 1980 race, Wirthlin advised putting forth "a comprehensive, credible, proprietary economic program." He added, "It must be identified as the Reagan plan and must never be referenced in whole or in part to Jack Kemp's economics." The Reagan economic plan would need to be publicized as soon as possible so that Carter would not be able to undercut it before the fall campaigning got under way. Credibility could be established by obtaining endorsements of the plan by some of the nation's leading economists.

Meanwhile, Reagan's foreign and defense policy should be based around a peace plan to avoid the perception that a Reagan presidency "would increase rather than decrease the chances of war." Although Wirthlin did not suggest emphasizing specific defense issues, he noted the importance of assuring voters that the United States could effectively manage the costs of increased defense spending. After all, Reagan had already told voters that guns-versus-butter trade-offs had no place in his defense and economic policies.

Carter's man, Pat Caddell, took a much more pessimistic position in a draft of an election strategy he wrote. The task that lay ahead of the Carter campaign was staggering, he wrote: "President Carter faces an extremely difficult reelection. Struggling against a persistent defeated primary challenger [Ted Kennedy], we face a united Republican party with a challenger posed to our right attempting to crowd our center. To our left, we face an Independent candidacy raiding our unhappy left leaning base and threatening the key electoral vote rich industrial belt. . . . A two front assault is of great concern."[3]

The Anderson and Reagan challenges were not Carter's only problems. Caddell was blunt: "Except for a weakened South, Carter has no real base, particularly when it comes to Democratic constituencies. Little enthusiasm." In effect, Caddell concluded that the absence of a sound base was rooted in the same problem Carter had encountered in the 1976 election, when he won with a mere 50.1 percent of the popular vote and 297 electoral votes to Ford's 48.0 percent and 240 electoral votes. Nonwhites had given Carter 85 percent of their vote in 1976, but they were the only segment of society to have supported him in such large numbers. Support from Jews, liberals, and urban Catholics had helped put the Georgia Democrat over the top, but Ford had outperformed him among independents and suburban Catholics. "In short," Caddell advised, "we must have essentially a Southern strategy *and* a Northern blue collar, liberal, suburban strategy. Blacks and Catholics become essential, Jews and Browns important."

Implicit in this summary was a recognition that Carter faced the same regional problems in 1980 that had almost cost him the 1976 race. In the 1980 primaries, Caddell recalled, "Carter basically repeated his 1976 performance—winning the South, doing well in the Midwest and being defeated decisively in the Atlantic Eastern states and California." In short, his electoral prospects had eroded during his four years in the White House.

Carter's pollster complained that the campaign was also repeating one of its worst 1976 errors by failing to put forward a strategic message. He wrote, "In 1976 neither side set the definition [of the election]—in fact neither side was all that cognizant of the framework." He added, "At the moment, the 1980 campaign is adrift—searching for a definition."

Caddell exhorted his colleagues to undertake "conceptual strategies" and eschew negative campaigning. At the same time, he encouraged the campaign's exploitation of mistakes made by the Anderson and Reagan campaigns, and urged the Carter team to attack Reagan's proposals, especially his tax reduction plan: "In his [Reagan's] record and his campaign," Caddell advised, "he is open to assault on a host of positions and ideas not the least of which is Kemp/Roth. Enough concern can be raised over these to inflict substantial damage." A Republican strategist was quoted in the *Wall Street Journal* in May 1980 as saying, "Politicians have seen that negative works, and most will have a go at it."[4]

The Rose Garden strategy was the final element in Caddell's plan. Carter was urged to run on his record of managing the United States in an uncertain international environment rocked by successive energy crises and the Iranian hostage standoff, among other problems. Instead of offering a conceptual strategy and definition for Carter's 1980 bid, Caddell was largely outlining rhetorical measures.

Caddell was confident that the Reagan camp would not put forth a conceptual strategy. He surmised, "It is unlikely Reagan will attempt the effort [of defining the election] for I don't think he or his people conceptually understand the process. This is our opportunity."

The Carter camp's opportunity depended on carrying the maximum number of states. Of the South's 139 electoral votes, Carter would need 110, along with 66 votes from small and medium states, including Hawaii, 19 electoral votes from Wisconsin and Connecticut, 27 from Pennsylvania, either New York's 41 or California's 45 votes, and either Iowa's eight or Washington's nine votes. This combination would yield 271 total electoral votes (or 276 if Carter took California instead of New York and Washington instead of Iowa). In either case, the incumbent would barely make it over the finish line.

With the race so close, the Midwest and Northeast were particularly coveted by both pollsters, and their respective candidates would devote much attention to these regions in the months ahead, albeit with very different appeals.

Anderson undertook a "Midwest strategy" as soon as he launched his campaign on June 8, 1979. He and his aides recognized that his best chance to make a respectable showing in the Republican primaries lay in the Midwest and the Northeast: if their candidate was unable to make a strong showing in these regions, he was unlikely to succeed anywhere else. As one of Anderson's strategists reminded him in a July 1979 memo:

> The Midwest is not only your home, but the home of the Party
> and its ideals. . . . The strength of the Midwestern commitment
> to moderate Republicanism has been shown in the area in its
> recent elections. The area is central not only geographically, but
> emotionally as well. Issues and solutions, which are accepted in
> the Midwest will have a large degree of acceptability throughout
> the U.S.

The memo identified Michigan and Ohio as essential components in
this strategy, but also urged what its author called "geographic concentration" in other parts of the Midwest and some New England
states. In addition to Michigan and Ohio, the list included New Hampshire, Illinois, Massachusetts, Wisconsin, Minnesota, Iowa, Connecticut, Vermont, Indiana, and Missouri.

The memo also suggested that Anderson forgo a southern strategy
or any attempt to focus on southern delegates: "We must be careful
that our terminology is not equated with the old Southern Strategy,
which was perceived as a sort of immoral plan to capitalize on the
weaknesses of our electoral system. Accordingly, we should not play up
the strength of 457 delegates."[5]

Another memo by the same strategist, issued just a few weeks earlier, had recommended that Anderson eschew negative campaigning in
favor of an upbeat tone. Sounding like Ronald Reagan, the strategist
suggested:

> Let's not talk to the American people about sacrifice and belt
> tightening; they are sick of it. Ours is a society of opportunity not
> limitation. If there is something that must be done the American
> people will do it. . . . We can and should inspire the people to
> meet today's responsibilities and tomorrow's obligations, but
> material martyrdom has never been a part of the American
> ethic.[6]

It is intriguing to wonder how Anderson might have fared if he had
taken this advice and chosen to compete with Reagan for the "politics
of more" space that the governor was carving out for himself. Instead,
the Illinois congressman's campaign more closely resembled Carter's,
warning that the nation would have to make sacrifices in order to
revive the economy, and that defense spending and other government
outlays would have to be cut back.

In April 1980, the month that Anderson announced as an independent, media specialist David Garth officially joined the Anderson campaign as its chief strategist. Garth wanted Anderson to capture traditional Democratic voters (blacks, Jews, city dwellers, and laborers) and to build upon Anderson's growing appeal among young professionals and liberal Republicans,[7] two groups that both Carter and Reagan would need in order to win.

Garth warned that the only way to win these blocs over was through caution. He advised Anderson to refrain from making any major policy pronouncements or accepting most national media requests in order to avoid peaking before the fall campaign began. At the same time, he encouraged Anderson to grant local interviews as he campaigned aggressively throughout the country. Garth advised a negative campaign against Anderson's two major contenders, but suggested that the attacks should be couched in broad terms that were consistent with the congressman's known positions on the issues. Garth did put his stamp on the campaign, but as Mark Bisnow, one of Anderson's closest advisers in the late 1970s, observed, "Ultimately Anderson had too independent a will to be muzzled."[8]

By Labor Day, it was clear to Garth that his strategy of carefully avoiding the major policy issues had failed to generate much momentum for Anderson's candidacy. Instead, Anderson began discussing specifics. He spoke out against the MX missile and in favor of federal budget cuts and a gas tax. Like Carter, he called for national sacrifice. In essence, he had reverted to the positions he had endorsed as a Republican presidential candidate earlier in the year without ever having run the kind of positive campaign that his adviser had suggested to him over the course of the summer. As Bisnow noted, once the congressman began repeating his original positions, many of his supporters reluctantly concluded that Anderson could not win.[9]

Jimmy Carter and Race Relations: July 4, 1980

Reagan declined an invitation to speak at the NAACP convention in Miami on July 4, 1980, due to a scheduling problem. Carter, who did attend, took the opportunity to get in a jab at Reagan: "As you can see, I did not have any trouble accepting my invitation to come to the NAACP convention." He reviewed his record of appointing minorities and women to the federal bench and discussed plans to revitalize cities and provide training and jobs for young people. Carter reminded his audience that "in Zimbabwe we stood firm for majority rule. . . . Zimbabwe is now free, democratic, and independent." He also reaffirmed the United States' commitment to defeat what he called Iranian terrorism.[10]

Reagan's absence was an easy target, but Carter's swipe did not automatically convince the convention-goers that he was the best candidate on race issues. As the *New York Times* reported the next day, "The President was warmly applauded by the 1,000 delegates and guests, but his reception was substantially less enthusiastic than the one given earlier this week to his opponent for the Democratic Presidential nomination, Senator Edward M. Kennedy of Massachusetts."[11]

Carter clearly enjoyed better standing among black voters than Reagan did, but this was hardly enough. The president's rhetorical message to the NAACP had the characteristic ring of pessimism:

> I cannot promise you everything will be better from this moment forward, that there will be no more sacrifice, because there will; no more delay in meeting treasured goals, because there's going to be delay. And I will not lie to you and say that all is right in the world, because it's not, or all right in our Nation, because it's not. . . . So, I just want to tell it to you straight. This is a time of controversy. This is a time of impatience. This is a time of pain. This is a time of struggle. But most of all, this is a time of making decisions.

Carter's sober message was the antithesis of Reagan's optimism. Loyal Democrats that so many of them were, African-Americans would deliver the majority of their votes to Carter on Election Day. But his message of sacrifice and national suffering did not help him win the hearts—or votes—of those Democrats who were frustrated with the candidate or his party.

Reagan's Acceptance Speech: July 17, 1980

As Michael Malbin has noted, "Ronald Reagan had three strategic goals for the Republican convention. . . . He wanted to maintain the enthusiasm of the conservative supporters who won him the nomination. He wanted to reach out to centrist and moderate Republicans, particularly to white-collar suburbanites who might be thinking about voting for independent candidate John Anderson. Finally, he wanted to build on his appeal to normally Democratic blue-collar workers."[12] Reagan's acceptance speech on July 17 was the most precise expression of these aspirations to date.

The Republican presidential nominee told the various constituencies that his party would help "build a new consensus with all those across the land who share a community of values embodied" in the campaign theme of "family, work, neighborhood, peace, and freedom." The centrist Reagan emerged: "As president, I will establish a liaison with the 50 governors to encourage them to eliminate, where it exists, discrimination against women." Meanwhile, he reassured his base by emphasizing his belief that reductions in taxes (through his plan to cut taxes by 30 percent over a three-year period) and the size of government, accompanied by the deregulation and private development of natural resources would help the United States overcome weaknesses in its current defense, economic, and energy policies. But Reagan's masterstroke was to present himself as a man of peace, committed to negotiations with the Soviet Union:

> Of all the objectives we seek, first and foremost is the establishment of lasting world peace. We must always stand ready to negotiate in good faith, ready to pursue any reasonable avenue that holds forth the promise of lessening tensions and furthering the prospects of peace. But let our friends and those who may wish us ill take note: the United States has an obligation to its citizens and to the people of the world never to let those who would destroy freedom dictate the future course of human life on this planet. I would regard my election as proof that we have renewed our resolve to preserve world peace and freedom.

Reagan was deploying a rhetorical arsenal that he had not yet amassed during the 1968 and 1976 Republican presidential contests. Carter would attempt to portray Reagan as a dangerous warmonger in the months ahead, but Reagan continued to tell voters that they should separate his strategy of rearmament from his objective of mutual cooperation with the Soviet Union—this was the heart of his interpretation of the conservative slogan "peace through strength."

Reagan, Race Relations, and
the South: August 3, 1980

The 1980 campaign raised the familiar issues of race, rights, and the South, but somewhat less empathically than had the 1968 race, when southerners controlled a deciding share of the delegates to the Republican Party's convention. Nonetheless, the South could not be discounted in 1980. Dick Wirthlin had suggested that Reagan might have to write off the region, yet at the same time recommended a campaign premised on the belief that no section of the country should be conceded to Carter. Thus it was no surprise that Reagan's first major campaign trip after the convention took him southward.

The Neshoba County Fair in Philadelphia, Mississippi, had a long tradition of hosting stump speeches, but Reagan's appearance marked the first visit from a presidential candidate. Reagan reiterated his most familiar campaign themes: Carter's economic policies had fueled inflation, and the United States was no longer respected by its enemies.

But the governor also made a number of rhetorical appeals to the conservative base—an essential tactic in a region where every state except Virginia had delivered its electoral votes to Carter four years earlier. In the sweltering Mississippi heat, Reagan told the crowd of listeners, "I believe in states' rights; I believe in people doing as much as they can at the private level." If elected president, Reagan promised, he would "restore to states and local governments the power that properly belongs to them."[13]

His message was enthusiastically received by his Mississippi audience, but it was not popular with all southerners. Reverend Andrew Young, former ambassador to the United Nations and a civil rights activist, wrote a *Washington Post* opinion essay about Reagan's remarks in which he warned that "code words like 'states' rights' and symbolic places like Philadelphia, Miss., leave me cold." Young was of course referring to the 1964 murders of civil rights workers James Chaney, Andrew Goodman, and Michael Schwerner in that Mississippi town. "Is Reagan saying that he intends to do everything he can to turn the clock back to the Mississippi justice of 1964?" he asked. "Do the powers of the state and local governments include the right to end the voting right of black citizens?"[14]

Reagan had been vying for the black vote throughout the campaign. His appearance in Mississippi did little for this cause, however—especially given that his campaign had declined an invitation to appear at the NAACP convention.

Two days after his speech at the Neshoba County Fair, Reagan was courting black votes at the Urban League convention in New York. This time he dropped any mention of states' rights, instead telling the audience, "I am committed to the protection and enforcement of the civil rights of black Americans. This commitment is interwoven into every phase of the programs I will propose." As an example of his commitment, Reagan outlined a plan to develop "enterprise zones" for urban renewal.[15]

His speech at the Neshoba Fair notwithstanding, Reagan's campaign rhetoric that fall was not dominated by code words. Instead, he relied on appeals to his economic program and its relationship to national defense.

The Democratic Convention and Carter's Acceptance Speech: August 11 to August 14, 1980

Carter's renomination was essentially assured when he arrived at the Democratic National Convention in New York on August 13. This is not to say the race was unproblematic, however. The Carter-Kennedy battle had been acrimonious and hard fought, and Kennedy would make his mark on the party's platform before the convention's end, exhorting Democrats to institute a new jobs-creation package. But the senator would also endorse Carter and call for the Democratic Party to unify and defeat Ronald Reagan.

Carter's acceptance speech, delivered on August 14, reflected the distinctly different directions in which the two parties were headed: "This election is a stark choice between two men, two parties, two sharply different pictures of what America is and what the world is, but it's more than that—it's a choice between two futures." The president contrasted his commitment to international cooperation with his opponent's policies, which, he argued, would lead to "the risk of international confrontation, the risk of an uncontrollable, unaffordable, and unwinnable nuclear arms race."

The president also spoke of his administration's "economic renewal program for the 1980's," declaring that it "will meet our immediate need for jobs and attack the very same, long-range problem that caused unemployment and inflation in the first place. It'll move America simultaneously toward our five great economic goals—lower inflation, better productivity, revitalization of American industry, energy security, and jobs." He claimed that his return to office would produce alternative sources of domestic energy and a transportation system that would allow American coal to compete with OPEC oil. Carter vowed he would support the technology and communications industries, expand job opportunities through training programs and investment in new energy-efficient homes and vehicles, and encourage investment in regions and communities struggling with unemployment.

But these economic promises aside, Carter failed to present a powerful economic agenda. Instead, he devoted his energy to attacking Reagan's platform, criticizing his promise to provide both guns and butter:

> They call it Reagan-Kemp-Roth. I call it a free lunch that Americans cannot afford. The Republican tax program offers rebates to the rich, deprivation for the poor, and fierce inflation for all of us. . . . Along with this gigantic tax cut, the new Republican leaders promise to protect retirement and health programs and to have massive increases in defense spending—and they claim they can balance the budget. If they are serious about these promises, and they say they are, then a close analysis shows that the entire rest of the Government would have to be abolished, everything from education to farm programs, from the G.I. bill to the night watchman at the Lincoln Memorial—and their budget would still be in the red.

Carter went on to promise equal opportunity and equal rights for all, and decry the Republican Party's record on social justice. The president also claimed his party had "reversed the Republican decline in defense." Unlike Reagan's speech, Carter's did not promise a rapid return to prosperity. Instead, he highlighted one of the distinguishing themes of his campaign: the need for sacrifice. Reagan's vision was "a make-believe world," Carter declared, which entailed "no hard choices, no sacrifice, no tough decisions—it sounds too good to be true, and it is." He added: "If we succumb to a dream world then we'll wake up to a nightmare. But if we start with reality and fight to make our dreams a reality, then Americans will have a good life, a life of meaning and purpose in a nation that's strong and secure."[16]

The president's strong performance at the convention notwithstanding, Patrick Caddell remained concerned. In an August 18 memo to the president, the pollster bluntly said: "Re-election is not something to be gambled. Risks ought to be minimized. However, your case is quite different. *You suffer because you are held to have no vision, no grand plan.* . . . To date you have shown no inclination in this direction. You have balked at second term agenda discussions, turning to us for campaign themes instead. Frankly, you are not going to get one from your Domestic Council or OMB. If you want to move, now is the time, while you're riding a comeback of sorts."[17]

The fall presidential campaign was a few weeks away, and the president had no major campaign themes in place. Caddell offered some—Carter's leadership ability, especially on issues on peace, human rights, and nuclear weapons; and his basic integrity and strong values. These were rhetorical messages, not the grand plan Caddell suggested was missing from the campaign. Reagan's message, however, was largely developed and well rehearsed.

On the Presidential Campaign Trail: August 15 to September 20, 1980

Rival Social Policies

Voters considered national defense and the economy as the main issues on which to evaluate presidential candidates in 1980. Social policies were also important to the electorate, of course, but none of the candidates provided novel approaches to pressing social issues or presented views that fundamentally enhanced their standing with a broad cross-section of voters.

The 1980 Democratic platform addressed the highly charged issue of abortion by stating, "The Democratic Party supports the 1973 Supreme Court decision on abortion rights as the law of the land and opposes any constitutional amendment to restrict or overturn that decision."[18] Carter was not in complete accord with this official position, as he opposed demands for expanded federal support for abortion services. The ACLU charged that the president had failed to implement his pledge to find alternatives to abortion.[19] Yet Carter scored high marks on other issues related to women. He supported the Equal Rights Amendment and had a solid record of appointing women and minorities to judicial posts and executive positions within his administration. The Democratic Party's 1980 platform proclaimed that "of the six women who have served in Cabinet positions, three have been Carter appointees. More women, Blacks and Hispanics have been appointed to senior government positions than during any other Administration in history." It was a record that neither Anderson nor Reagan could challenge. The president's performance on social issues disappointed some liberal and conservative Democrats, but it was generally well received, and Carter's rhetorical strategy was to campaign on the record he had built while in the White House.

Carter also appeared to take advantage of the Rose Garden effect when introducing policies that favored various sectors of society he was courting. For instance, the *New York Times* reminded its readers that Carter's September 30 announcement that he was relaxing environmental standards and raising import restrictions for the steel industry was geared toward voters in Illinois, Indiana, Michigan, Minnesota, Pennsylvania, and Ohio, key states in the upcoming election.[20]

Reagan's appeals on social issues were directed as much at conservative Democrats—union members and the working class, for example—as they were toward his own party. A number of Republican strategists believed, for example, that the governor's abortion stance would persuade some conservative Democrats to vote for their candidate.[21] "Very simply," Reagan wrote in a letter dated October 11, 1979, "my feeling is that an abortion is the taking of a human life and that can only be justified or excused in our society as defense of the mother's life."[22] Reagan's position was reflected in the 1980 Republican platform, which he endorsed: "[W]e affirm our support of a constitutional amendment to restore protection of the right to life for unborn children. We also support the Congressional efforts to restrict the use of taxpayers' dollars for abortion."[23] Reagan's long-standing and well-known posture on this issue carried the potential to garner votes from the conservative segment of the Democratic Party. Yet the abortion issue was not a dominant theme of his campaign, and Reagan stated that, if elected president, he would not use it as a criterion in making judicial appointments.[24]

Similarly, although Reagan did not attempt to hide or make light of his opposition to the Equal Rights Amendment, he did not make it a central issue while he was on the hustings. And during the platform fight on the ERA at the Republican convention in Detroit, he drafted a carefully worded letter expressing the position he had taken throughout his presidential campaign. "I am for equal rights and have a record to substantiate that claim," Reagan said, in reference to legislation he had supported as governor of California. He continued: "An amendment puts the matter in the hands of the courts and means years of court cases before a body of case law is established."[25] During the campaign, he promised that if he became president he would place a woman on the Supreme Court.[26]

In an August 22 speech in Dallas, Reagan campaigned for the vote of the newly emerging religious Right. Reagan told evangelical Christians, "I want you to know I endorse you and what you are doing. Religious America is awakening, perhaps just in time for our country's sake." But speaking in Virginia in early October, he expressed his belief in the importance of the separation of church and state.[27] In the full range of policy domains—the economy, defense, social policy, and so on—Reagan was seeking to command the center, albeit from a rightward tilt. He had become adroit at broadening his appeal by strategically adapting his rhetoric for the audience he was targeting.

It could be argued that the rhetorical refinement was less apparent in Reagan's earlier campaigns because he had never advanced beyond the primaries, where candidates tend to play to their natural bases. But the heresthetical beauty of what Reagan was doing is that even when he adapted his words, his philosophical themes remained consistent.

Anderson's appeals on social issues were not politically distinct. The gulf did not appear to be very wide between him and Carter on key social issues. Anderson was a stronger pro-choice advocate than Carter was, but both of them supported the ERA and gun control.[28]

All three candidates were known as religious Christians and thus they had the opportunity to be favored by faith-based communities. Of them all, Carter was the most favored candidate among evangelical Christians, according to a Gallup Poll report.[29]

Rival Defense and Foreign Policies

Throughout the presidential campaign, Carter both sought to hold his left flank and strengthen his position among moderate and conservative Democrats. He leaned toward the latter as he made appeals on defense and foreign policy. Speaking before the American Legion convention in Boston on August 21, the president responded to Reagan's attacks on his defense policy and even adopted rhetoric that seemed to echo Reagan's "peace through strength" message. In his stump speeches and radio commentaries, Reagan had been strongly critical of Carter's controversial decision to halt production of the B-1 bomber. The president told the Legionnaires that instead of B-1 bombers he was developing cruise missiles because "they represent a far more effective deterrent." Among the foreign policy goals he outlined was the prevention of war "through the assurance of our nation's strength and our nation's will."[30]

Carter asserted that the U.S. nuclear deterrent was adequate and that U.S. security could be ensured by modernizing the cruise missile, MX missile, and the Trident system; developing a rapid deployment force for various contingencies, especially in the Persian Gulf region; and negotiating nuclear arms control treaties with the Soviet Union.[31] He vowed to oversee "a steady, predictable, well-planned, orderly increase" in defense spending.[32] This shift toward a rearmament-oriented defense policy was due in no small measure to the Soviet invasion of Afghanistan and the mounting list of international crises (such as the Ogaden War of 1978) that the Carter administration came to view through a superpower lens. Furthermore, Democrats in Congress, such as Senator Sam Nunn (D-GA), had been exerting pressure on the president for increased defense spending and a more robust military posture—even before the Soviets invaded Afghanistan in December 1979.[33]

The president's shifts, then, were largely reactive. His strategic outlook remained intact, and this was evident even as specific policy decisions suggested a hardening of his position. He argued that a continuation of traditional containment, including especially nuclear arms control negotiations, would make the United States safe and war less likely. The essence of Carter's campaign was that he was running on his record. In other words, in every policy domain, including defense, Carter was running a rhetorical campaign.

Sometimes the Carter administration presented evidence of its moves in a more hawkish direction on defense matters. Presidential Directive 59 is a prime example. Approved by President Carter on July 25, 1980, the directive mandated the development of plans for counterforce strikes in the event of a nuclear war with the Soviet Union. PD-59 was classified, but the substance of the directive, which was made public, was reviewed by Secretary of Defense Harold Brown in his speech at the Naval War College on August 20.[34] Even though PD-59 was an extension of National Security Decision Memorandum 242 (also called the Schlesinger Doctrine) of 1974, which also planned for targeting U.S. nuclear weapons at Soviet military forces, some scholars have interpreted it in electoral terms. Political scientist Daniel Wirls has described PD-59 as "President Carter's eleventh-hour hawkish revision of American declaratory nuclear strategy" signed in the midst of the presidential campaign.[35] Historian Walter LaFeber has interpreted the policy as an attempt "to outflank the Republican nominee, Ronald Reagan, from the right—a mission impossible."[36]

It was an impossible mission because, as Wirls has observed, it simultaneously "showed Republicans that their political message had struck a sympathetic public chord" and was more fodder for the growing peace movement, which for a couple of years had being saying that President Carter had moved to the right on defense.[37] The hardening of the Carter administration's posture on defense was not producing domestic political dividends.

PD-59 represented deep thinking by a range of experts. Hank Cooper, a Republican scientist who was invited to work on the directive, recalls that "because of the bipartisan and broad way the Carter administration had pursed the Nuclear Targeting Policy Review within the entire nuclear/strategic community," Reagan's postelection strategic modernization program, reflected in National Security Decision Directive 13, included the core elements of PD-59.[38] President Carter's defense policy in 1979 and 1980 was not merely a response to electoral pressure. The public revelation of defense policies like PD-59, however, had the appearance of a president on the run and a president that was moving in the policy direction of his Republican opponent.

The revelation about the Stealth bomber program had a similar fate. Reports surfaced in print media and television news that the Carter administration had instituted a program to develop stealth weapons. An administration official was quoted in the *Washington Post* on August 14 as saying, "[Y]ou're going to hear about these new bomber breakthroughs sooner or later in this campaign."[39] On August 22, Brown confirmed the existence of the weapons program but denied that the Carter administration was trying to thwart criticism from the Republican Party and Ronald Reagan.[40] Richard V. Allen persuaded Reagan to "deliver [an] immediate counterpunch," which he did during a speech in Jacksonville, Florida, on September 4.[41] Reagan deemed the revelation as an attempt to help "Mr. Carter's troubled campaign" and charged the secretary of defense with making public "one of the nation's most closely held military secrets in a transparent effort to divert attention from the Administration's dismal defense record."[42] President Ford and other Republican leaders made similar statements.[43] The Republican response was not unexpected, but the exchange between the two sides highlighted how, in portraying itself as tough and resolved on national security, the Carter administration and the campaign were struggling to find a distinct policy definition on national defense, one of the most important issues for voters in 1980. The presidential election was only a few months away, and the Carter campaign had not found a unique appeal on national security.

While Carter labored to appear strong on defense, Reagan presented a more muted version of his own foreign policy and defense plans. Speaking at a Veterans of Foreign Wars gathering in Chicago on August 18, he expressed in peaceful terms his call for a military buildup: "Actually, I've called for whatever it takes to be so strong that no other nation will dare violate the peace. . . . World peace must be our number one priority. It is the first task of statecraft to preserve peace so that brave men need not die in battle. But it must not be peace at any price; it must not be a peace of humiliation and gradual surrender."[44] He said that since the Johnson era the United States steadily moved into the position of second place and proposed a return to military superiority as the solution for securing the peace. Military superiority entailed a buildup "both in conventional arms and the deployment of troops" as well as a robust "nuclear deterrent."[45] Reagan rejected the notion that this could not come about without domestic sacrifices when he invoked his heresthetical argument that there was no gun-versus-butter trade-off: "Our government must stop pretending that it has a choice between promoting the general welfare and providing for the common defense. Today they are one and the same."[46]

Reagan also returned to his theme about negotiating nuclear weapons agreements: "I think continued negotiation with the Soviet Union is essential. We need never be afraid to negotiate as long as we keep our long term objectives (the pursuit of peace for one) clearly in mind and don't seek agreements just for the sake of having an agreement. . . . I have repeatedly stated that I would be willing to negotiate an honest, verifiable reduction in nuclear weapons by both our countries to the point that neither of us represented a threat to the other. I cannot, however, agree to a treaty—specifically, the SALT II treaty, which, in effect, legitimizes a nuclear arms buildup."[47]

Reagan also presented a more moderate line on other foreign policy issues, including the status of Taiwan. Reporting on Reagan's Taiwan statements, China's *People's Daily* newspaper accused the governor of "interfering in China's internal affairs." The Reagan campaign responded quickly and forcefully. On August 22, George H. W. Bush, visiting China on behalf of the Reagan campaign, stated that "Governor Reagan, if elected, would not set back the clock . . . [on the] two-China policy." Soon thereafter, Reagan gave his assurance that, as president, he would abide by the Taiwan Relations Act.[48]

Anderson presented a moderate platform on defense policy. He supported the SALT II treaty, opposed the MX missile and the idea of striving for military superiority over the Soviets, and wanted drastic cuts in defense spending. Anderson tried to separate himself from the two main contenders by charging that they were both oriented toward fighting, at the very least, a limited nuclear war, but he was closer to the president on defense issues, including his support for SALT II. Anderson's positions on defense matters reinforced his standing with his natural political base but did not help him expand his reach.[49]

Rival Economic Plans

On August 28, President Carter gave a speech on his "economic renewal program." The program included about $27.6 billion in personal and business tax cuts, an increase in government assistance for energy conservation, renewed government support for revitalized industry, an extension of unemployment compensation, and the creation of an Economic Revitalization Board composed of leaders from industry, labor, and the public sector.[50]

The White House announced that it had sought the advice of a variety of leaders and opinion makers before unveiling the plan. And, indeed, Carter's proposal was favorably received by a range of prominent figures including Senator Kennedy, House Speaker Tip O'Neill, U.S. Steel chairman David M. Roderick, and the Conference of Mayors. But beneath the accolades few saw the proposal as a major leap forward. The response from Armco chairman C. William Verity, Jr., was typical: "My first reaction is that this is a disappointingly small step toward a very large problem. . . . I am a great deal more encouraged by the actions being considered by Congress, which respond directly to the need to rebuild the American economy." William M. Agee, the chairman of Bendix Corporation, offered a similar assessment: "It's a remarkable policy for its inconsistency with policies he has advocated in the past. The President is not creating an environment where psychological inflationary pressures will abate. I see him as part of the problem."[51]

Carter's August 28 announcement constituted the third economic package he had presented in eight months.[52] Policy analysts surmised that the president was searching for a platform that would "solve his own political problems, as well as . . . cure the nation's economic ills."[53] It was a tall order, and one that Carter's latest proposal was unable to fill.

Reagan had been advocating tax cuts, a reduction in government spending, and a host of familiar themes throughout the campaign, but until he rolled out his economic plan in Chicago on September 9, he had not integrated these ideas into a unified package. Speaking to the International Business Council, Reagan promised to reduce government regulations and spending; cut personal income tax rates at 10 percent a year across the board for three years; and institute a stable national monetary policy, thereby restoring international confidence in the American economy. The alternative policy vision Reagan was presenting was especially evident in his confidence that this economic plan could be used to facilitate a strategic military buildup.[54]

The International Business Council address was the public culmination of Reagan's many years of testing and refining his economic ideas through radio addresses, speeches, and newspaper columns. Behind the scenes, Martin Anderson had succinctly captured Reagan's thinking on the subject in his August 1979 policy memo. And Richard Wirthlin's June 1980 campaign plan had suggested that Reagan prepare a comprehensive economic message that could be endorsed by leading economists and delivered well before the fall.[55] Still, Reagan's strategists viewed developing a comprehensive economic agenda to be their most difficult election-year assignment.[56] Reagan's heresthetical message about economic prosperity and national security had been years in the making.

Forewarned that Reagan would be unveiling his economic program in Chicago, Carter delivered a counterattack that same day, telling New Jersey newspaper editors that "there is no way that you can have a Reagan-Kemp-Roth proposal intact, make an attempt to balance the budget, keep a strong defense, to which Reagan professes to be committed, and continue the routine programs that are designed to help the American people have a better life. It's just a ridiculous proposal, and any economist who studies it knows that." Reporters covering Carter's speech were given an analysis of Reagan's plan that had been prepared by the Office of Management and Budget. According to that assessment, Reagan's plan would increase inflation or decrease spending on government programs.[57]

Some Republican moderates, such as President Gerald Ford, also opposed Reagan's three-year tax cut. Ford doubted that it was possible to predict the economic situation three years down the road. Despite the criticism, Reagan's message was widely deemed to be moderate. Writing for the *Washington Post,* reporter (and later, Reagan biographer) Lou Cannon noted that "Reagan's plan as outlined today is far more modest than his campaign rhetoric over the last several months implied. It was in part an effort to assure voters that he could cut taxes, balance the budget and boost defense spending as promised without unduly slashing government programs."[58]

Reagan's message seemed to resonate with voters. In September, the same month in which Reagan gave his economic address, a Harris Poll reported that 45 percent of respondents 18 or older felt that Reagan would do a better job handling the economy than Anderson or Carter would. Only 27 percent endorsed Carter, and approximately 15 percent favored Anderson.

But despite strenuous campaigning around the country and carefully crafted messages that moderated his positions, Reagan was unable to maintain the immediate postconvention bounce of 45 percent support that he'd experienced in the Gallup Poll's presidential trial heat. Twenty-nine percent of those questioned in that early-August survey had indicated they would vote for Carter and 14 percent for Anderson if the election were held at that time. Yet, by mid-September, Carter and Reagan were tied with 39 percent each, while Anderson maintained his 14 percent support.[59]

It is not unusual for candidates to use their policies to bring together diverse voters who might otherwise not form a single coalition. What differentiates that behavior from a heresthetical strategy is their reliance on out-of-the-box policies and ideas. Reagan's economic program was radical as a campaign idea; no other presidential candidate in 1980 campaigned on a proposal of massive tax cuts, and most considered his plan a fantasy. Yet, as the economist Michael Boskin has observed, Reagan's proposal reflected a growing consensus among economists.[60] The California governor had latched onto a trend that the other candidates had ignored, disbelieved, or dismissed as too radical. A heresthetician typically sees possibilities beyond the confines of conventional wisdom, identifying emerging intellectual and policy opportunities that circumvent traditional assumptions and appeal to a broad swath of the electorate.

The radical nature of a heresthetical strategy might bind its proponent to a specific set of policy positions if he or she is elected. Thus, the heresthetician might find it difficult to abandon campaign proposals once in office. To do so would likely bring about the collapse of the very coalition the candidate worked so hard to construct, inasmuch as that coalition was the product of those very promises.[61]

On August 14 Anderson announced Mary Crisp, former cochairperson of the Republican Party, as the head of his campaign, and 11 days later he announced that Patrick Lucey, former Democratic governor of Wisconsin, would be his running mate. With Anderson's team in place and Carter and Reagan having won their party's nominations, the three-way race was officially under way.

On August 30, 1980, Anderson unveiled his National Unity Platform, which included his economic program.[62] Although Anderson had already put forward many of the individual elements of this program, they were now joined into a comprehensive economic statement that Anderson and his running mate would use to frame their fall campaign. The platform called for withholding personal tax cuts until the federal budget was balanced; imposing a $0.50 per gallon gasoline tax, the revenues of which would be used to decrease payroll taxes while increasing Social Security benefits; cutting Social Security taxes in half; exempting the first $750 in interest income from taxes; eliminating inheritance and gift taxes for spouses; creating tax incentives for the auto and steel industries, as well as small businesses; reducing taxes paid by families caring for elderly relatives in the home; and revoking tax credits traditionally offered against private primary and secondary school tuition.

But Anderson's program reached beyond taxes. He called for limits on federal spending as a percentage of the GNP. He endorsed the 1980 Youth Employment Act, which would provide $2 billion a year for job training as a means of decreasing unemployment. His ideas on voluntary wage-price guidelines enjoyed the support of labor and industry, when coupled with tax incentives for compliance with stated guidelines. And, finally, Anderson's "Urban Reinvestment" program called for the creation of a federal urban renewal fund, supported by nearly $4 billion a year in federal alcohol and tobacco taxes.[63]

Anderson, like Carter, warned the American people that they would have to sacrifice and change their energy-consumption patterns. The tax on gasoline was a prime example of this approach. Unlike Reagan, Anderson had little faith that tax cuts for individuals would stimulate the economy. Anderson and Carter were by no means in lockstep on the economy, but both candidates' rhetoric and proposals suggested that a shrinking pie would require that Americans make do with less. Only Reagan's plan promised economic recovery through tax cuts, and general prosperity without a substantial reduction in energy consumption, assuring voters that a revived American economy could lead to boundless opportunity for all.

The Fall Campaign Officially Begins: September 1, 1980

The three contenders each launched his campaign in regions where his strategists believed a strong showing was needed to win the election. Wirthlin had already calculated that Reagan's greatest challenge lay in the medium-sized states, particularly New Jersey. Reagan would need at least 82 electoral votes from these states to win. He opened his campaign on Labor Day in New Jersey.

Reagan's speech in Jersey City was an exercise in rhetorical flourish, but his focus on the president's economic performance also carried a heresthetical subtext. In reviewing Carter's record, Reagan signaled to voters of all political stripes that a vote for the incumbent was a vote for continued economic failure:

> Eight million out of work. Inflation running at 18 percent in the first quarter of 1980. Black unemployment at about 14 percent, higher than any single year since the government began keeping separate statistics. Four straight major deficits run up by Carter and his friends in Congress. The highest interest rates since the Civil War. . . . A recession is when your neighbor loses his job. A depression is when you lose yours. Recovery is when Jimmy Carter loses his.

The gloves were off. The bare knuckles did more damage later that same day, during a stop at the Michigan State Fair, where Reagan courted Michigan's substantial working-class vote—a category of voters essential to a Reagan victory. The governor told the crowd, "I'm happy to be here where you're dealing at first hand with the economic policies that have been committed and he's opening his campaign down in the city that gave birth to and is the parent body of the Ku Klux Klan."[64]

Reagan's attack misfired. Carter was simultaneously launching his campaign in Tuscumbia, Alabama. (As pollster Pat Caddell had noted, Carter needed to secure his southern base.) Carter's opening remarks that day were an appeal to his fellow southerners: "I remembered that in all our nation's wars young men from the South have led the rolls of volunteers and also led the rolls of casualties. We southerners believe in the nobility of courage on the battlefield. And because we understand the costs of war, we also believe in the nobility of peace." When members of the Klan, which had already endorsed Reagan, interrupted the speech, Carter responded by reminding the audience that he was the first candidate from the Deep South to become president in 140 years, adding, "I say these people in white sheets do not understand our region and what it's been through. . . . They do not understand that the South and all of America must move forward."[65]

Carter had taken a one-two punch from Reagan and the Klan and emerged unscathed. Reagan's remarks had made his Detroit audience uncomfortable. Worse yet, the governor had got his facts wrong: Tuscumbia was the national headquarters of the Klan, not its birthplace. Seven Democratic governors from the South issued a statement denouncing "Mr. Reagan's callous and opportunistic slap at the South." Carter chimed in during a September 2 appearance in Independence, Missouri, saying that he "resent[ed] very deeply what Ronald Reagan said about the South." The Reagan-Bush campaign issued what was, in effect, an apology for the blunder.[66]

Reagan would ultimately prevail in the South, but not because of his negative campaign rhetoric linking Carter to the Klan. After the debacle in Michigan, Reagan returned to his bedrock themes of defense and economic reform. Despite the Detroit blunder, his continued emphasis on these key issues eventually won southern Democrats over to his coalition.

Meanwhile, Anderson had launched his fall campaign in Illinois, consistent with the "Midwest strategy" that his advisers had suggested to him in 1979. And he proved no more immune to the temptations of negative campaigning than his competitors had, declaring that "Mr. Reagan isn't even a man for the 1950s. He is really a man of the 1920s." Of Carter, Anderson quipped, "He planned a recession, and by golly, it worked."[67]

The candidates offered little new information about themselves in their opening speeches. In the ensuing weeks, however, heresthetic would begin to win out over rhetoric, as the campaign played out the repeated drama of Reagan proposing his plans for the economy and defense and foreign policy, and Anderson and Carter denouncing them. The Californian was defining the terms of the campaign, something that Caddell had urged the president to do. Anderson and Carter found themselves devoting at least as much time to rhetorical attacks on Reagan's plan as they did to presenting their own ideas.

The president's predicament was reflected in a campaign document titled "Groping for a Central Message or Theme for the Autumn." The document decried the lack of a message: "*For the Carter candidacy,* the view ahead must be credible—cannot simply be a rhetorical vision. . . . Put another way, the view ahead must be stated in the context of this Presidency less as a driving dream than a few basic (almost but not quite programmatic) goals which are reiterated again and again."[68] As late as the fall of 1980, the Carter campaign remained in search of a direction.

Anderson versus Reagan:
The Debate, September 21, 1980

The League of Women Voters invited all three candidates to participate in a nationally televised debate in Baltimore in September. Desperate to maintain their incumbent advantage, the Carter campaign team advised the president to decline. Caddell was wary of a three-way race, and his comments on the subject were indicative of sentiments in the Carter camp as a whole: "In a general election sense Anderson is assaulting much of Carter's natural liberal base whose normal certainty would allow Carter to move right toward Reagan." Nor was this fact lost on the Reagan campaign. Wirthlin had long ago concluded that Anderson was likely to attract more Carter supporters than Reagan voters.[69] Thus, when the Carter campaign refused to participate in the three-way debate (at least until after a Carter-Reagan debate), Reagan's side insisted that the third-party candidate be included. Anderson himself very much wanted to participate, and the League ultimately found that he met their tripartite criteria of voter support, constitutional eligibility, and actual possibility of winning.[70]

Carter, fearing the damage that a decent Anderson showing could do to his base, formally declined the League's invitation. Carter also feared the effect of a strong Reagan performance on his tenuous standing in the polls. From Reagan's perspective, the debate offered a valuable opportunity to score points with voters; but an exceptional Anderson performance could just as easily eat into his shrinking lead. Anderson himself could hardly pass up an invitation to engage the GOP nominee in a nationally televised debate.

The independent and Republican candidates faced each other in Baltimore on September 21. The *Washington Post* headline the next day was "Debate Shows Rivals' Wide Differences."[71] And indeed the exchange between the two men reinforced, rather than weakened, the existing allegiances of the voters.

Early in the debate, Anderson called Reagan's proposal to curb inflation through tax cuts "irresponsible." Reagan responded by stating that the true sources of inflation were excessive federal spending and reduced productivity due to excessive government regulation. He then launched his heresthetical message that tax cuts could be used to reduce the federal deficit:

I believe we need incentive for the individual, and for business and industry, and I believe the plan that I have submitted, with detailed backing, and which has been approved by a number of our leading economists in the country, is based on projections, conservative projections out for the next five years, that indicates [*sic*] that this plan would, by 1983, result in a balanced budget.

When asked how Americans should respond to the energy crisis, Reagan described conservation as just one component of a larger solution. He advocated increased exploration for domestic coal and petroleum, as well as increased reliance on nuclear power. Anderson, on the other hand, asked Americans to change their lifestyle: "We will have to reduce the use of the private automobile. We are going to have to resort to van pooling, to car pooling. We are going to have to create a new conservation ethic in the minds of the American people." Reagan disagreed: "As for saving energy and conserving, the American people haven't been doing badly at that."

Anderson attacked the governor's economic plan, claiming that it was incapable of balancing the budget. This was Reagan's greatest vulnerability: Reagan's assurance that his economic plan would not fuel inflation or lead to further deficits was the glue holding together his coalition of social and economic conservatives. Reagan defended himself by reminding listeners that his Chicago speech was based on five-year projections made by the Senate Budget Committee.

Anderson dismissed this claim. The "Senate Budget Committee

Report does not accommodate all of the Reagan defense plans," he warned the audience, saying, "It doesn't accommodate the expenditures that he calls for. . . . I think the figures that he has given are simply not going to stand up." Reagan quickly moved in to defend his budget proposal: "We did factor in our own ideas with regard to increases in the projected military spending that we believe would, over a period of time, do what is necessary."

The two contenders struggled through their agreement on some issues, including opposition to reinstating the draft, but found their footing again in their profound differences on abortion, with Anderson openly opposing Reagan's call for a constitutional amendment banning the use of federal funding for abortion.

In his closing remarks, Reagan the optimist promised a better tomorrow:

> Today, we're confronted with the horrendous problems that we've discussed here tonight. And some people in high positions of leadership tell us that the answer is to retreat. That the best is over. That we must cut back. That we must share in an ever-increasing scarcity. . . . For 200 years, we've lived in the future, believing that tomorrow would be better than today, and today would be better than yesterday. I still believe that.

Anderson, who had the final word, again sounded like Carter: "A generation of office seekers has tried to tell the American people that they could get something for nothing. It's been a time, therefore, of illusion and false hopes, and the longer it continues, the more dangerous it becomes. We've got to stop drifting."[72]

Anderson's pragmatic rhetoric was obscured by Reagan's sunny optimism. In addition, the independent candidate did not offer a new or novel way of thinking about policy problems. Mark Bisnow, Anderson's press secretary from 1978 to 1980, has suggested in hindsight,

> It was not surprising that in the aftermath of the debate surveys indicated that liberals thought Anderson had won, and conservatives thought Reagan had won. In a sense, this amounted to a loss for Anderson, since his lower standing in the polls required him to broaden his base and attract whole new groups of voters. Overall, Anderson's performance was creditable, but ultimately disappointing. He had not shone as much as many had expected

he would in a match-up with Reagan. He did not jolt many into thinking differently about his candidacy.[73]

Reagan, on the other hand, hit his upbeat rhetorical stride, expounding a heresthetical vision in which his defense policy and his tax-reduction plan did not have to be inflationary or deficit producing.

On the Campaign Trail: September 22 to October 27, 1980

In mid-September, New York's Liberal Party endorsed Anderson, thereby breaking with its tradition of supporting the Democratic nominee.[74] The *New Republic* endorsed Anderson in its October 4 issue, although the endorsement was less than glowing: "[T]o vote for [Carter] a second time is an act of political decadence. . . . John Anderson's main asset is that he is not Jimmy Carter."[75] Despite picking up a few such endorsements and his continued accusations that Carter had betrayed his liberal base on issues such as energy and resource conservation and Reagan's unworkable economic plan, Anderson was unable to maintain his 14 percent voter support. That said, the voters who stayed with him were still primarily liberal and moderate Democrats and independents—the very groups that were essential to Carter's return to power. Although his hopes of reaching the White House were fading, Anderson was nonetheless a real force in the election.

Carter's most formidable challenge, of course, came from Reagan. While Anderson was attacking Carter, the president was moving to co-opt Reagan's positions while simultaneously throwing rhetorical punches at his GOP opponent. On September 30, he announced an assistance package for the steel industry that raised import restrictions and relaxed environmental rules. Reagan was quoted in the *New York Times* as having "an uneasy feeling that he [Carter] might not have done anything if I hadn't opened my mouth [by recommending a similar policy] on September 16." The *Times* went on to remind its readers that the steel industry was based in the key electoral states of Illinois, Indiana, Michigan, Minnesota, Ohio, and Pennsylvania.[76]

Carter invoked a classic negative campaign against Reagan. On October 6, the president told voters that Reagan's military policies were "an excellent way to lead our country toward war," and that under a Reagan presidency, "Americans might be separate, black from white,

Jew from Gentile, North from South, rural from urban." The next day, Reagan's running mate George H.W. Bush labeled the president's remarks "Carterism," which he defined as "rhetoric aimed for narrow political gain and inciting hatred and division among Americans." Carter quickly backed off, calling his earlier remarks "probably ill-advised."[77]

But just a few days later, Carter was back swinging. On October 10, he warned that Reagan's opposition to the SALT II treaty and his positions on economic and social policy meant the Californian "would not be a good President or a good man to trust with the affairs of this nation in the future."[78]

This negative style had become characteristic of Carter's campaign. As the incumbent, Carter believed his White House experience was his greatest asset, compared to Reagan's dangerous inexperience. This belief left him with little room to advocate any movement away from his existing policies.

This lack of a compelling policy agenda was apparent in mid-October when the president sought to counter the bad news about the Consumer Price Index by saying Reagan's tax cut would be bad for the economy. Secretary of State Muskie inadvertently highlighted Carter's indecision by emphasizing the White House's commitment to Senate ratification of SALT II, despite the fact that Carter had actually withdrawn the treaty from deliberation earlier that year in the wake of the Soviet invasion of Afghanistan.[79]

Reagan came back with the occasional rhetorical counterpunch, but for the most part his campaign focused on broadening his own appeal. These efforts were not always successful. Although Carter had long sought to paint a Reagan presidency as inimical to the interests of blacks and minorities, it was Coretta Scott King, widow of the Reverend Martin Luther King, Jr., who leveled the most damning criticism about the likely effects of a Reagan administration. In late September, Mrs. King supposed that "if Mr. Reagan becomes President, the Klan will be quite comfortable." A few days before the election, she repeated her warning: "I am scared that if Ronald Reagan gets into office, we are going to see more of the Ku Klux Klan and a resurgence of the Nazi Party."[80] Reagan found it harder to defend himself against Mrs. King's accusations than against those of his political opponents. He was not making much headway with black voters.

Although he failed to make much headway with black civil rights leaders, Reagan continued to present a moderate domestic program. In

October he declared that he would not make the issue of abortion a lit-
mus test for judicial appointments. He released a campaign circular
stating that he would not abolish the Occupational Safety and Health
Administration and would not advocate a federal law on the right-to-
work issue, but that he would apply antitrust laws to unions. The
Times, among others, interpreted these positions as "part of a broader
strategy to move his Republican candidacy closer to the center of the
political spectrum."[81]

Speaking to a crowd in Cincinnati on October 20, Reagan unleashed
one of his most thorough attempts to portray himself as a man of peace
and Carter as a hapless warmonger:

> The President of the United States seems determined to have me
> start a nuclear war. Well, I'm just as determined not to. As a mat-
> ter of fact, his foreign policy, his vacillation, his weakness is
> allowing our allies throughout the world to no longer trust us
> and depend on us and our adversaries to no longer respect us.
> There's a far greater danger of an unwanted, inadvertent war
> with that policy than there is with someone in there who believes
> that the first thing we should do is rebuild our defensive capabil-
> ity.[82]

The next day, Reagan publicly blamed Carter's Iran policy for the
ongoing hostage crisis. Carter charged that Reagan was using the crisis
as a political football, but Reagan refused to recant.[83]

Reagan also never lost sight of his heresthetical maneuvers during
this phase of the campaign. On October 24, four days before the
debate, Reagan gave a 30-minute televised address on his economic
program. He reviewed his heresthetical promise of economic and social
benefits for all, to which he added a new rhetorical gloss, vowing that
his presidential administration would promote "a humane economy."[84]
While Reagan was continually selling this ambitious economic agenda,
Carter was, as previously noted, talking about how ridiculous the plan
was.

A mid-October Gallup Poll showed 44 percent of respondents
choosing Reagan-Bush, 41 percent Carter-Mondale, and 9 percent
Anderson-Lucey. Reagan had once again surpassed the president in the
polls, while Anderson's share continued to shrink.[85] The League of
Women Voters decided not to invite Anderson to participate in its next
debate.

Reagan's message was clearly reaching a broader constituency: in October he was endorsed by the International Brotherhood of Teamsters and prominent Democrats Eugene McCarthy and Eugene Rostow.[86] Yet in the same period another Gallup Poll showed Reagan losing support, suggesting that the swings in voter support were within the margin of statistical error. Conducted in late October, just a few days before the Carter-Reagan debate, the poll found 39 percent of the voters choosing Reagan-Bush, 45 percent choosing Carter-Mondale, and 9 percent again choosing Anderson-Lucey.[87] At this late point in the election season, neither candidate enjoyed a secure lead, a fact that heightened public anticipation of the debate.

The Carter-Reagan Debate and the Anderson Response: October 28, 1980

Jimmy Carter had so far escaped meeting John Anderson and Ronald Reagan on a national platform, suggesting on several occasions that the debate would amount to a conversation between two Republicans.[88] A second debate had originally been proposed for early October, but was postponed after the candidates could not agree on the terms. By late October, however, the political dynamics had changed. Anderson's support had fallen below the 10 percent level required by the sponsoring League of Women Voters. With Reagan's postconvention lead narrowing, his camp felt that their candidate needed to debate the president, and agreed to do so even without Anderson's participation. In the Carter camp, pressure was mounting for the incumbent to interact directly with the Republican challenger. He acquiesced, and the first and only debate between the two men was scheduled to take place in Cleveland, Ohio, on October 28.

Moderator Howard K. Smith opened the debate with a question about how the candidates differed in their views on the use of American power. Reagan immediately portrayed himself as a peace advocate: "Our first priority must be world peace . . . use of force is always and only a last resort, when everything else has failed, and then only with regard to our national security."[89] Carter replied by portraying himself as strong on defense. He pointed to steady increases in defense spending during his first administration, and his amplification of the U.S. military presence in the Persian Gulf.

Seeking to preempt Carter's charge of warmongering—an accusation the president had made throughout the fall—Reagan countered by carefully emphasizing his defense plan's reliance on deterrence rather than aggression.

Carter countered with strong negative rhetoric. He attacked Reagan's economic proposals and praised the American people's willingness to sacrifice in the name of his own policies: "We have demanded that the American people sacrifice, and they have done very well." He echoed this sentiment just a few sentences later, attributing the promise of his new energy policy to two factors: "One is conservation, which requires sacrifice, and the other one, increase in production of American energy."

Reagan used his rebuttal to contrast Carter's call for sacrifice with his own, more optimistic approach. The president, Reagan declared, "has . . . accused the people of living too well and that we must share in scarcity, we must sacrifice and get used to doing with less. We don't have inflation because the people are living too well. We have inflation because the government is living too well."

Carter reminded the audience that even Reagan's running mate had once called his economic plan "voodoo economics." Later he called Reagan-Kemp-Roth "one of the most highly inflationary ideas that ever has been presented to the American public." This remark reflected Carter's approach throughout the debate; he attacked Reagan's proposals but failed to offer a coherent alternative. His strategy was almost entirely based on negative campaigning.

Reagan, meanwhile, relentlessly worked to broaden his appeal. He advocated the creation of urban development zones through tax incentives and private-sector support. He talked about ensuring "total equal opportunity for all people," and evinced optimism about America's future as a "multi-racial society." "I believe in it," Reagan said. "I am eternally optimistic, and I happen to believe that we've made great progress."

Asked about his solution for ending the Iran hostage crisis, Reagan advocated "quiet diplomacy" and a congressional investigation once the immediate situation was resolved. He claimed that a policy of more actively supporting the shah and encouraging him to improve human rights might have been more effective in averting the crisis than the course Carter had followed.

Reagan did not offer detailed responses, however, to Carter's remarks on terrorism and weapons of mass destruction. The president spoke at length about these matters:

Ultimately, the most serious terrorist threat is if one of those radical nations, who believe in terrorism as a policy, should have atomic weapons. Both I and all my predecessors have had a deep commitment to controlling the proliferation of nuclear weapons. In countries like Libya or Iraq, we have even alienated some of our closest trade partners because we have insisted upon the control of the spread of nuclear weapons to those potentially terrorist countries.

At one point, Carter declared that the most important difference in the campaign was the candidates' opposing stands on nuclear nonproliferation. This was a thinly veiled reference to a statement Reagan had made early in the year, "I just don't think it's [the spread of nuclear weapons] any of our business."[90] Reagan had promptly retracted that statement and endorsed nonproliferation, but Carter chose not to pass up an opportunity for negative campaigning.

Carter's own antiterrorism strategy included preventing the spread of nuclear weapons, imposing sanctions against countries involved with terrorist activities, and disallowing all commercial air travel to nations involved in terrorism or hijacking, or the harboring of hijackers. Reagan agreed with these proposals, but objected to the inaccurate portrayal of his views on nuclear nonproliferation, an issue that, he stated, "would be a major part of a foreign policy of mine."

As he had done throughout the campaign, Reagan based his opposition to SALT II on the grounds that it had required the United States to make too many concessions. Carter's rebuttal was more pointed than the vague lecturing that had characterized his past comments on this subject: "The control of these weapons is the single major responsibility of a President, and to cast out this commitment of all Presidents, because of some slight technicalities that can be corrected, is a very dangerous approach."

Carter proposed resolving the energy crisis through conservation and increased domestic oil production, whereas Reagan blamed the crisis on government restrictions on exploration. The debate then moved on to Social Security. Reagan, wary of weakening his support among those in the center, mildly proposed the formation of a task force to consider possible reforms. In fact, he returned to this moderate tone throughout much of the evening's exchange. When asked by moderator Smith about his opposition to the Equal Rights Amendment, Reagan warned against any move that would "take this problem out of the hands of elected legislators and put it in the hands of unelected judges," but also proclaimed his commitment to equal rights. He made a similarly moderate appeal to union members: "I'm the only fellow who ever ran for this job who was six times president of his own union and still has a lifetime membership in that union."

The candidates' closing remarks were studies in contrast. Carter reminded the audience that he and Reagan differed sharply on major policy issues, but the main part of his closing remarks took a different rhetorical tack. Carter asked the voters to stick with him because of his experience: "I've had to make thousands of decisions, and each one of those decisions has been a learning process. . . . I've learned in this last three and a half years that when an issue is extremely difficult, when the call is very close, the chances are the experts will be divided almost 50–50. And the final judgment about the future of the nation—war, peace, involvement, reticence, thoughtfulness, care, consideration, concern—has to be made by the man in the Oval Office." He also proclaimed his political centrism: "I consider myself in the mainstream of my party. I consider myself in the mainstream even of the bipartisan list of Presidents who served before me."

Reagan's now-famous closing remarks embodied the heresthetical use of rhetoric to reinforce a candidate's overall message. Reagan's criticism that Carter could deliver neither guns nor butter slyly implied that he could offer Americans both:

> Next Tuesday all of you will go to the polls, will stand there in the polling place and make a decision. I think when you make the decision, it might be well if you would ask yourself, are you better off than you were four years ago? Is it easier for you to go and buy things in the stores than it was four years ago? Is there more or less unemployment in the country than there was four years ago? Is America as respected throughout the world as it was? Do you feel that our security is as safe, that we're as strong as we were four years ago? And if you answer all of those questions yes, why then, I think your choice is very obvious as to whom you will vote for. If you don't agree, if you don't think that this course that we've been on for the last four years is what you would like to see us follow for the next four, then I could suggest another choice that you have. This country doesn't have to be in the shape that it is in. We do not have to go on sharing in scarcity with the coun-

try getting worse off, with unemployment growing. . . . I would like to have a crusade today, and I would like to lead that crusade with your help. And it would be one to take Government off the backs of the great people in this country, and turn you loose again to do those things that I know you can do so well, because you did them and made this country great. Thank you.

As Hedrick Smith wrote for the *New York Times*, "The presidential debate produced no knockout blow, no disastrous gaffe and no immediate, undisputed victor."[91] An ABC-TV phone survey had declared Reagan the winner, but there was no unanimous verdict among the media. Reagan had, however, gotten in a subtly powerful heresthetical jab in his closing remarks. One analyst described the governor's remark this way: "'Are you better off now than you were four years ago?' With that pointed question, Ronald Reagan defined the 1980 presidential election as a referendum on Jimmy Carter's economic policies."[92] Hamilton Jordan, Carter's chief of staff, recalls his reaction to Reagan's closing remarks thusly: "*What a narrow and selfish premise*, I thought, *asking people to choose their President based solely on their present condition.* Nevertheless, it was our idea, and now Reagan had turned it against us."[93]

Although John Anderson had been excluded from the October 28 forum because of his low numbers, the nascent Cable News Network had agreed to cover a simultaneous Anderson event at Constitution Hall in Washington. Anderson used the CNN coverage to respond to Carter's and Reagan's statements as their debate was taking place. On the topic of American military power, Anderson expressed a belief "that there really is no substantial difference between them on the issue of whether or not you can fight a limited nuclear war. . . . I do not believe that we can fight and win a nuclear war. I think there is no such thing as a limited nuclear war." He charged that the United States had descended into "deep trouble" during the Carter years, and declared that the essence of Reagan's policy prescriptions was "We'll turn back the clock."[94]

Anderson's commentary on the Carter-Reagan debate continued the negative rhetoric he had employed throughout his campaign. He used the CNN airtime to curry favor among his existing supporters, but offered no policy positions or arguments that were likely to broaden his appeal.

The Final Stretch: October 29 to November 4, 1980

The candidates reiterated familiar themes and appeals throughout the final week of the campaign. Both Anderson and Carter continued to go negative. On October 31, Anderson charged that a radio ad by the Carter campaign accusing him of failing to support civil rights legislation in the mid-1960s was "an effort desperately to hang onto the black vote."[95]

Carter's own negative rhetoric, meanwhile, was primarily directed against Reagan. On October 29, Carter reminded his audience of Reagan's statement in January in reference to Pakistan that the United States should not block the proliferation of nuclear weapons. Two days later, the president reached back into Reagan's political past and charged that his opponent had equated Medicare with socialism in 1961. "The President's constant quoting of old statements by his opponent . . . gave his campaign a dated quality," the Times wrote, reflecting the postelection analysis among Carter's advisers.[96]

The president saw a glimmer of hope when Deputy Secretary of State Warren Christopher notified him on November 2 that the Iranian parliament had outlined terms for releasing the American hostages in Tehran. That evening, Carter made a brief public statement about these "positive" developments, and assured voters that his response would not be "affected by the [electoral] calendar."[97] As he had done in the past, Anderson once again called for Carter to make the terms for releasing the hostages public. Reagan, who had been highly critical of Carter's Iran strategy, declined to comment on the grounds that the matter was "too sensitive."[98] The president, for his part, employed the Rose Garden strategy, emphasizing the importance of his White House experience during a crucial time in the nation's history.[99] Reagan kept up his heresthetical appeals in the final days of campaigning, but he, too, had occasional recourse to negative rhetoric. Speaking on October 30 to residents of an Arkansas community that had experienced an influx of Cuban émigrés, Reagan contended that Carter's policies exacerbated the refugee problem. In a New Jersey stop later that same day, he promised his audience that he was "committed to an economic program to reduce inflation and put people back to work," and that he would not "tax Social Security benefits."[100]

One day before voters headed to the polls, Reagan gave a televised address in which he reiterated various comments he had made during his debate with Carter. In declaring that the president's policies had produced "worsening economic conditions," Reagan once again combined rhetoric with heresthetical maneuvering.[101]

In repeating these questions, Reagan once again held out a promise of prosperity and happiness that Carter simply could not match. The president would have to admit to a host of failures in order to respond credibly. As the president's strategists later acknowledged, "Carter never went far enough in conceding that his first term had been less than successful—and in specifying just how his second term would be better . . . [he] never found a way to summarize his views in a single rousing, catchy, unifying theme."[102]

Caddell reported that, in the final days of the campaign, his polls showed voters to be increasingly dismayed by the hostage situation. Recent, heightened news attention was not helping matters, especially once the anticipated release of the hostages failed to materialize.

Lacking a message around which voters could rally, Carter needed a boost. In a September Harris Poll survey of voters, 73 percent responded affirmatively to a statement that the president was well-intentioned but his competence was questionable at times. An October survey of eligible voters by the same organization showed Carter with just over 34 percent of the vote to Reagan's 39 percent (and Anderson's 13 percent). A November Harris Poll reported that fewer than 4 percent of people 18 years of age and older believed the president had done a good job in the past four years. His performance was judged to be "pretty good" by 24 percent, "only fair" by 41 percent, and "poor" by approximately 30 percent of those surveyed. The Gallup Poll for October 30–November 1 showed support for Reagan-Bush climbing to 47 percent, while Carter-Mondale moved to 44 percent.[103]

On the eve of the election, Caddell informed the president and his closest advisers that Reagan was going to win by eight to 10 percentage points. He told the president, "We're losing the undecided voters overwhelmingly, and a lot of working Democrats are going to wake up tomorrow and for the first time in their lives vote Republican."[104] Caddell was right on target. On November 4, Reagan vanquished the president in a 10-point landslide, the third-largest margin in American presidential elections of the twentieth century.[105] Reagan won nearly 51 percent of the popular vote (44 million), 44 states, and 489 electoral votes. Carter received 41 percent of the popular vote (35.5 million), 49 electoral votes, and only seven electoral units (Georgia, Maryland, Minnesota, West Virginia, Rhode Island, Hawaii, and the District of Columbia), making him the first elected incumbent to lose the White

House since Herbert Hoover in 1932. Anderson, who failed to win a plurality in any state, received slightly less than 7 percent of the popular vote (5.7 million).

The demographic profile was consistent with the coalition of social and economic conservatives that Reagan had sought to construct. He had cut into the New Deal stronghold by taking 43 percent of the vote from households with union membership, while Carter won just 50 percent of the union vote—13 points less than he had received in 1976 (Anderson's support among union members was a mere 5 percent). Reagan ran exactly even with Carter on support from manual workers at 48 percent each, but not as well as Nixon had in 1972, when he received 57 percent of their votes. Nevertheless, it was a substantial improvement over the 41 percent that Ford had received from the group in 1976.

Reagan was also successful with white-collar workers, 51 percent of whom cast their ballots for him, compared to 40 percent for Carter, a 10-point decline from his 1976 share. Of those in Gallup's "professional and business" category, 55 percent voted for Reagan. Carter received 33 percent of these votes, again a decline from his 1976 level of 42 percent.[106]

Reagan also outperformed Carter among voters with high-school and college educations. High-school graduates voted 51 percent for Reagan versus 43 percent for Carter. College grads went 53 percent for Reagan and 35 percent for Carter. The only educational category in which Carter soundly beat Reagan was voters with a grade-school education, 54 percent of whom went for Carter, as opposed to 42 percent for Reagan.

In his strategy memo, Caddell had emphasized the importance of the Catholic and Jewish vote, but support for the president among Catholics had declined from 57 percent in 1976 to 46 percent in 1980. Jewish voters had backed Carter two-to-one in 1976, but delivered only 45 percent of their vote to the president in 1980. And Carter's 46 percent of the Protestant vote in 1976 diminished to 39 percent in 1980. Meanwhile, Reagan had carried 47 percent of the Catholic vote, 39 percent of the Jewish vote, and 54 percent of the Protestant vote, with Anderson taking the rest.[107]

Forty-six percent of whites stood with Carter in 1976, but in 1980, he received only 36 percent of their votes to Reagan's 56 percent. Nonwhites were the only racial category whose support for Carter held steady or increased: 85 percent of nonwhites had voted for Carter in

1976, rising to 86 percent in 1980. Reagan received only 10 percent of the nonwhite vote and Anderson 2 percent.

To win, Wirthlin noted in his campaign book, Reagan would have to score big among Democrats and independents. And in fact he did, attracting 26 percent of the Democratic vote, almost as much as Nixon (33 percent) had received in 1972. Among independents, 55 percent voted for Reagan (Nixon's plurality among these voters had been 69 percent in 1972). Reagan also performed well within his own party, garnering 86 percent of Republican support, but not matching either Ford's 91 percent or Nixon's 95 of the GOP vote.

Regionally, Wirthlin had been prepared to concede the South and parts of the East in the event Reagan prevailed in every other corner of the country. Reagan's actual geographic victory was impressive: he won 47 percent of the vote in the East (compared to Carter's 43 percent); 51 percent in the Midwest (Carter got 41); 52 percent in the South (44 percent for Carter); and 54 percent in the West (to Carter's 35).

The national election produced good results for Republicans more generally. Republicans gained 33 House seats and won control of the Senate, as well-known Democrats such as Birch Bayh, John Culver, Frank Church, Warren Magnuson, George McGovern, and Gaylord Nelson were defeated. The Democrats also lost control in top state-level posts. For instance, Arkansas governor Bill Clinton was defeated.[108]

Political scientist Robert Axelrod captured the thinking of many analysts following Carter's 1976 presidential victory: "For the Democrats, the New Deal coalition made a comeback in 1976. . . . The Democrats got a majority of the votes from each of the six diverse minorities which make up their traditional coalition: the poor, blacks, union families, Catholics, southerners, and city dwellers."[109] Carter had reactivated the Democratic Party's time-honored base in the "cities and the South," despite what appeared to be Nixon's undoing of the New Deal coalition in 1972. In 1980, however, Reagan did as well as Nixon had in 1972 among some New Deal segments, and better than Nixon among others. Reagan's presidential victory marked the second time in recent history that deep inroads had been made into the old New Deal constituency.

It has been argued by Greg Markus, among others, that there is no solid evidence on which to claim that Reagan's victory was due to his specific policy or ideological positions.[110] We are not asserting that Reagan's heresthetical message, which fully encompassed his policy positions, was the sole reason for his victory in 1980. We are suggesting that the governor's unanticipated move from the political Far Right to the center—redefined by him—of American politics was greatly facilitated by his unique appeals. Those appeals brought a diverse collection of voters into Reagan's political orbit; they also made it difficult for Carter to find policy alternatives that would not hurt him with his core constituencies.

William Riker's hypotheses are premised on the belief that issues and policies are of great consequence for any politician seeking to command the center. Going into the 1980 race, voter preferences on salient social issues such as abortion and the Equal Rights Amendment were much closer to the opinions of President Carter than they were to those of Governor Reagan. However, those issues "were essentially unrelated to voting choices," according to scholars Paul Abramson, John Aldrich, and David Rohde. A November 1980 *New York Times*/CBS Poll found that 68 percent of those who voted for Reagan opposed his lack of support for the ERA. Abramson and his coauthors also noted that "most people favored Reagan on defense spending but opposed him on abortion."[111] Political scientist Greg Adams has observed that "in 1980, most pro-lifers chose Carter over Reagan, while pro-choicers slightly favored Reagan. A number of scholars have looked at the 1980 presidential election and the years immediately following it and concluded that abortion was not a factor in voting or party identification."[112] The 1980 election clearly did not hinge on social issues, even though voters may have held strong opinions about them.

The analysis by Abramson et al. suggests that almost 90 percent of voters chose their candidate in 1980 according to their position on inflation and unemployment.[113] Voters wanted a drastic change in the direction of the economy, considering it even more important than foreign and defense policy positions. According to the University of Michigan's Survey Research Center, 56 percent of voters chose the economy as the most important issue in 1980, compared to 32 percent who chose defense. This margin was markedly narrower than it had been in earlier years, when 76 percent of voters ranked economic issues as most important and only 4 percent chose foreign policy.[114] Clearly, candidates in 1980 needed to focus significantly more attention on foreign and defense policy issues than had been necessary in previous elections.

Social scientists have demonstrated that the American electorate was also concerned about government spending and the size of bureaucracy. One study found that apparently broad support for the continuation of government services was diminished once this question was posed in terms of the need to reduce federal expenditures.[115] The 1980 election was all about the economy, defense, and government regulation.

Reagan's positions were important to many voters. According to Gallup Poll surveys, 17 percent of those who voted for him said they did so because of his economic policies; a further 14 percent backed him because of his overall policy stance. The November 1980 *New York Times*/CBS poll reported that 60 percent of those who voted for Reagan agreed with the governor that inflation was more important than unemployment.[116]

Reagan presented voters with a set of radical ideas about the economy and foreign relations, and linked these two issues in a way that suggested there need be no trade-off between guns and butter. In doing so, he staked out positions on the issues that most concerned voters and fundamentally shifted the debate about the economy and the role of the United States in the international system. This strategy directly contributed to some voters' decision to cast their ballots for the challenger. He built a heresthetically grounded coalition of voters, amassing a broad coalition that was satisfied that Reagan's approach to peace and prosperity was best. Many who voted for him seem to have been persuaded that they could have peace and they could have prosperity by reducing taxes, diminishing government regulations, and by increasing defense spending that would force the Soviet Union to adopt more realistic, cooperative policies.

Carter's explicit adoption of any part of Reagan's issue package would have been tantamount to admitting the failures of his administration. Yet the president's continual attacks on Reagan's policies made Carter appear disingenuous, suggesting that he lacked a plan of his own—a problem that his aides in fact acknowledged shortly after his defeat.[117] Carter's opposition to Reagan's ideas prevented the president from cultivating support from the wider constituency he urgently needed. Carter was trapped. Yes, he was a victim of retrospective voting, but he was also a victim of an unrelenting heresthetical strategy.

In Richard Nixon, a skillful rhetorician, Reagan had faced an opponent he could not overcome. Nor had he been able to establish rhetorical independence from President Ford in 1976. By early 1977, however, Reagan was formulating a heresthetical message and identifying the coalition with whom this message would resonate. This heresthetical strategy bore rich fruit during the 1980 campaign.

Reagan's positions on the economy, taxation, and defense spending are directly relevant to our understanding of the conclusion of the Cold War. If Jimmy Carter had been reelected in 1980, it is doubtful that relations with the Soviets (and later Russians) would have begun to thaw as they did in the late 1980s and early 1990s. Ronald Reagan's election was a major step in bringing an end to the long Cold War.

6

Fighting the
Nomenklatura's Privileges

*The Rhetorical Campaign
of 1986–88*

When Mikhail Gorbachev rose to power in March 1985, the Soviet Union was facing two simultaneous crises, one domestic and the other foreign. The domestic crisis was caused by inherent inefficiencies in the Soviet command economy. The foreign policy crisis was the result of the collapse of détente and the new challenge to Soviet expansionism posed by President Ronald Reagan's "peace through strength" strategy. Together, the two crises suggested that changes to traditional Soviet policies were critical to the regime's survival.

Reagan became the first U.S. president in the Cold War era to call for changes in the internal structure of the Soviet Union as a precondition for improved U.S.-Soviet relations. Aware of Reagan's demands, Gorbachev also recognized that internal reform was necessary if the USSR were to compete internationally and preserve the integrity of its socialist community. Remarkably, the two leaders had arrived at similar visions of the Soviet Union's future by very different paths. Both deemed internal change in the Soviet political and economic systems to be essential to transforming international affairs. Later in his tenure as general secretary, Gorbachev would advocate a radical vision of Soviet foreign policy that would provoke a backlash from the country's conservative forces. But it was his domestic reforms, not his suggestion to abandon the concept of international class struggle, that determined Gorbachev's political fate and the destiny of the USSR. The demise of the Soviet Union was attributable in large measure to internal political competition resulting from Gorbachev's conflicting attempts to liberalize the country while preserving its core Communist ideology.[1]

The series of domestic events that precipitated the end of the Soviet superpower are investigated in this chapter and the next. Rather than concentrating on Soviet or U.S. foreign policies, we show how internal political competition caused the disintegration of a Cold War rival, and we trace the origins of this competition to the very onset of Gorbachev's rule. In late 1985, at the suggestion of his deputy, Yegor Ligachev, the new Soviet leader invited a provincial first party secretary from Sverdlovsk, Boris Yeltsin, to run the city of Moscow. In five years, Yeltsin would be running for the presidency of the Russian Federation while Gorbachev would be desperately fighting to retain his quickly diminishing power. Political rivalry between these two men, exacerbated by their deep-seated personal animosity, contributed mightily to ending the decades of superpower contest between the United States and the Soviet Union. And once again, Riker's propositions about the principles of campaigning have a great deal to tell us about this global outcome.

Political competition under Gorbachev took place within a changing institutional structure. It involved a gradual expansion of the selectorate and the winning coalition responsible for keeping the leadership in office. Institutional changes also led to the redistribution of power from the Kremlin to the governing bodies of the Soviet republics, thus adding another dimension to the already-widening political space. Initially, however, the meaningful Soviet selectorate was limited to several hundred party functionaries in the Politburo and Central Committee, who directly participated in the process of selecting and sustaining the CPSU general secretary. Moreover, the relationship between the Central Committee and the Politburo was characterized by mutual bureaucratic accountability, which limited political competition in the Soviet Union to a power struggle within the highest party ranks.[2] In such cases where the winning coalition remains small, the range of policy preferences will generally be limited to satisfying the wants of the small coterie of essential supporters. This in turn greatly reduces the space for political maneuvering by aspiring leaders, even as it expands their discretion with regard to policies aimed at the general public. Such an institutional setup discourages politicians from taking radical positions on resource allocations that might alienate their core backers.

Pursuing his own reform agenda, Gorbachev decided to expand his baseline coalition and the national selectorate beyond the confines of the party leadership. He started with the introduction of multicandidate elections to the new legislative body, the Congress of People's Deputies, and subsequently introduced the office of president, whose occupant would be elected by the congress. Gorbachev also organized direct competitive elections to the legislative bodies in each republic, thus creating an additional layer of representative institutions accountable only to the local population. The selectorate's expansion was completed after some republics, including Russia, decided to have their republican heads elected by popular ballot.

Each stage of institutional development opened up wider opportunities for coalition-building and political contestation, since politicians could now appeal to a broader range of policy preferences among the electorate. This made pursuit of Gorbachev's broad policy objectives (especially perestroika) more feasible at the same time that it facilitated—we believe unwittingly on Gorbachev's part—the creation of viable political rivals for power that ultimately would lead to his downfall. After a period of personal political failure, Boris Yeltsin successfully used these opportunities to revive his career and divide Gorbachev's winning coalition of reformers and conservatives, bringing many of its members over to his side. In the process, Yeltsin won three election campaigns, thereby expanding his support group from the largely reform-oriented residents of Moscow to the more ideologically diverse population of the Russian Federation as a whole.

Yeltsin's initial attempts to climb the old Soviet institutional structure failed. During his period of failure, Yeltsin relied primarily on popular rhetoric rather than on the strategic choice of issues. As a result, he lost the support of key individuals whom he needed if he was to succeed. This period in Yeltsin's political career is important to consider for reasons similar to those that led us to address Reagan's 1968 campaign: it sets the scene and provides the context, as well as the emotional charge, for Yeltsin's later political battles. Here Yeltsin introduced and honed the issue that eventually defined him as a politician and showed his potential as a heresthetician. Through vigorous political maneuvering, he fractured the seeming unity of the top Soviet leadership. The ideological divides that resulted characterized further political competition and gave shape to his future coalition of support. His personal rivalry with Gorbachev, too, was destined to exhibit ramifications far beyond Soviet borders.

Radical-Conservative Split

In March 1985 the Communist leadership, recognizing the need for change, brought together reformist coalitions in the Politburo and the CPSU Central Committee (CC). They became Gorbachev's support base during his first two years in office.[3] Gorbachev was able to take advantage of uncertainty about his policy goals and his own extremely cautious approach to domestic reforms to maintain solidarity within the coalition. He successfully preserved this unity for a time despite varying levels of commitment to reform among members of the two groups. In fact, the first two years of Gorbachev's term as general secretary were marked by greater policy continuity than anyone who had heard his speeches in the year before taking office would have expected.[4] He resorted to traditional measures to improve administrative efficiency, adopting a policy of acceleration, calling for changes in the allocation of resources, and enforcing greater workplace discipline. Moreover, in his initial period of rule Gorbachev avoided questioning the ideological and organizational bases of the Soviet state, which looked to the Communist Party as its main guiding political force. Party conservatives took note of these differences between Gorbachev's revolutionary rhetoric and his policy decisions, and gradually warmed to his leadership. The first sign of Gorbachev's break with politics as usual came in December 1986, when he personally called the country's most prominent dissident, Andrei Sakharov, to inform him of his impending release from exile in Gorki.[5] But the coalition held even despite this unorthodox step. It was not until the following year that the first cracks began to surface.

During the January 1987 CC Plenum Gorbachev put forward plans to democratize the party and introduce multicandidate elections for party secretaries in the regions. If implemented, the elections would have been a momentous change in the decades-long practice of central party control over regional appointments and would have threatened the job security of current party bosses.[6] The strong opposition to Gorbachev's reform ideas was reflected in the failure of the participants in the CC Plenum to endorse the principle of multicandidate elections, allowing instead only a few limited experiments. Their opposition reflected any politician's natural concern for changes that jeopardize his or her hold on power.

By the end of Gorbachev's third year in office his support coalition was undergoing a tripartite split, sectioning off the factions who would engage in the emerging political battle. Two defining events were responsible for this split. The first was Boris Yeltsin's brief speech to the CC Plenum in October 1987. Yeltsin criticized the inability of the party apparatus to reform itself, and the resulting sluggishness of perestroika. In response, CC members, including Gorbachev, condemned Yeltsin's views and later relieved him of both his position as first secretary of the Moscow Party Committee and his Politburo candidate membership. These actions catalyzed the formation of a radical reformist wing within Gorbachev's coalition.[7]

Then, in March 1988, the ultraconservative newspaper *Sovietskaia Rossiia* published a letter by a committed Stalinist, Nina Andreyeva.[8] Comrade Andreyeva condemned the rise of political pluralism and called for the Communist Party to return to its role as the workers' champion. Her letter, entitled "I Cannot Forsake Principles," was vigorously denounced by Gorbachev and repudiated in a *Pravda* editorial. However, it quickly became an ideological manifesto for the conservatives, including the highly regarded and powerful Yegor Ligachev. It also reflected the growing unease of the conservatives with Gorbachev's attempts at liberalization.

The two episodes had much in common. Yeltsin's speech and Andreyeva's letter both criticized the pace of domestic reforms, albeit for opposite reasons. Gorbachev dismissed both incidents as irresponsible and ideologically erroneous attempts to reverse perestroika. And the whirlwind of public discussion that each episode produced delineated new divisions within Soviet society between the hard-line conservatives, gradualist reformers, and radical reformers. Ligachev commanded the loyalty of many party conservatives, Yeltsin monopolized the radical wing, and Gorbachev occupied the center.[9] Although Gorbachev attempted to prevent this tripartite split by reshuffling party apparatus members, his alliance was already beginning to come apart by early 1987.[10]

The tactics of Yeltsin and Ligachev each demonstrated certain heresthetical qualities. Gorbachev could not embrace either of their positions without alienating core parts of his own coalition. Conservatives viewed Yeltsin, campaigning against the privileges of the party elite, as a threat to the bedrock of the Communist hierarchy. Acceptance of Yeltsin's demands would have left Gorbachev without needed support from conservative majorities in the Politburo and the CC. On the other hand, repudiation of the Soviet totalitarian past was an indispensable element of Gorbachev's reform agenda. It was a matter of faith for Gorbachev's closest and most trusted allies, as well as for the wider Soviet intelligentsia. Granting the validity of Ligachev's concerns would therefore have tarnished Gorbachev's image as a committed reformer and estranged the very people Gorbachev was counting on to lead his reforms. The confrontation between Yeltsin and Ligachev had forcibly made Gorbachev into a centrist, a position that would soon become politically irrelevant.

Fighting Out the Differences

The most intense debates among conservatives and reformers swirled around Gorbachev's call to reform the party's governing bodies. The Soviet leader wanted to transform the party's organizational structure and its role in affairs of state, but was constrained by the intransigence of the party apparatus. The nomenklatura naturally feared losing power and influence, and Ligachev assured them of their continued dominance over the Soviet political system. Yeltsin shared Gorbachev's commitment to reform, but advocated more sweeping changes. Less than a year after Gorbachev assumed power, Yeltsin began to demand substantial reductions in the privileges given to the nomenklatura.

In February 1986, only two months after he was appointed first secretary of the Moscow Party Committee, Yeltsin condemned nomenklatura privileges at the Twenty-seventh CPSU Congress. Addressing the congress delegates, he pointed to the problem they were all familiar with but that none ventured to discuss in public: "Hearing of any manifestations of injustice—be they current or already chronic—makes one uncomfortable. But it is particularly painful when people talk bluntly about special benefits for leaders."[11] No doubt realizing the sensitivity of the issue he had raised, Yeltsin substantiated his concerns by citing Lenin's dim view of those Communist leaders who "lose the qualities they need—justice, party-minded modesty and complete selflessness." But his proposed change, abolishing all "unjustified" benefits for party officials, sounded almost heretical. Such a measure, in his view, was "bound to lead to a growth in people's labor and social agility" and would "give our ideological enemies no excuse for various speculations." One important indication of how far Yeltsin had moved into forbidden territory can be found in the fact that the transcript of his speech, published in the Communist mouthpiece *Pravda,* contained no trace of his criticisms of privileges.

Ironically, the subject had first surfaced in an article in *Pravda* several days before the congress.[12] The article "Cleansing—the Frank Discussion" was an overview of readers' letters with critical comments on various perceived negative policies within the party. One of these letters, written by a rank-and-file veteran Communist, took on the issue of excessive nomenklatura privileges. The writer accused "party, Soviet, trade-union, and Komsomol leaders" of exploiting access to special restaurants, stores, and clinics. While the author did not object to party bosses receiving higher wages, he disagreed with their access to any special privileges: "If the boss goes to the regular store and would stand in line as all other people," he wrote, "the lines might soon disappear."

The letter did not escape the notice of Politburo conservatives. Addressing the party congress, Ligachev accused *Pravda* of "lapses" that pushed the critique too far.[13] He emphasized that "criticism should be aimed at strengthening and developing socialist democracy and our social system." In contrast, the abolition of privileges would only weaken party discipline, because, according to Ligachev and other conservatives, the provision of perks helped ensure obedience at all levels of the Soviet power structure.

This premise was in line with the traditional party policy. According to Georgi Arbatov, adviser to several CPSU general secretaries, "Privileges have been an effective instrument for the maintenance of totalitarian rule ever since the revolution. The very existence of privileges brought along the fear that they could be lost and that your living standard could decline radically. Their weak side is the extremely negative reaction of envy and hatred from those who do not enjoy them."[14] By choosing to fight privileges, Yeltsin was appealing to the suppressed resentment of ordinary Soviet citizens. But he was also provoking outrage from those who held the reins of Soviet power.

Gorbachev could not afford to emulate Yeltsin's provocative rhetorical style. In his report to the party congress, delivered a day before Yeltsin's speech, he interpreted the issue of social justice in strictly ideological terms, proclaiming that "social justice permeates every aspect of socialist relations in society."[15] The essence of social justice was embodied in Lenin's famous slogan: "From each according to his ability, to each according to his labor." Therefore, the only expression of social injustice that Gorbachev acknowledged in Soviet society was "when the labor of a good worker and a negligent worker is remunerated equally," a practice known in party jargon as "leveling." Following the party line, Geidar Aliev, then the first secretary of Azerbaijan's Communist Party and a Politburo member, vehemently denied that Soviet leaders enjoyed any special privileges. At a press conference during the congress, Aliev argued that his salary was "no greater than that of a business manager," and that privileges simply compensated for the additional effort he and his party colleagues contributed to their work.[16]

Despite vehement disapproval from the party leadership, Yeltsin continued to portray himself as a selfless "fighter of privileges" throughout his short-lived tenure as Moscow's party boss. Moscow was an ideal place for Yeltsin to start his struggle for social justice, since in the Soviet capital alone 40,000 people were supplied with "special packages," including special buffets and access to normally unobtainable goods at half price; priority in the distribution of housing and summer vacation homes; free transportation; and the opportunity for one's offspring to attend specialized schools and the most prestigious universities.[17] These four types of privilege—food, housing, transportation, and education—would become the primary targets of Yeltsin's campaign.

In order to ward off criticism, Yeltsin linked his assault on privileges to Gorbachev's efforts to root out corruption and patronage from within the party. For example, he ordered an investigation into the Moscow State Institute of International Relations (MGIMO) to which children of the nomenklatura were given exclusive access. Yeltsin's memoir recounts his dismay at the investigation's results: "They [MGIMO] were riddled with nepotism and malpractice of every kind and it was our aim to bring proper order into these organizations, which for years had been immune to inspection and criticism."[18] So Yeltsin charged MGIMO's dean, N. I. Lebedev, with abuse of his position and removed him from his post

Yeltsin applied similarly radical measures in his efforts to fight other forms of social injustice. One of the local party bosses in Moscow's districts was fired after Yeltsin learned that he had built "a magnificent place for himself" within a regular apartment building.[19] Yeltsin also shut down an exclusive store located inside the building that housed

Moscow City's CPSU Committee, advising its employees to be "more sensitive to the outside shortages." Then, just eight months into his job, Yeltsin held an unprecedented meeting with journalists at which he condemned special cafeterias and shops and other privileges for ranking officials as an "outrage in [a] workers' state."[20] He called on reporters and citizens at large to publicize any examples of unequal treatment. Yeltsin was attempting to diminish private benefits to party insiders at a time when the country's exclusive, small-coalition institutional structure relied on the dispensation of privileges as the means to retain power. While his campaign might have been popular among the general public, the existing institutional arrangements were not favorable to his short-term political advancement.

As Yeltsin was waging his war on privileges, his political antagonist, Yegor Ligachev, was campaigning against excessive drinking. The antialcohol campaign started in May 1985, just weeks after Gorbachev came to power. It was viewed as a resumption of the fight against sloth and inefficiency that had been launched by Gorbachev's predecessor, Yuri Andropov. Presenting the antidrunkenness drive as a moral crusade, Ligachev advocated the adoption of tough administrative policies, including a drastic rise in alcohol prices, cuts in production, and restrictions on consumption. The results were endless queues, a black market for alcoholic beverages, and, for the first time since World War II, the introduction of nationwide rationing of sugar, which could be used for illicit distillery. A measure that was initially directed only against drunkenness had expanded to affect the entire population. In his memoirs, Ligachev acknowledged his responsibility for these policies, which "turned out to be excessively harsh and bureaucratic." He also recognized their damaging effect on his public image: "[I]nitially I appeared as a radical in the anti-alcohol campaign."[21]

The antialcohol campaign proved to be Gorbachev's first major policy disaster. His efforts to revitalize the Soviet economy through traditional methods—greater discipline and workplace sobriety—had failed. And the more radical economic measures Gorbachev introduced in late 1986 ran into considerable resistance from all levels of the party bureaucracy. So by the end of his second year in power Gorbachev had come to realize that only prompt liberalization of the political system could produce a much-needed economic turnaround. In January 1987 at the CC Plenum he unveiled his plan to democratize the party. The centerpiece of his proposal was an effort to increase the influence of rank-and-file party members by providing for secret, competitive, multicandidate elections for party secretaries at every level, from the local to the national. He carefully avoided imposing similar election procedures on the CPSU CC itself. Nevertheless, top party nomenklatura felt seriously endangered by Gorbachev's proposals.[22] As mentioned earlier, the extent of elite opposition to his reforms first became apparent in the CC's final resolution at this plenum, which declined to adopt the principle of competitive elections.

It was also during the January 1987 plenum that Gorbachev was first publicly criticized from the radical flank. Yeltsin, in his address to plenum members, charged that perestroika had not yet even started. His speech was a complete surprise to Gorbachev's liberal allies, who, nevertheless, thought that Yeltsin would make Gorbachev look less radical to the Politburo hard-liners.[23] Gorbachev, however, was distressed by Yeltsin's remarks and later criticized him for "extreme conservatism."[24] As recounted by Alexander Yakovlev, a Politburo member and eventual architect of perestroika, Gorbachev was concerned that Yeltsin's radicalism would scare the real party conservatives away from further democratization.

As the next CC Plenum—in June 1987—approached, rifts within Gorbachev's reform coalition were coming to the fore. Beyond his resistance to institutional changes within the party, Ligachev was also trying to limit the scope of glasnost and prevent a reassessment of Soviet history. He argued in *Pravda* against exaggerating the mistakes of the past, and demanded recognition of the Soviet achievements since the 1917 Revolution.[25] Ligachev also positively assessed Brezhnev's rule, which the reformers viewed as a period of economic stagnation. He obviously disagreed with Gorbachev's demands to eliminate all "blank spots" in Soviet history.[26]

By contrast, Yeltsin hailed Moscow's initial experiment with multicandidate elections as a success, and scorned the party nomenklatura for its exorbitant privileges. In an interview with the Moscow daily *Moskovskaia Pravda,* he pledged: "We must never again allow some people to live under the law, and others to live above the law. For that is precisely what happened. Not only fathers holding high posts in the party and Soviet apparatus or in trade were immune from the law. Their children and grandchildren sheltered in the shadow of their parents' immunity and did whatever they wanted."[27] He also argued that a campaign for social justice should accompany Gorbachev's reform policies since "this struggle [against privileges] will strengthen the unity of all strata of society, and perestroika will begin to pick up full speed if this unity becomes monolithic." The Soviet general secretary, however, was not tricked by Yeltsin's proreform rhetoric. Careful not to alienate nomenklatura, Gorbachev refused to accept the issue of party privileges as a legitimate criticism. In an interview with the Italian Communist newspaper *L'Unita* in May 1987, he argued that the privileges of party leaders were no worse than the existence of a workers' canteen in a factory.[28]

In the face of resistance to his reform agenda from conservative CC members, Gorbachev decided to present his plan at the CPSU conference scheduled for the summer of 1988, in the hope that the conference would take "measures for the further democratization of the life of the party and society."[29] Delegates to the party conference, last held in 1941, were to be elected by secret ballot at local party meetings. By engaging rank-and-file party members in the selection of delegates, Gorbachev hoped that the new party forum would be more sympathetic to his reforms than the rigid Central Committee.

While pushing for democratization and economic change, Gorbachev refrained from taking sides in the intensifying confrontation between Yeltsin and Ligachev in the Politburo. The two represented opposite visions of the reform process, but in open discussions they clashed mainly over the issues central to their individual campaigns. At Politburo meetings, when Ligachev would enthusiastically report on plummeting alcohol sales, Yeltsin would cite shocking reports of citizens drinking moonshine and even hair tonic.[30] And according to Yeltsin's close aide Mikhail Poltoranin, Ligachev considered the campaign against privileges to be social demagoguery, arguing that "one should not touch existing privileges but should improve conditions for those who do not enjoy certain opportunities."[31]

Yeltsin presented his conflict with Ligachev as a struggle between the supporters and adversaries of democratization. Gorbachev, however, viewed it differently. In a speech at the June CC Plenum he admonished those who used the new openness for narrow, self-serving purposes. Gorbachev believed that Yeltsin was attacking the party elite not out of idealism, but in order to curry support among Muscovites. Rather than accepting him as an ally, Gorbachev treated Yeltsin as a threat. Where Gorbachev demanded restraint and caution, Yeltsin favored bluntness. Where Gorbachev preached compromise and understanding, Yeltsin was stubborn and unforgiving. And while perestroika for Gorbachev was a gradual project, Yeltsin wanted it now.

The general secretary's distrust of Yeltsin was also reflected in his staff promotions. After coming to office, Gorbachev reshuffled leadership positions so that his personal appointees would form a majority in the Politburo and the CC. By March 1986, five out of the 12 full members of the Politburo had joined it under Gorbachev. Similarly, five out of the seven candidate members, including Yeltsin, owed their promotions to the new general secretary. The overall renewal rate was approximately 52 percent in just twelve months. And Gorbachev continued to make personnel changes throughout 1987. Two Brezhnev appointees were removed from the Politburo and Secretariat at the CC plenums in January and June of that year, while three Politburo members were moved from candidate to full status. Although all three had become candidate members after Yeltsin, they were promoted to full membership with voting rights in less than a year. By the fall of 1987, Boris Yeltsin was the only candidate member of the Politburo who had not advanced from the position he had been granted in February 1986. Yeltsin was effectively excluded from the country's main decision-making body, and his political prospects were uncertain. Gorbachev and Ligachev, his contemporaries, had reached the top of the party hierarchy, while his own power was confined to Moscow's boundaries. Not only was Boris Yeltsin less successful than his politically moderate party comrades, but Gorbachev was quietly tolerating Ligachev's constant interference in Yeltsin's Moscow affairs. Despite his immense popularity among Muscovites, Yeltsin was heading toward a political fiasco. He had masterfully enraged the only selectorate in the Soviet Union that mattered at the time.

How could a politician who later turned out to be such an exceptional campaigner miscalculate so badly? Yeltsin, as Reagan before him, and other, similarly skillful politicians, failed miserably in their early forays into high-level politics. Their heresthetical abilities may not always become manifest until after they have been plunged into, and seen how to escape from, the political wilderness. Institutional context matters as well. Rhetorical ingenuity and policy inventiveness, which herestheticians have to rely on, were not essential elements of success in Soviet politics. Reaching the apex of power mainly required political loyalty and conformity with the party line. As an experienced regional party boss, Yeltsin should have known as much.

While in Moscow, Yeltsin betrayed the instincts of an innate populist rather than a party apparatchik. This tendency would eventually serve him well, once his selectorate expanded beyond the Kremlin's walls. But in 1987, Yeltsin's only hope for saving his sinking career was to appeal directly to the general secretary.

The Point of No Return

Yeltsin's showdown with Ligachev reached a critical point in early September 1987. Ligachev questioned Yeltsin's tolerance for public demonstrations in Moscow and ordered a special commission to investigate.[32] Two days later, on September 12, Yeltsin wrote a personal letter to Gorbachev about what he perceived as "indifference to the matters concerning Moscow and coldness toward me personally, especially in several members of the Politburo and some secretaries of the Central Committee."[33] He pointed to Ligachev as being responsible for the "party's go-slow attitude to perestroika," and accused Politburo conservatives of insincerity in their support for Gorbachev's policies. Yeltsin also requested that the general secretary relieve him of his positions as Moscow party chief and Politburo candidate member—hoping, as he explained later in his memoirs, that his request would push Gorbachev toward a radical cadre reshuffle. The next CC Plenum was scheduled for October 21. Yeltsin asked Gorbachev to make a decision on his request before that meeting so that he would not have "to submit my request directly to a Plenum."

With the seventieth anniversary of the October Revolution looming, Gorbachev obviously preferred to avoid major personnel changes that might expose intraparty conflicts.[34] Therefore, he promised to consider Yeltsin's request some time "later."[35] Apparently, Gorbachev was unaware that Yeltsin's confrontation with Ligachev had reached a critical stage.

During the one-day October CC Plenum, Yeltsin decided to air his disagreement with Ligachev in front of all the members of the Central Committee. The primary function of the Central Committee was to lay down party policy in the five-year intervals between party congresses. With almost 500 members, the CC was largely a rubber-stamp body for the Politburo and the Secretariat, which held the real decision-making power; but in times of crisis the CC could facilitate the decisive resolution of conflicts within the party leadership. As long as Politburo members could agree among themselves, the CC exerted little influence. When Politburo members pursued conflicting agendas, however, they would turn to the CC members for support. Since Politburo members were formally selected by the CC, the composition of which was tightly controlled by the Politburo, the members of the two bodies were mutually dependent.[36]

The CC increased its influence during the decades after Stalin's death, and played a key role in several power transfers. Committee members defeated an attempt by Nikita Khrushchev's adversaries to oust him in 1957 and successfully removed the offenders from the Politburo. Seven years later, Politburo members Brezhnev and Podgornyi sought the support of the CC majority to depose Khrushchev himself. And in March 1985, Gorbachev's selection as the general secretary was facilitated by strong support for his candidacy from within the CC. Yeltsin, as the first secretary of the party committee in Sverdlovsk oblast, had been a member of the CC at the time. In his memoirs, he points out that Gorbachev became the party leader as a result of support from a large number of the first secretaries in the CC.

In October 1987, the CC comprised 307 voting members and 170 candidate members, all of whom had been elected by the CPSU Congress a year earlier.[37] Almost half were in their first term.[38] They included high-ranking party and state officials, representatives of the party and state bodies from the republics and provinces, leaders of trade unions and the Komsomol, as well as notable figures from the scholarly and artistic communities. The majority of career party apparatchiks at the CC were not only newcomers there, but also came fresh from the regions. As a result, conservatives within the party leadership could no longer count on their full support. Rather, it was Gorbachev who held sway. When Yeltsin unexpectedly took the floor during the October plenum, the thrust of his biting speech was directed against the top party leadership. He accused the CC Secretariat, headed by Ligachev, of lacking a "revolutionary energy" that the rest of the party displayed.[39] At the same time, Yeltsin conspicuously spared the Central Committee from his criticisms, calling it "the most trustworthy and open-minded assembly." He also pointed out two new and supposedly disturbing trends: the continued absence of tangible results from perestroika, and the increasing glorification of Gorbachev by the top leadership. In conclusion, he reasserted his inability to work within the Politburo due to the lack of support, "especially from Ligachev," and asked for permission to resign. The implication of his speech was clear: perestroika had been stalled by party hard-liners centered around Ligachev. They were only paying lip service to Gorbachev's reforms.

From Yeltsin's perspective, support for his resignation was a vote of confidence for the antiperestroika forces within the Politburo. And given that the largely conservative central party leadership was in the minority at the CC Plenum, most delegates might have been sympathetic to Yeltsin's charges. In order not to alienate potential supporters, Yeltsin shrewdly avoided his favorite subject, nomenklatura privileges. But by taking Ligachev on so publicly, Yeltsin left himself no room for political retreat. As revealed in his memoirs, he had no doubt that the odds were against him, yet he also knew then that the tone of the CC's response had to be set by the general secretary.

Gorbachev faced a difficult choice. After all, the inevitable result of Yeltsin's removal would be a strengthening of conservative elements in the party leadership. However, Yeltsin's speech was a challenge not only to Ligachev and conservatives, but also to Gorbachev's own reform strategy. During the earlier CC Plenum in June, Gorbachev blamed the slow pace of perestroika on the passivity of lower-level officials. He tried to avoid direct criticism of the central party apparatus, realizing that he would need its support in order to convene the 1988 party conference, where the radical reorganization of the party was to take place. Yeltsin's challenge undermined this evolutionary strategy by requiring Gorbachev to rid the party of the very conservatives he was relying on to implement his plan. By asking Gorbachev to choose between himself and Ligachev, Yeltsin was pushing the Soviet leader to expunge the conservatives from his coalition.

When the time came to speak, Gorbachev positioned himself as a defender of the interests of the party elite. He summarized Yeltsin's statement, emphasizing that it criticized not only the Politburo but the Central Committee as well. Setting the defamatory tone that would characterize his subsequent speeches on the topic, Gorbachev concluded: "This sounds like a wish to fight the Central Committee." He then encouraged members of the Central Committee to respond to Yeltsin's remarks. But first he gave the floor to Ligachev. The ensuing discussion made it readily apparent that even reformers like Alexander Yakovlev or Eduard Shevardnadze were unwilling to extend token support to Yeltsin. As one witness of the proceedings recalls, "I saw a completely different Central Committee then—many had been negative toward Yeltsin before, but this time it all burst through. The speeches were harsh, uncontrollable, full of aversion."[40]

The split between Yeltsin, now clearly perceived as a radical, and the moderate-conservative coalition behind Gorbachev was final.

Yeltsin was removed as a candidate member of the Politburo and Moscow first secretary. In his place Gorbachev appointed moderate loyalists, showing his preference for conformists over firebrands. Yeltsin's resounding political defeat was underscored by his new appointment as the first deputy chairman of the USSR Construction Committee, a position bereft of political weight. In a subsequent telephone conversation, Gorbachev made his intentions clear, vowing that he would "never let him [Yeltsin] into politics again." Yeltsin's challenge to Gorbachev's coalition had failed. But, as the next chapter will reveal, the lessons of this episode were not lost on him.

Changing the Rules of the Game

What impact did Boris Yeltsin's political defeat have on Gorbachev's support coalition? Conservatives and moderate reformers were united in their rejection of Yeltsin's radical challenge. However, since the hardline elements in the party leadership were the primary targets of his criticism, it was conservatives who went on the counteroffensive. Ligachev's new assertiveness was reflected in an interview he gave to *Le Monde* while visiting France. He emphasized that he, rather than the general secretary, chaired the meetings of the Secretariat at the behest of the Politburo, implying that he was nearly as powerful as Gorbachev.[41]

The publication of Nina Andreyeva's letter in March 1988 was a natural by-product of this conservative backlash. The power of the backlash also signaled to perestroika supporters, especially rank-and-file party members, that they should exhibit greater caution in calling for reform. And it showed that, rhetoric aside, Mikhail Gorbachev might not have been as serious about political change as he had professed to be. Sensing this shift in perceptions of his position, Gorbachev admitted to journalists two months after the Yeltsin affair that it came to be viewed among the intelligentsia and young people "as a blow to perestroika."[42] The moderate party leadership's willingness to side with conservatives against Yeltsin's radicalism was not shared by the more reform-oriented members of Gorbachev's coalition at the lower levels. For the first time since coming to power, Gorbachev risked losing his core support from the general public. Yeltsin's maneuver had failed, but it had instigated rifts in Gorbachev's coalition.

Public sympathy for Yeltsin's reform agenda was expressed in a series of unprecedented protests over his resignation. Pamphlets were distributed in his hometown of Sverdlovsk during early November, asking city residents to send protests to the Soviet government to prevent his resignation.[43] They warned that if Yeltsin were allowed to step down, "the saboteurs of perestroika would gain a free hand and political repression and dogmatism would return." Similar petitions were circulated in Moscow, where students demonstrated against Yeltsin's removal.[44] Public suspicions about the reversal of glasnost were reinforced by the Kremlin's refusal to publish Yeltsin's plenum speech. Various samizdat versions of the speech were circulated around the country and leaked to the international press. These versions differed in their interpretation of exactly who had been the intended targets of Yeltsin's criticisms, with opinions ranging from Ligachev and KGB chairman Chebrikov, to Gorbachev's wife Raisa and the general secretary himself. Ironically, the only topic all of them attributed to Yeltsin was the unjust nature of nomenklatura privileges, a subject that Yeltsin had not even raised in his speech.[45] In the presumed text of Yeltsin's address that circulated in Moscow and was published in *Le Monde,* Yeltsin was said to have blasted his Politburo colleagues by saying: "It is difficult for me to explain to a factory worker why, on the seventieth anniversary of the Socialist Revolution, he is forced to stand in line to buy sausages, which contain more starch than meat, whereas our tables are loaded with sturgeon, caviar and all kinds of delicacies easily acquired from a place he cannot even approach."[46] The privilege issue had become Yeltsin's trademark, and was seen by many as the true reason for his dismissal.

In order to limit potential damage to his coalition, Gorbachev quickly distanced himself from both the conservatives and the radicals, by portraying them as enemies of perestroika. Several weeks after the 1987 October plenum, the liberal Soviet weekly *Moscow News* published an essay by Gavriil Popov, a progressive economist from Moscow State University, who argued that in times of transition there was a need for "the unity of all forces . . . for solving the key tasks."[47] In Popov's view, Yeltsin's attempt "to counter the Plenary Meeting of the Central Committee with his 'special stand'" aimed to undermine such unity. A month later Popov published a longer article in which he argued against Yeltsin's position even more vigorously, defining it as "authoritarian conservative avant-gardism," "the haven for the devils of perestroika" and even tracing his views to Trotsky and Stalin. He concluded by calling for unity behind Gorbachev and urging efforts to overcome any resistance to perestroika.[48]

But Yeltsin continued to press the issue of privileges throughout 1988. In an interview with BBC Television in May, he reasserted the need to abolish all privileges, arguing that everyone in the Soviet Union should experience shortages to an equal degree.[49] He was also most outspoken about his differences with Ligachev, calling him "one of the main opponents on questions of social justice." Unwilling to abandon his politically costly confrontation with Ligachev, Yeltsin insisted that the number two man in the party should resign.

Yet Nina Andreyeva's letter had rendered Yeltsin's attack against Ligachev less controversial than it had been earlier. In her letter, the teacher from Leningrad criticized attempts to revise Soviet history and defended Stalin's cultural and historic achievements.[50] Although she professed support for perestroika, Andreyeva also attacked "left-liberals" and argued that the working class, rather than the intelligentsia, should be at the vanguard of the reform process. Since many in the Politburo thought that Ligachev was behind the letter's publication, they read it as his attack on the moderate reformers in the Gorbachev coalition.

Gorbachev recognized the threat and launched his own counteroffensive. Days after the letter's publication, *Pravda* printed an official rebuttal from two Politburo moderates, Alexander Yakovlev and Vadim Medvedev. Gorbachev also took immediate steps to downgrade Ligachev's role in the Secretariat, transferring most of his other responsibilities to moderate reformers. According to Anatoliy Lukianov, then a Politburo candidate member, Ligachev's marginalization in the party leadership was the direct result of the conflict surrounding Andreyeva's letter, and brought about the first serious divisions within the Politburo.[51] Despite this serious blow, Ligachev still tried to use Gorbachev's apprehension about Yeltsin to rehabilitate himself. During a speech in Togliatti he linked Yeltsin's thesis about resistance to perestroika to Stalin's idea that "as socialism is built the class struggle is exacerbated."[52] In an apparent effort to play on reformers' sensitivities, he concluded by reminding the audience about the "grave consequences that 'theory' led to."

Ligachev continued to position himself as the most outspoken of Yeltsin's critics during the Nineteenth CPSU Conference later that summer.

The July 1988 party conference marked Yeltsin's first public return from imposed political exile. Despite Gorbachev's attempts to prevent his opponent from speaking, Yeltsin managed to take the floor. His speech was even more significant because the conference was being broadcast live on Soviet television. Yeltsin therefore perceived it as his "last chance to break political isolation."[53] Yeltsin, ever the radical, insisted on the need to abolish "the food 'rations' for the so-to-speak 'starving nomenklatura,' eradicate elitism in society, eradicate the substance and the form of the word 'special' from our vocabulary, since we do not have any special Communists."[54] As in his BBC interview, Yeltsin reiterated his call on Ligachev and other conservative Politburo members to resign in order to quicken perestroika. He concluded by asking the stunned conference delegates for political rehabilitation. As Yeltsin later wrote, he hoped that the conference delegates could somehow reverse the decision to expel him from the Politburo, enabling him once again to strive for higher political office.[55]

His hopes were dashed when, after a short break, Gorbachev announced the first speaker: Yegor Ligachev. As he had done in October, Ligachev inveighed that Yeltsin had not drawn proper conclusions from his past errors.[56] And he rejected Yeltsin's plea for rehabilitation, arguing that there were no grounds for changing anything in the wording of the October plenum's decision. He also vigorously defended the system of nomenklatura privileges, claiming that party workers were grossly underpaid—"twenty-sixth in the country in terms of average wage."[57] Ligachev then rejected Yeltsin's proposal to eliminate privileges, calling it an attempt to win support from the masses that would lead to "parasitism." Subsequent speeches were filled with similar diatribes.

In conclusion, Gorbachev flatly rejected Yeltsin's request to review the plenum's decision, while ignoring Yeltsin's calls for the eradication of privileges. Instead of a turning point, the conference had become yet another political failure for Yeltsin. As he later recounted, "I felt that they are satisfied, they beat me, they are victorious. At that moment I was overcome with apathy. I did not want any further struggle, any explanations, only to forget everything and be on my own."[58]

Although the party conference was a major setback for Yeltsin, its decisions opened the way for Yeltsin's political comeback the following year. The single most far-reaching resolution of the gathering created a new legislative structure, the Congress of People's Deputies, consisting of 2,250 deputies, of which 1,500 were to be installed through direct popular election. Congress and the smaller Supreme Soviet, chosen from among the congress deputies, were expected to make the principal decisions on the political and economic development of the country.

This institutional innovation was a part of Gorbachev's design to transfer decision-making powers from the party to state bodies, in order to override conservative resistance to his reforms. Even more importantly, it provided Gorbachev with an alternative source of legitimacy. He could no longer rely on an increasingly uneasy and unstable coalition of moderates and conservatives within the party leadership to sustain his power. However, by creating the first multicandidate election in Soviet history, Gorbachev also enabled others to seek political power through public support rather than party approval.

Yeltsin, already sensing the full extent of his popularity, seized the opportunity to form a winning coalition drawn not from the party elite, but from the public at large.

Yeltsin's first attempt to gain political ascendancy in Moscow failed for reasons similar to those that had contributed to Reagan's failure in the 1968 presidential race. Both men had to compete in institutional settings with narrow selectorates and small winning coalitions of top party officials. In order to succeed they needed to appeal to the private interests of party bosses, rather than emphasize issues of concern to the wider public. Both Reagan and Yeltsin had misguidedly chosen to campaign on issues that resonated with the rank and file, but were irrelevant or even alarming to the elite. Even so, these early experiences established them as viable candidates, and prepared them to win future political battles under new institutional rules.

Yeltsin's Winning Campaigns

Down with Privileges and
Out of the USSR, 1989–91

The heresthetical maneuver that launched Yeltsin to the apex of power in Russia is a classic representation of Riker's argument. Yeltsin reformulated Russia's central problem, offered a radically new solution through a unique combination of issues, and engaged in an uncompromising, negative campaign against his political opponents. This allowed Yeltsin to form an unusual coalition of different stripes and ideologies that resulted in his election as Russia's first president. His rise to power, while certainly facilitated by favorable timing, should also be credited to his own political skill and strategic choices.

In addition to the institutional reforms introduced at the June party conference, the summer of 1988 was marked by two other significant developments in Soviet politics. In August, Gorbachev presented a draft plan for the radical reorganization of the Secretariat, which was to be replaced by six commissions, each dealing with a specific policy area. The Politburo's adoption of this plan in September was a major political blow for Ligachev, who had used the Secretariat as his principal power base. Once viewed as the second most powerful man in the party, Ligachev now found himself chairman of the CC commission on agriculture, a position with little real influence.[1] His ideological portfolio was transferred to Gorbachev's ally, Vadim Medvedev, who belonged to the new group of soft-line reformers. His colleague Alexander Yakovlev assumed responsibility for foreign policy.

According to Anatolii Chernyaev, Gorbachev's close adviser, the decision to curtail the Secretariat's power came in response to Ligachev's public and increasingly critical view of the reform process.[2] Gorbachev's surprise counteroffensive against the hard-liners also entailed removal of a few conservatives from the party leadership, including Gromyko and Solomentsev from the Politburo, and Demichev and Dolgikh from among the candidate members. By demoting Ligachev, Gorbachev neutralized one of his most prominent conservative challengers, but he also eliminated the traditional target of Yeltsin's political attacks, thus leaving himself exposed. With the conservatives in the Kremlin weakened, Gorbachev now had to bear sole responsibility for the consequences—and inadequacies—of the reform process.

National revival, combined with increased freedom of association, had led to the emergence that summer of a series of popular front movements in the three Baltic republics. These fronts initially represented themselves as committed supporters of perestroika. However, demonstrations that August made it clear that the groups endorsed reforms far beyond anything envisioned by Gorbachev. In addition to questioning the legality of the incorporation of the Baltic republics into the Soviet Union and insisting on the return of their historical national symbols, the fronts demanded full political and economic sovereignty for their republics as guaranteed by the Soviet constitution.

Gorbachev was not prepared to acknowledge the republics' right to secede, but he also could not reject outright their claim for sovereignty, which was a central principle of Soviet federalism. Palatable as the idea was to a broad political spectrum, "sovereignty" became an effective slogan for mobilization. Radical nationalists viewed it as the first step toward their long-term goal of independence, while moderate Communists believed that they were returning to fundamental Soviet principles. The call for greater autonomy was therefore compatible with both the goal of preserving the Union and that of dismantling it.

On November 16, 1988, the Estonian Supreme Soviet became the first to declare a republic's sovereignty and the primacy of republican over central laws. The issue of republican sovereignty suddenly posed a new threat to an already-fragile consensus among the top leadership behind Gorbachev's reform program. Gorbachev strongly objected to republican bids for legal supremacy over Moscow, warning of ensuing chaos and a conservative backlash.[3] Acquiescence to the nationalists' demands would radicalize the reform agenda to such a point that it would become unacceptable to the remaining conservatives. In Gorbachev's view, national radicals in the republics were playing into the hands of conservatives in Moscow, destabilizing the Soviet Union and making it ungovernable.

In an effort to consolidate his supporters, Gorbachev accused both radicals and conservatives of antiperestroika positions. During a speech in Krasnoyarsk in late September, Gorbachev fumed: "What the champions of extreme views have in common is the fact that both of them confuse people and sow doubts among them regarding the meaning and purpose of perestroika."[4] Calling these extreme views "scientifically erroneous and politically irresponsible," he confidently asserted that "we will not let ourselves be diverted from our chosen path."

But it was during this same visit to Krasnoyarsk that Gorbachev suddenly encountered a reaction different from any he had become accustomed to during his previous travels across the country. City residents, with whom he was meeting, openly expressed scorn and hostility over the lack of basic food items in the shops.[5] Yeltsin's warnings of popular dissatisfaction with perestroika's failure to produce material results caught up with Gorbachev on the streets of the Siberian city: "I heard much criticism about the food supply at that time . . . and had plenty to think about on my return from Krasnoyarsk. . . . Why were we spending billions on industry, but only petty sums on the things necessary for a comfortable life?"[6] By the end of 1988, as Yeltsin was preparing to jump into his first election campaign, food rationing was already being introduced in some parts of the country.

Campaign against Privileges: January–March 1989

Yeltsin had risen to national prominence while governing Moscow, and so the Soviet capital was a natural place from which to revive his flagging career. He registered as a candidate for the congressional seat in Moscow's first territorial election district. The district spanned the whole city, encompassing more than six million voters.

The campaign got off the ground with the publication of a Yeltsin interview in the holiday issue of the daily *Komsomolskaia Pravda*, under the title "Let Us Not Forget about a Human."[7] Conducted by Pavel Voshchanov, Yeltsin's future press secretary, the interview was confined to just two topics, the economy and social justice. Yeltsin immediately emphasized the connection between the two: "People were constantly told that in our humane country everything is done exclusively for their benefit. But what did they see in practice? Waiting lines of many years for any kind of housing. Empty counters. Extortion, corruption, and money-grubbing. The self-satisfied flourishing of bureaucracy. It all began to seem deceitful and economically unjustified." Responding to Ligachev's earlier charge of wage-leveling, Yeltsin was emphatic: "I am not in favor of leveling! No way. I am opposed to hierarchical benefits. . . . I think material benefits should be identically accessible to everyone. In other words, a minister's ruble should be no different than the janitor's ruble." Yeltsin also challenged Ligachev's argument that party apparatchiks were given privileges to compensate for their lower wages: "A system of double privileges emerges in society: on one hand you have higher wages, and on the other you have more goods for those wages." In his concluding message, Yeltsin reiterated the central theme of his future campaign: "Without a staunch, daily struggle for social justice, we could once again find ourselves hostages to bureaucracy."

It was a perfect example of Riker's dominance principle. Yeltsin noticed that his objection to elite perks generated a swell of support among reform-minded party members at the core of Gorbachev's coalition. The denials of party bosses rang hollow and hypocritical in contrast. Unable to offer a persuasive rejoinder to Yeltsin's argument, they instead opted for the kind of strategy advocated by Cicero's brother, and attacked Yeltsin's personal integrity: Riker's dispersion principle.

There were two components to Yeltsin's electoral strategy that attracted soft-line reformers. First, Yeltsin did not try to distance himself from his nomenklatura past. On the contrary, he presented himself as an apparat insider with firsthand knowledge of existing practices. As he wrote in his 1989 memoir: "Even at my level as a candidate member of the Politburo, my domestic staff consisted of three cooks, three waitresses, a housemaid, and a gardener with his own team of under-gardeners. And, surprisingly, all this luxury was incapable of producing either comfort or convenience. What warmth can there be in a marble-lined house?"[8] In contrast to his peers, he claimed to be appalled by existing practices and voluntarily relinquished them.

Yeltsin's other tactic was to justify his attacks against nomenklatura benefits by citing fundamental principles of Soviet socialism. In his interview with *Komsomolskaia Pravda*, Yeltsin explained that he was opposed to privileges because the practice "contradicts the economic law of the socialist society: 'To each according to his labor.'"[9] In another interview, he bemoaned the failure to achieve the socialist ideal of "bringing everyone to the same level regardless of the office they hold."[10] He thus emphasized his loyalty to the socialist system, which had not yet been discredited in the eyes of the pro-Gorbachev soft-liners.

Finally, he sought to refute the notion that he was personally opposed to Gorbachev: "I don't want people to portray me as a rival to Mr. Gorbachev, not under any circumstances. I am not the leader of an opposition party."[11] On another occasion he reaffirmed: "I am not and do not wish to be an alternative to Gorbachev. Who thinks this, in reality, does not think. I will never be against Gorbachev."[12] Moreover, he emphasized his agreement with Gorbachev on the strategy of reform and diminished their differences to a matter of "different opinions on tactics in internal politics." His aide, Mikhail Poltoranin, argued that Yeltsin's electoral program was strategically "in line with the CPSU platform."[13]

In the run-up to the election, the leadership made a concerted effort to undermine those elements of Yeltsin's electoral strategy that made him acceptable to soft-line reformers. First, the Politburo's spokesman on ideology, Vadim Medvedev, announced that a commission had been established to examine Yeltsin's party loyalty. The next day, *Pravda* reported that Yeltsin had been accused of campaign statements "contradictory to the guidelines of the Central Committee and party rules and ethics."[14] It warned that he faced expulsion from the top policy-making body and ultimately from the party—a signal to soft-liners that his policy proposals contradicted the official party line.

Three days later the Moscow-based daily *Moskovskaia Pravda* published an article by Vladimir Tikhomirov, a factory worker and Central Committee member. The article dismissed Yeltsin's image as a selfless fighter, claiming that members of his family continued to use the same privileged health services that Yeltsin so frequently criticized, and that the candidate himself retained a two-story nomenklatura dacha in one of Moscow's suburbs, as well as a luxury car.[15] Tikhomirov concluded his article with a call to all voters: "So let us not get confused: Comrade Yeltsin is sufficiently active in using those same 'benefits' that he is publicly 'fighting.'"

But the attacks proved counterproductive, burnishing instead Yeltsin's image as a martyr and mobilizing his supporters. Rallies protesting his treatment in the press were organized in Moscow and at least four other cities, including Leningrad and Lviv.[16] In the final week before the election, several rallies were held in Moscow to protest the accusations against him. Finally, on the day before the election, Moscow saw the biggest unofficial rally held there since the 1917 Revolution with tens of thousands demonstrating in support of Yeltsin.[17] Yeltsin's argument that the party apparatus opposed him because it feared losing its privileges convinced Moscow's proreform voters. Gorbachev's counteroffensive failed. Yeltsin had found an effective issue on which to build an electoral coalition.

One day before the election, *Moskovskaia Pravda* published Yeltsin's message to voters in which he emphasized that the only way out of the crisis was "through a struggle against the party-bureaucratic apparatus, corruption and social injustice." "Only this," he wrote, "will be able to achieve a new image of socialism and a new state of Soviet society." In effect, Yeltsin was proposing an alternative vision of the Soviet future characterized by a more "just" socialism. This vision had mass appeal among those who desired change, and the new large coalition electoral environment was an optimal setting for Yeltsin to capitalize on his vision. In the March 27, 1989, election to the Soviet Congress, Boris Yeltsin carried approximately 90 percent of the vote. Two months after his victory, in an interview with the Spanish newspaper *La Vanguardia,* he identified the central issue that had secured him such popularity as "the struggle for social justice—something that, certainly, earns people's respect."[18]

The tenets of Riker's theory of campaigning are readily apparent in Yeltsin's strategy. Yeltsin had found an issue that his opponent could not embrace without alienating core supporters. And he had linked his radical position on nomenklatura privileges to the issue of economic welfare to bring about new policy alternatives. While some soft-liners in Gorbachev's coalition—those connected to the party apparatus— might have disagreed with the need to abolish privileges, they nonetheless agreed with the complaint that perestroika had not brought economic improvement. Yeltsin was thus able to argue for eliminating privileges as a way to hasten perestroika and improve popular well-being.

Yeltsin's emphasis on the need for quicker reforms also reflected a broader societal consensus. According to a March 1989 public opinion poll, 70 percent of respondents identified themselves as active advocates of perestroika; another 15 percent claimed to be passively in favor of it, while only 5 percent opposed it.[19] At the same time, 80 percent of respondents said that perestroika was proceeding too slowly, and 75 percent judged perestroika by the state of the consumer goods market.[20]

In contrast, Gorbachev was still attempting to address each issue separately. On the one hand, he was defending the system of privileges as a reward for the extra work done by the party leadership. On the other hand, he was warning that a radical approach to perestroika would lead to major economic upheavals. As Yeltsin's antiprivilege drive gained momentum, and then eventually brought him victory, Gorbachev, following the dispersion principle, abandoned attempts to rebut his opponent. A month after the election, Gorbachev gave a speech in which he acknowledged that shortages in housing, food, and basic consumer goods were growing despite perestroika.[21] The next month, in a speech to the Soviet Congress, he proposed that a review of elite privileges be one of the main functions of the newly formed Supreme Soviet.[22]

Still, it was another year before Gorbachev took practical steps to neutralize Yeltsin's strategy. In late February 1990 the Soviet government announced that the country's current and former leaders were no longer entitled to extra privileges.[23] Party nomenklatura were left without summer homes, special food orders, household workers, or cars. By that time, however, Yeltsin had already begun to wage his second election campaign, using a different set of issues to form an even broader support coalition and further undermine Gorbachev.

Campaign for Russian Sovereignty: 1990–91

Despite his landslide victory in Moscow, Yeltsin still enjoyed less support, countrywide, than Gorbachev. According to a 1989 All-Union poll, the Soviet leader was named "Man of the Year" by 46 percent of respondents, while Yeltsin was mentioned by only 16 percent.[24] Yeltsin's support was concentrated in large cities such as Moscow, Leningrad, and his native Sverdlovsk, in contrast to the traditionally conservative rural areas.

The overwhelming dominance of the conservatives had virtually sidelined Yeltsin and his fellow radicals in the new Soviet legislature. The only way they could increase their influence was by winning additional seats in the republican and city soviets in the March 1990 elections. As Yeltsin later explained: "I was quick to understand that radical changes would not come from the All-Union bodies. . . . I was convinced that the role of the center must be sharply reduced . . . and we had to strengthen horizontal ties with greater independence for the republics."[25]

Yeltsin had to achieve two complementary goals in order to weaken the Kremlin's power: transfer decision-making power from the Communist Party apparatus to the elected deputy assemblies and from the center to the republics. He outlined these two goals in May 1989, during his first address to the Soviet Congress: "Power has to be transferred to the hands of the people whose interests are represented by the chief legislative body—the Congress of People's Deputies. . . . In order to speed up the reform process, we also need to give more political rights, as well as economic and financial self-rule, to every Union republic, give them territorial sovereignty."[26]

Yeltsin's call for expanded republican rights resonated in some circles of the Russian intelligentsia. A few Soviet literary figures had been expressing concern about the decay of Russian culture and about growing anti-Russian sentiment in other Soviet republics since at least the 1970s.[27] These anxieties were articulated by the prominent Russian writer Valentin Rasputin in his address at the First USSR Congress of People's Deputies, in May 1989: "Russophobia had spread into the Baltic countries and Georgia and is penetrating into other republics. Anti-Soviet slogans are being combined with anti-Russian ones. . . . Would it be better perhaps for Russia to leave the Union? This, incidentally, would help us solve many of our own problems, both current and future."[28]

By mid-1989 the intellectuals' concerns were being echoed by republican apparatchiks who raised the issue of the Russian Federation's sovereign rights. In August 1989, Vitaliy Vorotnikov, chairman of the Supreme Soviet of the Russian Soviet Federative Socialist Republic (RSFSR), proposed the use of world prices in trading with other Soviet republics.[29] During his address at the September Plenum of the Central Committee of the CPSU Vorotnikov also noted that "while other Union republics have become stronger, the underdeveloped economical and political mechanisms of the RSFSR have a negative effect on the country, and primarily for all the Russian people."[30] In an interview titled "Russia's Interests," another apparatchik, Alexander Vlasov, chairman of the RSFSR Council of Ministers, blamed the "undermined power of republican authorities" for Russia's worsening economic problems.[31] In his view, confusion about the interests of the USSR and RSFSR prevented Russia from quickly resolving its own problems. He argued in favor of strengthening republican power structures, and transferring Soviet industrial assets under Russia's control.

The Kremlin recognized the need to raise the Russian Federation's status in a new CPSU program called "Party's National Politics under the Present Conditions": "Up to now certain managerial functions in the republic were performed by the All-Union bodies. This had a negative effect on the interests of the republic and the Union."[32] However, the program made only a limited suggestion that the CPSU establish new governing bodies in Russia's administrative, economic, ideological, cultural, and scientific spheres. Still, it was enough to allow Vlasov to claim in December 1989 that Russia's sovereignty had been expanded.

But Yeltsin and the other radical reformers did not address the issue of Russian sovereignty. During his first visit to the United States in the fall of 1989, Yeltsin hardly mentioned the topic in any of his public appearances. His omission did not escape the notice of his opponents. In October 1989, the conservative newspaper *Sovietskaia Rossiia* published an interview with a Soviet deputy who was involved in forming a group to represent Russia. He claimed that the radical reformers in the Interregional Group of Deputies, which Yeltsin cochaired, never seriously discussed Russian problems.[33]

The campaign for the republican legislature seemed to bring about a turnaround in the reformers' attitudes. On December 28, Soviet news agencies reported that Yeltsin had not only announced his intention to run for a seat in the Russian parliament, but had also expressed his willingness to compete for the parliamentary chairmanship. In his first interview of the 1990 campaign, Yeltsin talked about the need to make Russia an independent republic, to address the needs of ethnic Russians, and to separate Russian authorities from the central government.[34] But aside from his vague promise to press for more radical change, his position was almost indistinguishable from that held by his more conservative opponents. Yeltsin's platform, published on February 5, contained only a passing appeal to Russian economic sovereignty.[35] He had not yet devised his heresthetical formula for success.

Two main electoral alliances formed in Russia in early 1990. Conservatives established the bloc of socialist-patriotic movements, uniting hard-line Communists and nationalists. Members of this somewhat unlikely coalition shared one important goal: reasserting Russian influence within the USSR, while preserving the latter's integrity. Nationalism became a popular ideological platform that could help the

Communists retain power and prevent the disintegration of the Soviet Union. The Communist nomenklatura became a major political ally in the nationalists' efforts to reverse democratic and market-oriented reforms, which they condemned as an attempt to westernize and further weaken Russia.[36] For both groups, preservation of the imperial Soviet state was paramount.

Radical reformers, for their part, organized an electoral bloc called Democratic Russia. According to one of its founders, Sergei Stankevich, the group's name reflected two popular tendencies in the Russian public: "Opinion polls had shown that the most powerful trends in Russian politics were pushing people to the left and to the right: toward democratic populism opposed to the power 'mafia' and toward Russian nationalism."[37] The combination of these two trends, however, precluded the neoimperial approach to relations with non-Russian republics that conservatives were advocating. The reformers felt that the republics should be granted the sovereign rights guaranteed by the Soviet constitution. They would then have to rely on their own economic resources, while Russia would be free to correct the economic distortions accumulated during its history of interrepublic relations. They also advocated limiting the power of the central authorities who, by that time, had been discredited in the eyes of reformers and conservatives alike.

This was a very attractive solution in the eyes of an increasingly disgruntled Russian public. Their non-Russian counterparts saw their economic and cultural degradation as the direct result of Moscow's exploitative policies. Russians, however, regarded the state of their culture and economy as being at least as pitiful as that of their peers. In their view, Russian decay was the result of sacrifices they had made on behalf of other republics with fewer natural resources and industrial capabilities. Thus, Russians perceived that other republics were living at their expense, not the reverse. This view was reinforced by a large number of articles published by Russian economists in the Moscow press, arguing that the other republics were receiving much more from the federal treasury than they were contributing.[38]

These sentiments were shared by many members of the intelligentsia, and even by Russian party officials. In the words of Valentin Rasputin: "We [Russians] are tired of being scapegoats, of enduring the slurs and the treachery. We are told that this is our cross to bear. But this cross is becoming increasingly unwieldy." Yuri Prokofiev, first secretary of the Moscow CPSU City Committee, struck a more plaintive note: "Russia put everything it could into the colonies, if you can call them that, and they are talking about seceding. And Russia is left, if you'll excuse me, with a bare butt."[39] The debate over ways to unburden Russia divided radical reformers from conservative nationalists and Communists.

Russian party bosses adopted a more ambiguous rhetoric, alternating between acknowledgments of the drive for republican self-rule and concessions to the demand for preserving Soviet cohesion. At the end of 1989 Vlasov still argued for giving the interests of the Union unequivocal priority over republican needs.[40] Vorotnikov expressed a similar view in which he saw Russia's role in enhancing the unity of Soviet republics.

In contrast, Yeltsin offered a radically different vision in which power was redistributed from the central authorities to the republics. In practical terms, Yeltsin suggested leaving Gorbachev with a substantially diminished and largely symbolic role of "strategic planning with a minimal apparat."[41]

This reformulation of Russia's fundamental problem would form the basis for Yeltsin's heresthetical future. Earlier political debates had focused on the growing economic crisis and ways to address it. Yeltsin also referred to the economic slump in order to buttress his antiprivileges campaign. This time, however, he argued that Russia's economic calamities were a by-product of the country's dysfunctional institutional structure. In an interview by the Soviet weekly *Argumenty i Fakty,* he pointed to the "superconcentration of power" as the sole reason for the country's dismal condition.[42]

Yeltsin's radical approach was best characterized in his interview with British ITV. In that interview, he named the three Baltic states, along with Georgia and Moldova, as the most likely republics to secede. Yeltsin added a caveat: "If Russia is treated the way it is being treated now, it can consider using this right the same way that Lithuania did."[43]

At the same time, Yeltsin was cautious enough to emphasize that, despite favoring maximum decentralization of power, he still did not advocate dissolution of the Union, saying, "I would only fight for maximum independence." In fact, he argued that his plan would prevent disintegration since, having strengthened their sovereign rights, republics would no longer want to secede from the Soviet Union.[44] This stance made his position acceptable to those who favored greater Russian sovereignty, but also supported Gorbachev's attempts to revitalize the Union as a whole. With the members of Democratic Russia running on his coattails, the Russian parliamentary election became the first true test of Yeltsin's widespread popularity. The party won nearly half the contested seats, while the conservative Communist-patriotic bloc failed to get even one. Still, Communists who ran independently of the two blocs won the majority of races.

The resounding defeat of the Communist-nationalist electoral alliance cannot be attributed simply to the unpopularity of their non-market, anti-Western, authoritarian vision of Russia. Nor can the strong showing of Democratic Russia be explained solely by the popularity of its progressive ideas.[45] The radical reformers succeeded because they identified an easily understood issue that appealed not only to their core constituency, but also to their ideological opponents. Many rank-and-file Communists with strong nationalist sentiments shared a sense of exhaustion with "imperial philanthropy" and a yearning for "contraction." For them, re-creating a more centralized empire, as the socialist-patriotic bloc advocated, would require that Russia still bear its costs. By contrast, divesting Russia of responsibility for the other Union republics, leaving them to make their own way in the world, seemed like an effective solution to Russia's imperial troubles. It also addressed the sentiment of Russians who felt they had been unjustly accused of exploiting the other republics. Even Evgenii Primakov, a career Soviet official and chairman of one of the Union parliament's chambers, pointed to the ironic unfairness of Russia's poor condition: "The paradox is that 'metropolis' RSFSR, having tremendous resources and potential, is worse off than other republics."[46]

Following on his electoral gains, Yeltsin decided to seek election as speaker of the parliament, a position that would allow him to directly challenge Gorbachev. Realizing this possibility, Gorbachev made every effort to prevent Yeltsin's rise. Gorbachev should have been ideologically sympathetic to many of Democratic Russia's positions. But Yeltsin's drive for decentralization, combined with personal animosity, instead pushed Gorbachev to tacitly support Yeltsin's ideological opponents, who advocated a stronger and more cohesive Union and hence a larger role for Gorbachev.

Gorbachev made his first attempts to satisfy the demands of the conservative Russian Communists during the September 1989 CPSU plenum. He promised to establish a Russian bureau in the Communist Party, grant more power to the regional authorities, and change the state structure of the Russian republic. When Democratic Russia was formed and Yeltsin emerged as a forceful advocate of republican sovereignty, Gorbachev sent another favorable signal to the conservatives by appointing two prominent Russian nationalists to his new 10-member Presidential Council. But Gorbachev's strongest expression of support for the nationalist-Communist conservatives came during the election of the chairman of Russia's Supreme Soviet.

In their opening remarks at the May 22, 1990 RSFSR Congress, Yeltsin and Vlasov, the Communist conservatives' representative, argued in favor of expanded Russian sovereignty. However, while Vlasov spoke mainly about economic sovereignty, Yeltsin emphasized the republic's expanded political rights and criticized the Union leadership, calling it "the cruel exploiter, the miserly benefactor who does not think about the future." He pledged to end the injustice in relations between Russia and the central authorities.[47]

Taking the floor, Gorbachev made his own preferences clear. First, he addressed the Communist conservatives, supporting their goal to strengthen Russia as a socialist republic within the Soviet Union "and promising them to create a Russian Communist party."[48] The focal point of his address, however, was a critique of Yeltsin's speech, calling it an attempt to distance Russia from socialism, which Yeltsin had allegedly failed to mention in his speech. In his rejection of socialism, Gorbachev argued, Yeltsin "contradicts the general course of perestroika, which is supposed to give socialism a fresh breath." The Soviet leader leveled his most serious charge when he concluded that Yeltsin's true goal was not so much the revival of Russian sovereignty as the dissolution of the Soviet Union. Thus, Gorbachev appealed not just to the nationalists and Communists, but also to soft-line reformers who were not yet prepared to accept the dissolution of the Union. Yeltsin immediately rebuffed the accusation, adopting a conciliatory tone: "I have never advocated Russia's secession. I am in favor of the independence of republics so that republics are strong and so that with this strength they reinforce our strong Union."[49]

Yeltsin was elected chairman of the parliament by a modest margin—535 to 467—after three rounds of voting. He clearly benefited from his opponents' drab style. But Yeltsin also managed to reassure many undecided deputies that his views were not as radical as Gorbachev had claimed. Repeating the party line that strong republics were needed for the sake of the stronger Union, Yeltsin presented his case for Russian sovereignty as a legitimate expectation, rather than a revolutionary goal. He was also quick to position himself as an independent candidate not beholden to any particular political group. One deputy reminded Yeltsin that many of his allies were supporting him not because he was the leader of Democratic Russia, but because of his personal qualities. Yeltsin responded by vowing to represent all Russians, and not just a particular political group. He then, quite suddenly, renounced his membership in Democratic Russia, saying he was no longer its hostage.[50]

Opinion polls revealed that Gorbachev's drift toward the conservatives was further straining his already-stressed coalition. Meanwhile, Gorbachev's approval rating had decreased from 52 percent in December 1989 to 39 percent the following May[51]—this despite the fact that Yeltsin had never directly challenged Gorbachev in his speeches and had even claimed to support his ultimate goals. However, as early as February 1990, Yeltsin called upon Gorbachev to renounce the conservative nomenklatura and side with the people. Nevertheless, the core of Gorbachev's coalition still held on.

Although the idea of greater sovereignty for Russia and the other republics had become widely popular by early 1990, Russians remained divided over the allocation of power between the Union elite and republican leaders. According to a May 1990 poll conducted in 20 RSFSR regions, 43 percent of respondents said that "Russia should receive political and economic independence (possibly seceding from the Union)," 35 percent believed the "economic and political rights of Russia should be expanded, but the final word should be left to the 'center,'" and 18 percent felt that the status of the Russian Federation in the Soviet Union "should remain the same way it is now."[52] Even after a parliamentary election held under the "Russia First" slogan, most Russians wanted the Union center to retain its hold on power. Yeltsin's task was to realign this majority in his favor.

Yeltsin had heresthetically wed the promise of swift economic reform to his crusade for Russian sovereignty. This strategic choice allowed him to attract to his side even those who were initially reluctant to devolve all power to the republics. His campaign focused on the idea that the center had for decades been draining Russian resources that could have been used to improve the republics' economies. Downsizing the central apparatus and providing the Russian leadership with the power to control their own resources seemed like a quick and effective way to stop economic deterioration. Yeltsin articulated this approach in his first speech at the Congress of People's Deputies on May 22, 1990, stressing that it was "not the center but Russia which must think about which functions to transfer to the center, and which to keep for itself."[53]

On June 12, 1990, the deputies of the Russian parliament overwhelmingly adopted a Declaration of Sovereignty, with 907 "yeas," 13 "nays," and nine abstentions. The declaration asserted primacy of Russian laws over Soviet ones and "reserved the right to leave the USSR freely." Yeltsin was even more specific about the role he envisioned for the Kremlin in an interview on the prime-time news program *Vremia:* "Russia should have both its own borders, its own sovereignty, and its independence in virtually everything apart from that share which we leave to the center. Not a large share, as we decided—six Union ministries."[54] This could be achieved by controlling the cash flow from republic to center: "If we do not need some Union program and we are not interested in it, be it space or any other Union program, we will not pay for it."[55] He called it "a question of elementary justice," which could be restored only if Russia "obtains real statehood."

Gorbachev clearly underestimated the appeal of Yeltsin's idea. As his adviser Vadim Medvedev wrote, the Politburo had viewed the RSFSR "as an artificial Stalinist creation, so the idea of Russia's independence was treated as absurd."[56] The Soviet leadership downplayed the significance of the election to the Russian parliament and was ill-prepared to offer an attractive alternative to Yeltsin in the republican legislature. Having failed to prevent the declaration of Russian sovereignty, Gorbachev now faced a challenge not only to his power, but also to his legitimacy. As the chairman of the USSR Supreme Soviet Anatoliy Lukianov later wrote, the "declaration of Russian sovereignty opened the way for a legal battle with the Union center."[57] Realizing this, Yeltsin used his TV appearance after the sovereignty vote to directly attack Gorbachev for the first time.

After arguing for several years that his main political opponents were Ligachev and other Politburo conservatives, Yeltsin suddenly changed his tune: "Gorbachev was the one who headed the campaign against me. He used Ligachev in this connection. . . . There were attempts to prevent my election as chairman of the Supreme Soviet of Russia and Gorbachev was most active here. . . . He gathered 250 loyal Communist deputies instructing them 'to stop Yeltsin with all possible means.' What may 'all means' be, a shot in the head?"[58] Yeltsin emphasized his opposition to Gorbachev and the center by publicly resigning from the Communist Party at the Twenty-eighth CPSU Congress in July 1990, a decision that he described as "a severe blow to Gorbachev."[59]

Yeltsin's campaign for republican rights anticipated Russia's establishment of it own ties with the other Soviet republics, especially those that supported his cause. Immediately after his election as head of the Russian parliament, Yeltsin declared that, as the titular head of Russia, he did not support the center's reactionary policies toward the breakaway republics. Distancing himself further from Gorbachev, he argued in favor of "developing direct horizontal ties between republics as sovereign and independent states and signing agreements, conditions for which are not determined by the center."[60] The first such agreement was signed with Latvia in August 1990: "The agreement will be the basis for our mutual relations," Yeltsin emphasized, "no matter how Latvia's relations with the center develop and independently of Latvia's participation in the Union treaty."[61] In other words, even if Latvia seceded from the Soviet Union, Russia would still be willing to maintain official ties. Later that year, he spoke even more forthrightly: "Say one, two, or three republics break away. What of it? We will conclude treaties; we will live; we will be friends."[62]

Yeltsin also used the standoff between the Kremlin and the Baltic republics to criticize the Union center and Gorbachev in particular: "I have a sharply negative attitude toward the economic blockade, as I have already said and written to Gorbachev. With regard to Lithuania, it is a major political mistake."[63] In response, Gorbachev continued to accuse Yeltsin of plotting the dissolution of the Soviet Union, while also calling for increased independence for autonomous republics within the Russian Federation.[64] Yeltsin responded to Gorbachev's move by upping the ante. Speaking in the autonomous Bashkir Republic, he magnanimously proposed that Bashkiri regional leaders "take as much sovereignty as one can digest."

Yeltsin continued to sharpen his anticenter rhetoric during an August 1990 trip across the Russian Federation. At a meeting with miners, he indicated that by adopting a declaration of state sovereignty for Russia, "We have repudiated the entire union bureaucracy, the top union leadership, all union ministers except six. We don't need them and we don't intend to feed them!"[65] Still, he emphasized that the Russian leadership had not been given enough power over the republic: "Today fifty billion rubles are leaving Russia, and we don't know where they are going. Today tens of billions in hard currency are leaving Russia, and we don't know where." When asked for his opinion about Gorbachev's attempt to overturn a specific resolution of the Russian parliament, Yeltsin reacted sharply: "If matters go that far, Gorbachev may be left without Russia."[66]

After several months in office, Yeltsin realized that Gorbachev had little leverage against an assertive and independent Russia: "You cannot blockade Russia, while it itself could blockade anyone."[67] On another occasion he noted how dependent the center was on Russia: "It is power over Russia that has always given power to the center itself. If it renounces power in Russia, it renounces everything."[68] That was precisely why Gorbachev could not outflank Yeltsin's heresthetical, pro-Russian position.

By September 1990, just two months after the declaration of Russian sovereignty, Yeltsin was already characterizing his relationship with the center by using the vocabulary of war: "A real struggle is going on. The center does not want to let Russia slip out of its clutches—not for anything. . . . There is a fierce struggle for the banks, for foreign currency, for gold, for diamonds, and so on and so forth. . . . We will fight for that declaration to the end." At the same time, he identified Gorbachev as his main opponent in this struggle, pledging not to make any concessions to the Soviet leader detrimental to Russian interests. A political commentator aptly noted at the time that once Yeltsin had been elected chairman of the parliament and Russia had declared its sovereignty, "All the central Union institutions seemed to be out of a job."[69]

Yeltsin and Gorbachev's disagreement was at the time focused on the economic reform program known as "500 Days." The program offered a road map for the transition from a planned economy to a market economy. Despite the two men's initial agreement to adopt this program on the Union level, Gorbachev rejected it in October as too radical. This made him even more vulnerable to Yeltsin's charges of being beholden to the conservative majority in the Soviet government.

Yeltsin presented Gorbachev's decision as an indication that the center was incapable of managing the economic disaster in the republic. He contrasted the central authorities' political interests with the basic needs of the Russian people, accusing Gorbachev of sabotaging reforms to discredit the republican authorities. Nor could the Soviet leader follow through on his initial promise for greater decentralization, at the very moment when he was attempting to strengthen his position by creating a Soviet presidency. Gorbachev had hoped that his election to this post by the Congress of People's Deputies in February

1990 would ensure him greater independence from the party apparatus. Instead, with his reformist allies defecting to Yeltsin, he was becoming increasingly dependent on Politburo conservatives.

The status quo was no longer acceptable to any of Gorbachev's key support groups. The intelligentsia traditionally favored expanded rights for Russia, and was discouraged by Gorbachev's flirtation with the Right. The nomenklatura blamed him for decentralization and viewed Russian sovereignty as a means to regain control. Even Yeltsin's former nemesis, Ligachev, called Russia's economic and political sovereignty "perfectly legitimate."[70] Most importantly, the reform-oriented majority among Gorbachev's backers was disillusioned by the unfulfilled promises of perestroika. Yeltsin's forceful challenge had gradually but irrevocably eroded Gorbachev's coalition.

In a last-ditch effort, Gorbachev swung to the right. By the end of 1990 he appointed hard-line conservatives to the top positions in the state apparatus, including the posts of prime minister (Pavlov), defense minister (Yazov), interior minister (Pugo), and KGB head (Kryuchkov). Moreover, conservative apparatchiks were also well positioned in the second tier of power, in the posts of vice president (Yanaev) and first deputy general secretary of the CPSU (Ivashko). With the exception of Ivashko, these men would eventually become the core of the State Emergency Committee (GKTchP) that tried to overthrow Gorbachev in an ill-fated coup attempt in August 1991.

The prevalence of hard-liners in key governmental posts strengthened public perception of Gorbachev as an obstacle to further reform. Yeltsin expressed this feeling in his December 1990 speech at the Fourth USSR Congress of People's Deputies, declaring an end to the revolution from the top: "The Kremlin ceased to be the initiator of improvements in the country. . . . The processes of renewal, which are blocked on the level of the center, transferred to the republics. There is a real possibility to start radical transformations within the republics."[71]

By late 1990, the original Gorbachev coalition had completely disintegrated. According to polls conducted by the All-Union Center for the Study of Public Opinion, his approval rating had dropped from 39 percent in May 1990, when Yeltsin was elected chairman of the Russian parliament, to 21 percent in October 1990, when Gorbachev rejected the "500 Days" plan of economic reforms.[72] Another poll, conducted in October 1990 by Monitoring, the Russian sociological service, showed an even greater popularity gap: 48 percent support for Yeltsin versus 11 percent for Gorbachev.[73] Yeltsin entered 1991 as the most popular politician in the country, attracting to his side most of Gorbachev's former supporters.

Working to maintain his newfound momentum, Yeltsin launched his most daring attack against Gorbachev and the central authorities in early 1991, after Soviet troops massacred peaceful demonstrators in Vilnius. Yeltsin characterized the attack as "a major onslaught on democracy,"[74] and vowed to interfere in case the conflict escalated.

Yeltsin thus positioned himself not only as a supporter of the republics' right to self-determination, but also as their protector against a Soviet assault on their sovereignty. In an extraordinary appeal, he urged Russian soldiers in Lithuania to disobey orders if they were asked to fire at civilian demonstrators: "You will not be court-martialed, and you will earn the respect of your people and your country—Russia."[75] Gorbachev, in turn, accused Yeltsin of violating the Soviet constitution and characterized his actions as a provocation.

But the president's warnings only seemed to stir Yeltsin to bolder provocations. Hardly a month later, in early March, Yeltsin openly condemned the center's interference in Russia's own affairs: "An extremely fierce offensive has been in progress for a long time in various forums, including the mass media. No methods are spurned. Persecution, slander, and dirt are again being hurled in ever greater quantities, with every passing day, at us."[76] In a moving speech to the meeting of the people's deputies from the Democratic Russia bloc on March 9, 1991, he charged that Gorbachev's actions against him were a threat to democracy.[77] Yeltsin portrayed Gorbachev not simply as a less radical reformer, but as an opponent of democratic forces: "He [Gorbachev] is constantly misleading both the people and, especially, democrats and democracy." In order to save Russia, Yeltsin called for the organization of a powerful party that could unite the disparate democratic forces. The reformist electorate was no longer choosing between a moderate Gorbachev and a radical Yeltsin, but between someone viewed as the main obstacle to change and its only consistent advocate.

Yeltsin continued to reassert the link between Russian sovereignty and economic welfare throughout early 1991. He blamed Russia's swift economic deterioration on Gorbachev's indecision, his half-measures, and, most importantly, his profound reluctance to concede full republican sovereignty. In an unprecedented live interview on Soviet television on February 19, 1991, Yeltsin addressed the people of the Russian Federation directly: "Will we live better? Yes, if Russia can live according to its own laws, if the center does not block republican bodies. . . .

We will not be able to live better with the existing center."[78] He accused Gorbachev of conducting an "antipeople policy" that resulted in price increases, military deployments against the civilian population, inter-ethnic hostilities, economic decline, and a low standard of living. Refer-ring to his fateful 1987 speech to the Politburo, he drew a clear line between himself and his once like-minded boss: "I warned in 1987 that Gorbachev has in his character an aspiration to absolutism of personal power. He has done this already, and has brought the country to dicta-torship, eloquently terming this presidential rule. I distance myself from the position and policy of the president, and advocate his immediate resignation." A week later, more than 400,000 people attended a pro-Yeltsin rally in Moscow, one of the largest unauthorized demonstra-tions ever held in the Soviet capital.[79]

By the spring of 1991, Yeltsin, campaigning on his outsider agenda, had succeeded in redefining the terms of Soviet political debate. The issue was no longer the Kremlin's willingness to allow liberalization, but instead the extent to which the Kremlin would remain an actor in Soviet politics. Yeltsin's unique combination of policies, which Gor-bachev was politically constrained from accepting, boxed the once-pro-gressive Soviet leader into a corner, with party conservatives as his only remaining allies. Yeltsin was able to attract the support of two crucial elements of the Gorbachev alliance: the intelligentsia, who were pri-marily concerned with democratic freedoms; and blue-collar workers in the Russian regions, who were the primary victims of the collapsing Soviet economy. In a poll conducted immediately after Yeltsin's Febru-ary interview on Soviet television, 77 percent of blue-collar workers and 78 percent of the intelligentsia expressed their trust in him, while only 22 percent of each group trusted Gorbachev.[80] The same poll showed that 62 percent of workers and 55 percent of the intelligentsia said they would vote for Yeltsin if he ran for the Russian presidency. As one observer of the Soviet political scene wrote: "Who was happy with Gorbachev? Neither Left nor Right; neither workers nor middle class; neither generals nor politically oriented intellectuals. The intellectuals, from economists Shatalin and Yavslinsky to Arbatov, who had served every Kremlin boss, jumped Gorbachev's ship en masse and swam to Yeltsin's."[81]

The writings of Vitaliy Tretiakov, then editor-in-chief of the liberal newspaper *Nezavisimaia Gazeta,* illustrate the intelligentsia's drift toward Yeltsin. Tretiakov had been an ardent Gorbachev supporter, but by February 1991 his view of the Soviet leader rang like a political death sentence: "In the present situation I am more attracted to the political figure of Yeltsin than to Gorbachev. The latter, who from being the people's favorite has become a reclusive politician almost isolated from the people, is not so much concerned with winning back people's sympathies as with robbing Yeltsin of them. Yeltsin, by contrast, is seeking more an alliance with the people than Gorbachev's further isolation."[82] In contrast, one of Gorbachev's earlier critics and a member of the conservative Soyuz group in the Soviet parliament, Viktor Alksnis, now endorsed Gorbachev: "The group to which I belong has never demanded President Gorbachev's resignation. It may sound surprising, but I am a supporter of President Gorbachev."[83] Yeltsin's successful erosion of Gorbachev's support was reflected in a spring 1991 *U.S. News and World Report* poll: only 14 percent of Soviet voters said that they would vote for Gorbachev in a national election, while 70 percent would vote for Yeltsin.[84] Yeltsin was entering Russia's first-ever presidential election with his popularity near its peak.

The creation of a Russian presidency had raised the republican leadership to a level equal with that of the Soviet president. In fact, since the Russian president was to be directly elected, his popular legitimacy would likely exceed that of Gorbachev. Gorbachev was voted into the Soviet presidency on March 16, 1990, at the regular session of the USSR Congress of People's Deputies, by less than two-thirds of the deputies.[85] In less than a year Yeltsin began pushing for the first direct presidential elections in Russia as early as possible in 1991. Although conservatives in the Russian parliament, lacking a strong leader, initially resisted, they finally agreed to put this issue up for a referendum scheduled for March. After it was approved by almost 70 percent of Russian voters, the election date was set for June 12, 1991.

In the referendum the majority of Russians endorsed the idea of a republican presidency, but they also voted overwhelmingly in favor of Gorbachev's proposal for a renewed union of sovereign republics. While Yeltsin never opposed the Union, he stressed on a number of occasions that his vision of its future differed substantially from Gorbachev's: "Gorbachev wants to have a strong center and weak republics. . . . I propose strong republics with a center without a president."[86] Democratic Russia called on its supporters to "say no to Gorbachev's model of the Union." However, fewer than 20 percent of Russians followed this call, while 71.3 percent turned out in favor of Gorbachev's proposal. Support for the Union was greater in Russia's autonomous republics and rural areas (82.6 percent) than it was in the

RSFSR overall. Voters there were also more cautious about the idea of introducing a Russian presidency (with 62.2 percent in favor) than was the republic as a whole.[87]

The results exposed the limitations of a purely democratic electoral base and proved that Yeltsin's popularity was founded on a wide coalition of various social groups. Yet it also showed that, despite strong support for Russian sovereignty, the majority of the republics' residents—especially ethnic non-Russians—wanted Russia to remain within the Union. In a poll conducted a few weeks before the referendum, 48.4 percent of those who identified themselves as democrats supported the idea of a union of sovereign republics, while another 10.6 percent even endorsed preserving the unified state.[88] The March referendum results served as a warning to Yeltsin that his radical confrontation with the Union center might backfire. Throughout the following three months of the campaign, Yeltsin presented himself as a politician capable of making compromises with the Union leadership.

In an address to the RSFSR Congress two weeks after the referendum, Yeltsin indicated that he was ready to work with Gorbachev on a union agreement, delineating the rights of the center and the republics, and gave his assurance that all the republics would sign it. The two men were symbolically reconciled at a meeting in Novo-Ogarevo on April 23 when they, along with eight other republican leaders, approved the so-called "9 + 1" agreement on the division of power between the center and the republics. This preliminary accord provided the republics with greater independence, while recognizing Gorbachev as the coordinator among them. In the interim between the signing of this accord and the election, Yeltsin avoided personal criticism of Gorbachev, emphasizing instead their new spirit of cooperation.

Yeltsin's main rival in the 1991 presidential election was Nikolay Ryzhkov, who headed the Soviet government from 1985 to late 1990. Ryzhkov was hardly a popular figure and was no longer a part of Gorbachev's close circle, but the Kremlin still favored him in the run-up against Yeltsin. Ryzhkov had been a surprise choice for the Communist apparatus. Widely blamed for the Soviet economic crisis, Ryzhkov ran on a pro-Union platform. While adopting strongly pro-Russian rhetoric, he also appealed to voter concerns about the integrity of the USSR: "I am most resolute in my intention to uphold Russians' interests. The task is to resurrect Russia, to consolidate compatriots without destroying the Union—unlike some, I believe that the Union must not be destroyed."[89] He aggressively criticized Yeltsin's focus on confrontation with the Union center, which Ryzhkov claimed came at the expense of Russia's well-being: "I personally think that Boris Yeltsin's position is groundless. I think we should not simply give power to a person who has not made any substantial contribution to the development of Russia or to the strengthening of the Union for that matter."[90]

In response, Yeltsin capitalized on his role in the 9 +1 agreement. In a *Pravda* interview published two days before the election, he explained that his vision of the Union was compatible with that held by Gorbachev and the other republican leaders: "The approach to the new center is defined in the joint statement signed at the first '9 + 1' meeting. And I fully share it. To put it briefly, the center will look the way the constituting union republics want to see it. . . . In a sense we advocate a strong center—but strong only in the sphere of its own competence and prerogatives."[91] As to his one real achievement as chairman of the Russian parliament, Yeltsin was quick to point out that "many citizens of the republic have remembered that their motherland is not only the Soviet Union, but first and foremost Russia."[92]

Yeltsin's awareness of the diversity of his coalition was reflected in his choice of vice presidential running-mate, the Soviet military hero Aleksandr Rutskoi. Since Rutskoi had never been among Yeltsin's close political allies, his selection came as a surprise to many. Yeltsin himself acknowledged the unlikeliness of the pairing, but credited Rutskoi with the ability to understand the needs of military veterans. He also praised Rutskoi's creation of the movement known as "Communists for Democracy."[93] In a television interview, Rutskoi in turn emphasized that he would remain a member of the Central Committee of the Russian Communist Party, but that he disagreed with its leadership, especially the hard-line conservative Ivan Polozkov.[94] He warned against labeling members of the Communist Party rank and file as criminals since they too supported the idea of a sovereign Russia. Rutskoi then appealed to all who sought the restoration of Russian greatness to vote for Yeltsin. The concerns of rank-and-file Communists about his candidacy were one of Yeltsin's biggest worries. In a February 1991 poll, only 28 percent of those identifying themselves as Communists had said they would vote for him in the presidential election, while 57 percent said they would not.[95]

Yeltsin's willingness to reach an accord with Gorbachev shortly before the election, and to form an alliance with the Communist Rutskoi, reassured those of his supporters who had voted to preserve the Union in the March referendum. It also undermined Ryzhkov, who was trying to present Yeltsin as the anti-Union candidate. In the end, Yeltsin's coalition gave him a strong victory in the first round, with 57.4 percent of the total vote.

In his memoirs, written three years later, Yeltsin singled out his support for the "new and incomprehensible idea of the sovereignty of Russia" as a factor that had worked against him in the campaign.[96] He may have been trying to portray himself as more of a maverick than he really was. From his parliamentary campaign in 1990 until his election as the first Russian president, Yeltsin had worked to wed, in voters' minds, full Russian sovereignty to radical economic transformation. He knew the Soviet president could never fully agree with this platform, thus allowing him to establish an independent power base and divide Gorbachev's supporters. The collapse of the Soviet economy helped Yeltsin transform this pairing from a radical idea into the only viable path for reform.

By linking the issues of Russian sovereignty and radical economic change, Yeltsin persuaded the Russian electorate that expanded republican rights were the only avenue to economic improvement. But his domestic platform also radically transformed the bipolar international system. As he put it while speaking at the Russian parliament, nine months before the Soviet collapse: "The status of a so-called superpower, which has drained the Russian economy, the stress on military force, and the striving for political domination should remain in the past."[97] It was a statement that would have been considered treasonous under the Soviets. But in the transformed political environment, Yeltsin was now able to sign the historic accords peacefully dissolving the Soviet Union.

Yeltsin would face many further political battles in the years to come. He would win another presidential campaign, but would lose most of his supporters by the end of his presidency. We will not analyze those years in this book. Our concern has been not Yeltsin as president, but Yeltsin as campaigner. Strategic campaigning, as we have argued, requires an ability to persuade or manipulate voters, rather than to govern. Heresthetical politicians win by formulating radically new policies, which create unusual coalitions. In the end, these policies might not be the most effective ones. But we believe it is vital to study how politicians acquire power, as well as how they exercise it. Heresthetical campaigners like Yeltsin and Reagan make history not by following rules, but by reinventing them.

8

Conclusions

....

We set out to examine political campaigns with four goals in mind: (1) to understand how candidates who are seemingly out of the mainstream of political life can maneuver themselves into position to win office through democratic processes; (2) to provide insights into how the domestic political maneuvers of Ronald Reagan and Boris Yeltsin transformed the international system in the late 1980s and 1990s; (3) to stimulate further research into a cross-national theory of campaigning, especially for the highest executive office; and (4) to illustrate, primarily through the Reagan analysis, how archives can be used to assist in investigating theories of political action. Now, having set out our theoretical claims and having probed successful and failed campaigns, we can offer some thoughts about what we have learned.

The first of these objectives provided the original motivation for this investigation, and it remains our most important concern. When Ronald Reagan first expressed national political aspirations, many thought his "extreme" views could never propel him to the presidency. Republican Party standard-bearer Barry Goldwater had gone down to decisive defeat in the 1964 presidential election. Little had happened in the years between Goldwater's defeat and Reagan's failed 1968 bid to alter the perception that Reagan was outside the American mainstream. Yet in 1976 he came close to wresting the Republican nomination away from incumbent Gerald Ford, and in 1980 he won a landslide victory to become President of the United States.

Reagan's story is about a campaigner who altered his approach from a purely rhetorical strategy to one infused with heresthetic. Most importantly he saw that the Democratic coalition could be challenged by redefining conservatism to embrace both the traditional fiscal conservatism that dominated the GOP and the social conservatism of millions of American blue-collar workers. In the process of building his own support base, Reagan introduced the idea that the Cold War could be won by launching an arms race that would force the Soviet leadership to choose between military strength and economic well-being. Reagan campaigned on the idea that his deterrence strategy could be financed by cutting taxes to stimulate economic growth. It was a wholly new linkage of guns and butter. With significant, if unintended, help from Boris Yeltsin, Reagan forced the Soviet's hand. Gorbachev's USSR was unable to keep up with the U.S. militarily or indeed even to sustain itself.

Boris Yeltsin's rise to prominence in the late 1980s and early 1990s owed much to Ronald Reagan's heresthetical campaign and his subsequent implementation of the policies that had dominated his campaign. Faced with dire economic conditions and a new arms race, Mikhail Gorbachev opened the door for radical change in Soviet politics. With the introduction particularly of his perestroika campaign, Gorbachev inadvertently planted the seeds of his own and the Soviet Union's eventual political demise.

Yeltsin's campaign for reform, like Reagan's before it, began unpromisingly. Like Reagan, Yeltsin initially failed to appreciate the importance of special privileges in any system whose leadership depends on a small coalition. His first effort to achieve national prominence was grounded in a campaign against the very special benefits that the Communist Party leadership doled out to party officials. Such a campaign could not succeed as long as the party's faithful—and the nomenklatura beneficiaries in particular—retained the power to choose leaders.

After Yeltsin was banished from even his candidate membership in the Politburo, few thought he had any further future in Soviet politics. But Yeltsin gradually came to see how he could exploit the slowness of Gorbachev's progress toward rebuilding the Soviet economy, and the Russian economy in particular. Through a series of artful maneuvers, he turned Gorbachev's own policies and political predilections against him. Yeltsin systematically weakened Gorbachev's coalition, gradually gaining the support of the Russian nomenklatura and a broad segment of the intelligentsia. He did so by arguing that the rights of Russian citizens should be guaranteed just as firmly as the rights of other citizens of the Soviet Union. In particular, he pressed for Russia's freedom to determine its own economic future, thereby ensuring that the Russian nomenklatura would be no worse off—and likely would be better off—under an autonomous Russian Republic than they were under Gorbachev's Soviet Union. He came to appreciate the need to alter the selection process, and maneuvered to promote broad-based real elections that would establish the legitimacy of his pro-Russian stance. To win high office, Yeltsin needed to transform the coalition and selectorate structure into one reliant on a large coalition, drawn from a large selectorate. He succeeded, in the process unraveling the Soviet Union and ensuring the end of the Cold War.

Ronald Reagan certainly set out to re-establish American dominance over the Soviet Union. He hoped that his strategy would lead not only to American dominance but to an end to the Soviet system. But it is unlikely that even he was so optimistic as to have believed that such a result could be achieved during his presidency and soon thereafter. Indeed, if he had not had to face pressure from Boris Yeltsin on Russian autonomy, or from the Baltic Republics on their sovereignty, Mikhail Gorbachev would probably not have allowed his client states to leave the Eastern bloc, or tolerated the tearing down of the Berlin Wall, or, ultimately, surrendered to the conditions that brought an end to the Soviet Union itself.

Gorbachev's efforts to hold the Union and its allied states together were hampered by Yeltsin's pressure, especially following the Baltic republics' declarations of sovereign rights under the Soviet constitution. The rise of nationalist movements within the federal Soviet structure pushed Gorbachev to allow competitive legislative elections and was central to Yeltsin's success. Thus, in his efforts to salvage support within his own coalition, Mikhail Gorbachev found himself cornered by the superior strategic maneuvering of his seemingly extreme-reformist rival, Boris Yeltsin. To be sure, Gorbachev made mistakes that created opportunities for Yeltsin, but just as Reagan showed great heresthetical skill in exploiting Carter's errors, Yeltsin too manifested enormous heresthetical ability—and institutional savvy—in forcing Gorbachev into errors and then turning Gorbachev's mistakes to his own advantage. Indeed, Yeltsin, perhaps even more than Reagan, proved himself master of his own destiny.

Gorbachev was dealt a tough hand, a hand made tougher by Reagan's policies, but without Yeltsin's prodding, probably Gorbachev's circumstances in the Soviet context would not have been as dire politically as Carter's were in the United States. After all, small coalition leaders, such as Gorbachev, are generally much better at surviving policy failures than are large-coalition, democratic leaders.[1] Their political survival depends on delivering private benefits, not effective public policy, to their support coalition and Gorbachev steadfastly protected those private benefits. Carter's bad luck, as we noted earlier, increased the odds that he would lose in 1980. Reagan's great skill was in putting together a policy-based coalition that neither his Republican rivals nor the incumbent president could pull apart without jeopardizing their own base of support. Yeltsin did that too, but first he had to change the context of debate so that policy grounded in a large coalition rather than the privileges of a select few would matter for his success. He, more than Gorbachev's errors, must be credited for seeing how to gain mastery over a situation that was structurally biased against his success.

While Yeltsin may have been an even more skilled heresthetician than Reagan, it is hard not to acknowledge that, unlike Ronald Reagan, Boris Yeltsin lacked a clear vision of what he wanted to do once he achieved high office. His heresthetical campaign for Russian autonomy set Russia on a path to freedom and democracy, but his failure to incorporate those changes into law has opened the door to deviations from this path. Still, whatever Yeltsin's weaknesses once in power, his creation of the opportunity for Russians and, indeed, all former Soviet citizens to define their own destiny, cannot be overstated. Nor can his role in ending the Cold War, even if, unlike Reagan, this was never his intention. We hope that this study will help future scholars explore this fact, which has, until now, largely been overlooked.

Lessons about Rhetorical Campaigns

All campaigns are rhetorical. A few are more than that. The puzzle of purely rhetorical campaigns is why anyone is persuaded to change allegiance from one candidate to another. After all, voters know that each candidate, to recall the words of Quintus Tullius, must "change his air and his statements in accordance with the opinions of the people he meets." In short, the successful rhetorical campaigner must lie. But knowing that they are being lied to, why would voters be persuaded by a candidate's promises? William Riker suggested the dominance and dispersion principles as a partial answer to this question.

Voters are not so much fooled into believing that the successful candidate will deliver on his or her promises as they are made to fear the awful things that one candidate persuades them might occur, if they mistakenly elect his or her opponent. Turning once again to Quintus Tullius, the successful rhetor must "Slander . . . opponents as often as possible, reckon their crimes, their sexual depravity, or their attempts to bribe other candidates—all according to the character of the individual opponent."

Negative campaigning is not some quirk of modern politics; nor is it a character flaw of this or that candidate. Rather, it derives its power from the fact that it will always be easier to persuade voters to fear an opponent's flaws, real or imagined, than to convince them of one's own merits. Negative campaigning should be understood as a rational strategy, a way to influence voters in one's own favor. Cicero learned this from his brother. Thomas Jefferson used it to impede the prospects of Alexander Hamilton, John Adams, and even—albeit cautiously— George Washington. Nor were the other founding fathers any more reluctant to enlist slanderous tales to advance their own prospects, at the expense of their political foes. Their use of negative campaigning is well-documented. And in this they were no different from many modern American or other politicians, who seek office at almost any cost to their own dignity or that of their political foes. We saw numerous examples of negative campaigning and mud-slinging in our examination of the 1968, 1976, and 1980 presidential campaigns in the United States and in the political struggles between Gorbachev, Ligachev, and Yeltsin in the Soviet Union and in the nascent Russian Republic.

But negative campaigning alone is rarely sufficient to win election. Candidates do not compete only by slinging dirt at each other. The campaigner's quiver contains arrows honed on slander and scandal, but these are not the only weapons with which to wound one's rivals. A rhetorical campaign also highlights a candidate's claim that they, and not their opponent, are best able to solve the problems of the day. The problems confronting voters change from election to election, of course; but negative campaigning and claims of competence are constants of the rhetorical landscape. Every now and again, however, candidates emerge who have honed a different type of strategy for seeking office. These are the heresthetical candidates. While they rely on rhetoric to persuade voters that their message is right, their message is fundamentally different from that of most campaigns. Theirs are messages that redefine political debate and that assemble previously seemingly impossible coalitions.

Lessons about Heresthetical Campaigns

The heresthete goes much further than the rhetor in establishing why voters should support his or her campaign. The heresthetical campaigner argues that politicians are debating the wrong issues; that the received wisdom about which problems need to be solved is misplaced. In doing so, they box their opponents into a corner from which it is difficult for them to escape. The opponent cannot embrace the heresthete's position without giving up core members of their coalition; nor can they deny the validity of the heresthetical agenda without losing core supporters. Indeed, the heresthetical campaigner's agenda is likely to be misunderstood by rivals (and voters) at the outset because it is founded on a completely novel set of assumptions about the political environment. The heresthetical campaign shifts debate to a new, previously undefined locus, where issues are linked together in novel ways and where formerly centrist, mainstream politicians seem askew, quaintly clinging to old ideas even after the new center has emerged.

Abraham Lincoln famously cornered Stephen Douglas with such a maneuver during their senate race. By recasting the slavery debate in the Illinois election to focus on the American Constitution's relevance to the territories—and, in particular, on the applicability of the Dred Scott decision—Lincoln ensured that Douglas would either have to give up his antislavery backers in Illinois, costing him the senate seat and thereby diminishing his future presidential prospects, or retain them at the expense of his appeal among Southern Democrats, without whom he would have little chance to win the presidency. Douglas chose the latter, gaining the senate seat but sinking his presidential prospects. Lincoln's maneuver succeeded in splitting the Democrats in 1860, thereby improving his own chances of becoming president. While both Lincoln and Douglas performed abysmally in the southern states during the 1860 election (garnering 3 and 7 percent of the popular vote, respectively), the outcome was much costlier to Douglas's electoral prospects than to Lincoln's.

As we have seen, Ronald Reagan and Boris Yeltsin both learned the pitfalls of rhetorical campaigning early in their quest for office. Each emerged as a heresthete capable of recasting national debate to their advantage, redefining the political mainstream to exclude their key opponents while placing themselves in the newly defined core.

Reagan entered the post-1976 electoral scene arguing, in essence, that the debate over how best to coexist with the Soviet Union was the wrong debate, on the wrong problem. He contended that the issue was not how to coexist, but rather how to defeat the Soviets peacefully, bringing an end to the Cold War and the global Communist threat. He also argued that the Republican Party had defined itself in a way that had alienated a vast array of potential allies. As early as January 15, 1977, before Jimmy Carter was inaugurated and long before he found himself hemmed in by double-digit unemployment, double-digit inflation, and the Iran hostage crisis, Reagan was arguing to his party that they needed to expand their view of conservatism to embrace socially conservative blue-collar workers. In doing so, he laid the foundation for a newly constructed Republican coalition that could draw support from Catholic blue-collar workers who had traditionally voted Democratically; from evangelical Christians who were little understood as an electoral bloc at the time, and who had no clear political home at all; and from national-security oriented Democrats like those in the Scoop Jackson wing of that party. To a significant degree, the broadened, conservative, "values"-oriented constituency that Reagan heresthetically created, remains central to the Republican Party's electoral prospects even now, decades later.

Boris Yeltsin, too, used heresthetical maneuvers to recast himself and his country in a way that advantaged him over his rivals, including both nearly forgotten figures such as Yegor Ligachev and the seemingly unchallengeable Mikhail Gorbachev. In some ways, as we have argued, Yeltsin's path was an even more difficult and more unlikely one than Reagan's. The platform on which Yeltsin settled required a fundamental redefinition of Soviet politics that would relegate the seemingly all-powerful central Soviet institutions virtually powerless in the face of a newly invented Russian Federation. Yeltsin needed first to convince a substantial portion of Russia's polity to abandon Gorbachev and the idea of Soviet rule, instead casting their political futures with an emerging Russian Republic. And he needed to attract support from key members of Gorbachev's small winning coalition despite his notoriety for waging an antiprivileges campaign that had challenged the personal interests of the very individuals whose support he needed. Perhaps even more dramatically, he needed to redefine the institutions of Soviet or at least Russian politics so that office-holding involved competition for support from a large electoral coalition, rather than a small, elite group of Communist Party members.

Both Reagan and Yeltsin found paths back from the wilderness of political defeat to the center of power. It is tempting to see their maneuvers as idiosyncratic manifestations of political genius, or as the confluence of circumstances that through serendipity brought them to power. We would not deny the value of good fortune, nor have we challenged the significance of personal genius. But neither do we endorse a "Great Man" theory of politics which suggests that history is governed by the decisions of unusual, great figures. Neither Ronald Reagan nor Boris Yeltsin is best understood in that light. Yeltsin, in particular, made decisions with momentous consequences for the end of the Soviet Union, as we have noted; but there is scant evidence to support the idea that this was his intention.

We have tried to show that neither Reagan nor Yeltsin was innately a heresthete (nor, for that matter, was Lincoln or any of the other successful examples). Each pursued high office for a long time without evident success. In those efforts, each acted as a rhetor who tried to persuade prospective constituents that he could most effectively advance their interests. This early, more populist period in their careers offered few hints of the ways in which they eventually would redefine political debate, box in their opponents, and secure a winning coalition forged out of a complex web of voters or selectors who only a short time earlier could not imagine themselves voting for Reagan or Yeltsin. Each saw how to reframe policy debate by linking issues in ways not previously done. Each saw how to create the perception among voters that their nation was headed for a political crisis if they did not embrace a new way of looking at old problems—if they did not eschew the received wisdom in favor of a totally new perspective.

Negative campaigning has a rather different meaning for the heresthetical campaigner than it does for the strategic rhetorician. The rhetorical campaigner follows the path exemplified by Cicero's campaign for Roman consul. The heresthetical campaigner may use slander as a rhetorical device, but is less reliant on it than the rhetor. The heresthete instead suggests that he or she sees the real problem, while the opponent does not. One might almost portray this as a positive method of negative campaigning. There is no need to slur the opponent's character or good intentions, nor even the opponent's competence to manage affairs as conventionally understood. Rather, the heresthete highlights the inadequacy of the rival's understanding of what the real problems are. We often observe successful heresthetical maneuvering in apparent crises because the heresthete is well-situated to accuse the rival or rivals of precipitating the crisis through their misunderstanding; or because the heresthete can actually foment a crisis (as Boris Yeltsin did) for political gain.

While Jimmy Carter argued that hard economic times required belt-tightening and changed expectations, Ronald Reagan argued that America's economic problems were the product of government policies rather than external forces that could only be overcome by personal sacrifice. While Jimmy Carter followed in the footsteps of Nixon and Ford by endorsing and encouraging détente with the Soviet Union, Reagan argued against détente. He went on to link economic policy and defense policy in a new way by contending that the American people could enjoy both economic prosperity and peace by increased spending on defense and by a reduced income tax.

While every seeker of the presidency since the end of World War II had debated how best to live with the Soviet threat (encirclement, mutually assured destruction, flexible response, détente, etc.), Reagan was the only major party candidate for president who argued that the Soviet threat could be defeated, rather than simply managed. While candidates debated how to balance the budget through spending cuts and changes in spending priorities, Reagan argued for massive spending that would supposedly produce what later came to be called a "peace dividend," and which would trickle down to benefit everyone in society. It did not matter for his electoral prospects whether hindsight would show him to be right. What mattered was that he could persuade voters to dismiss his rivals as archaic thinkers who did not understand the real problems of the day. That his success made it possible to spend the Soviet government into a rapid collapse was a bonus that few voters foresaw at the polls.

Boris Yeltsin likewise reframed political debate. While Gorbachev regarded the centrality of the Communist Party and the Soviet Union's core institutions of government as beyond dispute, Yeltsin argued that however effective these central organs of power might be for the national elite, they were unfair and ineffective from the perspective of Russians or Lithuanians or Georgians. In the process he showed his political opponents as incapable of unleashing the economic potential of their own citizens. He challenged the very idea that the central government was truly committed to socialist principles. In the process, he drove Russian bureaucrats, intellectuals, and—eventually—ordinary citizens and voters to look to their own government as the cause of their problems, rather than to the capitalist West, as they had always been taught to do. That these hardships were exacerbated for many Russians in the first decade after the collapse of the Soviet Union does not diminish the strategic insight of Yeltsin's heresthetical moves. He succeeded in redefining debate, fostering his own rise to power while rendering Gorbachev, the architect of glasnost and perestroika, politically irrelevant.

How Did Our Hypotheses Fare?

We began by sketching a theory of how heresthetical maneuvers and institutional constraints shape the strategy of campaigning. Our work implied several hypotheses, including the influence of the dominance and dispersion principles, the purpose of negative campaigning, the role of coalition size, and the implications of drawing a winning coalition from a larger or smaller pool of selectors. We have seen that the campaigns of Boris Yeltsin and Ronald Reagan support the ideas set out in our opening chapter.

We reported evidence of off-the-equilibrium-path thinking, as in Reagan's decision not to raise his ideas about a strategic defense initiative during the 1980 campaign. He suppressed his opinions not because he had doubts about their merits, but because he believed that expressing them would diminish, rather than expand, his coalition of support. Thus, while he may have told the truth to voters as he saw it, he did not tell the whole truth. He left out those elements of his heresthetical outlook that were likely to hinder his rhetorical mission to persuade voters to support him.

We have also seen that negative campaigning was used strategically to raise doubts about rivals and, thereby to invoke caution on the part of voters who were more concerned to avoid later regrets than to seek current gains. This was, of course, a hallmark of the anti-Goldwater campaign in 1964 and of Rockefeller's efforts in 1968. We have seen that messages, like Nixon's law and order message in 1968, were clung to as long as they resonated with relevant voters, whether they were the barons of the Republican Party or the broader base of Southern voters. And we have also seen how messages, like Romney's embrace of a Vietnam policy not very different from Lyndon Johnson's, were abandoned when they seemed no longer capable of attracting further supporters to a prospective electoral coalition.

We saw the elements of the dominance and dispersion principles, of heresthetic and rhetoric, of coalition size and off-the-equilibrium path calculations not only in the American context, where politicians were experienced with broad, open, public campaigning, but also in the Soviet context. Yeltsin learned the pitfalls of his message against special privileges when he needed to attract support from a small coalition of party apparatchiks whose very welfare was defined by their access to those privileges. He muted his opinions about privileges until the political climate was more hospitable—a change that came significantly through his own efforts to expand the voting coalition from a small elite group dependent on private rewards, to a broad-based electorate facing competing candidates in an American-style race for office. We also saw how Gorbachev backed away from the logical implications of his own perestroika campaign, as he came to recognize how its implementation would jeopardize his appeal to moderate conservatives in the Communist Party, even as Yeltsin was stripping him of backers by pushing for faster economic reform.

As we urged at the beginning, so we urge now that the reader recognize that we do not claim to have offered definitive proof that the strategic thinking we have highlighted is central to all campaigns. Nor do we claim to have proven that heresthetical maneuvers inevitably improve a candidate's prospects of political success. Rather, we have expanded the set of cases that reinforce the messages we laid out in our first chapter. And we have seen, by probing the archival records as well as secondary sources, that the candidates in question seem to have consciously and intentionally chosen courses of action that match the general principles we have presented.

Heresthetical maneuvering is difficult, but it appears capable of improving a candidate's prospects, offering a way to understand how apparent outlier candidates can nonetheless triumph over rivals in the political center. Finally, we have seen that in some cases radical, extraordinary changes in foreign policy can result from campaigns that were run largely on domestic issues. Boris Yeltsin's focus on internal Soviet and Russian questions nonetheless catalyzed the end of the Cold War. Domestic political maneuvering, more than grand strategy, contributed to the most important international political change of the latter half of the twentieth century—and, arguably, of modern history.

The more campaigns—both successful and unsuccessful—that we probe for insight into the forces governing strategic campaigning, the more we will learn to identify and gain confidence in general principles of electoral strategy, and the less likely we will be to rely on anecdote or idiosyncratic accounts. We close with the recognition that even after all his machinations, Quintus Tullius ultimately offers his brother Cicero—and all of us—a surprisingly hopeful instruction that we would do well to remember and apply to politics in the future: "When seeking a public position you must work in two directions: one is to ensure the support of your friends, the other is public benevolence."

Notes

....

CHAPTER I

1. Marshall Adesman, "The State of Pitching," http://www.thediamondan gle.com/archive/aug03/complete.html, consulted April 24, 2007.

2. Willard Manus, "Passing Recognition," *Michigan Today*, http://www .umich.edu/ news/MT/04/Fall04/story.html?passing, consulted April 24, 2007.

3. Many of these studies are referred to in the chapters on Reagan and Yeltsin.

4. Bruce Bueno de Mesquita and Randolph M. Siverson, "War and the Survival of Political Leaders: A Comparative Study of Regime Types and Political Accountability," *American Political Science Review* 89 (1995): 841–55; David A. Lake and Robert Powell, *Strategic Choice and International Relations* (Princeton, NJ: Princeton University Press, 1999); Randolph M. Siverson, ed., *Strategic Politicians, Institutions, and Foreign Policy* (Ann Arbor: University of Michigan Press, 1998); Bruce Bueno de Mesquita, Alastair Smith, Randolph M. Siverson, and James D. Morrow, *The Logic of Political Survival* (Cambridge: MIT Press, 2003).

5. Robert H. Bates, Avner Greif, Margaret Levi, Jean-Laurent Rosenthal, and Barry R. Weingast, *Analytic Narratives* (Princeton, NJ: Princeton University Press, 1998).

6. On campaigning see William H. Riker, *The Strategy of Rhetoric: Campaigning for the American Constitution* (New Haven: Yale University Press, 1996). See also James E. Campbell, *The American Campaign: U.S. Presidential Campaigns and the National Vote* (College Station: Texas A&M Press, 2000); Henry E. Brady and Richard Johnston, eds., *Capturing Campaign Effects* (Ann Arbor: University of Michigan Press, 2006); Nelson W. Polsby and Aaron Wildavsky, *Presidential Elections: Strategies and Structures of American Politics*, 10th ed. (New York: Seven Bridges Press, 2000). On institutionally driven leadership incentives see Bueno de Mesquita et al., *Logic of Political Survival*.

7. Bueno de Mesquita et al., *Logic of Political Survival*.

8. Polsby and Wildavsky, *Presidential Elections*, 43.

9. Gil Troy, *See How They Ran* (Cambridge: Harvard University Press, 1996), 191.

261

10. William H. Riker, *The Art of Political Manipulation* (New Haven: Yale University Press, 1986), x.

11. Riker, *Art of Political Manipulation,* ix.

12. Riker's theory of heresthetic is criticized by Gerry Mackie, "The Coherence of Democracy," unpublished manuscript, Research School of Social Sciences, Australian National University, 2001, on the grounds that many vote cycles identified by Riker, when more carefully examined, were not cycles at all. We agree, however, with Ian McLean in "William H. Riker and the Invention of Heresthetic(s)," *British Journal of Political Science* 32 (2002): 535–58, that Mackie is mistaken to emphasize cycles as essential to heresthetic. McLean demonstrates numerous examples of heresthetical maneuvers without requiring cycles. Maneuver, not preference cycles, is the essence of heresthetic.

13. William H. Riker, "Rhetorical Interaction in the Ratification Campaigns," in *Agenda Formation,* ed. Riker (Ann Arbor: University of Michigan Press, 1993), 83.

14. This type of manipulation is used in campaigns and a variety of other decision-making forums. For examples of heresthetical maneuvers in New Zealand, see Jack H. Nagel, "Social Choice in a Pluralitarian Democracy: The Politics of Market Liberalization in New Zealand," *British Journal of Political Science* 28 (1998): 223–65. For heresthetic in the founding of the American Constitution, besides Riker, "Rhetorical Interaction"; see also Jack N. Rakove, "The Madisonian Theory of Rights," *William and Mary Law Review* 31, no. 2 (1990): 245–66; and Norman Schofield, "Evolution of the Constitution," *British Journal of Political Science* 32 (2002): 1–23. For an application of heresthetic to coups see Youssef Cohen, "The Heresthetics of Coup Making," *Comparative Political Studies* 24 (1991): 344–64.

15. Riker, *The Strategy of Rhetoric,* 4.

16. Riker, *Art of Political Manipulation,* 1.

17. Riker, *The Strategy of Rhetoric,* 9.

18. Riker, "Rhetorical Interaction," 81.

19. See Riker, *Art of Political Manipulation* and *The Strategy of Rhetoric.*

20. See references in note 14 for a sampling of studies that use the concept of heresthetic to explain important political phenomena.

21. An appreciation of this dynamic is a driving force, for instance, behind the Downsian model of politics. See Anthony Downs, *An Economic Theory of Democracy* (New York: Harper, 1957).

22. During the campaign Reagan offered his thoughts about visiting the North American Aerospace Defense Command, which monitored missile activity but could not stop incoming missiles. In an interview with Robert Scheer, he said: "I think the thing that struck me was the irony that here, with this great technology of ours, we can do all of this yet we cannot stop any of the weapons that are coming at us. I don't think there's been a time in history when there wasn't a defense against some kind of thrust, even back in the old-fashioned days when we had coast artillery that would stop invading ships if they came." Robert Scheer, *With Enough Shovels: Reagan, Bush, and Nuclear War* (New York: Random House, 1982), 232–33.

23. Morris Fiorina, *Retrospective Voting in American National Elections* (New Haven: Yale University Press, 1981).

24. http://www.lakjer.dk/erik/comments/campaign.html, consulted May 10, 2005.

25. Duncan Black, *The Theory of Committees and Elections* (Cambridge: Cambridge University Press 1958).

26. Downs, *Economic Theory of Democracy*.

27. See Richard McKelvey, "Intransitivities in Multidimensional Voting Models and Some Implications for Agenda Control," *Journal of Economic Theory* 12 (1976): 472–82; and Norman Schofield, "Instability of Simple Dynamic Games," *Review of Economic Studies* 45 (1978): 575–94.

28. In the reframed issue environment that linked Russian autonomy to economic reform, Gorbachev might also have been able to sustain support from the nomenklatura, but to do so he would first have had to accept the principle that these two issues really were one. As we explain later, there were compelling political impediments to his doing so.

CHAPTER 2

1. Riker, "Rhetorical Interaction," 83.

2. Nelson W. Polsby and Aaron Wildavsky, *Presidential Elections: Strategies of American Electoral Politics* (New York: Scribner's, 1964), 64.

3. Bartels was referring to events that will be reviewed in this chapter: Senator Eugene McCarthy's near-victory in the New Hampshire primaries, President Johnson's surprise announcement that he would not compete for his party's presidential nomination, and the assassinations of Senator Robert Kennedy and Reverend Martin Luther King, Jr., all of which occurred in the span of a few months. Larry M. Bartels, *Presidential Primaries and the Dynamics of Public Choice* (Princeton, NJ: Princeton University Press, 1988), 19.

4. The number of Republican primaries in 1968 listed here includes delegate-selection primaries in Alabama and New York. In addition to 35 states holding Republican primaries in 1980, the District of Columbia and Puerto Rico held primaries. *CQ Press Guide to U.S. Elections*, 5th ed., vol. 1 (Washington, DC: Congressional Quarterly Press, 2005), 363–65, 377–85; and Austin Ranney, ed., *The American Elections of 1980* (Washington, DC: American Enterprise Institute for Public Policy Research, 1981), 369.

5. A key participant in and analyst of southern politics in the 1960s explains the origins of the strategy that was associated with Senator Goldwater's presidential campaign: "It is fitting that the term 'southern strategy' should have been coined in the Goldwater campaign of 1964 because that campaign planted the seed for a radical new direction in national politics, leading to a conversion of Democratic Dixie into a Republican heartland for presidential elections. For almost a century the Old South had been taken for granted by the Democrats and ignored by the Republicans. . . . Finally in 1964, the Republican Party nominated a presidential candidate who stood more with the South than the rest of the country." Harry S. Dent, *The Prodigal South Returns to Power* (New York: John Wiley, 1978), 6–7. Dent ran a southern operation for Goldwater during the 1964 presidential contest; encouraged Senator Strom Thurmond, whom he had worked for since the mid-1950s, to switch to the Republican Party in that year; and began running southern operations for Nixon and was elected Republican

Party state chairman for South Carolina in 1965. In 1971 and 1972, Dent was a White House adviser on southern strategy. Kevin P. Phillips, special assistant to Nixon campaign manager John Mitchell during the 1968 presidential race, was another key southern strategist. Nixon campaign aides studied Phillips's research on the evolving political landscape in the South, and Phillips published his findings after the election. His thesis that "the South is turning into an important presidential base of the Republican Party" turned out to be an accurate prediction. In his opinion, it would be easier to persuade voters in the states of the Outer South (Florida, North Carolina, Tennessee, and Virginia, for example) to vote for Nixon because Wallace controlled the Deep South. See his book *The Emerging Republican Majority*, 2d ed. (New Rochelle, NY: Arlington House, 1969), 22. The impact of Phillips's ideas on the Nixon campaign is discussed in another book on the Republican South, Wayne Greenhaw, *Elephants in the Cottonfields: Ronald Reagan and the New Republican South* (New York: Macmillan, 1982), 79–84. For a more recent analysis of the southern strategy, see Joseph A. Aistrup, *The Southern Strategy Revisited* (Lexington: University Press of Kentucky, 1996).

6. Lewis L. Gould, *1968: The Election that Changed America* (Chicago: American Ways Series, 1993), 25.

7. Quoted in "How Ray Bliss Plays the Cards for the GOP," *Business Week*, March 9, 1968, 28.

8. For a review of the 1966 election, see Thomas Byrne Edsall and Mary D. Edsall, *Chain Reaction: The Impact of Race, Rights, and Taxes on American Politics* (New York: Norton, 1991), 59–60.

9. In addition to California and Florida, the Republican Party won gubernatorial races in Arkansas, Arizona, Nevada, New Mexico, and Oklahoma. Both ends of the Republican Party had important electoral victories. Thurmond showed his political strength in 1966 by winning 25 percent more of the vote than his closest rival. Claude R. Kirk, Jr., won the governorship of Florida with the campaign slogan, "Your home is your castle." Yet moderate Republicans were elected in the South. Winthrop Rockefeller became governor of Arkansas, and Howard Baker, Jr., of Tennessee was elected to the Senate. See Lewis Chester, Godfrey Hodgson, and Bruce Page, *An American Melodrama: The Presidential Campaign of 1968* (New York: Viking, 1969), 188; Kirkpatrick Sale, *Power Shift: The Rise of the Southern Rim and Its Challenge to the Eastern Establishment* (New York: Random House, 1975), 115.

10. *Report of the National Advisory Commission on Civil Disorders* (New York: E. P. Dutton, 1968), 112, 113.

11. James W. Button, *Black Violence: Political Impact of the 1960s Riots* (Princeton, NJ: Princeton University Press, 1978), 10.

12. On the response of white elites and poor whites to black radicalism, see John Micklethwait and Adrian Wooldridge, *The Right Nation: Conservative Power in America* (New York: Penguin, 2004), 65–68.

13. Edsall and Edsall, *Chain Reaction*, 59.

14. Edsall and Edsall, *Chain Reaction*, 52.

15. Micklethwait and Wooldridge, *The Right Nation*, 66.

16. Philip E. Converse, Warren E. Miller, Jerrold G. Rusk, and Arthur C.

Wolfe, "Continuity and Change in American Politics: Parties and Issues in the 1968 Election," *American Political Science Review* 63 (1969): 1083–1105.

17. These figures were presented by Nelson Rockefeller throughout the Republican contest for the presidential nomination. See, for instance, his statement at a rally in San Francisco on July 8, 1968. Nelson A. Rockefeller Collection, Rockefeller Archive Center, Sleepy Hollow, New York (NAR), Record Group 15, Series 33, Box 62, Folder 2443. For other figures, see the data on party affiliation and orientation reported by American National Election Studies. According to it, in 1968, 55 percent of the respondents were either Democrat or leaning toward the party; 33 percent were Republican or leaning toward the party; and 11 percent were independent. See http://www.electionstudies.org/nesguide/toptable/ tab2a_2 .htm, consulted April 24, 2007.

18. Goldwater's successful 1968 bid to reenter the U.S. Senate after he had withdrawn to campaign for the presidency in 1964 assured him of continued involvement in Republican politics for years to come.

19. For a careful review of the activities of the Greenville Group and the role of the South in choosing the Republican Party's presidential nominee in 1968, see Dent, *Prodigal South Returns.*

20. Kirkpatrick Sale found that "Southern Republicans of all stripes were given at least limited help in establishing new and serious statewide organizations for the first time, and party machinery was established to continue tapping the new financial wells that the 1964 campaign had uncovered." Sale, *Power Shift,* 115.

21. See, for example, David S. Broder, "Romney Relaxes Pace in Contest with Nixon for '68 Nomination," *New York Times,* February 14, 1966, 19.

22. Nixon had been moving steadily toward the political center since his loss to incumbent Edmund "Pat" Brown in the race for governor of California in 1962. In fact, he credited that defeat in part to his denunciation of the John Birch Society, which he claimed cost him conservative votes. See Richard Nixon, *RN: The Memoirs of Richard Nixon* (New York: Simon & Schuster, 1990), 241.

23. Dirksen had opposed the Civil Rights Act of 1964 on the ground that defending the right of minorities to be served in any establishment intruded on the rights of property owners. He then voted for the measure, stating that it represented an idea whose time had come, and his leadership was instrumental in the Senate's affirmative decision. For a review of some of these issues see Byron C. Hulsey, *Everett Dirksen and His Presidents: How a Senate Giant Shaped American Politics* (Lawrence: University Press of Kansas, 2000), 175, 194–96.

24. For a discussion of Nixon's campaign activities in 1966 see Jonathan Martin Kolkey, *The New Right, 1960–1968, with Epilogue, 1969–1980* (Washington, DC: University Press of America, 1983), 253–54, 278–79.

25. Goldwater said: "I want to express my heartfelt thanks and gratitude to Dick Nixon who worked harder than any one person for the ticket this year. Dick, I will never forget it! I know that you did it in the interests of the Republican Party and not for any selfish reasons. But if there ever comes a time I can turn those into selfish reasons, I am going to do all I can to see that it comes about." Quoted in Kolkey, *The New Right,* 278. On March 7, 1968, Goldwater said: "I have stated on numerous occasions since 1965 that in my opinion the Republican

Party had, in Dick Nixon, a man who was singularly qualified to carry our banner in 1968." "Goldwater Shifts Rockefeller Stand," *New York Times*, March 8, 1968, 22; and Don Bolles, "Barry Is Brief: Nixon's His Man, Back Any Choice," *Arizona Republic*, March 8, 1968, 1, 11.

26. Chester, Hodgson, and Page, *An American Melodrama*, 185. Nixon's campaign activities were so extensive that shortly before the election President Johnson called the former vice president "a chronic campaigner." See Gould, *1968*, 28.

27. In 1965, Ford replaced Charles Halleck, a more conservative congressman, as House minority leader.

28. The address on behalf of Goldwater's candidacy is reprinted in Ronald Reagan, *A Time for Choosing: The Speeches of Ronald Reagan, 1961–1982* (Chicago: Regnery Gateway, 1983), 41–57.

29. Lou Cannon, *Reagan* (New York: G. P. Putnam's Sons, 1982), 98–118.

30. Warren Weaver, Jr., "G.O.P. Finds '68 Outlook Brighter as It Counts Election Successes: Gain of 47 in House, 8 Governors," *New York Times*, November 10, 1966, 1.

31. Kiron K. Skinner, Annelise Anderson, and Martin Anderson, eds., *Reagan, A Life in Letters* (New York: Free Press, 2003), 215.

32. *CQ Press Guide*, 360–62.

33. The potential for the Wallace vote to throw the presidential decision into the House of Representatives was so strong that Governor John Chafee (R-RI) proposed a deal between Democrats and Republicans to designate as president the candidate who received a plurality of votes. The proposal was rejected at the National Governors' Conference held in Cincinnati, Ohio, prior to the Republican National Convention of 1968. See "Governors Shun Two-Party Deal to Stop Wallace," *Cincinnati Enquirer*, July 24, 1968, 1.

34. Converse et al., "Continuity and Change," 1083.

35. Dent, *Prodigal South Returns*, 81.

36. On the convention rules and delegate counts see David English, *Divided They Stand* (Englewood Cliffs, NJ: Prentice Hall, 1969), 265; Chester, Hodgson, and Page, *An American Melodrama*, 189; Kolkey, *The New Right*, 279; and Dent, *Prodigal South Returns*, 88.

37. The Republican favorite sons in 1968 were Governor Walter J. Hickel of Alaska, Governor Winthrop Rockefeller of Arkansas, Governor George Romney of Michigan, Senator Frank Carlson of Kansas, Senator Hiram L. Fong of Hawaii, Senator Clifford P. Case of New Jersey, New York Mayor John V. Lindsay, and Governor James A. Rhodes of Ohio. Prior to the convention, Senator Strom Thurmond of South Carolina, Senator Howard Baker of Tennessee, and Senator John Tower of Texas shed their favorite-son status in order to endorse Nixon. Governor Ronald Reagan relinquished his designation as favorite son of the California delegation when he announced his presidential candidacy on August 5, 1968.

38. NAR, Record Group 15, Series 33, Box 62, Folder 2443.

39. This strategy was widely attributed to Nelson Rockefeller at the time. For instance, in a memo for the file dated August 23, 1967, Nixon reviewed a phone conversation he had with Goldwater about the upcoming presidential race: "I

had a talk with Barry Goldwater. . . . He feels that Rockefeller is quietly backing Romney, thinking that Romney will fall on his face and the Romney votes will shift to Rockefeller." Lyndon B. Johnson Library and Museum, Austin, Texas, Office Files of W. Marvin Watson, Box 23.

40. The documents, interviews, and analyses contained in these works are cited throughout this chapter: Chester, Hodgson, and Page, *An American Melodrama;* Dent, *Prodigal South Returns;* Richard J. Whalen, *Catch the Falling Flag: A Republican's Challenge to His Party* (Boston: Houghton Mifflin, 1972); and F. Clifton White and William J. Gill, *Why Reagan Won: A Narrative History of the Conservative Movement, 1964–1981* (Chicago: Regnery Gateway, 1981). These books provide some of the best firsthand accounts of the 1968 presidential race.

41. This was a reference to Romney's lack of support for Goldwater's candidacy in 1964. "Barry Denounces Romney; but He Likes Nixon in '68," *Free Press-Chicago Tribune* wire, August 29, 1966. This wire, as well as a set of testy exchanges between Romney and Goldwater, including a Romney letter to Goldwater that became public, are found in George Romney Papers, Bentley Historical Library, University of Michigan, Ann Arbor (GRP), Romney Associates, Box 45, Folder Goldwater, Barry.

42. Bachelder's campaign document is found in GRP, Romney Associates, Box 47, Folder Issues: General.

43. The day after the midterm election, Romney disavowed that he would immediately begin preparing to seek the Republican presidential nomination but also left open the possibility of such a move. His intentions became much clearer two months later when Romney Associates, a pre-presidential-campaign organization, opened offices in Lansing, Michigan, near his office at the State Capitol. See Walter Rugaber, "Romney Edges toward Race for '68 Nomination," *New York Times,* November 10, 1966, 28; and Paul Hofmann, "A Romney Group Opens '68 Office," *New York Times,* January 20, 1967, 21.

44. Romney made this statement in his February 18, 1967, speech in Anchorage, Alaska. GRP, Gubernatorial, Box 262, Folder Lincoln Day Banquet. Copies of speeches and interviews he gave on his tour in February are found in this box.

45. Quotes in this paragraph are found in Bob Miller, "Michigan Governor Sure GOP Has Big Win Ahead," *Anchorage Daily Times,* February 20, 1967, 1. See also George H. Gallup, *The Gallup Poll: Public Opinion, 1935–1971,* 3 vols. (New York: Random House, 1972), 2049, 2052, 2053, 2055, and 2060; and Theodore H. White, *The Making of the President, 1968* (New York: Atheneum, 1969), 64.

46. GRP, Romney, Box V-8, Folder April 1967.

47. Michael S. Kramer and Sam Roberts, *"I Never Wanted to be Vice-President of Anything!": An Investigative Biography of Nelson Rockefeller* (New York: Basic Books, 1976), 327.

48. The letter was dated April 10, 1967. GRP, Romney Associates, Box 44.

49. GRP, Romney Associates, Box 49, Folder Memoranda (9).

50. This was Nixon's assessment of Romney as reported by Richard Whalen in *Catch the Falling Flag,* 11.

51. "Romney Asserts He Underwent 'Brainwashing' on Vietnam Trip," *New York Times,* September 5, 1967, 28.

52. GRP, Romney Associates, Box 51, Folder Polls.

53. See Romney's "Statement on Conclusion of Urban Tour," September 30, 1967, GRP, Box 265.

54. Robert B. Semple, Jr., "Romney Sees Need for a Major Effort to Prevent Rioting," *New York Times*, September 13, 1967, 1, 32.

55. Warren Weaver, Jr., "Romney Pays Visit to Coast Hippies," *New York Times*, September 23, 1967, 16.

56. GRP, Box 265.

57. "Republicans," *Time*, October 20, 1967, 17–21.

58. See the November 9, 1967, memo by Henry A. Berliner, Jr., on the stationery of the Romney for President Committee. GRP, Romney Associates, Box 49, Folder General—Romney for President Committee.

59. Romney's address at Dartmouth College in Hanover, New Hampshire, on October 30, 1967, is found in GRP, Box 265.

60. "Romney Says Plight of Poorer Nations Is a Threat to U.S.," *New York Times*, December 7, 1967, 32.

61. Jerry M. Flint, "Romney Terms War in Vietnam His Key Issue in New Hampshire," *New York Times*, February 16, 1968, 18. The text of his speech is found in GRP, Gubernatorial, Box 266, Folder Keene, New Hampshire 1–15–68 Keene State College.

62. GRP, Gubernatorial, Box 266, Folder Sigma Delta Chi (New England Chapter) Concord, New Hampshire, February 15, 1968.

63. Gallup, *Gallup Poll, 1935–1971*, 2090 and 2094.

64. English, *Divided They Stand*, 81.

65. "Statement by Romney," *New York Times*, February 29, 1968, 22. See also Warren Weaver, Jr., "Romney Suddenly Quits; Rockefeller Reaffirms Availability to a Draft," *New York Times*, February 29, 1968, 1, 22.

66. See Tom Reed, diary notes about Reagan's 1968 campaign, 5. The document is found in Reed's private papers in Healdsburg, California.

67. Reed, diary, 7.

68. Reed, diary, 8.

69. For a review of the Reagan-Kennedy debate, see Cannon, *Reagan* (1982), 260; and Joseph Lewis, *What Makes Reagan Run? A Political Profile* (New York: McGraw-Hill, 1968), 196–97. See also Jack Gould, "TV: Dialogue with London Students," *New York Times*, May 16, 1967, 91. The transcript of the debate is in Ronald Reagan Gubernatorial Papers (RRGP), Ronald Reagan Presidential Library, Simi Valley, California, Box P20. See page 4 of the document for the quotation.

70. See page 8 of the speech, which is found in RRGP, Box P17, Press Unit—Speeches.

71. Reed, diary, 10.

72. Reed, diary, 11.

73. Reed, diary, 12. For Reagan's speech in South Carolina, as well as his speech to the Republican State Central Committee in Milwaukee, Wisconsin, on September 30, 1967, see RRGP, Box P17, Press Unit—Speeches.

74. Reed, diary, 13.

75. Glawdin Hill, "Reagan Says Indecisive Action in War Is Immoral," *New York Times,* November 12, 1967, 60.

76. Tom Wicker, "In the Nation: The Republicans and Vietnam," *New York Times,* November 14, 1967, 46. For a more thorough review of the positions of leading Republicans on Vietnam see Terry Dietz, *Republicans and Vietnam, 1961–1968* (Westport, CT: Greenwood, 1986).

77. E. W. Kenworthy, "Eisenhower Joins Truman in Group Backing the War," *New York Times,* October 26, 1967, 1, 10.

78. On August 25, 1967, a group of aides and supporters reported to the governor that Phil Battaglia, his executive assistant (chief of staff in modern parlance), was recruiting homosexuals in the governor's inner office. Three days later, Battaglia resigned. On October 31, columnist Drew Pearson broke the story. On November 10, despite the fact that the *New York Times* verified that Nofziger had told reporters that some members of the governor's staff had been dismissed for immoral behavior, Reagan stated publicly that there were no homosexuals serving in top positions in his administration. This story is recounted in Lou Cannon, *Governor Reagan: His Rise to Power* (New York: Public Affairs, 2003), 238–53. See also Drew Pearson and Jack Anderson, "Scandal in Sacramento," *New York Post,* October 31, 1967, 46; and George H. Smith, *Who Is Ronald Reagan?* (New York: Pyramid Books, 1968), 13–23. According to Theodore White, the scandal took the wind out of the sails of the Reagan presidential drive. "Shocked, Reagan purged his immediate staff, then withdrew to the circle of only his oldest friends, making trusted personal lawyer, William French Smith, an amateur in politics, master of all his political enterprises and surrogate for all decisions. The plans of Reed and White were put on ice. From this blow, the Reagan campaign never recovered." *Making of the President,* 40–41. For a similar analysis, see David S. Broder, "Reagan Banks Prairie Fire," *Washington Post Times Herald,* January 14, 1968, B1, B3. Others hold that the homosexual scandal did not divert Regan's attention away from his campaign, but the governor's concern about undertaking a presidential bid early in his governorship dampened his enthusiasm for the effort. See White and Gill, *Why Reagan Won;* and William A. Rusher, *The Rise of the Right* (New York: William Morrow, 1984), 206.

79. This story is recounted in Reed, diary.

80. Chester, Hodgson, and Page, *An American Melodrama,* 185.

81. English, *Divided They Stand,* 79.

82. White, *Making of the President,* 59.

83. Goldwater dictated this letter to Charles F. Conrad on December 26, 1966. It is found in GRP, Romney Associates, Box 45, Folder Goldwater, Barry.

84. For a review of these events, see White, *Making of the President,* 60; and Whalen, *Catch the Falling Flag,* 57.

85. According to Harry S. Dent, chairman of the Republican Party in South Carolina in the mid-1960s, he "sold a 'southern strategy' to citizen Nixon in 1966 while he was campaigning for congressional candidates in Columbia, South Carolina." Dent, *Prodigal South Returns,* 6.

86. Following his defeat to Edmund Brown in the gubernatorial race in California in 1962, Nixon moved to New York and joined a prestigious law firm as a

senior partner. Although he enjoyed his new life on the East Coast and the new political network he developed, Nixon was never fully accepted by the eastern Establishment.

87. Sale, *Power Shift,* 115.

88. Sale, *Power Shift,* 6. When Nixon became president, Dent was appointed special counsel to the president, serving as a liaison between Nixon and Republican organizations throughout the country. Dent was also Nixon's adviser on the South. During the 1968 campaign, Dent was the Republican state chairman for South Carolina. He participated in Nixon's southern strategy during the 1968 campaign, but Howard "Bo" Callaway of Georgia ran the former vice president's operation in the South.

89. Cannon, *Governor Reagan,* 258–29.

90. Quote found in Robert B. Semple, Jr., "Nixon's Campaign Is Stately, Dignified, Proud—and Slow," *New York Times,* February 18, 1968, 164.

91. Nixon, *RN,* 298.

92. Quoted in Whalen, *Catch the Falling Flag,* 83.

93. Cannon, *Governor Reagan,* 260.

94. Nixon had reflected on and explained his unusual decision to travel abroad and take a six-month hiatus from politics as the Republican contest for the presidency was gaining momentum in 1967. See Richard Nixon, *In the Arena: A Memoir of Victory, Defeat, and Renewal* (New York: Simon & Schuster, 1990), 197.

95. Reagan's address before the Economic Club in New York on January 17, for instance, was a critique of the Great Society and a call to reduce "the heavy spending programs and the extravagant credit policies that have brought inflation back." A copy of the speech is found in RRGP, Box P17. In mid-January, Reagan further lambasted the Great Society in speeches at fund-raisers for the Republican Party in Tulsa, Washington, New York, Pittsburgh, and Philadelphia. See "A Reagan Speaking Tour to Begin Jan. 16 in Tulsa," *New York Times,* January 4, 1968, 13; Alvin Rosensweet, "Gov. Reagan Derides Government Handouts," *Pittsburgh Post-Gazette,* January 19, 1968, 1; James Helbert, "GOP Wants Youth Support, Reagan Says," *Pittsburgh Press,* January 19, 1968, 6; and Joseph H. Miller, "Nixon in Lead for GOP Bid, Reagan Says," *Philadelphia Inquirer,* January 19, 1968, 1, 3.

96. "Goldwater Shifts Rockefeller Stand," *New York Times,* March 8, 1968, 22; and Bolles, "Barry Is Brief."

97. Chester, Hodgson, and Page, *An American Melodrama,* 220.

98. Rockefeller's decidedly moderate positions on policy issues were published in a book during the election year. See Nelson A. Rockefeller, *Unity, Freedom & Peace: A Blueprint for Tomorrow* (New York: Random House, 1968). See also Tom Wicker, "Impact of Romney Move," *New York Times,* February 29, 1968, 22; and "Presidential Politics: A New Race with Romney Out," *New York Times,* March 3, 1968, E2.

99. Barely two days after Romney withdrew, Rockefeller came close to declaring his candidacy in a press conference: "I am not going to create dissension within the Republican Party by contending for the nomination, but I'm ready and willing to serve the American people if called." The governor in effect entered the field with this statement, even though it would be two more months before he

made his candidacy official. See Warren Weaver, Jr., "Rockefeller Says That He Will Run If Asked by G.O.P.," *New York Times,* March 2, 1968, 1, 21.

100. Louis Harris, "President Tops GOP Field in Polls," *Washington Post Times Herald,* January 8, 1968, A1, A2.

101. Sydney Kossen, "Reagan Would Support Nominee, Even Rocky," *Washington Post Times Herald,* March 6, 1968, A1, A16.

102. Whalen, *Catch the Falling Flag,* 97.

103. Quoted in Whalen, *Catch the Falling Flag,* 82.

104. Whalen, *Catch the Falling Flag,* 128.

105. Whalen, *Catch the Falling Flag,* 91.

106. Whalen, *Catch the Falling Flag,* 83.

107. Whalen, *Catch the Falling Flag,* 132.

108. Whalen, *Catch the Falling Flag,* 135.

109. The draft of the speech is reproduced in Whalen, *Catch the Falling Flag,* appendix.

110. Chester, Hodgson, and Page, *An American Melodrama,* 221. See also Richard Witkin, "Rockefeller Urged by G.O.P. Leaders to Get into Race," *New York Times,* March 11, 1968, 1, 32.

111. The transcript of Rockefeller's announcement is found in NAR, Record Group 18, Series 33, Box 59, Folder 2322.

112. Reed, diary, 14.

113. See "April 1, 1968. Statement. Vietnam bombing halt," Richard Nixon Library and Birthplace, Yorba Linda, California (RNLB), Speech Files, Box 94, Folder 18.

114. Gould, *1968,* 56.

115. "Gallup Poll Finds Nixon Leads 3 Chief Democratic Contenders," *New York Times,* April 21, 1968, 44.

116. The speech is found in "April 25, 1968. Bridges to Human Dignity. RN's copy," RNLB, Speech Files, Box 94, Folder 27. Nixon would not expend considerable time and energy courting the black vote once he became the Republican Party's presidential nominee. According to Lewis L. Gould, "When asked to appear [during the general election] in black districts, he declined. 'I am not going to campaign for the black vote at the risk of alienating the suburban vote.' His attitude toward black voters was stark. 'If I am President, I am not going to owe anything to the black community.'" Gould, *1968,* 139–40.

117. Whalen, *Catch the Falling Flag,* 149.

118. This statement is found in RRGP, Box P8, Press Unit—Press Releases, Box P8.

119. A copy of the speech can be found in the RRGP, Box P17, Press Unit—Speeches.

120. The quotes in this paragraph are found in Tom Wicker, "Reagan on the Move," *New York Times,* April 28, 1968, E19. In addition to speaking in Boise, Idaho, Reagan gave a stump speech in Boulder, Colorado, on April 27, 1968. His speeches in both states are found in RRGP, Box P17, Press Unit—Speeches.

121. R. W. Apple, Jr., "'Choice' Offered by Rockefeller as He Joins Race," *New York Times,* May 1, 1968, 1, 30.

122. Rockefeller discusses his campaign strategy in his June 19 speech in Cleveland, Ohio; his June 26 speech in New Haven, Connecticut; and his July 2

speech in Boise, Idaho. See NAR, Record Group 15, Series 33, Box 61, Folder 2397; Record Group 15, Series 33, Box 61, Folder 2413; and Record Group 15, Series 33, Box 62, Folder 2434.

123. Quoted in Darcy G. Richardson, *A Nation Divided: The 1968 Presidential Campaign* (Lincoln, NE: Writers Club Press, 2002), 243–44.

124. One undated and unsigned confidential document was obviously written before Romney's withdrawal: "For the time being, the contest is openly between Romney and Nixon. It seems that *Nixon* will win that contest. My analysis is that the more support Nixon gains, the better it is for Rockefeller because all the ground gained by Nixon reduces the power of the Goldwater-Reagan conservatives who enter the convention fight with a tough, unyielding but manageable minority. . . . Romney's experience has dramatically shown the fatal danger that exists for anyone aspiring to national leadership in changing one's position purely for political reasons." NAR, Record Group 15, Series 35.3, Box 19, Ann Whitman Series, Folder 241.

125. Rockefeller presented these figures on July 31 in a speech at his New York headquarters. See NAR, Record Group 15, Series 33, Box 63, Folder 2493.

126. The quotes in this paragraph are found in R.W. Apple, Jr., "Rockefeller Says U.S. Policy Lags," *New York Times*, May 2, 1968, 1, 21.

127. NAR, Record Group 18, Series 33, Box 59, Folder 2321.

128. See R. W. Apple, Jr., "Rockefeller Sees Reagan in South," *New York Times*, May 21, 1968, 1, 28. Rockefeller's speeches in Florida, Georgia, and South Carolina are found in NAR, Record Group 18, Series 33, Box 59, Folder 2338; Record Group 18, Series 33, Box 60, Folder 2344; and Record Group 18, Series 33, Box 60, Folders 2346 and 2348.

129. Quoted in Richard L. Madden, "Rockefeller Scores Talks by Kennedy," *New York Times*, May 25, 1968, 16.

130. Reed, diary, 15.

131. RRGP, Box P24, Governor's Daily Schedules, 1968 (5–1-68 to 7–30-68) Press Unit.

132. Chester, Hodgson, and Page, *An American Melodrama*, 200. The quote from Reagan's speech is also found on page 200 of Chester et al. See also Paul Atkinson, "Humphrey-RFK Possible Demo Team—Reagan," *Times-Picayune*, May 20, 1968, sec. 1, pp. 1, 3.

133. White and Gill, *Why Reagan Won*, 109.

134. These speeches are reviewed in Reed, diary, 15–16. See also Sam Jacobs, "GOP Lands: Rocky, Reagan Tour Florida," *Miami Herald*, May 21, 1968, 1A, 19A; and James M. Naughton, "JFK's 'Missile Gap' Now Exists—Reagan," *Plain Dealer* (Cleveland), May 23, 1968, 1, 5. Copies of Reagan's speeches in Miami and Cleveland can be found in RRGP, Box P17, Press Unit—Speeches.

135. Reed, diary, 16.

136. White and Gill, *Why Reagan Won*, 109.

137. The document is found in RNLB, Speech Files, Box 94, Folder 31.

138. Excerpts from Nixon's speech are found in RNLB, Speech File 1968 (Jan. 27–May 26), Box 94, Folder 34.

139. The radio address is found in RNLB, Speech File 1968 (Jan. 27–May 26), Box 94, Folder 37. See also Donald Janson, "Nixon Discerns a New Coalition," *New York Times*, May 17, 1968, 25.

140. For Nixon's statement of May 16, 1968, see RNLB, Speech File 1968 (Jan. 27–May 26), Box 94, Folder 36.

141. Dent, *Prodigal South Returns*, 80–81.

142. Dent, *Prodigal South Returns*, 82.

143. Nixon, *RN*, 305.

144. The ABM commitment is recounted in Jules Witcover, *The Resurrection of Richard Nixon* (New York: G. P. Putnam's Sons, 1970), 310–11; and Adam Clymer, "Strom Thurmond, Senate Institution Who Fought Integration, Dies at 100," *New York Times*, June 28, 2003, A13.

145. Thurmond wrote: "For our future peace and security, our ABM defenses should be expanded. . . . [T]he United States must now proceed with development of a reliable anti-satellite system for use in conjunction with the ABM." Strom Thurmond, *The Faith We Have Not Kept* (San Diego: Viewpoint Books, 1968), 72, 73.

146. Nixon, *RN*, 305. "Nixon on the Issues" was a campaign circular that presented the former vice president's views on policy issues. It is in the Richard Nixon Book Collection at the Nixon Library and Birthplace Foundation, Yorba Linda, California.

147. White and Gill, *Why Reagan Won*, 108–9.

148. In a June 6, 1968, letter to a resident of Georgia, Thurmond wrote: "I had a talk with Richard Nixon in Atlanta. . . . I was very much pleased with his position on matters and the statements he made. I realize that he will not favor every position that we take, but on balance he seems to be far the superior candidate to any of the Democrats that have been mentioned. I feel that as time has gone by he has seasoned a great deal and will stand for principles in which you and I believe." See Letter, June 6, 1968, from Strom Thurmond to Hugh G. Grant, Folder Political Affairs 2 (Elections) January 30—December 11, 1968, Box 26 Subject Correspondence 1968. Strom Thurmond Collection, Clemson University.

149. According to William A. Rusher, "After the primaries, Everett Dirksen—having given his junior colleague, Charles Percy, a badly needed pointer or two on political footwork—let it be known that he would go along [with Nixon]." "What Happened at Miami Beach?" *National Review*, December 3, 1968, 1209. Mindful of his position as chairman of the Platform Committee for the 1968 Republican convention and the need for party unity, Dirksen consulted with Nixon, Reagan, and Rockefeller and fully expressed his endorsement of Nixon after the convention. See Neil MacNeil, *Dirksen: Portrait of a Public Man* (New York: World Publishing, 1970), 330. As chairman of the Republican National Convention of 1968, Ford refrained from publicly supporting any candidate before the convention. He reportedly stated, however, that he "was a Nixon man even before the 1968 campaign began. No equivocation. No question. He knew that, and so did everybody else." James Cannon, *Time and Chance: Gerald Ford's Appointment with History* (Ann Arbor: University of Michigan Press, 1998), 94. In a September 11, 1967, telegram to Harold Hayes, editor of *Esquire*, Congressman Ford said: "In order to build a unified and constructive Republican record in the House I have refrained from endorsing any Republican as a candidate for the Presidency. To sponsor any individual candidate prior to action by national convention delegates would undermine my unifying efforts in

the House. At this point with the Johnson Administration in such trouble at home and abroad it is necessary to have a public discussion of all potential Republican candidates." Ford Congressional Papers, Box A68, Folder 21, Gerald R. Ford Library, Ann Arbor, Michigan (GRF).

150. Quoted in Gould, *1968*, 101.

151. Richardson, *A Nation Divided*, 249–50; and R. W. Apple, Jr., "Rockefeller Links His Goals to Those of Kennedy," *New York Times*, June 12, 1968, 22.

152. Kramer and Roberts, *I Never Wanted*, 326.

153. NAR, Record Group 4, Series 6, Box 1, Folder 5.

154. Whalen, *Catch the Falling Flag*, 174–75.

155. Whalen, *Catch the Falling Flag*, 175.

156. Whalen, *Catch the Falling Flag*, 177–78.

157. Whalen, *Catch the Falling Flag*, 182.

158. See pages 13–14 of Nixon's press conference, found in RNLB, Speech File 1968 (May 27–Aug. 8), Box 95, Folder 15, Press Conference.

159. The quotes in this paragraph are found in Whalen, *Catch the Falling Flag*, 189–91.

160. The text of the Vietnam statement that Nixon submitted to the Platform Committee of the Republican National Convention is found in RNLB, Speech Files, Box 95, Folder 19.

161. Robert O. Conoley, "GOP Delegates to Back Nixon," *State and the Columbia Record*, June 23, 1968, 1A, 8A; "Sen. Strom Thurmond Gives Support to Richard Nixon," *News and Courier* (South Carolina), June 23, 1968, 1A; and "Tower Backs Nixon," *New York Times*, July 2, 1968, 24.

162. The quotes from Nixon's June 27, 1968, radio address, "Toward an Expanded Democracy," are found on pages 3 and 9. See RNLB, Speech File 1968 (May 27–Aug. 8), Box 95, Folder 4. The quote from his June 29, 1968, statement is found in Robert B. Semple, Jr., "Nixon: Keeping Cool," *New York Times*, June 30, 1968, E3.

163. See RNLB, Speech File 1968 (May 27–Aug. 8), Box 95, Folder 6. The quotes from Nixon's June 23, 1968, statement are found in Clayton Knowles, "Nixon Fears Cuts in Defense Funds," *New York Times*, June 24, 1968, 16.

164. See Apple, "Rockefeller Links His Goals," 22; Sydney H. Schanberg, "Governor Vetoes Marijuana Bill," *New York Times*, June 25, 1968, 26; "Rockefeller Urges State Poverty Plan," *New York Times*, July 1, 1968, 17; and "Rockefeller Urges New Crime Studies," *New York Times*, July 6, 1968, 8. Rockefeller's views on economic and social policy are reviewed in the June 11 and July 10, 1968, "Speakers Kit." See NAR, Record Group 7, Series G, Box 4, Folders 26 and 27.

165. Richardson, *A Nation Divided*, 255. Rockefeller explicitly reached out to black voters in a speech in Baltimore on July 12. In the speech, he mentioned his familiar themes regarding social policy that would cure urban ills such as poor schools and unemployment. See NAR, Record Group 15, Series 33, Box 62, Folder 2455.

166. NAR, Record Group 15, Series 33, Box 61, Folder 2420.

167. The full text of Rockefeller's Vietnam plan is found in NAR, Record Group 7, Series G, Box 2, Folder 12.

168. For instance, at a press conference in Cincinnati, Ohio, on July 23, 1968,

Reagan told reporters that "a third party vote is a throwaway vote. It would mean literally disenfranchising themselves." Warren Wheat, "Reagan Attempts to Woo Wallace Backers to GOP," *Cincinnati Enquirer,* July 24, 1968, 10.

169. The point here is not that the Democratic presidential contenders were insulated from Wallace; indeed, Wallace came out of the Democratic Party. In the 1968 election, however, he was competing with Republicans for some of the same voters. Lou Cannon has concisely explained the problem: "Polls taken in 1967 and 1968 showed that any Republican nominee would defeat President Johnson (and later Hubert Humphrey) in most southern states in a two-way race. With Wallace in the mix as a third-party candidate, however, Republicans trailed Democrats in some states and Wallace in others." Cannon, *Governor Reagan,* 264.

170. Barry Goldwater, "Don't Waste a Vote on Wallace," *National Review,* October 22, 1968, 1060–61, 1079.

171. Cannon, *Governor Reagan,* 264.

172. These speeches are found in RRGP, Box P17, Folder RR GP Press Unit and Folder 1966–75 Press Unit—Speeches.

173. See "State Seeks Racial Gains While Keeping Law, Order—Reagan," *Los Angeles Times,* July 15, 1968, 1; "Reagan on the Racial Problem," *San Francisco Chronicle,* July 15, 1968, 12; and Cannon, *Governor Reagan,* 263

174. This review of Reagan's activities on behalf of minority communities is based on the analysis found in Cannon, *Governor Reagan,* 263.

175. Cannon, *Governor Reagan,* 264.

176. Cannon, *Governor Reagan,* 264.

177. See, for instance, Earl C. Behrens, "Reagan Says Wallace Makes Sense," *San Francisco Chronicle,* July 17, 1968, 1, 30; and Tom Goff, "Reagan-Wallace Differences Blurred, Governor Admits," *Los Angeles Times,* July 17, 1968, 3, 18.

178. The text of Reagan's press conference is found in RRGP, Box P2, Folder Press Conference Transcripts June 25, 1968; July 2, 1968; July 8, 1968; and July 16, 1968.

179. Lou Cannon described Reagan's tour as a "southern solicitation." See Cannon, *Governor Reagan,* 265.

180. "Reagan Disowns Vice Presidency," *Baltimore Sun,* July 22, 1968, A1, A4; Bob Webb, "Reagan Rests Hopes with 'Winds of Change,'" *Cincinnati Enquirer,* July 22, 1968, 14; and "Reagan Dines 7 Months Late," *Cincinnati Enquirer,* July 23, 1968, 11.

181. For instance, see his speech in Amarillo, Texas, on July 19 and in Charlottesville, Virginia, on July 20. RRGP, Box P17, Folder RR GP Press Unit. See also Peter Boisseau, "Reagan Says Democrats Weighing Superstates," *Richmond Times-Dispatch,* July 21, 1968, A1, A13.

182. Reagan's statement in Amarillo is found in James E. Jacobson, "Not Active Candidate, Reagan Still Insists," *Birmingham News,* July 21, 1968, 1,6,8. His speech in Little Rock is found in RRGP Box P17, Folder RR GP Press Unit.

183. Quotes found in Charles Richardson, "Reagan Rips Third Party as Futile, but Favors Much of Wallace Platform," *Birmingham News,* July 25, 1968, A1, A6; and Al Fox, "Reagan Fails to Sweep GOP Delegates," *Birmingham News,* July 25, 1968, 2.

184. "Back Nixon, Barry Urges State GOP," *Birmingham News,* July 24, 1968, 2.

185. "Reagan States His Conditions to Enter Race," *Courier-Journal* (Louisville, KY), July 31, 1968, A3.

186. RRGP, Box P17, Press Unit, Folder Speeches—Gov Ronald Reagan [5/21/68 thru 7/31/68].

187. Reed, diary, 17.

188. GRP, Gubernatorial, Box 362, Folder GOP Convention Nominating Speech.

189. The polls regarding Nixon and Rockefeller are cited in Warren Weaver, Jr., "Nixon Men Claim Victory," *New York Times,* July 30, 1968, 1, 26.

190. Cited in Robert S. Boyd, "Nixon Loses a Few Votes but Still Has Big Lead," *Miami Herald,* August 5, 1968, 1A, 19A.

191. "Dent Advised Reagan Not to Announce His Candidacy," *State* (South Carolina), August 6, 1968, A8.

192. Robert S. Boyd, "Reagan Jumps into Race to Halt Nixon Stampede," *Miami Herald,* August 6, 1968, 1A, 14A.

193. English, *Divided They Stand,* 288; Warren Weaver, Jr., "Nixon Said to Want Rockefeller, Lindsay or Percy for 2d Place," *New York Times,* August 5, 1968, 1, 24; and Remer Tyson, "Sen. Thurmond Rallied Dixie for Nixon," *Atlanta Journal and Atlanta Constitution,* August 11, 1968, 1A,18A,19A.

194. The telegram is quoted in Dent, *Prodigal South Returns,* 87.

195. English, *Divided They Stand,* 288–89; and Barry M. Goldwater, *With No Apologies: The Personal and Political Memoirs of United States Senator Barry M. Goldwater* (New York: William Morrow, 1979), 207.

196. Quoted in Philip G. Grose, Jr., "S.C. Delegation Takes Dim View of Reagan Candidacy," *State,* August 6, 1968, A1, A8.

197. Boyd, "Nixon Loses a Few"; and Chester, Hodgson, and Page, *An American Melodrama,* 455.

198. Reed discusses the issue of Reagan's running mate in his diary, 17.

199. Quoted in Sale, *Power Shift,* 117–18.

200. Robert S. Boyd, "Reagan, Rocky Fail to Dent Nixon Ranks," *Miami Herald,* August 7, 1968, 1A, 2A.

201. White and Gill, *Why Reagan Won,* 103.

202. English, *Divided They Stand,* 291; and Chester, Hodgson, and Page, *An American Melodrama,* 460–74.

203. *CQ Press Guide to U.S. Elections,* 5th ed., vol. 1 (Washington, DC: Congressional Quarterly Press, 2005), 650.

204. The front-page article was written by Don Oberdorfer. See also Robert Eells and Bartell Nyberg, *Lonely Walk: The Life of Senator Mark Hatfield* (Chappaqua, NY: Christian Herald Books, 1979), 59–60.

205. NAR, Record Group 15, Series 33, Box 63, Folder 2502.

206. Quoted in Whalen, *Catch the Falling Flag,* 177–78. See also Tom Reed's April 29, 2007, e-mail correspondence to Kiron Skinner. This correspondence is found in Skinner's private files at Carnegie Mellon University and the Hoover Institute.

207. Another view about the vice presidential selection was that Nixon chose Agnew because he "could take orders." See Robert E. Hartley, *Charles H. Percy: A Political Perspective* (New York: Rand McNally, 1975), 96.

208. For the text of Agnew's statement, see *Baltimore Sun,* April 12, 1968, C7.

See also Gene Oishi, "Negroes Quit Conference with Agnew," *Baltimore Sun,* April 12, 1968, C22, C7; and "Agnew Angers Negroes," *New York Times,* April 12, 1968, 20.

209. Sale, *Power Shift,* 118.

210. Richard Reeves, *President Reagan: The Triumph of Imagination* (New York: Simon & Schuster, 2006), xi. ·

CHAPTER 3

1. Bill Boyarsky, "Reagan Isn't Sure If Car Was Speeding," *Los Angeles Times,* December 30, 1974, 3; Lee Fremstad, "Newspaper Column, Talks Are Reagan's Next Career," *Sacramento Bee,* December 30, 1974, B1; Peter Hannaford, *The Reagans: A Political Portrait* (New York: Coward-McCann, 1983), 57–81; Kiron K. Skinner, Annelise Anderson, and Martin Anderson, eds., *Reagan, In His Own Hand: The Writings of Ronald Reagan That Reveal His Revolutionary Vision for America* (New York: Free Press, 2001), xiii–xxiii; and Kiron K. Skinner, Annelise Anderson, and Martin Anderson, eds., *Reagan's Path to Victory: The Shaping of Ronald Reagan's Vision, Selected Writings* (New York: Free Press, 2004), xi–xvii.

2. Skinner, Anderson, and Anderson, *A Life in Letters,* 335.

3. "Reagan's Radio Producer," *Television/Radio Age,* September 8, 1980, 16; and Skinner, Anderson, and Anderson, *Reagan's Path to Victory,* xiv.

4. "Reagan Key to Conservative Hopes," *Human Events,* March 1, 1976, 5.

5. Marquis Childs, "Reagan: More Serious Than Ever," *Washington Post,* May 16, 1978, A13.

6. Riker, *Art of Political Manipulation,* 1.

7. For examples of Reagan's ideas on the economy see his discussion of Proposition 13, the June 1978 ballot initiative approved by California voters. Skinner, Anderson, and Anderson, *In His Own Hand,* 258–62. The quotes in this paragraph are from pages 274 and 255. Proposition 13 was a property-tax-cutting measure.

8. Skinner, Anderson, and Anderson, *In His Own Hand,* 284–85.

9. Skinner, Anderson, and Anderson, *In His Own Hand,* 4–9 and 12.

10. Skinner, Anderson, and Anderson, *A Life in Letters,* contains more than 1,000 letters Reagan wrote by hand during 72 years of his life. The authors collected a database of more than 5,000 letters drawn from private collections, President Reagan's private papers, and public archives throughout the United States. Writing responses to those who heard his radio commentary and disliked it was one of the ways in which Reagan communicated with people about both his radio program and his philosophy. In the spring of 1977, Reagan wrote a lengthy response to a critic who believed his radio station should discontinue broadcasting Reagan's commentaries. At the end of the letter he encouraged his critic to "listen at least for the next few weeks because I'm doing a broadcast about our great generosity. Another about the difference between ourselves and Russia as to what we give medals for, and three broadcasts about the government of Chile." Page 271. For another response to a critique of his radio commentary see his March 1, 1978, letter found on pages 276–77.

11. Bartels, *Presidential Primaries,* 13–27; William J. Crotty, *Political Reform*

and the American Experiment (New York: Thomas Y. Crowell, 1977), 193, 255; John L. Moore, *Elections A to Z*, 2nd ed. (Washington, DC: Congressional Quarterly Press, 2003), 369, 370; and Nelson W. Polsby, *Consequences of Party Reform* (New York: Oxford University Press, 1983), 16, 54, 55, 59, 61, and 62.

12. Ranney, *American Elections of 1980*, 369.

13. An example of Goldwater's support for Ford is found in the senator's March 7, 1976, memo to the president on campaign strategy. The letter is found at http://www.fordlibrarymuseum.gov/library/exhibits/campaign/goldwat1.htm, consulted April 24, 2007.

14. Reagan's political activities are reviewed extensively in a later section of this chapter.

15. These ratings are based on Gallup surveys. Some of the ratings herein listed are found in George H. Gallup, *The Gallup Poll: Public Opinion, 1972–1977*, 2 vols. (Wilmington, DE: Scholarly Resources, 1978), 2:787, 944, 950–51.

16. Gallup, *Gallup Poll, 1972–1977*, 1:601.

17. Lou Cannon, *Reagan* (New York: G. P. Putnam's Sons, 1982), 193–94; Francis X. Clines, "'My Options Open,'" *New York Times*, December 12, 1973, 91; and Lyle Emerson Nelson, *American Presidents, Year by Year*, vol. 3 (Armonk, NY: M. E. Sharpe, 2004), 662.

18. Russell Baker, "Not Those Old Wings Again!" *New York Times*, February 8, 1975, 22; James Reston, "Thunder on the Right," *New York Times*, March 5, 1975, 39; James M. Naughton, "Ford Hopes to Have Rockefeller on Slate," *New York Times*, June 17, 1975, 1; "Gallup Poll Sees Reagan Ahead of Rockefeller," *New York Times*, August 28, 1975, 14; John Robert Greene, *The Presidency of Gerald R. Ford* (Lawrence: University Press of Kansas, 1995), 159–60; and Yanek Mieczkowski, *Ford and the Challenges of the 1970s* (Lexington: University Press of Kentucky, 2005), 311–12.

19. Frank Lynn, "Rockefeller Acting as If He's Running," *New York Times*, June 1, 1976, 1; Frank Lynn, "The Party That Roared," *New York Times*, June 6, 1976, 417; and James M. Naughton, "Ford Announces Candidacy for '76 'To Finish Job,'" *New York Times*, July 9, 1975, 77.

20. "Text of Reagan Statement," *New York Times*, July 27, 1976, 15; David Keene, "Why Reagan Chose Schweiker: An Insider's Account," *The Alternative: An American Spectator*, November 1976, 13–15; and Jon Nordheimer, "A Total Surprise," *New York Times*, July 27, 1976, 1.

21. White and Gill, *Why Reagan Won*, 179. See also Jules Witcover, *Marathon: The Pursuit of the Presidency, 1972–1976* (New York: Viking, 1977), 462–63.

22. Peter G. Bourne, *Jimmy Carter: A Comprehensive Biography from Plains to Post-Presidency* (New York: Scribner's, 1977), 167–69 and 231–36; David Chagall, *The New Kingmakers: An Inside Look at the Powerful Men behind America's Political Campaigns* (New York: Harcourt Brace Jovanovich, 1981), 51; and Nelson, *American Presidents*, 640–41.

23. See "1976 Presidential Campaign, Campaign Director's Office, Campaign Director—Hamilton Jordan, 'Memorandum—Hamilton Jordan to Jimmy Carter, 11/4/72,'" Box 199, Jimmy Carter Library, Atlanta (JCL).

24. Wayne King, "Georgia's Gov. Carter Enters Democratic Race for President," *New York Times,* December 13, 1974, 1.

25. Walter R. Mears, *Deadlines Past: Forty Years of Presidential Campaigning: A Reporter's Story* (Kansas City, MO: Andrews McMeel, 2003), 131; and Ted Widmer, *Campaigns: A Century of Presidential Races from the Photo Archives of the New York Times* (New York: DK Publishing, 2001), 280–81.

26. Carter's campaign themes are reviewed in Michael G. Krukones, "Campaigner and President: Jimmy Carter's Campaign Promises and Presidential Performance," in *The Presidency and Domestic Policies of Jimmy Carter,* ed. Herbert D. Rosenbaum and Alexej Ugrinsky (Westport, CT: Greenwood, 1994), 138–39. Carter's 1976 and 1980 presidential campaign themes are discussed in greater depth in the next chapter.

27. On Carter's selection of Mondale, see Bourne, *Jimmy Carter,* 330–33; and Jimmy Carter, *Keeping Faith: Memoirs of a President* (New York: Bantam, 1982), 36–39.

28. B. Drummond Ayres, Jr., "Wallace Opens 1976 White House Drive," *New York Times,* November 13, 1975, 81; and Jules Witcover, "Wallace Announces He'll Run," *Washington Post,* November 13, 1975, A1.

29. B. Drummond Ayres, Jr., "Wallace Isolated by Tight Security," *New York Times,* February 1, 1976, 34; and Tom Wicker, "Sending the Message," *New York Times,* February 27, 1976, 31. For a review of the many factors complicating Wallace's 1976 presidential bid, see Jody Carlson, *George C. Wallace and the Politics of Powerlessness: The Wallace Campaigns for the Presidency, 1964–1976* (New Brunswick, NJ: Transaction Books, 1981), 203–20.

30. Prior to the official announcement of Wallace's candidacy, Melvin Laird, former secretary of defense and one of Ford's longtime political associates, stated that the governor's candidacy would be a boost for the president because Wallace would receive the votes of the conservatives in the Democratic primaries who would otherwise oppose Ford in the Republican primaries. See Christopher Lydon, "Laird Expects Challenge to Rockefeller," *New York Times,* May 14, 1975, 10. In his retrospective analysis of Republican politics from the 1960s to the 1980s, Harry Dent includes Wallace in his analysis of Ford's loss but places the blame squarely on Reagan: "When Reagan became a candidate, George Wallace was abandoned by the John Birch Society. This, more than the 1972 wound, caused the demise of Wallace and the consequent loss to Carter in the big southern primary stakes between the two southern Democratic hopefuls, Wallace and Carter." *Prodigal South Returns,* 55–56.

31. Paul Hope, "Reagan Eyes Road to White House," *Washington Star,* June 3, 1973, A12.

32. See William F. Buckley, Jr., "Say It Isn't So, Mr. President," *New York Times Magazine,* August 1, 1971, 36.

33. In a May 21, 1971, letter to Robert Docksai, the chairman of YAF, Reagan denounced the movement to have him seek the presidency in 1972: "The move you've announced can only divide and destroy our chance to go forward. I am pledged to support the president and have told him I'll lead a California delegation to the convention in his behalf." See Skinner, Anderson, and Anderson, *A Life in Letters,* 174.

34. "A Declaration," *National Review,* August 10, 1971, 842; and Tad Szulc, "11 Conservatives Criticize Nixon," *New York Times,* July 29, 1971, 7.

35. George H. Nash, *The Conservative Intellectual Movement in America* (New York: Basic Books, 1976), 337.

36. Micklethwait and Wooldridge, *The Right Nation,* 70.

37. Frank S. Meyer, "Reform without Principle," *Modern Age,* Spring 1961, 196.

38. William A. Rusher, *The Making of the New Majority Party* (New York: Sheed and Ward, 1975), xviii.

39. Quoted in Lou Cannon, "The Reagan Years," *California Journal,* November 1974, 365.

40. Quoted in Richard Bergholz, "Reagan Future: Which Office to Aim For?" *Los Angeles Times,* August 13, 1974, 3, 16.

41. The speech is reprinted in a collection of Reagan's speeches, *A Time for Choosing: The Speeches of Ronald Reagan, 1961–1982* (Chicago: Regnery Gateway, 1983), 139, 146.

42. These remarks were not part of Reagan's GOP speech in Atlanta, but were typical of those he made during the Watergate crisis. The remarks are quoted in Cannon, *Reagan* (1982), 198.

43. Russell Kirk, "New Directions in the U.S. Right?" *New York Times Magazine,* August 7, 1966, 28.

44. William A. Niskanen, *Reaganomics: An Insider's Account of the Policies and the People* (New York: Oxford University Press, 1988), viii–ix.

45. Cannon, *Governor Reagan,* 446; Skinner, Anderson, and Anderson, *A Life in Letters,* 179.

46. Skinner, Anderson, and Anderson, *In His Own Hand,* 258–59; Skinner, Anderson, and Anderson, *Reagan's Path to Victory,* 354–55.

47. The statement by Peter Schrag is from his book *Paradise Lost: California's Experience, America's Future* (New York: New Press, 1998), which Lou Cannon cites in *Governor Reagan,* 381. The Cannon quote above is found on the same page.

48. Larry Stammer, "Reagan Checks His Options for '76 White House Drive," *San Jose Mercury News,* December 16, 1973, 3.

49. Cannon, *Reagan* (1982), 192.

50. Bergholz, "Reagan Future," 3.

51. See for example the August 10, 1974, telegram from Mr. and Mrs. Jack Christian and President Ford's August 30 response in GRF, White House Central Files, Box 20, Folder PL/Reagan, Ronald 8/9/74–8/31/74. Ford's response was a form letter, perhaps written as such due to the high volume of critical letters the president received about his choice of Rockefeller as vice president.

52. Skinner, Anderson, and Anderson, *Reagan's Path to Victory,* xiv.

53. These statistics and assessments are found in Lou Cannon, *Governor Reagan,* 394. William Rusher reported different figures for identification with the Republican Party than Teeter did. Rusher reported that 23 percent of Americans described themselves as Republican. See *New Majority Party,* xvi.

54. Rusher, *New Majority Party,* xiii–xiv, xviii.

55. Rusher, *New Majority Party,* 36, 37.

56. See two books by Phillips: *The Emerging Republican Majority,* and *Medi-*

acracy: American Parties and Policies in the Communications Age (New York: Doubleday, 1975).

57. Phillips, *Mediacracy*, 2, 3, and 8.

58. See, for example, The Ripon Society and Clifford W. Brown, Jr., *Jaws of Victory* (Boston: Little, Brown, 1974).

59. David S. Broder, "Conservatives Eye 3d-Party Option," *Washington Post*, February 15, 1975, A2.

60. Jon Nordheimer, "Reagan's Shift to Left," *New York Times*, August 14, 1976, 13.

61. White and Gill, *Why Reagan Won*, 167–68.

62. Hannaford, *The Reagans*, 63.

63. GRF, Richard Cheney Files, Box 18, Folder President Ford Committee—Establishment. See also http://www.fordlibrarymuseum.gov/library/exhibits/campaign/planning.htm, consulted April 24, 2007.

64. James M. Naughton, "President Names a Campaign Chief," *New York Times*, June 19, 1975, 1.

65. GRF, Presidential Handwriting File, Box 71, Folder 7/1/75 (Jerry Jones to Don Rumsfeld). See also http://www.fordlibrarymuseum.gov/library/exhibits/campaign/jones1.htm, consulted April 24, 2007.

66. GRF, Robert Teeter Papers, Box 62, Folder 11/12/75—Analysis of Early Research and Strategy Recommendations (Memo, Robert Teeter to Richard Cheney). See also http://www.fordlibrarymuseum.gov/library/exhibits/campaign/themes.htm, consulted April 24, 2007.

67. GRF, Richard Cheney Files, Box 16, Folder Goldwater, Barry.

68. "The Ford Strategy," *New York Times*, November 5, 1975, 42.

69. Craig Shirley, *Reagan's Revolution: The Untold Story of the Campaign That Started It All* (Nashville, TN: Nelson Current, 2005), 61.

70. GRF, President Ford Committee Records, Box B2, Folder Marik File—Market Opinion Research (Memo, Robert Teeter to Bo Callaway, 12/11/75) or http://www.fordlibrarymuseum.gov/library/exhibits/campaign/121175.htm, consulted April 24, 2007. See also GRF, Foster Chanock Files, Box 4, Folder Robert Teeter—Memoranda and Polling Data (3) (Memo, Robert Teeter to Richard Cheney, 12/24/75), or http://www.fordlibrarymuseum.gov/library/exhibits/campaign/polls.htm, consulted April 24, 2007.

71. Witcover, *Marathon*, 394.

72. PH Box 5, Folder (Research) Sears, John.

73. Cannon, "The Reagan Years," 364.

74. Cannon, *Reagan* (1982), 201.

75. Christopher Lydon, "G.O.P. Right Wing Seems to Rule Out Support for Ford for 1976 Campaign," *New York Times*, February 10, 1975, 18; and "Transcript of President's News Conference on Foreign and Domestic Matters," *New York Times*, April 4, 1975, 12.

76. White and Gill, *Why Reagan Won*, 166.

77. "Transcripts of President's News Conference on Domestic and Foreign Matters," *New York Times*, February 15, 1975, 16.

78. "Ford vs. Solzhenitsyn," *New York Times*, July 4, 1975, 22; "Reagan Lays Snub to Policy," *Los Angeles Herald Examiner*, July 19, 1975; "Jerry Don't Go," *Wall Street Journal*, July 23, 1975; and David S. Broder, "Détente

Criticism behind Ford Talk," *Washington Post,* August 20, 1975. For Reagan's July 21, 1975, newspaper column on Ford and Solzhenitsyn see Deaver and Hannaford Collection, Hoover Institution Archives, Stanford, California (DH), Box 61.

79. Carroll Kilpatrick, "Critics of Trip Put President on Defensive," *Washington Post,* July 25, 1975, A2; and Rudy Abramson, "Ford Attempts to Soothe Critics of Europe Pact," *Los Angeles Times,* July 26, 1975, 1.

80. James F. Clarity, "Soviet Wary of the Internal Effects of Détente Abroad," *New York Times,* August 2, 1975, 8; "Ford Overruled Kissinger on Helsinki Summit Talk," *Los Angeles Times,* August 9, 1975, A3; and James M. Naughton, "Ford Sees 35-Nation Charter as a Gauge on Rights in East Europe," *New York Times,* July 26, 1975, 2.

81. James M. Naughton, "Ford Bids Nations Live Up to Spirit of Helsinki Pact," *New York Times,* August 2, 1975, 1; "Ford Overruled Kissinger on Helsinki Summit Talk," *Los Angeles Times,* August 9, 1975, 3; and Endre Marton, "Kissinger Overruled by Ford," *Washington Post,* August 9, 1975, A3.

82. Broder, "Détente Criticism."

83. The speech is found in Ronald Reagan Subject Collection, Hoover Institution Archives, Stanford, California (RRSC), Box 1, Folder RR Speeches 1975–76. See also Neil Mehler, "Reagan: Cut Spending $82.4 Billion," *Chicago Tribune,* September 27, 1975, 3.

84. Reagan's September 24, 1975, speech is found in DH, Box 9, Folder Ronald Reagan Press Releases and Speeches, 1973–75.

85. "Address at the University of Hawaii," December 7, 1975. See http://www.presidency.ucsb.edu/ws/index.php?pid=5422&st=&st1=.

86. Bill Kovach, "Government's Role in Economy, an Issue as Old as the Nation, Is Debated," *New York Times,* January 4, 1976, NES 22, 23.

87. Eileen Shanahan, "President to Ask 10-Billion Tax Cut with Spending Lid," *New York Times,* January 4, 1976, 1, 22; James M. Naughton, "State of the Union: Congress Urged to Act with 'Common Sense' to Meet U.S. Needs," *New York Times,* January 20, 1976, 1, 19; and Philip Shabecoff, "A Vision of America," *New York Times,* January 20, 1976, 19.

88. Both speeches are found in RRSC, Box 1, Folder RR Speeches 1975–76.

89. Rhodes Cook, *United States Presidential Primary Elections, 1968–1996: A Handbook of Election Statistics* (Washington, DC: Congressional Quarterly Press, 2000), 258.

90. John W. Finney, "Defense: Long-Term Rise in 'Real' Outlay Projected with No Cut in Forces," *New York Times,* January 22, 1976, 25.

91. GRF, Foster Chanock Files, Box 4, Folder Research re Ronald Reagan.

92. Cannon, *Reagan* (1982), 202. See also White and Gill, *Why Reagan Won,* 175–76.

93. James M. Naughton, "Ford Says 'In Time' He Expects to Talk with Nixon on China," *New York Times,* March 2, 1976, 12.

94. Reagan's March 4, 1976, statement in Florida is found in Citizens for Reagan Collection, Hoover Institution Archives, Stanford, California (CFR), Box 40, Folder Presidential Campaign 1976, Policy Statements . . . Speeches, Press releases, January 15, 1976–April 22, 1976.

95. Greene, *Presidency of Ford,* 164.

96. Greene, *Presidency of Ford,* 166; and Joseph Kraft, "Foreign Policy: The Issue for '76," *Washington Post,* March 28, 1976, 35.

97. Philip Shabecoff, "Ford Threatens a Defense Veto," *New York Times,* March 30, 1976, 1, 18.

98. Excerpts from Reagan's March 31, 1976, televised speech are found in CFR, Box 101.

99. GRF, Foster Chanock Files, Box 3, Folder Polls—Sindlinger.

100. GRF, Foster Chanock Files, Box 3, Folder Polls—Sindlinger.

101. "Ford Says Reagan's Position on Canal Could Lead to a 'Blood Bath' in Panama," *New York Times,* April 23, 1976, 16; and David Binder, "Panama Canal Pact Plays Big Role in Texas Voting," *New York Times,* April 30, 1976, 16.

102. Ellen Hume, "Reagan Clarifies Remarks on Rhodesia," *Los Angeles Times,* June 4, 1976, 12. See also a statement on the flap by Lyn Nofziger and John Sears in CFR, Box 40 Folder Presidential Campaign 1976, Policy Statements . . . Speeches, Press Releases, June 1, 1976–August 4, 1976.

103. "Effects of Tuesday Voting," *New York Times,* June 10, 1976, 41.

104. Hannaford, *The Reagans,* 130.

105. The Morality and Foreign Policy statement in the 1976 Republican platform is found in http://www.ford.utexas.edu/LIBRARY/document/platform/platform.htm. Reagan's convention speech was reproduced as a pamphlet titled "Will They Say We Kept Them Free?" RRSC, Box 1, Folder RR Remarks—1976 Convention (1-Staff; 2-Convention).

106. Hannaford, *The Reagans,* 137.

107. Phil Williams, "Carter's Defense Policy," in *The Carter Years: The President and Policy Making,* ed. M. Glenn Abernathy, Dilys M. Hill, and Williams (New York: St. Martin's Press, 1984), 86–87.

108. CFR, Box 9 Folder Goldwater, Barry—Letter Announcing Support for GRF 6/29/76.

109. Copley News syndicated Reagan's newspaper column in 1975 and distributed it once a week.

110. Skinner, Anderson, and Anderson, *In His Own Hand,* 235–37; and Skinner, Anderson, and Anderson, *Reagan's Path to Victory,* 58 and 61–64.

111. Hannaford, *The Reagans,* 137.

112. White and Gill, *Why Reagan Won,* 203–4.

113. Skinner, Anderson, and Anderson, *A Life in Letters,* 220.

114. Skinner, Anderson, and Anderson, *A Life in Letters,* 222.

115. Martin Anderson, *Revolution: The Reagan Legacy* (Stanford, CA: Hoover Institution Press, 1990), 151.

116. For instance, see Reagan's July 9, 1979, radio commentary titled "Nigeria." In it, he asks: "Are we choosing paths that are politically expedient and morally questionable? Are we in truth losing our virtue?" Skinner, Anderson, and Anderson, *In His Own Hand,* 17.

CHAPTER 4

1. See Wirthlin, "Reagan for President Campaign Plan," June 29, 1980. Skinner obtained this document from Wirthlin before he donated his private papers to the Hoover Institution Archives. The campaign document should now be available to the public in the Richard B. Wirthlin Papers at the Hoover Archives.

2. Gerald M. Pomper, "The Nominating Contest," in Gerald Pomper et al., *The Election of 1980: Reports and Interpretations,* ed. Marlene Michels Pomper (Chatham, NJ: Chatham House, 1981), 2. See also James W. Davis, *National Conventions in an Age of Party Reform* (Westport, CT: Greenwood, 1983), 34–35.

3. Pomper, "The Nominating Contest," 2.

4. Dent, *Prodigal South Returns,* 18.

5. Hannaford, *The Reagans,* 140–42.

6. Dent, *Prodigal South Returns,* 14.

7. JCL, Staff Secretary Files, Box 1, Folder Caddell, Patrick 12/76–1/77.

8. Gallup, *Gallup Poll: Public Opinion, 1972–1977;* Gallup Poll, *Public Opinion, 1978* (Wilmington, DE: Scholarly Resources, 1980); Gallup Poll, *Public Opinion, 1979* (Wilmington, DE: Scholarly Resources, 1981); Gallup Poll, *Public Opinion, 1980* (Wilmington, DE: Scholarly Resources, 1981); Gallup Poll, *Public Opinion, 1981* (Wilmington, DE: Scholarly Resources, 1982). For Carter's early 1977 rating mentioned herein see 1972–1977, 2:1036; for the late July 1978 rating see page 212 of the 1978 volume; and for the July 1980 rating and assessment of that rating see page 158 of the 1980 volume.

9. Jonathan Moore, ed., *The Campaign for President: 1980 in Retrospect* (Cambridge, MA: Ballinger, 1981), 263–75.

10. The statements by Baker and Dole are found in Bill Peterson, "Behind Front-Runners Plod the 'Other Republicans,'" *Washington Post,* December 18, 1979, A2.

11. Pomper, "The Nominating Contest," 10.

12. Peter Schweizer and Rochelle Schweizer, *The Bushes: Portrait of a Dynasty* (New York: Anchor, 2004), 288.

13. Adam Clymer, "Anderson in New York to Spur New Hampshire Drive," *New York Times,* February 6, 1980, 20; and Richard Harwood, ed., *The Pursuit of the Presidency, 1980* (New York: Berkley Publishing, 1980), 212–13.

14. See "The ANES Guide to Public Opinion and Electoral Behavior," *The American National Election Studies* (Ann Arbor: University of Michigan Center for Political Studies), http://www.electionstudies.org/nesguide/nesguide.htm, consulted on May 22, 2007.

15. William Safire, "Third Party A-Comin'?" *New York Times,* March 20, 1980, A27.

16. Mark Bisnow, *Diary of a Dark Horse: The 1980 Anderson Presidential Campaign* (Carbondale: Southern Illinois University Press, 1983), 297.

17. Norman H. Nie, Sidney Verba, and John R. Petrocik, *The Changing American Voter* (Cambridge: Harvard University Press, 1976), 312–18.

18. Adam Clymer, *Edward M. Kennedy: A Biography* (New York: William Morrow, 1999), 295.

19. *CQ Press Guide,* 377–83.

20. Adam Clymer, "Carter Rejects Specifics of Job Plan but Endorses Its 'Spirit and Aims,'" *New York Times,* August 14, 1980, A1.

21. Michael J. Boskin, *Reagan and the Economy: The Successes, Failures, and Unfinished Agenda* (San Francisco: Institute for Contemporary Studies, 1987), 51.

22. Reagan's January 15, 1977, September 5, 1978, and March 24, 1979, speeches are found in RRSC, Box 3, Folder RR Speeches—1977, Folder RR Speeches—1978,

and Folder RR Speeches—1979. Delivered before the American Conservative Union Banquet in Washington, DC, Reagan's February 6, 1977, speech has the same theme as his January 15 speech and is found in CFR, Box 104, Folder Speeches 1977, and in Baltizer, *A Time for Choosing*, 183–201. The quote from Reagan's June 8, 1977, speech is found in "Reagan Calls for 'New Majority' Party," *Daily-Record* (York, PA), June 10, 1977, 12.

23. See the following Reagan speeches: June 9, 1977, before the Foreign Policy Association in New York; March 17, 1978, before the Conservative Political Action Conference in Washington, DC; April 10, 1978, before the Bonds for Israel Dinner; January 12, 1979, Pepperdine University, Malibu, California; December 13, 1979, St. Petersburg, Florida; and March 17, 1980, Chicago Council on Foreign Relations. See also the foreign and defense policy sections of Skinner, Anderson, and Anderson, *In His Own Hand*, 21–218, and the two Cold War chapters in *A Life in Letters*, 372–431. The speeches listed here are found in CFR, Box 104, Folder 1–5 and Folder 1–6; RRSC, Box 3, Folder RR Speeches—1977, Folder RR Speeches 1978, Folder Speeches 1979; CFR, Box 107, Folder 4–3 and Peter Hannaford Collection, Box 5, Folder Reagan—March, 1980, Hoover Institution Archives, Stanford, California.

24. For a few radio commentaries in which the Kemp-Roth bill is discussed see Skinner, Anderson, and Anderson, *In His Own Hand*, 279–80; Skinner, Anderson, and Anderson, *Reagan's Path to Victory*, 382.

25. RRSC, Box 3, Folder RR Speeches 1978.

26. For instance, see "Avis of Superpowers?" *Public Opinion*, May–June 1978, 28–29.

27. Gary Hart, "American Idol," *New York Times Book Review*, December 24, 2006, 14.

28. Hannaford, *The Reagans*, 200–201; Bill Peterson, "Reagan-for-President Committee Is Formed, but He Hasn't Announced Candidacy—Yet," *Washington Post*, March 8, 1979, A2.

29. Anderson, *Revolution*, 112–13.

30. Anderson, *Revolution*, 116–21.

31. Skinner, Anderson, and Anderson, *In His Own Hand*, 441–42; and Leslie Zaitz, "Reagan Sees Arms Threat as Way to Impress Soviets," *Oregonian*, June 27, 1977, B1.

32. For a major statement of Reagan's assessment of Soviet expansionism, including its control of Eastern Europe, see his June 9, 1977, speech before the Foreign Policy Association in New York. CFR, Box 104, Folder 1–4; and RRSC, Box 3, Folder RR Speeches 1977.

33. CFR, Box 105 Folder 2–5 Reagan Column 1978.

34. RRSC, Box 3, Folder RR Speeches 1978.

35. Skinner, Anderson, and Anderson, *In His Own Hand*, 442.

36. Allen's meeting with Reagan is reviewed in Richard V. Allen, "Peace through Strength: Reagan's Early Call: Win Cold War," *Human Events*, October 24, 2003, http://www.humanevents.com/article.php?id=2175, consulted April 24, 2007; and Peter Robinson, *How Ronald Reagan Changed My Life* (New York: HarperCollins, 2003), 71 and 72.

37. DH, Box 3, Folder Ronald Reagan Collection, Ronald Reagan—General Memos and Allen.

38. The interviewing dates for this survey were April 26–27, 1980. *Gallup Poll, 1980,* 103.

39. Skinner, Anderson, and Anderson, *In His Own Hand,* 120.

40. CFR, Box 104.

41. Adam Clymer, "Reagan: The 1980 Model," *New York Times,* July 29, 1979, SM6.

42. Box 3, Folder Official Announcement Speech 11/13/79 New York.

43. *Public Papers of the President, Jimmy Carter* (Washington, DC: GPO, 1977), 629. See also Charles Mohr, "Two-Year Package of $30 Billion Aims for 800,000 New Jobs," *New York Times,* January 8, 1977, 1; Clyde Farnsworth, "Carter Aides Aiming for 1976 Tax Rebate of up to $11 Billion," *New York Times,* January 23, 1977, A1; and Clyde Farnsworth, "Carter Widens Plan to Aid the Economy to $31 Billion Total," *New York Times,* January 26, 1977, 1.

44. "Carter to Trim Budget $13 billion and Curb Credit to Cut Inflation; Sees Need for Pain and Discipline," *New York Times,* March 15, 1980, 1.

45. Bruce J. Schulman, "Slouching toward the Supply Side: Jimmy Carter and the New American Political Economy," in *The Carter Presidency: Policy Choices in the Post–New Deal Era,* ed. Gary M. Fink and Hugh Davis Graham (Lawrence: University Press of Kansas, 1998), 54.

46. Schulman, "Slouching toward Supply Side," 56.

47. Pat Caddell's campaign strategy document is reviewed in the next chapter.

48. "Carter Budget Message and Some Proposals," *New York Times,* January 23, 1979, B9.

49. Terence Smith, "Carter Discusses Oil and Inflation with Top Aides," *New York Times,* March 20, 1979, A1 and D6.

50. The link to President Carter's speech is http://www.presidency.ucsb.edu/ws/?pid=32596, consulted April 24, 2007. See also Hedrick Smith, "Part Homily, Part Program," *New York Times,* July 16, 1979, A1.

51. DH, Box 9, Folder 9–9.

52. "Changing the Way Things Are," *Washington Post,* July 15, 1979, E6.

53. Henry A. Plotkin, "Issues in the Presidential Campaign," in *The Election of 1980: Reports and Interpretations,* Pomper et al., 48.

54. The quote is from the Trilateral Commission's web site, http://www.trilateral.org/about.htm, consulted April 24, 2007.

55. Bourne, *Jimmy Carter,* 240–41; and Zbigniew Brzezinski, *Power and Principle: Memoirs of the National Security Adviser, 1977–1981,* rev. ed. (New York: Farrar, Straus and Giroux, 1985), 5.

56. See JCL, Jimmy Carter Presidential Campaign, 1976 Presidential Campaign Materials, Box 21, "Issues Press Packet—Pre- and Post-Convention Index 1/76–7/76."

57. http://www.presidency.ucsb.edu/ws/?pid=7552, consulted April 24, 2007.

58. Brzezinski, *Power and Principle,* 147–50; Cyrus Vance, *Hard Choices: Critical Years in America's Foreign Policy* (New York: Simon & Schuster, 1983), 45–46; and Zaikie Laidi, *The Superpowers and Africa: The Constraints of a Rivalry, 1960–1990,* trans. Patricia Badoin (Chicago: University of Chicago Press, 1990), 129.

59. Bourne, *Jimmy Carter,* 382.

60. For a history of the Panama Canal negotiations see William J. Jorden, *Panama Odyssey* (Austin: University of Texas Press, 1984).

61. Hannaford, *The Reagans,* 144–45.

62. Don McLeod, "Carter Policies Draw Active Reagan criticism," *San Diego Evening Tribune,* June 10, 1977.

63. The transcript of Reagan's May 1, 1977, interview on *Meet the Press* is found in DH, Box 13, Folder 13–2, Correspondence 1977–1980; the August 11, 1977, press release is found in DH, Box 9, Folder Ronald Reagan Press Releases 1977–79 and RRSC, Box 3, Folder RR Speeches 1977; the September 8, 1977, Senate testimony is found in Peter Hannaford Collection, Box 5, Folder Reagan Speeches 1977, Hoover Institution Archives, Stanford, California; the October 4 newspaper column is in CFR, Box 105, Folder 2–4 Reagan Column 1977; and excerpts from Reagan's October 20 speech are in RRSC, Box 3, Folder RR Speeches 1977. For radio commentaries on the Panama Canal treaties see Skinner, Anderson, and Anderson, *In His Own Hand,* 198–212.

64. The declassified document in which this quote is found is reprinted in Odd Arne Westad, ed., *The Fall of Détente: Soviet-American Relations during the Carter Years* (Oslo: Scandinavian University Press, 1997), 267.

65. Martin Tolchin, "President Says U.S. Is Able to Monitor Treaty with Soviet," *New York Times,* April 26, 1979, A1, A17; and *Public Papers of the President, Jimmy Carter, 1979,* 1:834 and 1:835.

66. "Jackson Calls Approval of Pact 'Appeasement,' " *New York Times,* June 13, 1979, A14; and Robert G. Kaiser, "Jackson Rips 'Appeasement' of Moscow," *Washington Post,* June 13, 1979, A1.

67. Jay Winik, *On the Brink* (New York: Simon & Schuster, 1996), 101, 102.

68. Richard Halloran, "Joint Chiefs Dissent on Carter-Brown Military Budget," *New York Times,* May 30, 1980, D14; and George C. Wilson, "Joint Chiefs of Staff Break with Carter on Budget Planning for Defense Needs," *Washington Post,* May 30, 1980, A1.

69. "Transcript of President's Interview on Soviet Reply," *New York Times,* January 1, 1980, 4. President Carter declared that "we are now free of that inordinate fear of communism" in his commencement address at the University of Notre Dame on May 22, 1977. The speech is found at http://www.presidency.ucsb.edu/ws/?pid=7552, consulted April 24, 2007.

70. For President Carter's January 4, 1980, address to the nation on the Soviet invasion of Afghanistan see http://www.presidency.ucsb.edu/ws/index.php?pid=32911&st=&st1, consulted April 24, 2007. For his January 23, 1980, State of the Union address see http://www.presidency.ucsb.edu/ws/index.php?pid=33079, consulted April 24, 2007.

71. Winik, *On the Brink,* 103.

72. Skinner, Anderson, and Anderson, *In His Own Hand,* 74–128.

73. Seyom Brown, *The Faces of Power: Constancy and Change in United States Foreign Policy from Truman to Clinton,* 2nd ed. (New York: Columbia University Press, 1994), 384–85.

74. See Lawrence J. Korb, "National Security Organization and Process in the Carter Administration," in *Defense Policy and the Presidency: Carter's First Years,* ed. Sam C. Sarkesian (Boulder, CO: Westview Press, 1979), 166–68.

75. JCL, Carter, Rafshoon, Box 24, Folder Campaign Themes Memorandum.

76. JCL, Carter, Jordan, Box 34, Folder Comprehensive Test Ban Treaty, SALT 1978 and Box 80, Folder Themes.

77. Warren Weaver, Jr., "Conservatives Fear Bush Profits from the Reagan-Crane Rivalry," *New York Times,* February 8, 1980, A17.

78. Theodore H. White, *America in Search of Itself: The Making of the President, 1956–1980* (New York: Harper and Row, 1982), 250.

79. Adam Clymer, "Missing Republican in Iowa," *New York Times,* January 7, 1980, A1; and Walter R. Mears, "Word for GOP Debaters: Cautious," *Cedar Rapids Gazette,* January 7, 1980, 10A.

80. "Excerpts from Forum in Iowa of 6 G.O.P. Presidential Candidates," *New York Times,* January 7, 1980, B4. See also Douglas E. Kneeland, "Reagan Offers Plan to Cut Taxes, Balance Budget, 'Restore Defenses,' " *New York Times,* September 10, 1980, A1.

81. Hannaford, *The Reagans,* 230–36; Edwin Meese III, *With Reagan: The Inside Story* (Washington, DC: Regnery Gateway, 1992), 3–13; White, *America in Search of Itself,* 250–52.

82. "Excerpts from Transcript of Debate among 7 G.O.P Candidates," *New York Times,* February 21, 1980, B12. See also Warren Weaver, Jr., "Financial Support Problem Imperils Campaign Debates," *New York Times,* February 20, 1980, A18; and Lou Cannon and David S. Broder, "GOP Debaters Restate Basic Positions," *Washington Post,* February 21, 1980, A1.

83. Moore, *The Campaign for President,* 121.

84. Ronald Reagan, *An American Life* (New York: Pocket Books, 1990), 213. The editor's name was Jon Breen. In his anger, Reagan had a slip of the tongue. See Cannon *Reagan,* 253.

85. Reagan, *An American Life,* 213.

86. Hedrick Smith, "Excluded from G.O.P. Debate, Four Attack Bush," *New York Times,* February 24, 1980, 1.

87. Hugh E. Gibson, "GOP Candidates Find Few Major Differences," *News and Courier* (Charleston, SC), February 29, 1980, 1A. See also David S. Broder and Bill Peterson, "Despite Barbs, GOP Debate Produces Little Disagreement," *Washington Post,* February 29, 1980, A6; and Douglas E. Kneeland, "4 G.O.P. Contenders Find Much Harmony in 'Debate,' " *New York Times,* February 29, 1980, B5.

88. Broder and Peterson, "Despite Barbs," A6.

89. Warren Weaver, Jr., "Baker Says His Drive Was Going Nowhere," *New York Times,* March 6, 1980, D16.

90. David S. Broder and Bill Peterson, "Rivals Take Turns Ripping Anderson's Loyalty to GOP," *Washington Post,* March 14, 1980, A6; and Jon Margolis, "Candidates Gang Up on Rep. Anderson," *Chicago Tribune,* March 14, 1980, section 1, 1.

91. Adam Clymer, "3 Rivals Attack John Anderson in Illinois Forum," *New York Times,* March 14, 1980, A16.

92. Steven V. Roberts, "Crossovers Are Forsaking Tradition in Wisconsin Vote," *New York Times,* March 30, 1980, 18.

93. Adam Clymer, "Ford Declines Race for the Presidency to Avoid G.O.P. Split," *New York Times,* March 16, 1980, 1.

94. Warren Weaver, Jr., "An Independent Anderson Seen as a 'Problem' for Carter," *New York Times*, March 20, 1980, B11.

95. "Crane to Withdraw from Contest and Support Reagan," *New York Times*, April 17, 1980, D17; Hedrick Smith, "Connally Drops Bid for the Presidency after Carolina Loss," *New York Times*, March 10, 1980, A1, B10; "Crane Urges Supporters to Back Reagan's Drive," *New York Times*, March 21, 1980, A17; and Francis X. Clines, "Anderson Is 'Mulling Over' Possible Bid as Independent," *New York Times*, March 26, 1980, B6.

96. Norman Baxter and Cragg Hines, "Bush, Reagan Find Lots of Common Ground in Forum," *Houston Chronicle*, April 24, 1980, sec. 1, p. 1; and Howell Raines, "Reagan and Bush Debate in Texas but Disagree on Few Major Points," *New York Times*, April 24, 1980, A25.

97. Moore, *The Campaign for President*, 6.

98. Steven V. Roberts, "Carter's Political Rivals React Cautiously to His Announcement of Steps on Iran," *New York Times*, April 8, 1980, A7.

99. *New York Times*, May 12, 1980, D13.

100. Adam Clymer, "Bush Wins Michigan; Reagan and Carter Are Oregon Victors," *New York Times*, May 21, 1980, A1.

101. Hedrick Smith, "George Bush Running Hard, with Brand New Track Suit," *New York Times*, April 27, 1980, E4.

102. Hedrick Smith, "Carter's Foreign Policy Draws Fire on Eve of Caucuses," *New York Times*, January 21, 1980, A1, A13.

103. Robert Lindsey, "Reagan Urges Bases in Mideast and Missiles for Afghan Rebels," *New York Times*, January 10, 1980, B8; and Frank Lynn, "Reagan, in New York, Is Backed by Conservative Party Leaders," *New York Times*, January 16, 1980, A19.

104. "Bush Sees 'a Factual Gap' in Reagan's Campaigning," *New York Times*, April 12, 1980, 10.

105. "Excerpts from Transcripts of Debate among 7 G.O.P. Candidates," *New York Times*, February 21, 1980, B12.

106. Adam Clymer, "Reagan Presses in Speech on Coast for 'Born Again' Protestants' Vote," *New York Times*, May 27, 1980, B9.

107. "Transcript of Kennedy's Speech at Georgetown University on Campaign Issues," *New York Times*, January 29, 1980, A12; Steven Rattner, "Kennedy Urges Energy Plan Based on Liberal Ideas," *New York Times*, February 3, 1980, 16; John Herbers, "Nuclear Power Emerging as Key Issue in Presidential Race," *New York Times*, February 21, 1980, B10; and Clymer, *Edward M. Kennedy*, 305.

108. Bernard Weinraub, "Kennedy Makes a Blunt Attack on Carter Policy," *New York Times*, January 15, 1980, D15; Edward Cowan, "Carter Plan Is Attacked by Rival," *New York Times*, March 15, 1980, A1; and Clymer, *Edward M. Kennedy*, 295.

109. Leslie Bennetts, "Feminists Believe in Anderson Difference," *New York Times*, March 17, 1980, A14.

110. E. J. Dionne, Jr., "Despite Memories of the 60's Blacks Lean toward Carter," *New York Times*, May 11, 1980, E5.

111. "Major News," *New York Times*, June 8, 1980, E1; and "Reagan, Carter

Sew Up Nominations Early," *The Gallup Opinion Index* (December 1980), Report No. 183, 31.

CHAPTER 5

1. *Gallup Poll, 1980*, 139.

2. Wirthlin, "Reagan for President Campaign Plan."

3. Caddell's campaign plan is found in JCL, Carter, Chief of Staff Jordan, Box 77, Folder Campaign Strategy—Caddell, Patrick General Election.

4. Albert R. Hunt, "Voters, Suffering Lowered Expectations, May View the Nastiest Media Blitz Ever," *Wall Street Journal,* May 30, 1980, 7.

5. The July 5, 1979, memo from Brad to John [Anderson] is titled "Initial Proposals for General Strategy (July–March)," John Anderson Campaign Collection, Box 27, Folder 1.2, New Hampshire Political Library, Concord.

6. The quote is from a June 4, 1979, memo to John [Anderson] from Brad titled "Random thoughts." John Anderson Campaign Collection, Box 27, Folder 1.2, New Hampshire Political Library, Concord.

7. Bisnow, *Dark Horse,* 216.

8. Bisnow, *Dark Horse,* 210.

9. This review of David Garth's strategy is based on Bisnow, *Dark Horse,* 208–49 and 301.

10. President Carter's speech is found at http://www.presidency.ucsb.edu/ws/index.php?pid=44730&st=st1=, consulted April 24, 2007.

11. Steven Weisman, "'Fanatics' in Regime in Tehran Blamed by Carter for Crisis," *New York Times,* July 5, 1980, 1, 7.

12. "The Conventions, Platforms, and Issue Activists," in Ranney, *American Elections of 1980,* 100. For Reagan's acceptance speech see http://www.nationalcenter.org/ReaganConvention1980.html.

13. Douglas E. Kneeland, "Reagan Campaigns at Mississippi Fair," *New York Times,* August 4, 1980, A11. See also Anne Q. Hoy, "Reagan Speaks Part on Unique Rural 'Set,'" *Clarion Ledger,* August 4, 1980, 3A; and Jo Ann Klein, "Reagan Wows Crowd at the Neshoba Fair," *Clarion Ledger,* August 4, 1980, 1A.

14. Andrew Young, "Chilling Words in Neshoba County," *Washington Post,* August 11, 1980, A19.

15. Douglas E. Kneeland, "Reagan Urges Blacks to Look Past Labels and to Vote for Him," *New York Times,* August 6, 1980, A1.

16. President Carter's 1980 acceptance speech is found at http://www.presidency.ucsb.edu/ws/index.php?pid=44909&st=speech&st1=, consulted April 24, 2007.

17. JCL, Carter, Chief of Staff Jordan, Box 77, Folder Carter-Mondale Presidential Campaign General. In a July 16, 1979, memo to President Carter, Hamilton Jordan wrote: "Pat [Caddell] had yelled 'wolf' so many times that I discounted his harsh analysis of our situation as well as his unconventional approach to our problems. However, after exposure to his work and time for reflection, there is no question that Pat's original concept was sound and that many of his suggestions were and are valid." Carter, Jordan, Box 34, Folder Image Analysis & Changes, 7/16/79.

18. http://www.presidency.ucsb.edu/ws/index.php?pid=29607, consulted April 24, 2007.

19. See M. Glenn Abernathy, "The Carter Administration and Domestic Civil Rights," in *The Carter Years: The President and Policy Making,* ed. Abernathy, Dilys M. Hill, and Phil Williams (New York: St. Martin's Press, 1984), 117.

20. Edward Cowan, "Carter Sets Steel Aid Program," *New York Times,* October 1, 1980.

21. Darrell M. West, *Making Campaigns Count: Leadership and Coalition-Building in 1980* (Westport, CT: Greenwood, 1984), 44–45.

22. Skinner, Anderson, and Anderson, *A Life in Letters,* 199.

23. http://www.presidency.ucsb.edu/ws/index.php?pid=25844, consulted April 24, 2007.

24. Wallace Turner, "Reagan Says He Would Not Use Single-Issue Test to Pick Judges," *New York Times,* October 2, 1980, A1, B14.

25. Peter Hannaford Collection, Box 7–2, Folder Reagan for President Committee File, 1980, Hoover Institution Archives, Stanford, California.

26. Steven R. Weisman, "President Sees Politics in Reagan Vow to Put Woman on High Court," *New York Times,* October 16, 1980, A1, B6.

27. Howell Raines, "Reagan Backs Evangelicals in Their Political Activities," *New York Times,* August 23, 1980, 8; and Howell Raines, "Reagan Is Balancing 2 Different Stances," *New York Times,* October 4, 1980, 9.

28. Clifford W. Brown, Jr., and Robert J. Walker, *A Campaign of Ideas: The 1980 Anderson/Lucey Platform* (Westport, CT: Greenwood, 1984).

29. "Dissatisfaction Motivated Voters," *The Gallup Poll Index* (December 1980), Report No. 183, 4.

30. "Excerpts from Carter Address to American Legion," *New York Times,* August 22, 1980, B7.

31. Plotkin, "Issues in the Presidential Campaign," 57.

32. Frank Lynn, "Carter Hails Defense Record at 'Town Meeting' on L.I.," *New York Times,* October 17, 1980, A1, A22.

33. "Nunn Again Demands Arms Rise," *New York Times,* November 2, 1979, A8.

34. Raymond L. Garthoff, *Détente and Confrontation: American-Soviet Relations from Nixon to Reagan* (Washington, DC: Brookings Institution, 1994), 864–65 and 870. The partially declassified version of PD 59 is found at http://www.jimmycarterlibrary.org/documents/pddirectives/pd59.pdf, consulted April 24, 2007.

35. Daniel Wirls, *Buildup: The Politics of Defense in the Reagan Era* (Ithaca, NY: Cornell University Press, 1992), 38 n. 20.

36. Walter LaFeber, *America, Russia, and the Cold War, 1945–2006,* 10th ed. (Boston: McGraw-Hill, 2006), 318.

37. Wirls, *Buildup,* 65.

38. Ambassador Hank Cooper, e-mail to coauthor (Kiron Skinner), March 5, 2007. NSDD 13, Nuclear Weapons Employment Policy, is partially declassified and is found in Records Declassified and Released by the National Security Council Box 1, Ronald Reagan Presidential Library, Simi Valley, California.

39. George C. Wilson, "Carter to Support New U.S. Bomber," *Washington Post,* August 14, 1980, A1. See also Walter J. Boyne, "A Tale of Two Bombers," *Air Force Magazine,* July 2006; and Richard Burt, "Brown Says Plane Report Was Meant to Hide Details," *New York Times,* September 5, 1980, A13.

40. Richard Burt, "Brown Says Radar-Evading Planes Shift Military Balance Toward U.S.," *New York Times,* August 23, 1980, 12.

41. Richard V. Allen, e-mail to coauthor (Kiron Skinner), January 5, 2007. This correspondence is found in Skinner's private files.

42. "Brown Responds to Reagan View on Plane Report," *New York Times,* September 6, 1980, 8; and Hedrick Smith, "Reagan's Campaign Shifts Tactics and Moves to Curb Misstatements," *New York Times,* September 5, 1980, A18.

43. Douglas E. Kneeland, "Kissinger Backs Reagan on Secret Plane Charge," *New York Times,* September 6, 1980, 8; and "Ford Assails Disclosure of Secret Plane," *New York Times,* September 9, 1980, D18.

44. Skinner, Anderson, and Anderson, *In His Own Hand,* 480, 481.

45. Skinner, Anderson, and Anderson, *In His Own Hand,* 483.

46. Skinner, Anderson, and Anderson, *In His Own Hand,* 485.

47. Skinner, Anderson, and Anderson, *In His Own Hand,* 484.

48. Mike Tharp, "China Rift Follows Bush on Japan Visit," *New York Times,* August 20, 1980, B9; James P. Sterba, "Bush Explains Reagan Words," *New York Times,* August 23, 1980, 8; and Howell Raines, "Reagan, Conceding Misstatements, Abandons Plan on Taiwan Office," *New York Times,* August 26, 1980, A1, B7.

49. Brown and Walker, *A Campaign of Ideas.*

50. "White House Fact Sheet on Carter's Economic Program for 80's," *New York Times,* August 29, 1980, D12.

51. The statements by business leaders are found in Peter J. Schuyten, "Carter's Proposals Get Mixed Reviews," *New York Times,* August 29, 1980, D13. See also Julie Connelly, "Carter's Plan for U.S. Industry," *Time,* September 1, 1980; Lee Lescaze, "$27.6 Billion in '81 Tax Cuts Would Boost Deficit," *Washington Post,* August 29, 1980, A1; and Steven Rattner, "Bid to Widen Voter Support," *New York Times,* August 29, 1980, 1.

52. On January 28, 1980, President Carter delivered his budget to the U.S. Congress, and on March 14, he introduced his anti-inflation package.

53. Rattner, "Bid to Widen Voter Support," 1.

54. Lou Cannon, "Reagan Scales down Plan for Patching up Economy," *Washington Post,* September 10, 1980, A1; and Kneeland, "Reagan Offers Plan," A1.

55. Niskanen, *Reaganomics,* 12–13.

56. Kneeland, "Reagan Offers Plan," A1.

57. Lee Lescaze, "Carter Attacks Reagan Program, Defends His Handling of 'Stealth,'" *Washington Post,* September 10, 1980, A6.

58. Cannon, "Reagan Scales down Plan," A1.

59. *Gallup Poll, 1980,* 163–64, 196; and Louis Harris and Associates, *Harris 1980 Presidential Election Survey,* no. 80212 (New York: Harris and Associates, 1980), http://www.irss.unc.edu/data_archive/pollsearch.html.

60. Boskin writes, "By 1980, discontent with the policies of the previous two decades and the disappointing economic performance of the 1970s led a growing number of economists, businessmen, and politicians to support different economic policies than those in favor since 1960. These changing attitudes were not limited to a narrow ideological band, but were embraced by a broad group of

people drawn from various political and economic persuasions. President Reagan's economic program, which represented a significant departure from previous policies, reflected this new outlook and differed only in degree and packaging from what was rapidly becoming a consensus among economists. Although Reaganomics was oversold ideologically and politically, it was simply something of an exaggerated expression of mainstream economic thinking at the time. It was not an aberration." *Reagan and the Economy*, 11.

61. Reagan won the 1980 presidential election, of course, and he certainly did not abandon his revolutionary campaign proposals once in the White House. On February 18, 1981, four weeks after his inauguration, he proposed an economic program to Congress under the title "America's New Beginning: A Program for Economic Recovery." Considerable debate ensued, and in August 1981 Reagan signed into law a compromise version, the Economic Recovery Act of 1981. This legislation was consistent with the proposals Reagan had laid out in his September 9, 1980, speech in Chicago and throughout his presidential campaign: income tax rates were to be cut by 25 percent, with a 5 percent cut in October 1981; a 10 percent cut in July 1982, and a 10 percent cut in July 1983. The top income tax rate would be reduced from 70 percent to 50 percent, tax rates would be indexed to soften the impact of inflation, and the exemption for estates and gifts would be increased. Lee Edwards, *The Essential Ronald Reagan: A Portrait in Courage, Justice, and Wisdom* (Lanham, MD: Rowman and Littlefield, 2005), 93; and John W. Sloan, *The Reagan Effect: Economics and Presidential Leadership* (Lawrence: University Press of Kansas, 1999), 145–46. *Newsweek* described ERTA as the "second New Deal potentially as profound in its import as the first was a half century ago." Peter Goldman with Thomas M. DeFrank, Eleanor Clift, John J. Lindsay, Gloria Borger, and Howard Fineman, "RWR's Own New Deal," *Newsweek*, March 2, 1981, 22. Following the enactment of ERTA, the United States experienced 60 months of uninterrupted economic growth, the longest period of economic growth since the U.S. government began recording such statistics in 1854.

62. According to national newspapers, the Anderson/Lucey program was unveiled on August 30, 1980. Anderson and Lucey, however, signed an August 29 letter in which they outlined their national program. Their program was attached to the letter. See Brown and Walker, *A Campaign of Ideas*, 7–11.

63. "Excerpts From Platform Issued by the Anderson-Lucey Presidential Campaign," *New York Times*, August 31, 1980, 20; Bill Peterson and Kathy Sawyer, "Anderson Unveils National Unity Platform," *Washington Post*, August 31, 1980, A1; T. R. Reid, "Anderson Favors Tax Credits, Penalties to Direct Economy," *Washington Post*, September 8, 1980, A5; and Warren Weaver, Jr., "Anderson Platform Urges Votes to Put Country over Party," *New York Times*, August 31, 1980, 1.

64. "Reagan Jabs Carter on Choice of Area with Klan Strength," *Washington Post*, September 2, 1980, A3. See also "Candidates' Labor Day Speeches Mark Start of Presidential Race," *Washington Post*, September 1, 1980, A5.

65. Edward Walsh, "Carter: Appealing to the South to Support One of Its Own," *Washington Post*, September 2, 1980, A1.

66. Martin Schram, "Reagan Beats a Retreat on Klan Remark," *Washington*

Post, September 3, 1980, A1; and Terrence Smith, "Carter Assails Reagan Remark about the Klan as an Insult to the South," *New York Times,* September 3, 1980, B8.

67. "Anderson Opens Campaign in Midwest," *New York Times,* September 2, 1980, B8; and Bill Peterson, "Anderson: Mocking the Republican, Denouncing the Democrat," *Washington Post,* September 2, 1980, A1.

68. JCL, Carter, Chief of Staff Jordan, Box 77, Folder Campaign Strategy—Caddell, Patrick.

69. Patrick Caddell's document is found in JCL, Carter, Chief of Staff Jordan, Box 77, Folder Campaign Strategy—Caddell, Patrick General Election.See page 33 of the campaign document. See page 87 of Wirthlin's "Reagan for President Campaign Plan."

70. Newton N. Minow, Clifford M. Sloan, and Carlos T. Angulo, *Opening Salvos: Who Should Participate in Presidential Debates?* (New York: Century Foundation, 1999), 17–18; and Edward Walsh and Lou Cannon, "Reagan, Carter Plan Debate," *Washington Post,* October 18, 1980, A1.

71. David S. Broder and Lou Cannon, "Debate Shows Rivals' Wide Differences," *Washington Post,* September 22, 1980, A1.

72. The debate is found at http://www.debates.org/pages/trans80a.html, consulted on May 7, 2007.

73. Bisnow, *Dark Horse,* 304–5.

74. Maurice Carroll, "Liberals Follow Leadership and Back Anderson Ticket," *New York Times,* September 14, 1980, A32.

75. "Campaign Report: New Republic Endorses Anderson for Presidency," *New York Times,* September 28, 1980, 37.

76. Cowan, "Carter Sets Steel Aid"; and Howell Raines, "Carter Accused of Copying Reagan Plan for Steel Mills," *New York Times,* October 3, 1980, A19.

77. Steven R. Weisman, "Carter Presses Issue of 'War and Peace,'" *New York Times,* October 7, 1980, D21; "Campaign Report: Bush, Back Home in Texas, Aims Barrage at Carterism," *New York Times,* October 7, 1980, B7; and Steven R. Weisman, "Carter Plans Shift in Campaign Tactics," *New York Times,* October 9, 1980, B8.

78. Terence Smith, "Carter Asserts Reagan Presidency Would Be 'Bad Thing' for Country," *New York Times,* October 11, 1980, 8.

79. Richard Burt, "Muskie Urges Arms Treaty Action Despite Soviet Role in Afghanistan," *New York Times,* October 17, 1980, A1, A22; and Steven R. Weisman, "Californian's Plan Attacked," *New York Times,* October 25, 1980, 1, 9.

80. "Campaign Report: Mrs. King Calls the Klan 'Comfortable' with Reagan," *New York Times,* September 30, 1980, A20; and "Mrs. King Fears Result of Victory by Reagan," *New York Times,* November 3, 1980, D15.

81. Turner, "Single-Issue Test"; and Howell Raines, "In Move to the Center, Reagan Plans to Alter 2 Antiunion Positions," *New York Times,* October 9, 1980, A1, B8.

82. Douglas E. Kneeland, "Reagan Presses Theme of Peace in Ohio and Kentucky," *New York Times,* October 21, 1980, A1.

83. Terence Smith, "President Critical," *New York Times,* October 22, 1980, A1, A25.

84. Howell Raines, "Pocketbook Issues Stressed," *New York Times,* October 25, 1980, 1, 10.

85. The poll represented questioning on October 10–13, 1980. *Gallup Poll, 1980,* 240.

86. "Campaign Report: Teamsters Executive Board Unanimously Backs Reagan," *New York Times,* October 9, 1980, B8; Eric Planin, "McCarthy Backs Reagan, with Much Explanation," *Minneapolis Tribune,* October 24, 1980, 1A, 10A; "McCarthy Gives Reagan His Vote, Mentioning Arms and Tax Stances," *New York Times,* October 24, 1980, A16; and "Clean Gene Did *What?*" *St. Paul Pioneer Press,* October 24, 1980, 12.

87. *Gallup Poll, 1980,* 240.

88. Broder and Cannon, "Debate Shows Wide Differences," A1.

89. The Carter-Reagan debate is found at http://www.debates.org/pages/trans80b.html, consulted April 24, 2007.

90. Robert Lindsey, "Reagan Says America Should Not Bar Others from A-Bomb Output," *New York Times,* February 1, 1980, A12.

91. Hedrick Smith, "No Clear Winner Apparent; Scene Is Simple and Stark," *New York Times,* October 29, 1980, A1.

92. Schulman, "Slouching toward Supply Side," 51.

93. Hamilton Jordan, *Crisis: The Last Year of the Carter Presidency* (New York: G. P. Putnam's Sons, 1982), 357. See pages 357–58 for reference to the ABC-TV poll.

94. "Excerpts from Anderson Responses to Questions at the Carter-Reagan Debate," *New York Times,* October 29, 1980, A29.

95. Warren Weaver, Jr., "Anderson Charges Democratic 'Lie' for Black Vote," *New York Times,* November 1, 1980, 8.

96. Terence Smith, "Carter Sharpens Attacks on Reagan's Arms Stand," *New York Times,* October 30, 1980, B14; and Terence Smith, "Carter Post-Mortem: Debate Hurt but Wasn't Only Cause for Defeat," *New York Times,* November 9, 1980, 1. For Reagan's statement on Pakistan and nuclear weapons see Robert Lindsey, "A-Bomb Output," A12, and "Reagan Charges Carter Policies Raise War Risk," *Washington Post,* February 1, 1980, A3.

97. Terence Smith, "Iran Move Disrupts Carter's Campaign," *New York Times,* November 3, 1980, A17; and "Transcript of Carter's Statement," *New York Times,* November 3, 1980, A17.

98. "Anderson Calls for Details," *New York Times,* November 3, 1980, A17; and A. O. Sulzberger, "Reagan Terms Hostage Situation Too Sensitive for Him to Comment," *New York Times,* November 3, 1980, A1, A17.

99. Adam Clymer, "Carter and Reagan Make Final Appeals before Vote Today," *New York Times,* November 4, 1980, A1.

100. Douglas E. Kneeland, "Reagan Steps up Attack on Carter's Performance," *New York Times,* October 31, 1980, A16; and South Bergen County, New Jersey, Ronald Reagan Library, Reference Copy from Vertical File.

101. Clymer, "Carter and Reagan Make Final Appeals," A1.

102. Smith, "Carter Post-Mortem," A1.

103. *Gallup Poll, 1980,* 240; and Harris and Associates, *Harris 1980 Presidential Election Survey,* nos. 802119, 802121, 802125.

104. Jordan, *Crisis,* 368.

105. "Facts That Help Put Election in Focus," *U.S. News and World Report,* November 17, 1980, 38.

106. Statistics are from the Gallup Poll unless otherwise noted.

107. See "Gallup Brain" at http://brain.gallup.com/content/Default.aspx?ci= 9460; Paul T. David, and David H. Everson, eds., *The Presidential Election and Transition, 1980–1981* (Carbondale: Southern Illinois University Press, 1983), 161.

108. Clymer, *Edward M. Kennedy,* 319–20.

109. Robert Axelrod, "1976 Update: An Analysis of Electorial Coalitions, 1952–1968," *American Political Science Review* 72 (1978): 622.

110. Gregory B. Markus, "Political Attitudes during an Election Year: A Report on the 1980 NES Panel Study," *American Political Science Review* 76 (1982): 538.

111. Paul R. Abramson, John H. Aldrich, and David W. Rohde, *Change and Continuity in the 1980 Elections* (Washington, DC: Congressional Quarterly Press, 1982), 135; and Adam Clymer, "Displeasure with Carter Turned Many to Reagan," *New York Times,* November 9, 1980, 28.

112. Greg D. Adams explains that "only for the last few years have Democrats been the more pro-choice party, although the changes producing this result have been clearly underway for a much longer period. . . . Republicans were more pro-choice than Democrats up until the late 1980s. . . . Among those who recalled voting for president in 1968, most pro-lifers voted Democrat for Humphrey (by a five-point margin), while most pro-choicers voted Republican for Nixon (by an 11-point margin)." "Abortion: Evidence of an Issue Evolution," *American Journal of Political Science* 41 (1997): 731, 732.

113. Abramson, Aldrich, and Rohde, *Change and Continuity,* 135.

114. The data from the University of Michigan is reported in Andrew E. Busch, *Reagan's Victory: The Presidential Election of 1980 and the Rise of the Right* (Lawrence: University Press of Kansas, 2005), 130.

115. J. Merrill Shanks and Warren E. Miller, "Policy Direction and Performance Evaluation: Complementary Explanations of the Reagan Elections," *British Journal of Political Science* 20 (April 1990): 168.

116. "The 1980 Election One of the Most Unusual," *Gallup Poll Index,* Report No. 183, December 1980, 29; and Clymer, "Displeasure with Carter," 28.

117. Smith, "Carter Post-Mortem," 1.

CHAPTER 6

1. For alternative explanations of the USSR's collapse, see, among others, Mark Beissinger, *Nationalist Mobilization and the Collapse of the Soviet State* (Cambridge: Cambridge University Press, 2002); Valerie Bunce, *Subversive Institutions: The Design and the Destruction of Socialism and the State* (Cambridge:

Cambridge University Press, 1999); Steven L. Solnick, *Stealing the State: Control and Collapse in Soviet Institutions* (Cambridge: Cambridge University Press, 1998); Ronald Grigor Suny, *The Revenge of the Past: Nationalism, Revolution, and the Collapse of the Soviet Union* (Stanford, CA: Stanford University Press, 1993); and Philip G. Roeder, *Red Sunset: The Failure of Soviet Politics* (Princeton, NJ: Princeton University Press, 1993).

2. For the analysis of the impact of Soviet institutional constraints, see Roeder, *Red Sunset*.

3. For discussion of Gorbachev's support coalition within the CPSU leadership, see Graeme Gill, *The Collapse of a Single-Party System: The Disintegration of the CPSU* (Cambridge: Cambridge University Press, 1994); George W. Breslauer, *Gorbachev and Yeltsin as Leaders* (Cambridge: Cambridge University Press, 2002); and Jonathan Harris, *Subverting the System: Gorbachev's Reform of the Party's Apparat, 1986–1991* (Lanham, MD: Rowman and Littlefield, 2004).

4. Gorbachev's close adviser Vadim Medvedev points out that perestroika started de facto only in 1987. See Vadim Medvedev, *V komande Gorbacheva, Vzgliad iznutri* (Moscow: Bylina, 1994), 42. The most prominent example of Gorbachev's strong reformist rhetoric prior to 1985 was his speech at a party conference in December 1984. See Breslauer, *Gorbachev and Yeltsin,* 49.

5. Sakharov gained international prominence in the late 1960s as the leading Soviet human rights activist. In 1980, Soviet authorities arrested Sakharov, charging him with "anti-Soviet activity," and exiled him from Moscow to Gorki (now Nizhniy Novgorod), an industrial center that was closed to foreigners. In *Memoirs*, Gorbachev wrote that from the time he became general secretary he wanted to "rescue Sakharov from exile." See Mikhail Gorbachev, *Memoirs* (New York: Doubleday, 1996), 296. For Sakharov's discussion of his release from exile, see Andrei D. Sakharov, *Memoirs* (New York: Knopf, 1990).

6. On the significance of Gorbachev's proposals, see Medvedev, *V komande Gorbacheva,* 44.

7. For the first extensive discussion of the repercussions of Yeltsin's speech, see Seweryn Bialer, "The Yeltsin Affair: The Dilemma of the Left in Gorbachev's Revolution," in *Inside Gorbachev's Russia: Politics, Society and Nationality,* ed. Bialer (Boulder, CO: Westview Press, 1989), 110–18.

8. Nina Andreyeva, "Ne mogu postupat'sia printsipami," *Sov'etskaia Rossiia,* March 13, 1988.

9. In addition to Ligachev, the conservative coalition in the Politburo included Solomentsev, Chebrikov, and Iazov. See Mikhail Gorbachev, *Zhizn' i Reformy* (Moscow: Novosti, 1995), 1:378.

10. Gordon M. Hahn, *Russia's Revolution from Above, 1985–2000: Reform, Transition and Revolution in the Fall of the Soviet Communist Regime* (New Brunswick, NJ: Transaction Publishers, 2002), 59.

11. "Boris Yeltsin's Speech at the 27th CPSU Congress," quoted in Foreign Broadcast Information Service, FBIS-SOV-86-39, Supplement 042, February 27, 1986, O20–O21.

12. "Ochishenie—Otkrovenny'i Razgovor," *Pravda,* February 15, 1986.

13. "Vystupleniia delegatov XXVII s'ezda KPSS," *Pravda,* February 28, 1986.

14. Georgi Arbatov, *The System: An Insider's Life in Soviet Politics* (New

298 Notes to Pages 212–18

York: Random House, 1992), 86.

15. "Political Report of the Central Committee of the CPSU Delivered by M. S. Gorbachev at the 27th CPSU Congress," quoted in FBIS-SOV-86-38, Supplement 041, February 26, 1986, O20.

16. The press conference of Geidar Aliev during the Twenty-seventh CPSU Congress, quoted in FBIS-SOV-86-40, February 28, 1986, O33.

17. Vladimir Solovyov and Elena Klepikova, *Boris Yeltsin. Politicheskie Metamorfozy* (Moscow: Vagrius, 1992), 44.

18. Boris Yeltsin, *Against the Grain: An Autobiography* (New York: Summit, 1990), 103.

19. Leon Aron, *Yeltsin: A Revolutionary Life* (New York: St. Martin's Press, 2000), 169.

20. Alison Smale, "Moscow Party Boss Decries Special Privilege," Associated Press, August 22, 1986.

21. Yegor Ligachev, *Inside Gorbachev's Kremlin* (New York: Pantheon, 1993), 337.

22. Aleksandr Yakovlev, *Sumerki* (Moscow: Materik, 2003), 405.

23. During Yeltsin's speech at the plenum, Yakovlev wrote to Medvedev: "It turns out there is someone more radical than us, and that is good." See Medvedev, *V komande Gorbacheva*, 46.

24. Yakovlev, *Sumerki*, 405.

25. Yegor Ligachev, "Na vstrechu 70-letiu velikogo Oktiabria," *Pravda*, March 24, 1997.

26. *Pravda*, February 14, 1987.

27. "Yeltsin Addresses Progress of Restructuring," *Moskovskaia Pravda*, April 14, 1987, in FBIS-SOV-87-77, April 22, 1987, R9–R10.

28. John Morrison, *Boris Yeltsin: From Bolshevik to Democrat* (New York: Dutton, 1991), 49.

29. "O sozyve XIX Vsesoiuznoi konferentsii KPSS," *Pravda*, June 27, 1988.

30. Anthony D'Agostino, *Gorbachev's Revolution* (New York: New York University Press, 1998), 153.

31. From Poltoranin's interview with *Corriere della Sera*, May 12, 1988, as quoted in Aron, *Yeltsin*, 199.

32. Yeltsin refers to the September 10, 1987, Politburo meeting in his letter to Gorbachev and cites it as an example of "systematic persecution" on the part of Ligachev; this account is confirmed in Aleksandr Yakovlev, *Gor'kaya Chasha: Bol'shevizm i Reformatsiya v Rossii* (Yaroslavl': Verkhne-Volzhskoe knizhnoe izd-vo, 1994), 216.

33. Yeltsin, *Against the Grain*, 178.

34. According to his adviser, Gorbachev was notably irritated after discussing the resignation letter with Yeltsin. In Gorbachev's view, Yeltsin was just looking for scapegoats after failing in Moscow. See V. Boldin, *Krushenie P'edestala. Shtrikhi k Portretu M. S. Gorbacheva* (Moscow: Respublika, 1995), 327.

35. Yeltsin, *Against the Grain*, 11. Yeltsin's interpretation of his appeal and Gorbachev's response were corroborated by Gorbachev at the October 1987 CC Plenum.

36. Roeder, *Red Sunset*, 30.

37. Ronald J. Hill and Peter Frank, *The Soviet Communist Party* (Boston: Allen and Unwin, 1986), 64.

38. J. H. Miller, "How Much of a New Elite?" in *Gorbachev at the Helm: A New Era in Soviet Politics?* ed. R.F. Miller et al. (London: Croom Helm, 1987), 71.

39. Yeltsin, *Against the Grain,* 189.

40. Boldin, *Krushenie P'edestala,* 328.

41. "Ligachev Discusses Working with Gorbachev," in FBIS-SOV-87-233, December 4, 1987, 42.

42. "Demokratizatsiia—sut' perestroiki, sut' sotsializma," *Pravda,* January 13, 1988, 1–3.

43. "Yeltsin Pamphlets Circulated in Sverdlovsk," in FBIS-SOV-87-214, November 5, 1987, 49.

44. Francis Clines, "Campus Rally for Yeltsin, a Rare Sight," *New York Times,* November 14, 1987.

45. Solovyov and Klepikova, *Boris Yeltsin,* 71.

46. "Presumed Text of 21 Oct Yeltsin Speech," in FBIS-SOV-88-021, February 2, 1988, 52.

47. Gavriil Popov, "Learning Our Lessons," *Moscow News,* N47 (Nov. 29–Dec. 6, 1987), 3.

48. Gavriil Popov, "The Kind of Perestroika We Want: Some Ideas about Political Avant-Gardism," *Moscow News,* N51 (Dec. 27, 1987–Jan. 3, 1988), 15.

49. "Sacked Moscow Party Chief Calls for Ligachev's Resignation," United Press International, May 30, 1988.

50. Andreyeva, "Ne mogu postupat'sya printsipami," 3.

51. Michael McFaul Collection, 1989–2000, Box 1, tape interview with Anatoliy Lukianov, 1993, Hoover Institution Archives.

52. "Kursom sozidaniia," *Pravda,* June 5, 1988, 2.

53. Boris Yeltsin, *Ispoved' na Zadannuyu Temu* (Sverdlovsk: Sredne-Uralskoe Knizhnoe idz-vo, 1990), 191.

54. "Vystuplenie tovarisha Yeltsina," *Pravda,* July 2, 1988, 10.

55. Yeltsin, *Ispoved' na Zadannuyu Temu,* 195.

56. "Yegor Ligachev's Speech at the Party Conference," ITAR-TASS, July 1, 1988.

57. "Vystuplenie tovarisha Ligacheva," *Pravda,* July 2, 1988, 11.

58. Yeltsin, *Ispoved' na Zadannuyu Temu,* 210–11.

CHAPTER 7

1. Gill, *Collapse of Single-Party System,* 72.

2. Anatolii Chernyaev, *Shest' Let s Gorbachevym: Po Dnevnikovym Zapisiam* (Moscow: Progress, 1993), 230–33.

3. Edward W. Walker, *Dissolution: Sovereignty and the Breakup of the Soviet Union* (Lanham, MD: Rowman and Littlefield, 2003), 64.

4. "Vremia deistvii, vremia prakticheskoi raboty. Vystuplenie M. S. Gorbacheva v Krasnoiarske," *Pravda,* September 18, 1988, 1–3.

5. "Perestroika: vremia prakticheskih del. Prebyvanie M. S. Gorbacheva v Krasnoiarskom krae," *Pravda,* September 13, 1988, 1.

6. Gorbachev, *Memoirs,* 264–65.

7. Pavel Voshchanov, "Ne Zabudem o Cheloveke," *Komsomolskaia Pravda*, December 31, 1988, 4.

8. Yeltsin, *Against the Grain*, 147.

9. Voshchanov, "Ne Zabudem o Cheloveke," 4.

10. V. Ivanov, "B. N. Yeltsin: Liudiam ochen' vazhna pravda," *Sovetiskaia Estoniia*, February 19, 1989, 2.

11. BBC World Service, "Yeltsin Denies Leading Opposition," in FBIS-SOV-89-056, March 24, 1989, 37.

12. *La Repubblica*, "Italian Daily Interviews Yeltsin," in FBIS-SOV-89-056, March 24, 1989, 38-39.

13. *Moskovskie Novosti*, January 29, 1989.

14. FBIS-SOV-89-51, March 17, 1989, no. 51, 72-73.

15. V. Tikhomirov, "Pismo Redaktoru," *Moskovskaia Pravda*, March 19, 1989.

16. Jerusalem Domestic Service, "Further on Demonstrations in Support of Yeltsin," in FBIS-SOV-89-053, March 21, 1989, 35.

17. Agence France-Presse, "Yeltsin Rally Biggest since 1917," in FBIS-SOV-89-057, March 27, 1989, 46.

18. *La Vanguardia*, "Yeltsin on Campaign, Ethnic Issues, Congress Talks," in FBIS-SOV-89-104, June 1, 1989, 38-39.

19. TASS, "Sociologist Views Reactions to Restructuring," in FBIS-SOV-89–052, March 20, 1989.

20. TASS, "Sociologist Views Reactions."

21. Andrew Katell, "Yeltsin Says He Still Talks to Gorbachev Despite Criticism," Associated Press, May 9, 1989.

22. Alison Smale, "Congress, Supreme Soviet to Have New Legislative Oversight," Associated Press, May 30, 1989.

23. Andrew Katell, "Government to Politburo: No More Plush Palaces," Associated Press, February 20, 1990.

24. Alexei Levinson, "Tri cheloveka goda. Kak i prezhde, sovetskie politiki populyarnee telezviozd," *Nezavisimaia Gazeta*, February 28, 1991, 2.

25. Morrison, *Boris Yeltsin*, 143; Geoffrey Hosking notes Yeltsin's ambiguous use of the words *independence (nezavisimost')* and *sovereignty (suverenitet)*, which he used interchangeably. See Geoffrey Hosking, *Rulers and Victims: The Russians in the Soviet Union* (Cambridge: Belknap Press of Harvard University Press, 2006), 383. Yeltsin's reference to independence was largely rhetorical, while substantively he demanded expansion of Russia's rights and powers within the weakened Soviet Union.

26. M. Gorchakov and V. Zhuravliov, eds., *Gorbachev-Yeltsin: 1500 Dnei Politicheskogo Protivostoianiia* (Moscow: Terra, 1992), 138.

27. See Yitzhak M. Brudny, *Reinventing Russia: Russian Nationalism and the Soviet State, 1953–1991* (Cambridge: Harvard University Press, 1998); and Hedrick Smith, *The New Russians* (New York: Random House, 1990).

28. Quoted in Smith, *The New Russians*, 384-85.

29. "Pro ravenstvo prav i obiazannostei: V. I. Vorotnikov otvechaet na voprosy redkollegii," *Sovetskaia Rossiia*, August 10, 1989, 1.

30. "Na leninskih printsipah—k novomu kachestvu mezhnatsional'nyh

otnoshenii," *Izvestiia,* September 21, 1989.

31. A. Vlasov, "Interesy Rossii," *Izvestiia,* September 1, 1989.

32. "Natsional'naia politika partii v sovremennyh usloviiah," *Pravda,* September 20, 1989.

33. Yu. Shatalov, "Ponimat i deistvovat: interviu pered vstrechei deputatov s narodnym deputatom SSSR S. V. Vasilevym," *Sovetskaia Rossiia,* October 27, 1989.

34. "B. N. Yeltsin: Dumayu, chto menia podderzhat," *Literaturnaia Gazeta,* January 24, 1990, 2.

35. Walker, *Dissolution,* 78.

36. For more on the nationalist-Communist alliance in the election of 1990, see Brudny, *Reinventing Russia;* and Smith, *The New Russians.*

37. Smith, *The New Russians,* 531.

38. Dimitri K. Simes, *After the Collapse: Russia Seeks Its Place as a Great Power* (New York: Simon & Schuster, 1999), 58–59.

39. Smith, *The New Russians,* 384.

40. "Vtoroi S'ezd Narodnyh Deputatov SSSR," *Izvestiia,* December 15, 1989.

41. R. Amos, "U russkogo cheloveka vse-taki est Rodina. Interviu s narodnym deputatom SSSR B. N. Yel'tsinym," *Sovetskaia Estoniia,* February 20, 1990, 4.

42. P. Lukianchenko and A. Binev, "Ia vse-taki optimist," *Argumenty i Fakty,* March 3–9, 1990, 4–5.

43. ITV, "Yeltsin Grants Television Interview in London," in FBIS-SOV-90-086, May 3, 1990, 27.

44. Amos, "U russkogo cheloveka vse-taki est' Rodina," 4.

45. See Brudny, *Reinventing Russia,* 20.

46. "O vlasti i privilegiiakh," *Argumenty i Fakty,* March 10–16, 1990, 2.

47. "Yeltsin Speaks at 22 May RSFSR Congress," in FBIS-SOV-90-100, May 23, 1990, 96.

48. Gorchakov and Zhuravliov, *Gorbachev-Yeltsin,* 194.

49. Gorchakov and Zhuravliov, *Gorbachev-Yeltsin,* 196.

50. TASS in English, in FBIS-SOV-90-105, May 31, 1990, 81.

51. "The popularity ranking of Mikhail Gorbachev prepared by the All-Union center for the study of the public opinion under supervision of Professor Yurii Levada," in Gorchakov and Zhuravliov, *Gorbachev-Yeltsin,* 281.

52. "Kaikim putiom my poidiom . . . ," *Argumenty i Fakty,* May 26–June 1, 1990, 2.

53. "Yeltsin Speaks," 96.

54. Moscow TV Service, "Russian Sovereignty," in FBIS-SOV-90-123, June 26, 1990, 84.

55. Moscow TV Service, "Yeltsin News Conference on Congress Results," in FBIS-SOV-90-124, June 27, 1990, 92.

56. Medvedev, *V komande Gorbacheva,* 137.

57. A. Lukianov, *Perevorot, Mnimyi i Nastoiashchii: Otvety na Voprosy, Prishedshie v "Matrosskuiu Tishinu"* (Moscow: Nezavisimoe izd-vo "Manuskript," 1993), 45.

58. "Yeltsin Interviewed on CPSU, Gorbachev," in FBIS-SOV-90-142, July 23,

1990, 82–83.

59. Ibid.

60. Moscow TV Service, in FBIS-SOV-90-149, August 2, 1990, 65.

61. Ibid.

62. Moscow TV Service, in FBIS-SOV-90-212, November 1, 1990, 80.

63. A. Olbik, "Boris El'tsin: V Rossiiu vsio esho mozhno verit'," *Komsomolskaia Pravda,* August 8, 1990, 1–2.

64. Simes, *After the Collapse,* 59.

65. Quoted in John Dunlop, *The Rise of Russia and the Fall of the Soviet Empire* (Princeton, NJ: Princeton University Press, 1993), 50.

66. "Iz teletaipa TASS," *Komsomolskaia Pravda,* August 25, 1990, 2.

67. "Boris Yeltsin: v Rossiiu vsio eshcho mozhno verit'," *Komsomolskaia Pravda,* August 8, 1990, 2.

68. Moscow TV Service, "Yeltsin Outlines 'Struggle," in FBIS-SOV-90-178, September 13, 1990, 78.

69. Andronik Migranian, "Soyuz nerushymyi? Pro perspektivy sovetskoi gosudarstvennosti," *Izvestiia,* September 21, 1990, 3.

70. "Ligachev Interviewed on Current Issues," in FBIS-SOV-90-106, June 1, 1990, 31–35.

71. Yeltsin's Address at the Fourth Congress of the USSR People's Deputies, December 19, 1990, in Gorchakov and Zhuravliov, *Gorbachev-Yeltsin,* 287–89.

72. Gorchakov and Zhuravliov, *Gorbachev-Yeltsin,* 281.

73. "Chem zhyviosh', narod? Kak dela?" *Gospodin Narod,* N1, 1991, 3, in Demokraticheskaia Rossiia, Records, 1989–1993, Box 2, Hoover Institution Archives.

74. *Moscow News,* January 20–27, 1991, 4.

75. As quoted in Solovyov and Klepikova, *Boris Yeltsin,* 221.

76. "Yeltsin Addresses Democratic Russia Bloc," in FBIS-SOV-91-047, March 11, 1991, 68.

77. "Yeltsin Addresses Democratic Russia Bloc," 68.

78. "Yeltsin 19 Feb Moscow Television Interview," in FBIS-SOV-91-034, February 20, 1991, 79.

79. "400,000 Attend Pro-Yeltsin Rally in Moscow," in FBIS-SOV-91-037, February 25, 1991.

80. "Posle televystupleniia Yeltsina," in Demokraticheskaia Rossiia, Records, 1989–1993, Box 2, Hoover Institution Archives.

81. Solovyov and Klepikova, *Boris Yeltsin,* 232.

82. Quoted in Mitrokhin, "Vechnyi Opponent? Detali politicheskogo portreta B. Yeltsina," *Pravda,* March 5, 1991, 3.

83. "Alksnis Stresses Support for Gorbachev," in FBIS-SOV-91-045, March 7, 1991.

84. *U.S. News and World Report,* April 8, 1991, 38–39.

85. A. Grachev, *Gorbachev* (Moscow: Vagrius, 2001), 245.

86. "Yeltsin Sees No Reconciliation with Gorbachev," in FBIS-SOV-91, March 14, 1991.

87. Walker, *Dissolution,* 117.

88. "Posle televystupleniia Yeltsina," in Demokraticheskaia Rossiia, Records, 1989–1993, Box 2, Hoover Institution Archives.

89. S. Pashaev, "N. I. Ryzhkov: Dlia menia eto bylo tiazheloe reshenie," *Krasnaia Zvezda*, May 11, 1991.

90. Yu. Makartsev, "Esli ia stanu Prezidentom Rossii . . . ," *Rabochaia Tribuna*, May 14, 1991, 1–2.

91. *Pravda*, June 10, 1991, 1–2.

92. R. Lynev, "Tsel'—vozrozhdenie Rossii: B. N. Yel'tsin otvechaet na voprosy 'Izvestii,'" *Izvestiia*, May 24, 1991.

93. Yeltsin's speech in the Moscow theater Oktiabr, June 1, 1991, videotape in Demokraticheskaia Rossiia, Records, 1989–1993, Box 8, Hoover Institution Archives.

94. Interview with Aleksandr Rutskoi, "5 koleso," May 22, 1991, videotape in Demokraticheskaia Rossiia, Records, 1989–1993, Box 8, Hoover Institution Archives.

95. "Posle televystupleniia Yeltsina," in Demokraticheskaia Rossiia, Records, 1989–1993, Box 2, Hoover Institution Archives.

96. Boris Yeltsin, *Zapiski Prezidenta* (Moscow: Ogoniok, 1994), 51.

97. "Yeltsin Addresses on Conditions in Republic," *Radio Rossii*, in FBIS-SOV-91-062, April 1, 1991, 68.

CHAPTER 8

1. See Bueno de Mesquita et al., *Logic of Political Survival*, especially chapter 7.

Bibliography

....

ARCHIVES

John Anderson Campaign Collection, New Hampshire Political Library, Concord

Jimmy Carter Library, Atlanta (JCL)

Gerald R. Ford Library, Ann Arbor, Michigan (GRF)

Hoover Institution Archives, Stanford, California

    Citizens for Reagan Collection (CFR)

    Deaver and Hannaford Collection (DH)

    Demokraticheskaia Rossiia (Political party)

    Peter Hannaford Collection (PH)

    Ligachev, E. K. (Egor Kuzmich), Hoover Institution Records.

    Michael McFaul Collection, 1989–2000

    Ronald Reagan Subject Collection (RRSC)

    University of California Center for Slavic and East European Studies collection, 1986–90

    Richard B. Wirthlin Papers

Lyndon B. Johnson Library and Museum, Austin, Texas

Richard Nixon Library and Birthplace, Yorba Linda, California (RNLB). [This archive will soon be administered by the National Archives and Records Administration as the Richard Nixon Library and Museum.]

Ronald Reagan Presidential Library, Simi Valley, California

    Ronald Reagan Gubernatorial Papers (RRGP)

    Records Declassified and Released by the National Security Council

Rockefeller Archive Center, Nelson A. Rockefeller Collection, Sleepy Hollow, New York (NAR)

George Romney Papers, Bentley Historical Library, University of Michigan, Ann Arbor (GRP)

Strom Thurmond Collection, Special Collections, Clemson University Libraries, Clemson, South Carolina

ARTICLES

Adams, Greg D. "Abortion: Evidence of an Issue Evolution." *American Journal of Political Science* 41 (1997): 731–32.

Allen, Richard V. "Peace through Strength: Reagan's Early Call: Win Cold War." *Human Events,* October 24, 2003. http://www.humanevents.com/article.php?id=2175.

"Avis of Superpowers?" *Public Opinion,* May–June 1978, 28–29.

Axelrod, Robert. "1976 Update: An Analysis of Electoral Coalitions, 1952–1968." *American Political Science Review* 72 (1978): 622–24.

Boyne, Walter J. "A Tale of Two Bombers." *Air Force Magazine,* July 2006, 72–76.

Buckley, William F., Jr. "Say It Isn't So, Mr. President." *New York Times Magazine,* August 1, 1971, 8–9, 36–40.

Bueno de Mesquita, Bruce, and Randolph M. Siverson. "War and the Survival of Political Leaders: A Comparative Study of Regime Types and Political Accountability." *American Political Science Review* 89 (1995): 841–55.

"Bush Breaks Out of the Pack." *Newsweek,* February 4, 1980, 30–31.

Cannon, Lou. "The Reagan Years." *California Journal* 5 (November 1974): 360–66.

Cohen, Youssef. "The Heresthetics of Coup Making." *Comparative Political Studies* 24 (1991): 344–64.

Connelly, Julie. "Carter's Plan for U.S. Industry." *Time,* September 1, 1980, 40–42.

Converse, Philip E., Warren E. Miller, Jerrold G. Rusk, and Arthur C. Wolfe. "Continuity and Change in American Politics: Parties and Issues in the 1968 Election." *American Political Science Review* 63 (1969): 1083–1105.

"A Declaration." *National Review,* August 10, 1971, 842.

Goldman, Peter, with Thomas M. DeFrank, Eleanor Clift, John J. Lindsay, Gloria Borger, and Howard Fineman. "RWR's Own New Deal." *Newsweek,* March 2, 1981, 22–24.

Goldwater, Barry. "Don't Waste a Vote on Wallace." *National Review,* October 22, 1968, 1060–61, 1079.

Hart, Gary. "American Idol." *New York Times Book Review,* December 24, 2006, 14.

"How Ray Bliss Plays the Cards for the GOP." *Business Week,* March 9, 1968, 28.

Keene, David. "Why Reagan Chose Schweiker: An Insider's Account." *The Alternative: An American Spectator,* November 1976, 13–15.

Kirk, Russell. "New Directions in the U.S. Right?" *New York Times Magazine,* August 7, 1966, 20–28.

Manus, Willard. "Passing Recognition." *Michigan Today,* 2005. http://www.umich.edu/news/MT/04/Fall04/story.html?passing.

Markus, Gregory B. "Political Attitudes during an Election Year: A Report on the 1980 NES Panel Study." *American Political Science Review* 76 (1982): 538–60.

McKelvey, Richard. "Intransitivities in Multidimensional Voting Models and Some Implications for Agenda Control." *Journal of Economic Theory* 12 (1976): 472–82.

McLean, Ian. "William H. Riker and the Invention of Heresthetic(s)." *British Journal of Political Science* 32 (2002): 535–58.

Meyer, Frank S. "Reform without Principle." *Modern Age,* Spring 1961, 194–96.

Nagel, Jack H. "Social Choice in a Pluralitarian Democracy: The Politics of Market Liberalization in New Zealand." *British Journal of Political Science* 28 (1998): 223–65.

Rakove, Jack N. "The Madisonian Theory of Rights." *William and Mary Law Review* 31, no. 2 (1990): 245–66.

"Reagan Key to Conservative Hopes." *Human Events,* March 1, 1975, 1–5.

"Republicans." *Time,* October 20, 1967, 17–21.

"Republicans Run a Different Race." *Business Week,* March 9, 1968, 27–30.

Rusher, William. "What Happened at Miami Beach?" *National Review,* December 3, 1968, 1206–9, 1231.

Schofield, Norman. "Evolution of the Constitution." *British Journal of Political Science* 32 (2002): 1–23.

Schofield, Norman. "Instability of Simple Dynamic Games." *Review of Economic Studies* 45 (1978): 575–94.

Shanks, J. Merrill, and Warren E. Miller. "Policy Direction and Performance Evaluation: Complementary Explanations of the Reagan Elections." *British Journal of Political Science* 20 (April 1990): 143–235.

"Reagan's Radio-Producer." *Television/Radio Age,* September 8, 1980, 16.

"Surprise Harvest in Iowa." *Time,* February 4, 1980, 24–25.

"Facts that Help Put Election in Focus." *U.S. News and World Report,* November 17, 1980, 38–39.

BOOKS AND CHAPTERS

Abernathy, M. Glenn. "The Carter Administration and Domestic Civil Rights." In *The Carter Years: The President and Policy Making,* ed. Abernathy, Dilys M. Hill, and Phil Williams. New York: St. Martin's Press, 1984.

Abramson, Paul R., John H. Aldrich, and David W. Rohde. *Change and Continuity in the 1980 Elections.* Washington, DC: Congressional Quarterly Press, 1982.

Aistrup, Joseph A. *The Southern Strategy Revisited.* Lexington: University Press of Kentucky, 1996.

Ambrose, Stephen E. *Nixon: The Triumph of a Politician, 1962–1972.* Vol. 2. New York: Simon & Schuster, 1989.

American Enterprise Institute. *The Candidates 1980: Where They Stand.* Washington, DC: American Enterprise for Public Policy Research, 1980.

Anderson, Martin. *Revolution: The Reagan Legacy.* Stanford, CA: Hoover Institution Press, 1990.

Arbatov, Georgii. *The System: An Insider's Life in Soviet Politics.* New York: Random House, 1992.

Aron, Leon. *Yeltsin: A Revolutionary Life.* New York: St. Martin's Press, 2000.

Bakshian, Aram, Jr. *The Candidates 1980.* New Rochelle, NY: Arlington House, 1980.

Barone, Michael. *Our Country: The Shaping of America from Roosevelt to Reagan.* New York: Free Press, 1990.

Bartels, Larry M. *Presidential Primaries and the Dynamics of Public Choice.* Princeton, NJ: Princeton University Press, 1988.

Bates, Robert H., Avner Greif, Margaret Levi, Jean-Laurent Rosenthal, and Barry R. Weingast. *Analytic Narratives.* Princeton, NJ: Princeton University Press, 1998.

Beissinger, Mark. *Nationalist Mobilization and the Collapse of the Soviet State.* Cambridge: Cambridge University Press, 2002.

Beschloss, Michael. *The Presidents.* New York: American Heritage, 2003.

Bialer, Seweryn, ed. *Inside Gorbachev's Russia: Politics, Society and Nationality.* Boulder, CO: Westview Press, 1989.

Bisnow, Mark. *Diary of a Dark Horse: The 1980 Anderson Presidential Campaign.* Carbondale: Southern Illinois University Press, 1983.

Black, Duncan. *The Theory of Committees and Elections.* Cambridge: Cambridge University Press, 1958.

Black, Earl, and Merle Black. *The Rise of Southern Republicans.* Cambridge: Harvard University Press, 2002.

Black, Earl, and Merle Black. *The Vital South: How Presidents Are Elected.* Cambridge: Harvard University Press, 1992.

Boskin, Michael J. *Reagan and the Economy: The Successes, Failures, and Unfinished Agenda.* San Francisco: Institute for Contemporary Studies, 1987.

Bourne, Peter G. *Jimmy Carter: A Comprehensive Biography from Plains to Post-Presidency.* New York: Scribner's, 1977.

Brady, Henry E., and Richard Johnston, eds. *Capturing Campaign Effects.* Ann Arbor: University of Michigan Press, 2006.

Brady, John. *Bad Boy: The Life and Politics of Lee Atwater.* Reading, MA: Addison-Wesley, 1997.

Brennan, Mary C. *Turning Right in the Sixties: The Conservative Capture of the GOP.* Chapel Hill: University of North Carolina Press, 1995.

Breslauer, George W. *Gorbachev and Yeltsin as Leaders.* Cambridge: Cambridge University Press, 2002.

Brown, Clifford W., Jr., and Robert J. Walker. *A Campaign of Ideas: The 1980 Anderson/Lucey Platform.* Westport, CT: Greenwood, 1984.

Brown, Seyom. *The Faces of Power: Constancy and Change in United States Foreign Policy from Truman to Clinton.* 2nd ed. New York: Columbia University Press, 1994.

Brudny, Yitzhak M. *Reinventing Russia: Russian Nationalism and the Soviet State, 1953–1991.* Cambridge: Harvard University Press, 1998.

Brzezinski, Zbigniew. *Power and Principle: Memoirs of the National Security Adviser, 1977–1981.* Rev. ed. New York: Farrar, Straus and Giroux, 1985.

Buchanan, Patrick J. *Conservative Votes, Liberal Victories: Why the Right Has Failed.* New York: Quadrangle/New York Times Book Company, 1975.

Bueno de Mesquita, Bruce, Alastair Smith, Randolph M. Siverson, and James D. Morrow. *The Logic of Political Survival.* Cambridge: MIT Press, 2003.

Bunce, Valerie. *Subversive Institutions: The Design and the Destruction of Socialism and the State.* Cambridge: Cambridge University Press, 1999.

Busch, Andrew E. *Reagan's Victory: The Presidential Election of 1980 and the Rise of the Right.* Lawrence: University Press of Kansas, 2005.

Button, James W. *Black Violence: Political Impact of the 1960s Riots.* Princeton, NJ: Princeton University Press, 1978.

Campbell, James E. *The American Campaign: U.S. Presidential Campaigns and the National Vote.* College Station: Texas A&M Press, 2000.

Cannon, James. *Time and Chance: Gerald Ford's Appointment with History.* Ann Arbor: University of Michigan Press, 1998.

Cannon, Lou. *Governor Reagan: His Rise to Power.* New York: Public Affairs, 2003.

Cannon, Lou. *Reagan.* New York: G. P. Putnam's Sons, 1982.

Cannon, Lou. *Ronnie and Jesse: A Political Odyssey.* Garden City, NY: Doubleday, 1969.

Carlson, Jody. *George C. Wallace and the Politics of Powerlessness: The Wallace Campaigns for the Presidency, 1964–1976.* New Brunswick, NJ: Transaction Books, 1981.

Carter, Jimmy. *Keeping Faith: Memoirs of a President.* New York: Bantam, 1982.

Chagall, David. *The New Kingmakers: An Inside Look at the Powerful Men behind America's Political Campaigns.* New York: Harcourt Brace Jovanovich, 1981.

Chester, Lewis, Godfrey Hodgson, and Bruce Page. *An American Melodrama: The Presidential Campaign of 1968.* New York: Viking Press, 1969.

Clymer, Adam. *Edward M. Kennedy: A Biography.* New York: William Morrow, 1999.

Cohodas, Nadine. *Strom Thurmond and the Politics of Southern Change.* New York: Simon & Schuster, 1993.

Connally, John, and Mickey Herskowitz. *In History's Shadow: An American Odyssey.* New York: Hyperion, 1993.

Connery, Robert H., and Gerald Benjamin. *Rockefeller of New York.* Ithaca, NY: Cornell University Press, 1979.

Cosman, Bernard, and Robert J. Huckshorn, eds. *Republican Politics: The 1964 Campaign and Its Aftermath for the Party.* New York: Frederick A. Praeger, 1968.

Crotty, William J. *Political Reform and the American Experiment.* New York: Thomas Y. Crowell, 1977.

D'Agostina, Anthony. *Gorbachev's Revolution.* New York: New York University Press, 1998.

David, Paul T., and David H. Everson. *The Presidential Election and Transition, 1980–1981.* Carbondale: Southern Illinois University Press, 1983.

Davis, James W. *National Conventions in an Age of Party Reform.* Westport, CT: Greenwood, 1983.

Dent, Harry S. *The Prodigal South Returns to Power.* New York: John Wiley, 1978.

Dietz, Terry. *Republicans and Vietnam, 1961–1968.* Westport, CT: Greenwood, 1986.

Donaldson, Gary. *Liberalism's Last Hurrah: The Presidential Campaign of 1964.* Armonk, NY: M. E. Sharpe, 2003.

Downs, Anthony. *An Economic Theory of Democracy.* New York: Harper, 1957.

Drew, Elizabeth. *Portrait of an Election: The 1980 Presidential Campaign.* New York: Simon & Schuster, 1981.

Dunlop, John. *The Rise of Russia and the Fall of the Soviet Empire*. Princeton, NJ: Princeton University Press, 1993.

Edsall, Thomas Byrne, and Mary D. Edsall. *Chain Reaction: The Impact of Race, Rights, and Taxes on American Politics*. New York: Norton, 1991.

Edwards, Lee. *The Essential Ronald Reagan: A Portrait in Courage, Justice, and Wisdom* Lanham, MD: Rowman and Littlefield, 2005.

Eells, Robert, and Bartell Nyberg. *Lonely Walk: The Life of Senator Mark Hatfield*. Chappaqua, NY: Christian Herald Books, 1979.

English, David. *Divided They Stand*. Englewood Cliffs, NJ: Prentice Hall, 1969.

Evans, Rowland, Jr., and Robert D. Novak. *Nixon in the White House: The Frustration of Power*. New York: Random House, 1971.

Ferguson, Thomas, and Joel Rogers. *The Hidden Election*. New York: Pantheon, 1981.

Fiorina, Morris. *Retrospective Voting in American National Elections*. New Haven: Yale University Press, 1981.

Ford, Gerald. *A Time to Heal: The Autobiography of Gerald R. Ford*. New York: Harper and Row, 1979.

Garthoff, Raymond L. *Détente and Confrontation: American-Soviet Relations from Nixon to Reagan*. Washington, DC: Brookings Institution, 1994.

Germond, Jack W., and Jules Witcover. *Blue Smoke and Mirrors: How Reagan Won and Why Carter Lost the Election of 1980*. New York: Viking, 1981.

Gill, Graeme. *The Collapse of a Single-Party System: The Disintegration of the CPSU*. Cambridge: Cambridge University Press, 1994.

Goldberg, Robert Alan. *Barry Goldwater*. New Haven: Yale University Press, 1995.

Goldwater, Barry M. *With No Apologies: The Personal and Political Memoirs of United States Senator Barry M. Goldwater*. New York: William Morrow, 1979.

Gorbachev, Mikhail. *Memoirs*. New York: Doubleday, 1996.

Gould, Lewis L. *1968: The Election That Changed America*. Chicago: American Ways Series, 1993.

Greene, John Robert. *The Presidency of Gerald R. Ford*. Lawrence: University Press of Kansas, 1995.

Greenfield, Jeff. *The Real Campaign: How the Media Missed the Story of the 1980 Campaign*. New York: Summit Books, 1982.

Greenhaw, Wayne. *Elephants in the Cottonfields: Ronald Reagan and the New Republican South*. New York: Macmillan, 1982.

Hahn, Gordon M. *Russia's Revolution from Above, 1985–2000: Reform, Transition, and Revolution in the Fall of the Soviet Communist Regime*. New Brunswick, NJ: Transaction Publishers, 2002.

Hannaford, Peter. *The Reagans: A Political Portrait*. New York: Coward-McCann, 1983.

Harris, Jonathan. *Subverting the System: Gorbachev's Reform of the Party's Apparat, 1986–1991*. Lanham, MD: Rowman and Littlefield, 2004.

Hartley, Robert E. *Charles H. Percy: A Political Perspective*. New York: Rand McNally, 1975.

Harwood, Richard, ed., *The Pursuit of the Presidency, 1980*. New York: Berkley Publishing, 1980.

Hess, Stephen, and David S. Broder. *The Republican Establishment: The Present and Future of the GOP.* New York: Harper and Row, 1967.

Hill, Ronald J., and Peter Frank. *The Soviet Communist Party.* Boston: Allen and Unwin, 1986.

Hodgson, Godfrey. *The World Turned Right Side Up: A History of the Conservative in America.* Boston: Houghton Mifflin, 1996.

Hosking, Geoffrey. *Rulers and Victims: The Russians in the Soviet Union.* Cambridge: Belknap Press of Harvard University Press, 2006.

Huebner, Lee W., and Thomas E. Petri, eds. *The Ripon Papers, 1963–1968.* Washington, DC: National Press, 1968.

Hulsey, Byron C. *Everett Dirksen and His Presidents: How a Senate Giant Shaped American Politics.* Lawrence: University Press of Kansas, 2000.

Isserman, Maurice, and Michael Kazin. *America Divided: The Civil War of the 1960s.* New York: Oxford University Press, 2000.

Jordan, Hamilton. *Crisis: The Last Year of the Carter Presidency.* New York: G. P. Putnam's Sons, 1982.

Jorden, William J. *Panama Odyssey.* Austin: University of Texas Press, 1984.

Knapman, Edward W., ed. *Presidential Election 1968.* New York: Facts on File, 1970.

Kolkey, Jonathan Martin. *The New Right, 1960–1968, with Epilogue, 1969–1980.* Washington, DC: University Press of America, 1983.

Korb, Lawrence J. "National Security Organization and Process in the Carter Administration." In *Defense Policy and the Presidency: Carter's First Years,* ed. Sam C. Sarkesian. Boulder, CO: Westview Press, 1979.

Kramer, Michael S., and Sam Roberts. *"I Never Wanted to be Vice-President of Anything!": An Investigative Biography of Nelson Rockefeller.* New York: Basic Books, 1976.

Krukones, Michael G. "Campaigner and President: Jimmy Carter's Campaign Promises and Presidential Performance." In *The Presidency and Domestic Policies of Jimmy Carter,* ed. Herbert D. Rosenbaum and Alexei Ugrinsky. Westport, CT: Greenwood, 1994.

Kurlansky, Mark. *1968: The Year That Rocked the World.* New York: Ballantine, 2004.

Lachicotte, Alberta. *Rebel Senator: Strom Thurmond of South Carolina.* New York: Devin-Adair, 1966.

LaFeber, Walter. *America, Russia, and the Cold War, 1945–2006.* Boston: McGraw-Hill, 2006.

LaFeber, Walter. *The Deadly Bet: LBJ, Vietnam, and the 1968 Election.* Lanham, MD: Rowman and Littlefield, 2005.

Laidi, Zaikie. *The Superpowers and Africa: The Constraints of a Rivalry, 1960–1990.* Trans. Patricia Badoin. Chicago: University of Chicago Press, 1990.

Lake, David A., and Robert Powell. *Strategic Choice and International Relations.* Princeton, NJ: Princeton University Press, 1999.

Leipold, L. Edmond. *Ronald Reagan: Governor and Statesman.* Minneapolis: T. S. Dennison, 1968.

Lesher, Stephan. *George Wallace: American Populist.* Reading, MA: Addison-Wesley, 1994.

Lewis, Joseph. *What Makes Reagan Run? A Political Profile.* New York: McGraw-Hill, 1968.

Ligachev, Yegor. *Inside Gorbachev's Kremlin.* New York: Pantheon, 1993.

Lurie, Leonard. *The Running of Richard Nixon.* New York: Coward, McCann and Geoghegan, 1972.

MacNeil, Neil. *Dirksen: Portrait of a Public Man.* New York: World Publishing, 1970.

Malbin, Michael J. "The Conventions, Platforms, and Issue Activists." In *The American Elections of 1980,* ed. Austin Ranney. Washington, DC: American Enterprise Institute for Public Policy Research, 1981.

McCarthy, Eugene J. *The Limits of Power: America's Role in the World.* New York: Holt, Rinehart and Winston, 1967.

McGinniss, Joe. *The Selling of the President, 1968.* New York: Washington Square Press, 1969.

Mears, Walter R. *Deadlines Past: Forty Years of Presidential Campaigning: A Reporter's Story.* Kansas City, MO: Andrews McMeel, 2003.

Meese, Edwin, III. *With Reagan: The Inside Story.* Washington, DC: Regnery Gateway, 1992.

Micklethwait, John, and Adrian Wooldridge. *The Right Nation: Conservative Power in America.* New York: Penguin, 2004.

Mieczkowski, Yanek. *Ford and the Challenges of the 1970s.* Lexington: University Press of Kentucky, 2005.

Miller, J. H. "How Much of a New Elite?" In *Gorbachev at the Helm: A New Era in Soviet Politics,* ed. R. F. Miller, J. H. Miller, and T. H. Rigby. London: Croom Helm, 1987.

Minow, Newton N., Clifford M. Sloan, and Carlos T. Angulo. *Opening Salvos: Who Should Participate in Presidential Debates?* New York: Century Foundation, 1999.

Moore, John L. *Elections A to Z.* 2nd ed. Washington, DC: Congressional Quarterly Press, 2003.

Moore, Jonathan, ed. *The Campaign for President: 1980 in Retrospect.* Cambridge, MA: Ballinger, 1981.

Morrison, John. *Boris Yeltsin: From Bolshevik to Democrat.* New York: Dutton Books, 1991.

Murphy, Reg, and Hall Gulliver. *The Southern Strategy.* New York: Charles Scribner's Sons, 1971.

Nash, George H. *The Conservative Intellectual Movement in America.* New York: Basic Books, 1976.

Nie, Norman H., Sidney Verba, and John R. Petrocik. *The Changing American Voter.* Cambridge: Harvard University Press, 1976.

Niskanen, William A. *Reaganomics: An Insider's Account of the Policies and the People.* New York: Oxford University Press, 1988.

Nixon, Richard. *In the Arena: A Memoir of Victory, Defeat, and Renewal.* New York: Simon & Schuster, 1990.

Nixon, Richard. *RN: The Memoirs of Richard Nixon.* New York: Simon & Schuster, 1978.

Parmet, Herbert S. *Richard Nixon and His America.* Boston: Little, Brown, 1990.

Pemberton, William E. *Exit with Honor: The Life and Presidency of Ronald Reagan.* Armonk, NY: M. E. Sharpe, 1998.

Persico, Joseph E. *The Imperial Rockefeller.* New York: Simon & Schuster, 1982.

Phillips, Kevin P. *The Emerging Republican Majority.* 2nd ed. New Rochelle, NY: Arlington House, 1969.

Phillips, Kevin P. *Mediacracy: American Parties and Policies in the Communications Age.* New York: Doubleday, 1975.

Pilat, Oliver. *Lindsay's Campaign: A Behind-the-Scenes Diary.* Boston: Beacon Press, 1968.

Plotkin, Henry A. "Issues in the Presidential Campaign." In *The Election of 1980: Reports and Interpretations,* by Gerald Pomper et al. Ed. Marlene Michels Pomper. Chatham, NJ: Chatham House, 1981.

Polsby, Nelson W. *Consequences of Party Reform.* New York: Oxford University Press, 1983.

Polsby, Nelson W., and Aaron Wildavsky. *Presidential Elections: Strategies and Structures of American Politics.* 10th ed. New York: Seven Bridges Press, 2000.

Polsby, Nelson W., and Aaron Wildavsky. *Presidential Elections: Strategies of American Electoral Politics.* New York: Scribner's, 1964.

Pomper, Gerald M., ed. *The Election of 1976.* New York: Longman, 1977.

Pomper, Gerald M. "The Nominating Contest." In *The Election of 1980: Reports and Interpretations,* by Gerald Pomper et al. Ed. Marlene Michels Pomper. Chatham, NJ: Chatham House, 1981.

Ranney, Austin, ed. *The American Elections of 1980.* Washington, DC: American Enterprise Institute for Public Policy Research, 1981.

Reagan, Ronald. *An American Life.* New York: Pocket Books, 1990.

Reagan, Ronald. *The Creative Society.* New York: Devin-Adair, 1968.

Reagan, Ronald. *Speaking My Mind.* New York: Simon & Schuster, 1989.

Reagan, Ronald. *A Time for Choosing: The Speeches of Ronald Reagan, 1961–1982.* Ed. Alfred A. Baltizer and Gerald M. Bonetto. Chicago: Regnery Gateway, 1983.

Reeves, Richard. *President Reagan: The Triumph of Imagination.* New York: Simon & Schuster, 2006.

Richardson, Darcy G. *A Nation Divided: The 1968 Presidential Campaign.* Lincoln, NE: Writers Club Press, 2002.

Riker, William H. *The Art of Political Manipulation.* New Haven: Yale University Press, 1986.

Riker, William H. "Rhetorical Interaction in the Ratification Campaigns." In *Agenda Formation,* ed. Riker. Ann Arbor: University of Michigan Press, 1993.

Riker, William H. *The Strategy of Rhetoric: Campaigning for the American Constitution.* New Haven: Yale University Press, 1996.

Ripon Society and Clifford W. Brown, Jr. *Jaws of Victory.* Boston: Little, Brown, 1974.

Robinson, Peter. *How Ronald Reagan Changed My Life.* New York: HarperCollins, 2003.

Rockefeller, Nelson A. *Unity, Freedom & Peace: A Blueprint for Tomorrow.* New York: Random House, 1968.

Roeder, Philip G. *Red Sunset: The Failure of Soviet Politics*. Princeton, NJ: Princeton University Press, 1993.

Rusher, William A. *The Making of the New Majority Party*. New York: Sheed and Ward, 1975.

Rusher, William A. *The Rise of the Right*. New York: William Morrow, 1984.

Safire, William. *The New Language of Politics: An Anecdotal Dictionary of Catchwords, Slogans, and Political Usage*. New York: Random House, 1968.

Sakharov, Andrei D. *Memoirs*. New York: Knopf, 1990.

Sale, Kirkpatrick. *Power Shift: The Rise of the Southern Rim and Its Challenge to the Eastern Establishment*. New York: Random House, 1975.

Saloma, John S. *Ominous Politics: The New Conservative Labyrinth*. New York: Hill and Wang, 1984.

Sandbrook, Dominic. *Eugene McCarthy and the Rise and Fall of Postwar American Liberalism*. New York: Anchor, 2005.

Scheer, Robert. *With Enough Shovels: Reagan, Bush and Nuclear War*. New York: Random House, 1982.

Schoenwald, Jonathan M. *A Time for Choosing: The Rise of American Conservatism*. New York: Oxford University Press, 2001.

Schrag, Peter. *Paradise Lost: California's Experience, America's Future*. New York: New Press, 1998.

Schulman, Bruce J. "Slouching toward the Supply Side: Jimmy Carter and the New American Political Economy." In *The Carter Presidency: Policy Choices in the Post–New Deal Era*, ed. Gary M. Fink and Hugh Davis Graham. Lawrence: University Press of Kansas, 1998.

Schuparra, Kurt. *Triumph of the Right: The Rise of the California Conservative Movement, 1945–1966*. Armonk, NY: M. E. Sharpe, 1998.

Schweizer, Peter, and Rochelle Schweizer. *The Bushes: Portrait of a Dynasty*. New York: Anchor, 2004.

Sherrill, Robert. *Gothic Politics in the Deep South: Stars of the New Confederacy*. New York: Grossman, 1968.

Shirley, Craig. *Reagan's Revolution: The Untold Story of the Campaign That Started It All*. Nashville: Nelson Current, 2005.

Simes, Dimitri K. *After the Collapse: Russia Seeks Its Place as a Great Power*. New York: Simon & Schuster, 1999.

Siverson, Randolph M., ed. *Strategic Politicians, Institutions, and Foreign Policy*. Ann Arbor: University of Michigan Press, 1998.

Skinner, Kiron K., Annelise Anderson, and Martin Anderson, eds. *Reagan, A Life in Letters*. New York: Free Press, 2003.

Skinner, Kiron K., Annelise Anderson, and Martin Anderson, eds. *Reagan, In His Own Hand: The Writings of Ronald Reagan That Reveal his Revolutionary Vision for America*. New York: Free Press, 2001.

Skinner, Kiron K., Annelise Anderson, and Martin Anderson, eds. *Reagan's Path to Victory: The Shaping of Ronald Reagan's Vision, Selected Writings*. New York: Free Press, 2004.

Sloan, John W. *The Reagan Effect: Economics and Presidential Leadership*. Lawrence: University Press of Kansas, 1999.

Smith, George H. *Who Is Ronald Reagan?* New York: Pyramid Books, 1968.

Smith, Hedrick. *The New Russians*. New York: Random House, 1990.

Solnick, Steven L. *Stealing the State: Control and Collapse in Soviet Institutions.* Cambridge: Cambridge University Press, 1998.

Stacks, John F. *Watershed: The Campaign for the Presidency, 1980.* New York: Times Books, 1981.

Suny, Ronald Grigor. *The Revenge of the Past: Nationalism, Revolution, and the Collapse of the Soviet Union.* Stanford, CA: Stanford University Press, 1993.

Thimmesch, Nick. *The Condition of Republicanism.* New York: Norton, 1968.

Thurmond, Strom. *The Faith We Have Not Kept.* San Diego: Viewpoint Books, 1968.

Troy, Gil. *See How They Ran: The Changing Role of the Presidential Candidate.* Cambridge: Harvard University Press, 1996.

Van der Linden, Frank. *The Real Reagan.* New York: William Morrow, 1981.

Vance, Cyrus. *Hard Choices: Critical Years in America's Foreign Policy.* New York: Simon & Schuster, 1983.

Wainstock, Dennis. *The Turning Point: The 1968 Presidential Campaign.* Jefferson, NC: McFarland, 1988.

Walker, Edward W. *Dissolution: Sovereignty and the Breakup of the Soviet Union.* Lanham, MD: Rowman and Littlefield, 2003.

West, Darrell M. *Making Campaigns Count: Leadership and Coalition-Building in 1980.* Westport, CT: Greenwood, 1984.

Westad, Odd Arne, ed. *The Fall of Détente: Soviet-American Relations during the Carter Years.* Oslo: Scandinavian University Press, 1997.

Whalen, Richard J. *Catch the Falling Flag: A Republican's Challenge to His Party.* Boston: Houghton Mifflin, 1972.

White, F. Clifton, and William J. Gill. *Suite 3505: The Story of the Draft Goldwater Movement.* Ashland, OH: Ashbrook Press, 1992.

White, F. Clifton, and William J. Gill. *Why Reagan Won: A Narrative History of the Conservative Movement, 1964–1981.* Chicago: Regnery Gateway, 1981.

White, Theodore H. *America in Search of Itself: The Making of the President, 1956–1980.* New York: Harper and Row, 1982.

White, Theodore H. *The Making of the President, 1968.* New York: Atheneum, 1969.

Wicker, Tom. *One of Us: Richard Nixon and the American Dream.* New York: Random House, 1991.

Widmer, Ted. *Campaigns: A Century of Presidential Races from the Photo Archives of the New York Times.* New York: DK Publishing, 2001.

Williams, Phil. "Carter's Defence Policy." In *The Carter Years: The President and Policy Making,* ed. Glenn Abernathy, Dilys M. Hill, and Williams. New York: St. Martin's Press, 1984.

Wills, Garry. *Nixon Agonistes: The Crisis of a Self-Made Man.* Boston: Houghton Mifflin, 1970.

Wills, Garry. *Reagan's America: Innocents at Home.* New York: Penguin, 2000.

Winik, Jay. *On the Brink.* New York: Simon & Schuster, 1996.

Wirls, Daniel. *Buildup: The Politics of Defense in the Reagan Era.* Ithaca, NY: Cornell University Press, 1992.

Wirthlin, Dick, and Wynton C. Hall. *The Greatest Communicator: What Ronald Reagan Taught Me about Politics, Leadership and Life.* Hoboken, NJ: John Wiley and Sons, 2004.

Witcover, Jules. *Marathon: The Pursuit of the Presidency, 1972–1976.* New York: Viking, 1977.

Witcover, Jules. *The Resurrection of Richard Nixon.* New York: G. P. Putnam's Sons, 1970.

Yeltsin, Boris. *Against the Grain: An Autobiography.* New York: Summit, 1990.

PERIODICALS AND NEWS AGENCIES

Agence France-Presse
Air Force Magazine
The Alternative: An American Spectator
American Journal of Political Science
American Political Science Review
Anchorage Daily Times
Arizona Republic
Associated Press
Atlanta Journal and the Atlanta Constitution
Baltimore Sun
BBC World Service
Birmingham News
British Journal of Political Science
Business Week
California Journal
Cedar Rapids Gazette
Chicago Tribune
Cincinnati Enquirer
Clarion Ledger
Courier-Journal (Louisville, KY)
Comparative Political Studies
Daily Record (York, PA)
Dallas Morning News
Honolulu Star-Bulletin
Houston Chronicle
Human Events
Jerusalem Domestic Service
Journal of Economic Theory
Los Angeles Herald Examiner
Los Angeles Times
Miami Herald
Michigan Today
Milwaukee Journal
Minneapolis Tribune
Modern Age
National Review
New York Times
New York Times Magazine

News and Courier (South Carolina)
Newsweek
Oregonian
Philadelphia Inquirer
Pittsburgh Post-Gazette
Pittsburgh Press
Plain Dealer (Cleveland)
Public Opinion
Review of Economic Studies
Richmond Times-Dispatch
Sacramento Bee
San Diego Evening Tribune
San Diego Union
San Francisco Chronicle
San Francisco Examiner
San Jose Mercury News
St. Louis Post-Dispatch
St. Paul Pioneer Press
State (South Carolina)
Time
Times Picayune
United Press International
U.S. News and World Report
Wall Street Journal
Washington Post
Washington Post Times Herald
Washington Star
William and Mary Law Review

REFERENCE SOURCES

Cook, Rhodes. *United States Presidential Primary Elections, 1968–1996: A Handbook of Election Statistics.* Washington, DC: Congressional Quarterly Press, 2000.

CQ Press Guide to U.S. Elections. 5th ed. Vol. 1. Washington, DC: Congressional Quarterly Press, 2005.

DeGregorio, William A. *The Complete Book of U.S. Presidents.* 5th ed. New York: Gramercy Books, 2002.

Drake University School of Journalism and Mass Communication. "Caucus History in Iowa." 1980. http://www.drake.edu/journalism/CyberCaucus2004/history1.html#1980. Consulted April 29, 2005.

Driscoll, James G. *Newsbook: Elections, 1968.* Silver Spring, MD: National Observer, 1968.

Farber, David, and Beth Bailey. *The Columbia Guide to America in the 1960s.* New York: Columbia University Press, 2001.

Ferrell, Robert H. *The Twentieth Century: An Almanac.* New York: World Almanac, 1984.

Gallup, George H. *Gallup Poll: Public Opinion, 1935–1971*. New York: Random House, 1972.

Gallup, George H. *The Gallup Poll: Public Opinion, 1972–1977*. 2 vols. Wilmington, DE: Scholarly Resources, 1978.

Gallup Poll. *Public Opinion, 1978*. Wilmington, DE: Scholarly Resources, 1980.

Gallup Poll. *Public Opinion, 1979*. Wilmington, DE: Scholarly Resources, 1981.

Gallup Poll. *Public Opinion, 1980*. Wilmington, DE: Scholarly Resources, 1981.

Gallup Poll. *Public Opinion, 1981*. Wilmington, DE: Scholarly Resources, 1982.

Gallup Poll Index. "Dissatisfaction Motivated Voters" and "The 1980 Election One of the Most Unusual." Report No. 183 (December 1980).

Gould, Lewis L. *Grand Old Party: A History of the Republicans*. New York: Random House, 2003.

Harris, Louis and Associates. *Harris 1980 Presidential Election Survey*. Various Surveys. New York: Harris and Associates, 1980.

Matuz, Roger. *The Presidents Fact Book*. New York: Black Dog and Leventhal, 2004.

Nelson, Lyle Emerson. *American Presidents, Year by Year*. Vol. 3. Armonk, NY: M. E. Sharpe, 2004.

"The ANES Guide to Public Opinion and Electoral Behavior." *The American National Election Studies*. Ann Arbor: University of Michigan Center for Political Studies.

Official Report of the Proceedings of the Twenty-Ninth Republican National Convention. Republican National Committee, 1968.

Report of the National Advisory Commission on Civil Disorders. New York: E. P. Dutton, 1968.

Republican National Convention, Miami Beach, August 1968 Official Program. Republican Party, 1968.

Schlesinger, Arthur M., Jr. *The Election of 1968 and the Administration of Richard Nixon*. Philadelphia: Mason Crest, 2003.

Schlesinger, Arthur M., Jr. *The Election of 1976 and the Administration of Jimmy Carter*. Philadelphia: Mason Crest, 2003.

Witcover, Jules. *Party of the People: A History of the Democrats*. New York: Random House, 2003.

GOVERNMENT DOCUMENTS

Carter, Jimmy. *The Presidential Campaign, 1976*. Vol. 1. 2 parts. Washington, DC: United States Government Printing Office, 1978.

Foreign Broadcasting Information Service, Soviet Union, 1985–91.

Public Papers of the President. Washington, DC: United States Government Printing Office, various years.

UNPUBLISHED MANUSCRIPTS

Mackie, Gerry. "The Coherence of Democracy." Unpublished manuscript, Research School of Social Sciences, Australian National University, Canberra, 2001.

Reed, Tom, Diary notes. The diary notes referred to in this book are from an unpublished manuscript by Reed that is derived from his diary. Reed's unpublished manuscript and diary are held in his private papers in Healdsburg, California.

Vorobiova, Elena V. "The Republican Party in the South in the 1968 Presidential Election." Ph.D. diss., Auburn University, 1997.

ARTICLES (RUSSIAN)

Amos, R. "U russkogo cheloveka vse-taki est' rodina. Interviu s narodnym deputatom SSSR B. N. Yel'tsinym." *Sovietskaia Estoniia,* February 1990.

Andreyeva, Nina. "Ne mogu postupat'sia printsipami." *Sovietskaia Rossiia,* March 13, 1988.

Argumenty i Fakty. no. 10 (March 1990).

"B. N. Yeltsin: Dumayu, chto menia podderzhat." *Literaturnaia Gazeta,* January 24, 1990.

Ivanov, V. "B. N. Yeltsin: Liudiam ochen' vazhna pravda." *Sovietskaia Estoniia,* February 19, 1989.

"Kaikim putiom my poidiom. . . ." *Argumenty i Fakty,* May 26–June 1, 1990.

Luk'ianchenko, P., and A. Binev. "Ia vse-taki optimist." *Argumenty i Fakty,* March 3–9, 1990.

Popov, Gavriil. "Learning Our Lessons." *Moscow News,* no. 47 (1987).

Popov, Gavriil. "The Kind of Perestroika We Want: Some Ideas about Political Avant-gardism." *Moscow News,* no. 51 (1987).

"Varianty Borisa Yeltsina." October 18–24, 1990.

BOOKS (RUSSIAN)

Boldin, V. *Krushenie P'edestala. Shtrikhi k Portretu M. S. Gorbacheva.* Moscow: Respublika, 1995.

Chernyaev, Anatolii. *Shest' Let s Gorbachevym: Po Dnevnikovym Zapisiam.* Moscow: Progress, 1993.

Falin, V. M. *Konflikty v Kremle: Sumerki Bogov Po-russki.* Moscow: Sentrpoligraf, 2000.

Gorbachev, Mikhail. *Zhizn' i Reformy.* Vol. 1. Moscow: Novosti, 1995.

Gorchakov, M., and V. Zhuravliov, eds. *Gorbachev-Yeltsin: 1500 Dnei Politicheskogo Protivostoianiia.* Moscow: Terra, 1992.

Grachev, Andrei. *Gorbachev.* Moscow: Vagrius, 2001.

Lukianov, Anatoliy. *Perevorot, Mnimyi i Nastoiashchiy: Otvety na Voprosy, Prishedshie v "Matrosskuiu Tishinu."* Moscow: Nezavisimoe izd-vo "Manuskript," 1993.

Medvedev, Vadim. *V komande Gorbacheva. Vzgliad iznutri.* Moskva: Bylina, 1994.

Solovyov, Vladimir, and Elena Klepikova. *Boris Yeltsin. Politicheskie Metamorfozy.* Moscow: Vagrius, 1992.

Yakovlev, Aleksandr. *Sumerki.* Moscow: Materik, 2003.

Yakovlev, Aleksandr. *Gor'kaya Chasha: Bol'shevizm i Reformatsiya v Rossii.* Yaroslavl': Verkhne-Volzhskoe knizhnoe izd-vo, 1994.

Vorotnikov, Vitalii. *A Bylo Eto Tak* . . . Moscow: Sovet Veteranov Knigoizdaniia SI-MAR, 1995.

Yeltsin, Boris. *Ispoved na Zadannuyu Temu*. Sverdlovsk: Sredne-Uralskoe Knizhnoe idz-vo, 1990.

Yel'tsin, Boris. *Zapiski Prezidenta*. Moscow: Ogoniok, 1994.

Ziankovich, Mikalai. *Boris Yel'tsin: Raznye Zhizni*. Moscow: OLMA-PRESS, 2001.

PERIODICALS AND NEWS AGENCIES (RUSSIAN)

Argumenty i Fakty
Gospodin Narod
ITAR-TASS
Izvestiia
Komsomolskaia Pravda
Krasnaia Zvezda
Literaturnaia Gazeta
Moscow News
Moskovskaia Pravda
Nezavisimaia Gazeta
Ogoniok
Pravda
Rabochaia Tribuna
Radio Rossii
Sovietskaia Estoniia
Sovietskaia Rossiia

Index

ABM. *See* Antiballistic missile
Abortion
  Anderson, 177
  Carter ACLU rating, 175
  Reagan, 120, 130, 132, 176, 189, 192
  republicans/democrats on, 120, 130, 175, 296n112
  rights, 175–76
  voter preferences on, 157, 202
Adams, Greg D., 202, 296n112
Afghanistan, 159–60, 287n70
Agenda
  CPAC, 107
  Carter reelection, 175
  for economy, 174–75, 182, 192, 284n103
  heresthetical, 27, 254
  importance of, 10, 23
  issue-based, 32
  outsider, Yeltsin, 244
  Politburo, 217
  policy, 46
  Reagan's, 99, 103, 160, 182, 191
  reform, of Gorbachev, 207–8, 210, 215, 224, 226–27, 263n28
  reform, of Yeltsin, 220–21
  rhetoric, 32–33
  Romney policy, 46
  setting (using rhetoric and heresthetic), 12
  strategy of setting, 12, 32
Agnew, Spiro, 57, 60, 88, 94, 101, 105, 276n207, 277n208
Aliev, Geidar, 298n212
Allen, Richard V., 73, 118, 139–40, 154, 179, 285n36, 292n41
All-Union
  bodies, 231, 233
  polls, 231
All-Union Center for the Study of Public Opinion, 242, 301n51
American Independent Party, 41, 58, 97
Anderson, Annelise, 277n10
Anderson, John, 119, 129–31, 163, 284n16, 290n5, 290n6, 293n62
  announcing running mate, 184
  campaign strategy, 167–69, 294n67, 295n95, 295n98
  on Carter-Reagan debate, 193, 197, 295n94
  on defense, 181
  in debate, Chicago, 156, 288nn90–91
  in debate, Manchester 153–54
  in debate, Nashua, 155
  election results, 200–201
  on handling economy, 183
  negative campaigning of, 168–69, 186–87, 198
  (performance in) primaries, 156–58, 284n13
  platform, 184, 291n28, 293nn62–63
  popularity among liberals, 161, 190, 294n74, 294n75

Anderson, John (*continued*)
  Reagan debating, 153–54, 187–90
  running as independent, 156, 158,
    164, 169, 289n95
  on social issues, 177, 289n109
  third-party threat, 164, 166, 171,
    187, 289n94
  Wallace differing from, 131
Anderson, Martin, 118, 122, 136–37,
    139, 182, 277n10
Andreyeva, Nina
  conservative backlash, 220
  letter by, 209, 220, 297n8
  Stalin defended by, 222
Andropov, Yuri, 213
Antiballistic missile (ABM), 70,
    273nn144–45
anti-Communist, 56, 71, 97, 137. *See
    also* Communism; Communist
    Party
Antiperestroika, 219, 227. *See also* Per-
    estroika
Antiterrorism, 195. *See also* Terrorism
Approval ratings, 95, 109, 116, 128,
    238, 242
Arbatov, Georgi, 211, 244, 297n14
Ashbrook, John, 100
"Asia after Vietnam" (Nixon), 56
Axelrod, Robert, 201, 296n109

Bachelder, Glen, 45–46, 267n42
Baker, Howard, 69, 125, 129–30,
    153–56, 264n9, 266n37, 284n10,
    288n89
Barons
  conservative, 37–38, 43–44, 85
  nomination procedure, 9–10, 63, 82,
    93
  at Republican convention, 55–58
  support from, 9–10, 40, 42, 47, 51,
    61, 64, 71, 258
  threat from Wallace, 78
Battaglia, Phil, 269n78
BBC Television, 222–23
Berlin Wall, 52, 251
Birmingham News, 82, 275nn182–84
Bisnow, Mark, 169, 189–90, 284n16
Black Americans

as activists, 36
Nixon's relationship with, 63, 66,
    69, 75, 271n116
  vote of, 133–34, 169–70, 172–73,
    271n116, 274n165
Black power movement, 36–37
Bliss, Ray, 35, 39, 264n7
Blue-collar workers, 100, 105–6
  Reagan and, 12, 165, 171, 250, 255
  Yeltsin gaining support of, 244
Boskin, Michael, 183, 284n21, 292n60
Bourne, Peter, 96, 146, 278n22
Brezhnev, Leonid, 113, 148, 214, 216,
    218
Brown, Edmund, 265n22, 269n86
Brown, Harold, 149, 178–79, 287n68,
    291n39, 292n40, 292n42
Brown, Jerry, 131
Brown, Seyom, 151–52, 287n73
Brown, Ron, 152
Brzezinski, Zbigniew, 145–47, 286n55,
    286n58
Buchanan, Pat, 72–73, 88
Buckley, William F., Jr., 99, 279n32
Bueno de Mesquita, Bruce, 8, 261n4
Bush, George H. W., 13, 153, 162n22,
    284n12, 288n77, 288n86
  campaigning for Reagan, 129–30,
    191, 280, 292n48, 294n77
  candidacy gaining momentum, 154,
    157–58, 289nn100–101
  on foreign policy, 160
  Reagan vs., 13, 125, 129, 154,
    155–57, 289n96, 289n104
  rhetoric of, 159–60

Caddell, Patrick, 96, 128, 143, 284n7,
    290n17, 294n69
  campaign plan, 290n3
  on Carter campaign, 175, 199
  Rose Garden strategy of, 143, 167,
    176
  strategies of, 163–64, 166–67,
    186–87, 200
  on voters' reaction to hostage situa-
    tion, 199
Callaway, Howard "Bo," 108, 110,
    270n88, 281n, 70

Campaign(s). *See also* Negative campaign(s)
  Anderson, J., 130–31, 167
  antialcohol, of Ligachev, 213
  Caddell's, plan, 290n3
  Carter, 175, 187
  examples of three successful, vii
  Goldwater, 38, 41, 47, 258, 263n5
  governance relating to, vii
  heresthetic, 13–14, 248, 250, 252, 254–58
  issues, 55–56
  leading aggressive, 77–78
  manipulation used in, 262n14
  memos, 73
  1976 presidential, 121–23, 165–66, 171, 200–203, 249, 253–54
  Nixon, 69, 84–86, 88
  principles of, 11–13, 206
  rhetoric, 16, 19–20, 173, 183, 186 252–53
  strategy, 31, 45–46, 248–49
  studies of, 6
  themes, 14, 153, 172, 175, 279, 279n26, 281n66, 287n75
  theory, 249
  Whalen on, 63
  Yeltsin redirecting, 6–7
Candidate(s)
  attracting voters, 27–28
  Bush as, 157–58
  commanding political center, 2, 13, 20, 25, 249
  Debs, Eugene as, 27
  heresthetic/rhetoric used by, 11–13, 26
  issue-driven, 17–18
  maneuvering to win office, 4–5
  persuasive, 16–17
  Reagan as, 84
  rhetorical vs. heresthetical, 253–58
  Rockefeller as, 65
  third-party, 78
  voters' opinions of, 18, 33, 252–53
  Wallace as, 41, 58–59, 279n30
  Yeltsin removed as, 219–20
Cannon, Lou, 56–57, 266n29, 275n169, 275n179

  on "Let the People Rule," 115
  on Proposition 1, 103
  on Reagan's tax plan, 183
  on Wallace/Reagan, 78–80, 275n169
Carter, Jimmy
  appeal to Kennedy democrats, 130–31
  budget of, 292n52
  campaign seeking new direction, 187
  campaign themes of, 279n26
  carrying South, 126
  CDM and, 148–51
  coalition (1976) of, 127–28
  combining issues, 89
  on communism, 287n69
  convention acceptance speech of, 173–75
  détente, 139
  defense policies of, 179–80
  economic stimulus package proposed by, 142
  economy and, 132, 142, 145, 174, 181, 183, 257
  election of, 121
  election strategy, 166, 176–78
  election results (1980), 201
  environmental standards, 176
  Ford vs., 122
  foreign/defense policy and, 145–46, 151, 170, 204
  in Gallup Poll, 140, 164, 200
  inauguration of, 255
  Iranian hostage crisis and, 124, 150
  Iran policy of, 157–58, 192
  Kennedy, E., challenging, 161–62, 173
  misfortune, 125
  on national energy problems, 144, 195
  negative campaigning of, 190–91, 194, 198–99
  political demise of, 151
  precarious political situation of, 128, 153
  race relations and, 169–70
  Reagan debating, 193–97
  Reagan vs., 3, 6, 13, 26, 28, 33, 89,

Carter, Jimmy (*continued*)
    130, 135, 141, 143, 147, 152,
    163–64, 167, 179–80, 185, 194–95,
    197–200, 203
    Reagan as similar to, 96–97
    regional problems faced by, 166–67
    rhetoric of, 150
    SALT II and, 147–48
    Soviet relations and, 204
    Wallace endorsing, 98
Casey, William, 154, 156
CC. *See* CPSU Central Committee
CDM. *See* Coalition for a Democratic
    Majority
Centrist(s), 15, 25
    Carter as, 196
    Gorbachev as, 210
    ideas in a heresthetical campaign,
    254
    Nixon as, 39, 56, 85–86, 98–99,
    265n22
    Reagan as, 171
CFTR. *See* Citizens for the Republic
Chamberlain, Neville, 30
Cheney, Dick, 108–9, 115
Chernyaev, Anatolii, 226, 299n2
Christopher, Warren, 198
Churchill, Winston, 2, 30
Cicero, 19, 228, 253, 256, 260
Citizens for Peace with Freedom in
    Vietnam, 54
Citizens for the Republic (CFTR),
    127–28
Civil rights, 39
    Carter administration, 291n19
    in Democratic Party, 36–37
    GOP recovery, 35, 37
    legislation, 34, 198, 265n23
    Nixon on, 32
    Reagan on, 52, 64, 85, 173, 191
    Romney campaign on, 45
    Young, Andrew on, 172
Civil Rights Act of 1964, 39
    Dirksen's opposition to, 265n23
Clymer, Adam, 131, 273n144, 284n13,
    284n18, 284n20, 286n41, 288n79,
    288n91, 288n93, 289n100,
    289n106, 295n99, 296n111

Coalition
    Gorbachev, 206–8, 214 219–21, 228,
    238, 242, 250–51, 297n3
    New Deal, 128, 201
    Nixon, 272n139
    Reagan constructed, 200, 203,
    249–50, 252
    small vs. large, 17, 126, 206, 213,
    250, 252, 255, 258–59
    winning, 8, 224
    Yeltsin's, 225, 230–31, 233, 246–48,
    251
Coalition for a Democratic Majority
    (CDM), 148–51
"Coherence of Democracy, The"
    (Mackie), 262n12
Cold War
    analysis of, by Reagan, 93, 137
    end of, 4, 29–30, 204, 251–52, 255
    era of, 205
    foreign policy, 36, 132
    leadership and, 4–5
    misunderstanding of, 141
    Reagan and, 12–13, 93, 112–13, 126,
    134, 137, 204, 205, 250–52, 255
    Yeltsin's rise at end of, viii, 255
Committee on the Present Danger
    (CPD), 151
Communism, 29
    Carter on, 146, 150, 287n69
    ideology of, 206
    Reagan on, 93
    Romney on, 48–49
Communist Party, 247, 298n37
    commanding median, 21, 208
    competition within, 4
    conservatives in, 259
    decision-making powers of, 232
    Gorbachev and, 10, 236–37, 257
    leadership of, 10, 208, 250
    members and special privileges, 17,
    250
    officials, 7
    as workers champion, 209
    Yeltsin and, 4, 7, 239–40, 251, 255,
    257, 259
    Yeltsin's resignation from, 239–40
Conformity to party line, 216

Congress of People's Deputies, 207, 223, 232, 245
  Yeltsin's speech at, 238–39
Conservation, 181, 188, 190, 194–95
Conservatism, 37–38, 105, 132–33
  compassionate, 75
  democrats and, 107, 149
  Gorbachev and, 214, 238–39
  Reagan and, 53, 57, 65, 101–2, 105–6, 110, 114, 160, 255
  social/economic, 106, 132–33, 138–39, 160
  southern, 43, 85
Conservative(s)
  barons of, 37–38, 43–44
  CC members as, 215
  in Communist Party, 214–15, 218–20 259
  democrats as, 149
  Ligachev as, 209
  Nixon's appeal to, 68
  Politburo members, 217, 223
  Republicans as, 48–49, 51
Conservative Political Action Committee (CPAC), 107
Constitution
  amendments to, 137
  ratification of, 26–28
  Soviet, 234, 243, 251
Context
  institutional, 11, 55, 125, 216
  political, 127–32
  of political contest, 7–8, 127
  for political debate, 12, 252
Cooper, Hank, 179
Corruption, 16–17, 212, 228, 230
CPAC. *See* Conservative Political Action Committee
CPD. *See* Committee of the Present Danger
CPSU (Communist Party of the Soviet Union)
  general secretaries, 206, 211, 242
  "Party's National Politics under the Present Conditions" program, 233
CPSU Central Committee (CC), 208, 214, 229, 232

conservative member of, 215
  Plenum, 208–9, 211, 217–18, 220–21, 232, 236
Crane, Philip, 129, 153, 155–57, 160
Crime rates, 36, 48–49
Crisp, Mary, 184

Dean, John, 101
Deaver, Michael, 91, 104
Debate(s)
  Anderson, J., vs. Reagan, 187–90
  Carter vs. Reagan, 193–97
  context for political, 12
  on economic crisis, 235
  heresthetical, 254–55
  Reagan vs. Kennedy, E., 268n69
  on reform (in USSR), 210, 235, 244
  reframing, 7, 252–53, 256–58
  Republican Party, 153–62
Declaration of Sovereignty, 239
Defeat
  of Goldwater, 55, 249
  of Gorbachev, 23
  political, 2
Defense
  ABM, 70, 273n145
  initiative, 258
  national, 13, 57, 69–70, 74, 108, 140, 173, 175, 180
  policy, 57, 70, 114–15, 117, 134–35, 137, 139, 141, 145–46, 151, 165, 177–81, 190, 202, 257
  Reagan's view on national, 140–41
Defense spending, 75, 97, 100, 115–16, 120, 123, 126, 135, 141, 145, 149–50, 152, 154, 160, 168, 174, 178, 181, 183, 202–4, 257
Democratic convention, 131, 161, 173–75
Democratic leaders, 36, 252
Democratic National Convention, 37, 44, 173
Democratic Party, 36–37, 151, 161, 173, 175–76, 201, 296n112
  conservatism within, 106–7, 132
  1968 convention, 93–94
  presidential contenders of, 275n169
  status of, 128

Democratic Russia, 234
　deputies of, 243
　members of, 236–38
　supporters of, 245
Democrats
　on abortion, 296n112
　blue-collar workers as, 127, 171
　conservative, 101–2, 105, 107, 122,
　　149
　electoral support for, 85
　gain in legislatures, 34–35, 105
　geographical appeal, 97
　liberal, 152
　as southern voters, 100, 127
　views of, 37
　voting of, 39, 41, 65, 71, 77, 85
Dent, Harry S., 38, 55–56, 66, 69–70,
　84
　southern strategy and, 263n5
　as special counsel to president,
　　270n88
　on Wallace, 279n30
Dirksen, Everett M., 39–40, 51, 71,
　85
　opposition to Civil Rights Act of
　　1964, 265n23
Dispersion principle, 15–20, 26,
　115–16, 228, 231, 252, 258–59
Dole, Bob, 125, 129, 153, 155, 156
Domestic energy, 144–45, 174
Dominance principle, 15–20, 23, 24,
　60, 116, 160, 228, 252, 259
Douglas, Stephen, 254

"Economic Bill of Rights," 137
Economic Recovery Act of 1981, 103,
　293n61
Economic renewal program, 173–74,
　181
Economic welfare, 230, 243
Economy
　agenda, 103, 174, 182, 192
　Anderson, M., plan for transform-
　　ing, 137
　Carter and, 132, 257
　conditions of, 4, 10–11, 48, 199, 250
　crisis of, 235, 246
　growth of, 92, 136–37, 154, 250

plan for, 111, 136–37, 159, 165,
　181–82, 188, 190, 194
Reagan's philosophy of, 93, 138,
　154–55, 203, 292n60
rival plans for, 181–85
Russian, 24, 137, 242, 248, 250
of Soviet Union, 21–22, 137, 213,
　244, 248, 250
Yeltsin on, 228–31
Edwards, Lee, 293n61
Ehrlichman, John, 101
Election(s)
　of Carter, 121
　direct presidential, in Russia,
　　245–46
　multicandidate, 207–8, 214, 224
　1980 presidential, 6, 18, 92, 96, 103,
　　122–23, 126, 130–31, 134–35, 141,
　　163–64, 197, 202, 253
　scholarly literature of, 15
Electoral system, 34, 168
Energy. See Domestic Energy
Energy crisis, 124, 144, 161, 188, 195
Environment, 144, 167, 176, 190
Equal opportunity, 79, 80, 81, 174, 194
Equal Rights Amendment, 130, 165,
　175–77, 195, 202
Europe, 49, 68, 112–13
Extremists, 2, 25

Faith We Have Not Kept, The (Thur-
　mond), 70
Farley, James A., 11, 14
Favorite son(s), 39, 47, 57, 65, 69, 75,
　83, 87, 89
　definition of, 43
　Reagan as, 40, 51, 67
　Republican, 266n37
Federalists, 11, 16
500 Days, 241
Food rationing, 227
Ford, Gerald R., 6, 94–95, 104, 122,
　128, 157, 160, 166, 182–83, 201
　détente, 139, 257
　Goldwater on, 120
　as incumbent, 94, 108–9, 249
　Kissinger influencing, 110, 113, 119
　as moderate, 40, 85

New York Times, 109, 113–14
Nixon supported by, 71, 273n149
on Panama Canal, 117
as president, 104–6, 179
in primaries, 117–20
Reagan vs., 94–96, 111–21, 203, 249
Reagan attacking administration of,
   108
strategy of, 109–11
Foreign policy, 5, 177–81
   Carter and, 145–51, 161, 177, 195
   choices regarding, 5, 29–31, 259
   Ford, 110, 116, 117
   Gorbachev and, 206
   Johnson administration's, 49
   Nixon, 3, 73
   Reagan on, 61, 67–68, 118, 122, 125,
      139–41, 148, 154, 160, 165–66,
      180–81, 192, 205
   Romney's, 48, 50
   reorientation of, 151
   speeches, 68
   Vietnam War as main issue of, 56
   voter choices on, 202
   voters offered alternatives for,
      159–60
   Yakovlev and, 226
Freedom, Reagan on individual,
   119–20
Friedman, Benny, 1–2

Gallup Polls, 46, 50, 95, 105
   Carter in, 128, 140
   Nixon in, 63, 74, 83
   ratings based on, 278n15
   Reagan/Carter in, 131, 140, 164, 177,
      183, 192–93, 199–200, 203
Gardner, James, 86
Garth, David, 163–64, 169
Gergen, Dave, 116
Ginsburg, Bob, 143
Globalists, 146
Goldwaithe, Alfred W., 84, 87
Goldwater, Barry, 34, 37–38, 139, 258
   bid to reenter U.S. Senate of, 265n18
   defeat of, 55, 249
   on Ford/Reagan, 120
   1964 presidential bid of, 42

on Nixon, 55
Nixon endorsed by, 71
on Rockefeller, 65
Romney and, 267n41
strategy of, 263n5
Thurmond collaborating with, 86
Wallace campaigning for, 41
GOP. *See* Republican Party
Gorbachev, Mikhail, vii–viii, 3, 4, 10,
   15, 18
   accusations of Yeltsin by, 243
   attempts to revitalize Soviet Union,
      235–36
   Communist Party and, 239–40, 257
   conservatism of, 238–39
   defeat of, 23
   defending privileges, 231
   disagreement over 500 Days pro-
      gram, 241–42
   erosion of support for, 245
   liberalization attempts of, 209–10
   nomenklatura and, 214, 263n28
   as party leader, 218
   policies, 217
   Politburo appointees of, 216
   popularity of, 301n51
   reform agenda of, 205, 207–8, 215,
      224, 226–27, 263n28
   rise to power of, 205–6
   Soviet politics and, 250
   support coalition of, 220–21, 238,
      297n3
   Yeltsin reaching accord with,
      247–48
   Yeltsin vs., 4, 7, 18–19, 21, 23, 223,
      229–31, 236–37
Governance, vii, ix, 29
Government
   anti-big, 40, 49, 52–53, 69, 79, 92, 97,
      101, 109, 132, 136–37, 142–43,
   challenging central, 257
   democratic, 8
   interference, 144
   spending, 64, 100, 103, 114, 145,
      154
   Soviet, 221, 231, 241, 246, 257
   Vietnamese, 48, 56, 59, 77
   voters' views of, 19

Great Society, 81–85
  Reagan's critique of, 64, 270n95
Greenspan, Alan, 73
Greenville Group, 38, 53, 87, 265n19
Gun control, 165, 177. *See also*
  Weapons

Hadelman, H. R., 101
Hall, Leonard, 50
Hannaford, Peter, 91, 104, 108, 118,
  146
Harris Poll, 58, 83, 105, 158, 183,
  199
Hart, Gary, 136
Hatfield, Mark, 85
Helms, Jesse, 94, 107, 116, 119
Heresthetic, 6, 31, 125, 136, 216,
  262n20
  campaigning, 26–27, 141–42, 183–84,
    203, 253–58
  linkage of issues, 25
  Nixon using, 32–33, 71
  Reagan utilizing, 99, 103, 121–23,
    126, 132–33, 135, 137, 142–43, 154,
    158–59, 161, 177, 180, 182, 184,
    188, 190, 192, 196–99, 201, 248,
    249–52, 255
  recasting debate, 20, 23, 92
  rhetoric vs., 163, 186–87, 250, 259
  Riker defining, 11–14, 92, 262n12
  successful, 33, 203
  Yeltsin utilizing, 207, 209, 225–26,
    233, 235, 238, 241, 248, 251–52,
    255–58
Hickel, Walter J., 46
Hitler, Adolf, 30
Homosexuality, 54, 269n78
Hosking, Geoffrey, 300n25
House of Representatives, 34–35, 41
Human Events, 92
Humphrey, Hubert, 63, 72, 73–74, 83,
  88
Hypotheses, 5, 33, 137, 202, 258–60

Indochina, 37, 49, 54, 59, 62
Inflation, 93
  concern about, 132–33
  in United States, 135–36

Intelligentsia, 210, 220, 222, 232, 242,
  244, 250
International affairs, 28–31, 205
International Business Council, 182
Iran
  hostage crisis in, 6, 124, 131, 149–50,
    158, 198–99, 255
  Kennedy, E., on, 161
  policy, 171, 192
  Reagan on, 156, 192, 194
  terrorism and, 170
  USSR bordering, 150
Issue(s)
  agenda based on, 32
  campaign, 16, 55–56
  combining, 11–12, 14, 19, 89
  domestic political, 29–30
  linkage, 12, 22, 24
  main, for voters, 175
  Nixon's strategic combination of,
    33
  one-dimensional, 20, 22
  privilege, 212–13
  reframing, vii, 2–4, 6, 13–14, 263n28
  strategy of avoiding particular,
    169
  voters concerned with single, 165

Jobs, 152, 154, 170, 173. *See also*
  Unemployment
Johnson, Lyndon B., 39, 51, 56, 59, 61,
  67, 74–76, 81, 100, 180, 258
  administration of, 49, 74–75,
    273n149
  election of, 34–35, 38
  in Gallup Polls, 46
  in Harris Polls, 58
  peace talks called for by, 62, 64, 74
  on Romney, 46–47
  war on poverty, 27
Johnson, William, 50
Jordan, Hamilton, 96, 153, 197,
  290n17

Kahneman, Daniel, 28
Kemp, Jack, 134, 165
Kennedy, Edward M., 97, 130, 170,
  181

Carter challenged by, 152–53, 158,
    161–62, 166, 170, 173
  Reagan debating, 268n69
Kennedy, John F., 39, 67–68, 122
Kennedy, Robert F., 46, 52, 61–63, 66,
    68, 71–72, 76, 130
  reconsidering bid for office, 59
  supporters of, 71
Khrushchev, Nikita, 218
King, Coretta Scott, 63, 191
King, Martin Luther, Jr., 36, 161
  assassination of, 63–64, 88
Kirk, Russell, 102
Kissinger, Henry, 72
  Ford influenced by, 113, 119
  policy contributions of, 116, 118,
    139
Kramer, Michael, 47
Kremlin, 206, 216–17, 226, 232–33, 239,
    240, 242, 246
  liberalization and, 244
  refusal to publish Yeltsin's speech,
    220–21
Ku Klux Klan, 185–86, 191

LaFeber, Walter, 179
Laird, Melvin, 279n30
Language, 36, 71, 74, 111, 119
  corruption of, 16–17
  for persuasion, 11
Law and order, 36–37, 42, 48–49, 58,
    69
  Nixon on, 32, 35, 55, 68, 73–77, 79,
    84, 258
  policies, 36, 79–80
  Reagan on, 52, 79–82, 85, 132
Laxalt, Paul, 94, 111, 136
Leader(s), 110, 125, 136, 141, 147, 191,
    205–6, 210, 212, 218, 231, 244
  Democratic, 36, 252
  Gorbachev as, 218
  liberal/moderate, 38–40
  Republican, 109, 120, 125–26, 174,
    179
Leadership
  Cold War and, 4–5
  of Communist Party, 10, 208, 212,
    217–20, 222, 224, 226, 231, 250

Hart on, 136
  policy choices of, 8–11
  of Reagan, 136
  Yeltsin's critique of, 218
League of Women Voters, 103,
    157–58, 187–90, 192–93
Lebedev, N. I., 212
Lenin, Vladimir, 210, 212
"Let the People Rule" (Reagan), 113,
    115
Liberals
  Anderson, J., appealing to, 130–31,
    190
  Democrats as, 152
  Gorbachev and, 209–10
  Kremlin and, 244
  leaders, 40
  Rockefeller as, 38–39, 47
Life in Letters, A. (Skinner, A. Ander-
    son, and M. Anderson), 277n10
Ligachev, Yegor, 18–19, 206, 211,
    225–26, 228, 255
  antialcohol campaign of, 213
  as conservative, 209–10
  role in Secretariat, 222
  on Russian economy, 242
  Yeltsin's confrontation with, 210,
    213–23, 239, 242, 253
Lincoln, Abraham, 2, 133, 174, 254–56
Linowitz, Sol, 146
Logic of Political Survival, The
    (Bueno de Mesquita), 8
Lucey, Patrick J., 130, 184, 293n62
Luck, 3–4, 6, 19, 252
Lukianov, Anatoliy, 222, 239
Lyon, Charlton, 87

Mackie, Gerry, 262n12
Making of the New Majority Party,
    The (Rusher), 105–6
Markus, Greg, 201
Martin, Jim, 87
McCarthy, Eugene J., 59, 63, 66, 74,
    83, 193, 263n3
McKelvey, Richard, 22
Mediacracy: American Parties and
    Policies in the Communications
    Age (Phillips), 106

Median voter theorem, 20–25
Medvedev, Vadim, 222, 225, 229, 239, 297n4
Meese, Edwin, 104, 154
Meet the Press, 147
Meyer, Frank, 100
MGIMO. *See* Moscow State Institute of International Relations
Miami Herald, 85, 87
Midwestern states, 61,167–68, 186
Military
  power of United States, 54, 115, 123, 135, 151, 197
  Russian, 243, 248
  spending, 12, 138–40, 149–51, 189
  strategy, 120–21, 132
  superiority, 81, 84, 134, 151, 180–81
  weapons, 178–80
Minimax regret, 28
Mondale, Walter, 97
Moscow, 62, 150, 206–7, 212, 216–17, 220–21, 224, 226–28
  exploitative policies of, 234
  multicandidate elections in, 214
  Yeltsin attempt to gain political ascendancy in, 224
Moscow News, 221
Moscow Party Committee, 209–10
Moscow State Institute of International Relations (MGIMO), 212
Multicandidate elections, 207–9, 214
Murfin, Bill, 38, 39
Muskie, Edmund, 2, 158, 191

NAACP, 169–71, 173
National appeal, 53
Nationalists, 226, 227, 233–45, 237
National Unity Platform, 184
Natural resources, 171, 234
Negative campaign(s), 19–20, 256, 258
  of Anderson, J., 168–69
  of Bush, 159
  of Carter, 166–67, 190–91, 194–95, 198–99
  of Ford, 110
  gaining support through, 28
  heresthetical campaign and, 256

  of Reagan, 61, 110–11, 120, 158, 185–86
  of Romney, 50–51
  strategy of, 253, 258
  of Yeltsin, 225
"New Alignment For American Unity, A" (Nixon), 69
New Deal, 103, 200
  coalition, 106–7, 128, 201
"New Direction for America's Economy, A." (Nixon), 76
New Politics, 107
New Right, 35, 51, 58
  preferences of, voters, 37
  Rockefeller and, 77
New York Times
  on Carter, 142, 170, 190
  on Carter's environmental standards, 176
  on Ford, 109, 113–14
  on Nixon's potential running mates, 84
  on presidential debate, 197
  on Reagan, 40, 54, 102, 141, 155–57
  on Reagan-Bush, 155, 159
  on Reagan's defense policy, 141
  on Rockefeller, 77, 95
New York's Liberal Party, 190
Nezavisimaia Gazeta, 244–45
Nixon, Richard, vii–ix, 2, 6, 32, 44–45, 76
  appeal to conservatives, 68
  attempt to sway Wallace supporters, 73
  black voters and, 271n116
  as centrist, 39, 40, 56, 85–86, 98–99, 265n22
  challenges to, 43–44
  Ford supporting, 71, 273n149
  in Gallup Poll, 46, 50, 63, 83
  Meyer on, 100
  negative campaigning against, 50–51
  on new alignment, 69
  party politics utilized by, 9–10
  Reagan's attempt to prevent victory for, 87
  rhetoric used by, 12, 32
  Romney and, 55, 272n124

selecting running mate, 88
Southern support for, 66, 82–84, 263n5
strategic combination of issues, 33
strategy to win southern conservatives, 43
Thurmond supporting, 70–71, 273n148
tours of, 54–55
on Vietnam, 56, 59–60, 62, 74–75
Nofziger, Lyn, 53, 127
Nomenklatura, 21–24
as ally to nationalists, 234
fear of losing power/influence, 210
Gorbachev's proposals threatening, 214
Gorbachev supported by, 263n28
privileges, 211–12, 219, 221, 223, 228, 230–31, 250–51
Yeltsin's attacks against, 228–31
Nonviolent movement, 36
Northeast, 35, 39, 43, 55, 83, 85–86, 95, 167
Northern states, 167
Nuclear Targeting Policy Review, 179
Nuclear weapons, 119, 141, 175, 178–80, 195, 198
Nunn, Louie B., 81
Nunn, Sam, 178

Occupational Safety and Health Administration, 100, 192
O'Donnell, Peter, 38
Opportunities
capitalizing, 26
creating, 4
equal, 174
exploiting, 3, 11
fostering, 25, 251

Pakistan, 159–60, 198
Panama Canal, 115, 146
opposition to, treaties, 113, 147, 151, 165
Reagan vs. Ford on, 117
Paris Peace Talks, 74, 82
Party affiliation, 38
Party bosses, 6, 32, 34, 84, 89, 93–94

higher wages of, 211
Russian, 208, 212, 224, 228, 235
Wirthlin on, 125
Peace, 62, 71, 74, 83, 93, 115, 117, 151, 175, 180
plan, 140, 165–66
Reagan as man of, 132, 138–40, 171, 192, 193
People's Republic of China (PRC), 56, 65, 99, 114–15, 130, 145, 180–81
Perestroika, 18, 207, 215, 222–23, 226–27, 230, 237, 250, 258–59
failures of, 242, 227
Medvedev on, 297n4
results from, 218
supporters of, 220, 226
Yeltsin on, 209, 214, 217–19, 221, 231
Persian Gulf Crisis, 150, 178
Persuasion
language used for, 11–13
rhetoric for, 32, 94, 253
Petitions, 221
PFC. *See* President Ford Committee
Phillips, Kevin, 106–7, 263n5
Pierce, Franklin, 162
Platform Committee, 74, 82, 85
Plenum, 208–9, 211, 214, 215
Plotkin, Henry, 145
Podhoretz, Norman, 149
Policy. *See also* Foreign policy
agenda, 32, 46, 191
analysts, 181–83
Boskin on, 183, 292n60
choices, 8–11, 22
defense, 141, 145–46, 177–81
domestic, 45, 81, 103, 136
entrenched, positions, 27
equilibrium, 14
of Gorbachev, 217
intent, 19–20
Iran, 192
Kissinger and, 116
law and order, 79–80
Moscow and, 234
objectives of Gorbachev, 207
priorities, 143
Reagan on, 25, 53

Policy (*continued*)
  Rockefeller, positions, 270n98
  social, 50, 114, 152, 175–77, 191
  Vietnam, 39, 50, 56, 62, 258
  voters' preferences of, 20–21
  Yeltsin on, 25
Policy Memorandum Number 1, 137
Politburo, 3–4, 206, 208–12, 214
  antiperestroika forces within, 219
  Gorbachev's appointees in, 216
  members of, 217
  moderates, 222
  Yeltsin on, 298n32
  Yeltsin/Ligachev confrontation in,
    215
  Yeltsin's speech to, 244
Political analysts, 65–66
Political center, 47–48, 56, 259
Political context, 127–32
Political institutions, 2, 7, 41
Political outliers, 14–15
Politicians
  centrist, 25, 39
  heresthetical, 248
  insightful, 27
  redefining issues/changing institu-
    tions, 2
  strategic, 5
  successful, 16–18
  Wall Street Journal on, 167
Politics, 260
  changes in, 125
  contest within, 7–8
  domestic, 5, 29–30, 34, 147
  loyalty and, 216, 229
  luck in, 3–4
  New, 107
  party, 9–10, 72
  of Southern states, 263n5
  in Soviet Union, 250
  sports compared to, 1–2
  success in, 259
Poltoranin, Mikhail, 215, 229
Pomper, Gerald, 125–26, 129
Popov, Gavriil, 221
Popularity, 3, 60, 116, 131, 216, 224,
    230, 236, 242, 245–46
Position(s)

entrenched policy, 27
median, of voters, 20–25
Rockefeller, on policy, 270n98
Romney, on convention, 83
winning, 20–26
Powell, Jody, 143
Pravda
  Ligachev arguing against, 214
  Yeltsin interview in, 247
  Yeltsin's speech in, 211
PRC. *See* People's Republic of China
President. *See also* Presidential nomi-
    nation
  Democratic contenders for, 275n169
  Dent as special counsel to, 270n88
  Ford as, 104–6
  1980 election for, 163–64, 202
  Russian, 245
President Directive 59, 178–79
President Ford Committee (PFC), 108
Presidential nomination
  contenders for, 40–41
  1968 competition for Republican, 6,
    32–34
Presidential race, contender of, in
    1976, 94–96
Price, Ray, 74
Primaries
  Ford vs. Reagan in, 117–20
  McCarthy's near-victory in, 263n3
  proliferation of, 93–94
  Reagan in, 96–97, 159–60
  Republican Party, 153–62, 263n3
  significance of, 10, 126
Principles, 18
Privileges, 7–10, 17–18
  four types of, 212
  Gorbachev defending, 231
  nomenklatura, 210–12, 223, 250–51
  Yeltsin on, 7, 259
Proposition 1, 103
Proposition 13, 103

Rafshoon, Jerry, 152
Ranney, Austin, 94
Rasputin, Valentin, 234
Reader's Digest, 57
Reagan for President Committee, 136

Reagan Presidential Library, 91
Reagan Revolution, 6
Reagan, Ronald, vii–ix, 32
  aggressive campaigning of, 77–78
  Allen advising, 285n36
  Anderson, J., debating, 187–90
  attempts to prevent Nixon victory,
    87
  Bush, H. W., vs., 155–56
  Cannon on, 78–80, 275n169
  Carter vs., 6, 13, 28, 200, 203
  Carter debating, 193–97
  Carter as similar to, 96–97
  challenges to, 43–44
  on civil rights, 64
  Cold War and, 12–13, 112, 134, 139,
    204
  conservative message of, 57, 101–2,
    105–6, 255
  convention acceptance speech of,
    170–71
  declaration of candidacy, 84
  defense initiative and, 258
  domestic political maneuvers of, 5
  economic philosophy of, 93, 138,
    154–55, 203, 292n60
  first planning session of, 51
  Ford vs., 94–95, 111–21, 249
  Ford administration attacked by,
    108
  foreign policy of, 122, 139–40, 148,
    165–66, 180–81
  in Gallup poll, 164
  geographic victory of, 201
  as governor, 40
  Great Society critiqued by, 270n95
  as heresthetician, 132–33, 142–43,
    248, 251–52
  homosexuality and, 269n78
  Kennedy, E., debating, 268n69
  on law and order, 79–82, 85
  leadership of, 136
  lessons learned in 1968, 90
  letters written by, 277n10
  as man of peace, 192
  on national defense, 140–41
  negative campaigning of, 110–11,
    185–86

  policy preferences of, 25, 53
  political gain for, 151–52
  in primaries, 96–97, 159–60
  race relations and, 172–73
  radio program/newspaper column,
    91–93
  reconstituting national effort, 61
  Reeves on, 89
  as rhetorician, 92, 121–23, 161, 177
  rise to presidency of, 3, 124–25
  running mate selected by, 86, 118
  on SALT II, 141, 180–81, 191
  Southern states and, 80–81, 126–27
  on Soviet expansionism, 285n32
  speeches of, 40, 67–68, 284nn22–23
  strategic insights of, 6–7, 249
  supporters of, 156–57
  tax reform and, 122–23, 134–35,
    182–83
  tours of, 52–53
  on Vietnam War, 53–54
  Wallace vs., 80
  Washington Post on, 156
  on weapons, 262n22
  in White House, 293n61
  Wirthlin's suggestions to, 172
  Yeltsin compared to, 99, 224, 256
Reed, Clarke, 38, 84, 87
Reed, Tom, 51, 53, 54, 61, 68, 77,
    268n66, 276n206
Reeves, Richard, on Reagan, 89
Reform. *See also* Tax reform
  agenda of Gorbachev, 207–8, 215,
    224, 226–27, 263n28
  agenda of Yeltsin, 220–21
  institutional, 10
  rhetoric of, 297n4
Regionalists, 146
Relationships
  international, 29–31
  Nixon's, with black Americans, 75,
    271n116
  of United States/Soviet Union, 52,
    251
Religion, 177
Republic, independent, 233
Republican National Convention,
    83–85

Republican Party, 296n112
  contenders, 88–89
  debates, 153–62
  electoral prospects of, 255
  favorite sons, 266n37
  fundraising for, 80–81
  liberals of, 38–39
  as "new majority" party, 134
  new party to replace, 106
  1968 presidential nomination, 6,
    32–34
  political center of, 47–48
  primaries, 153–62, 263n3
  social justice record of, 174
  winning nomination of, 42
Republicans
  on abortion, 296n112
  conservative, 48–49, 51
  Wallace supported by, 72–73
Rhetoric, 11–13
  of Anderson, J., 189
  anticenter, 240
  of Bush, 159–60
  campaign, 19–20, 252–53
  of Carter, 150
  as continuum, 32
  heresthetic vs., 186–87, 250
  ingenuity in, 216
  negative, 194, 198
  persuasion of, 253
  of Reagan, 92, 121–23, 161, 177
  refinement of, 177
  reformist, 297n4
  of Republican contenders, 88–89
  Riker on, 13, 155
Riker, William, 6, 16
  analysis of candidates, 33
  dispersion principle of, 115–16
  dominance principle of, 23, 228,
    252, 259
  early work of, 31
  on heresthetic/rhetoric, 11–14, 92,
    262n12
  hypotheses of, 202
  principles of campaigning, 206
  theories of, 16, 155, 230
  Yeltsin representing argument of,
    225

Riots, 35–36, 47–49, 88
Roberts, Sam, 47
Roberts, Stephen, 153
Rockefeller, Nelson, 9, 15, 32
  announcement of candidacy, 65
  appealing to moderate/liberal wings
    of party, 76–77
  black voters and, 274n165
  figures presented by, 265n17,
    272n125
  as liberal, 38–39, 57
  policy positions of, 270n98
  Reagan and, 86–87
  strategy of, 266n39, 271n122
  tours of, 65–66
  as vice president, 95
Roe v. Wade, 120
Romney, George, 9, 32
  campaign strategy of, 45–46
  Goldwater and, 267n41
  initial lack of support for, 44–45
  as liberal, 38–39
  Nixon and, 55, 272n124
  plan for neutralization, 49–50
  position on convention, 83
  tours of, 46–49
  on Vietnam War, 46–47
  withdrawal from race of, 50–51,
    57–58
Romney Associates, 48, 267n43
Roosevelt, Franklin, 11
Rose Garden Strategy, 167, 176, 198
Roth, William, 134
RSFSR. See Russian Soviet Federative
    Socialist Republic
Rumsfeld, Donald, 100, 108
Running mate
  Lucey as, to J. Anderson, 184
  Nixon selecting, 88
  Nixon's choice of, 73
  Reagan selecting, 86, 118
  Rutskoi as, to Yeltsin, 247
Rusher, William, 100, 105–7
Russia. See also Soviet Union
  authoritarian vision, 236
  autonomy of, 21–23, 263n28
  central problems of, 225
  creation of presidency in, 245

economy of, 242, 248
expanded rights for, 242
military of, 243
party bosses of, 235
sovereignty of, 233, 238–44, 246
Soviet Union and, 237
Russian Federation, 206–7, 232, 233,
  238, 240, 243, 255
Russian parliament, 239, 248
Russian Republic, 7, 21, 236, 252
autonomy of, 251
political struggles in, 253
Russian Soviet Federative Socialist
  Republic (RSFSR), 232, 237
Politburo view of, 239
Yeltsin addressing, 246
Rutskoi, Aleksandr, 247
Ryzhkov, Nikolay, 246–47

Sakharov, Andrei, 208
international prominence of, 297n5
SALT II, 145–48
Reagan on, 141, 180–81, 191
Senate ratification of, 150–51
Samuelson, Don, 64
San Diego Evening Tribune, 147
Scheer, Robert, 262n22
Schofield, Norman, 22
Scholars
on elections, 15
on 1980 presidential election,
  163–64, 202
Schrag, Peter, 103
Schreiber, Taft, 54
Schweiker, Robert, 96, 118
Sears, John, 96, 153
Secretariat, 222
reorganization of, 225
Selectorate
size of, 8, 93
theory, 9–11, 33, 126
Senate. *See also* Government; United
  States
Goldwater's bid to reenter, 265n18
ratification of Panama Canal treaty,
  146
ratification of SALT II, 150–51
Senate Budget Committee, 188

Shevardnadze, Eduard, 219
Sindlinger, Al, 116
Skinner, Kiron K., 277n10, 283n1
Slander, 20
Sloan, John W., 293n61
Smith, Hedrick, 197
Smith, Howard K., 193
Social justice
Republican Party record of, 174
Yeltsin on, 228–31
Social policies, 97, 175–77
Social Security 27, 67, 130, 195
benefits, 184
taxes, 156, 198
Socialism, 222
loyalty to, 229
new image of, 230
Solzhenitsyn, Alexander, 118
Southern states, 172–73
politics of, 263n5
Reagan seeking support of, 80–81,
  126–27
Romney's support from, 45–46
strategy and, 263n5
support of, 42–43
support for Nixon from, 66, 82–84,
  263n5
Soviet Union, 21–22, 138
Afghanistan invaded by, 150, 157,
  159–61, 178, 191, 287n70
changes for, 205
collapse of, 296n1
economy of, 21–22, 213
expansionism, 285n32
federalism and, 226
Gorbachev attempting to revitalize,
  235
Iran's border with, 150
military competition with, 140
military strategy and, 120–21
negotiations with, 171
nuclear arms control treaties with,
  178
politics in, 250
relations with United States, 52, 251
Russia and, 237
threat to United States from, 257
Vietnam War relating to, 60

Sovietskaia Rossiia
  Andreyeva's letter published by, 209
  interview in, 233
Speeches. *See also* specific titles
  platform, 82–83
  Reagan, 40, 67–68, 284nn22–23
  Yeltsin's plenum, 209, 211, 220–21
Spencer, Stuart, 51, 109
Sports, 1–2
Stalin, 218, 221–22
Stealth weapons, 179
Stengel, Casey, 1–2
Strategists, 58, 125, 163–64
Strategy
  of agenda setting, 12
  antiterrorism, 195
  of avoiding certain issues, 169
  of Caddell, 166, 200
  campaign, 31, 45–46, 248–49
  of Ford, 109–11
  future campaigners benefiting from, vii–ix
  general principles of electoral, 260
  of Goldwater, 263n5
  grand, 139
  military, 120–21
  negative campaigning as, 253, 258
  politicians implementing, 5
  in presidential election of 1980, 163–64
  of Reagan, 78
  of Rockefeller, 266n39, 271n122
  Rose Garden, 167, 176, 198
  Southern, 263n5
  of Wirthlin, 182
  of Yeltsin, 230–31
" 'Strategy for Peace', The" (Allen), 139
Strategy of Rhetoric, The (Riker), 16
Supreme Court, 68–69
  decision on abortion rights, 175
  decision in *Roe v. Wade*, 120

Tax(es)
  reduction of, 171, 181–83, 203, 257
  social security, 156, 184
Tax Reduction Act of 1975, 112
Tax reform, 103, 188

Reagan advocating, 122–23, 134–35, 182–83
Teeter, Robert, 105, 109
Terrorism, 170, 194
Tet Offensive, 59, 62
Third-party candidate, 78. *See also* Wallace, George C.
  Anderson, J., as, 130–31
Thurmond, Strom, 37–38, 42, 51, 53, 74, 264n9
  on ABM defense, 273n145
  campaign for Nixon, 84–87
  Nixon supported by, 70–71, 75, 273n148
  Wallace influenced by, 41
Tikhomirov, Vladimir, 229
Time, 49
"Time for Choosing, A" (Reagan), 40
"Timing, Issues & Strategy" (Bachelder), 45–46
Tours
  of Nixon, 54–55
  of Reagan, 52–53
  of Rockefeller, 65–66
  of Romney, 46–49
Tower, John, 37–38, 42, 51, 71, 76, 84
  Nixon endorsed by, 75
  Reed meeting with, 53
  Romney supported by, 47
  Thurmond collaborating with, 86
Tretiakov, Vitaliy, 244
Trotsky, 221
Truth, 20
Tullius, Quintus, 20, 27, 252, 260
Tuttle, Holmes, 54
Tversky, Amos, 28

Unemployment, 28, 50, 99, 112, 114, 132, 142–43, 173–74, 181, 184–85, 196–97, 202–3, 255
United States
  ethics in, 168
  inflation in, 135–36
  involvement in Vietnam War, 36–37, 54
  military power of, 123, 151
  party politics in, 9
  political landscape of, 99

problems within, 144
safety of, 178
Soviet Union's relations with, 52, 251
Soviet Union threatening, 257
Unit rule, 43, 57, 89
USSR. *See* Soviet Union

Vance, Cyrus, 146–48, 150, 158
Vice president, 95. *See also* Running mate
Vietnam War
  arguments about, 52
  as foreign policy issue, 56
  Nixon on, 62, 74–75
  opposition to, 36–37
  Reagan on, 53–54
  Rockefeller's plan to end, 76–77
  Romney on, 46–47, 50
  Soviet Union relating to, 60
Volpe, John A., 65, 88
Voshchanov, Pavel, 227–28
Vote(s)
  of black Americans, 133–34, 169–70, 172–73, 271n116, 274n165
  cycles, 262n12
  number of, to win presidency, 164
Voters
  abortion preferences of, 202
  alternatives on foreign policy offered to, 159–60
  black, 133–34, 169–70, 172–73, 271n116, 274n165
  breakdown of, 200
  candidates appealing to, 18, 33, 252–53
  governmental views of, 20
  Iran hostage crisis and, 199
  main issues concerning, 175
  median position of, 20–25
  Russian presidency and, 246
  single-issue, 165
  skepticism of, 17
  supporting Vietnam War, 37
  Yeltsin's message to, 230

Wall Street Journal, 167
Wallace, George C.

Anderson, J., differing from, 131
candidacy of, 41, 58–59, 279n30
Cannon on, 275n169
challenge presented by, 78–80
endorsing Cater, 98
Reagan vs., 80, 81
Republican support for, 72–73
War. *See also* Cold War; Vietnam War
  avoiding, 135
  decreasing chances of, 165
Washington Post, 113, 188
  on Carter, 145, 179
  on Ford, 113
  on Reagan, 92, 156, 172, 183
  on stealth weapons, 179
Watergate scandal, 3, 101
  changes in wake of, 94
  impact of, 102, 105
Weapons
  of mass destruction, 194
  Reagan on, 262n22
Whalen, Richard J., 59–60
  on campaign, 63
  on Nixon, 74
"Where Are We Now in the Campaign?" (Kissinger), 72
White, Clif, 51–52, 64, 86
  meeting with Thurmond, 70
  on Reagan, 67
White House, 108–9
  Carter's experience in, 191
  Reagan in, 293n61
  rivalry for, 163
White, Theodore, 269n78
Wicker, Tom, 64
Wills, Gary, 86
Wirls, Daniel, 178–79
Wirthlin, Richard
  as key strategist to Reagan, 125
  on Reagan, 154, 201
  strategies of, 163–65, 182, 185, 187
  suggestions to Reagan, 172
Women, 87, 103, 157–58, 175–76, 187–90

Yakovlev, Alexander, 214
  foreign policy and, 226

Yakovlev, Alexander (*continued*)
  rebuttal of Andreyeva's letter, 222
  as reformer, 219
Yeltsin, Boris, vii–ix
  advocating direct presidential elec-
    tions, 245–46
  early political career of, 207–8
  on economy/social justice, 228–31
  failures vs. successes of, 31, 216
  Gorbachev vs., 18–19, 21, 223,
    229–31, 236–37
  heresthetical maneuvering of,
    225–26, 251–52, 255–58
  Hosking on, 300n25
  interview with BBC Television,
    222–23
  Ligachev's confrontation with, 210,
    215–18
  message to voters, 230
  on perestroika, 214
  policy preferences of, 25
  on Politburo, 298n32

  political maneuvers of, 5, 249
  on privilege issue, 212–13, 259
  public resignation of, 239–40
  Reagan compared to, 99, 224, 256
  redirecting campaign, 6–7
  reform agenda of, 220–21
  removal from candidacy of, 219–20
  rise to prominence of, 250
  Russian presidency of, 3–4
  on Russian sovereignty, 233,
    238–44
  Rutskoi as running-mate of, 247
  Ryzhkov v, 246–47
  speech to CC Plenum, 209, 211
  speeches of, 297n7, 303n93
  strategy of, 230–31
  top party leadership criticized by,
    218
  victory of, 248
Young, Andrew, 146, 149, 161, 172
Young Americans for Freedom, 99
Youth Employment Act, 184